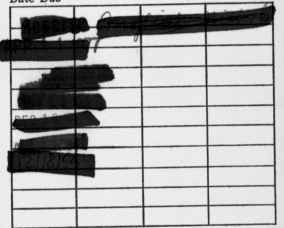

The Multiple Plot in English Renaissance Drama

The
Multiple Plot
in
English Renaissance
Drama

Richard Levin

The University of Chicago Press
Chicago and London

International Standard Book Number: 0-226-47526-3
Library of Congress Catalog Card Number: 75-130306
The University of Chicago Press, Chicago 60637
The University of Chicago Press, Ltd., London
© 1971 by The University of Chicago
All rights reserved. Published 1971
Printed in the United States of America

To my mother and the memory of my father

Contents

Contents

Preface

This book is a study of the structures and functions of the multiple plot in English Renaissance drama. Although I say something about the origins and development of this convention, the emphasis throughout is analytical rather than historical; each of the central chapters deals with a specific kind of structure which is examined in its own terms without regard to chronology. I have not covered all of these multiple-plot structures, but only those that seemed most important; and I certainly have not covered all of the multiple-plot plays, but have concentrated on a relatively small number of examples of each kind, chosen mainly for their illustrative value. The period I am concerned with extends from the beginnings of the secular theater in the 1560s to its demise in 1642, though most of my examples are naturally drawn from the fifteen or so years of its greatest achievement, coinciding roughly with Shakespeare's professional career.

Any general investigation of this drama is faced with the problem of what to do with Shakespeare. He cannot be left out, yet if he is given his proper weight he will not leave much room for anyone else. The difficulty is compounded here because his multiple plots have already accumulated such a substantial body of fine criticism (since almost from the start the critics were prepared to take seriously his use of this convention which they ignored or condemned in his fellow playwrights) that there seemed to be little point in repeating it. I have therefore settled on a compromise by selecting only one of his plays (*Troilus and Cressida*) as a primary example for extended analysis, but discussing a number of others more briefly under the class to which they belong. For the structures employed by Shakespeare were usually not different in kind from those of his contemporaries, and some further insight into his practice may be gained by seeing it in relation to theirs.

With a single exception, I have limited my study to the best of these contemporaries, although not always to their best known plays if they did not serve my purpose. Within this select group the reader will notice that Thomas Middleton is given a place of special prominence. I have gone to his canon to exemplify so many of the categories because I believe him to be one of the most inventive and effective architects of multiple plots in the period, and one of the most neglected. And I confess to a fascination with the man and his work. The reader will also notice that a particular critical approach, which might be called "structural," is adopted here, although I have tried not to make a big thing of the theory behind it, or the system of classification derived from it that marks off the chapters. No mode of criticism can ever bring all aspects of the literary object into equally sharp focus, and I have therefore not felt obliged to "disprove" the other studies of these plays, based on premises different from my own, which I call to the reader's attention. And no classification of literature can ever satisfy all conditions; the one worked out in Chapters 2 through 5 makes no claim to being anything more than a useful, if necessarily imprecise, instrument for the investigation I have undertaken. Whatever value that investigation has will be determined, not by a theoretical defense of its approach or its categories—still less by a refutation of some alternative possibility—but by their practical application in the analyses of the individual plays, and on these my case must rest.

To facilitate reference I have listed in Appendix B each play mentioned in the text, with its author, date of production, and the edition used for quotations and citations. This list also serves as an index. In quoting from old-spelling editions I modernize the spelling and some of the punctuation; in citing from editions which do not number lines I give the act, scene, and page number (I.iii.p.29).

I am especially indebted to Professors Mark Ashin, S. F. Johnson, and Norman Rabkin for their careful criticism of the first draft of this book and very helpful suggestions for its improvement. I would also like to thank the American Council of Learned Societies for a generous fellowship which enabled me to begin this project, the Research Foundation of the State University of New York and the

Graduate School of the State University at Stony Brook for continued support in its later stages, and the staff of the Henry E. Huntington Library for their many kindnesses during my year of work there. Portions of the book have appeared in different form in various journals, noted among the Acknowledgments, and I am grateful to their editors and publishers for permission to make use of this material. I also want to express my appreciation to Miss Mary Bruno and Mrs. Rose Williams, who prepared the manuscript, and most of all to my wife, who conscientiously refrained from reading it.

RICHARD LEVIN

STATE UNIVERSITY OF NEW YORK
STONY BROOK

Acknowledgments

Material from the following articles has been incorporated into this book, in somewhat different form, with the kind permission of the original editors and publishers: "The Double Plot of *The Second Maiden's Tragedy*," *Studies in English Literature*, 3 (Spring 1963); "The Three Quarrels of *A Fair Quarrel*," *Studies in Philology*, 61 (April 1964); "The Dampit Scenes in *A Trick to Catch the Old One*," *Modern Language Quarterly*, 25 (June 1964); "The Four Plots of *A Chaste Maid in Cheapside*," *Review of English Studies*, 16 (February 1965); "The Structure of *Bartholomew Fair*," *PMLA*, 80 (June 1965), by permission of the Modern Language Association of America; "*The Staple of News*, the Society of Jeerers, and Canters' College," *Philological Quarterly*, 44 (October 1965); "The Subplot of *The Atheist's Tragedy*," *Huntington Library Quarterly*, 29 (November 1965); "Elizabethan 'Clown' Subplots," *Essays in Criticism*, 16 (January 1966); "Sexual Equations in the Elizabethan Double Plot," *Literature and Psychology*, 16 (Winter 1966); "The Family of Lust and *The Family of Love*," *Studies in English Literature*, 6 (Spring 1966); "The Triple Plot of *Hyde Park*," *Modern Language Review*, 62 (January 1967), by permission of the Modern Humanities Research Association and of the Editors; "The Double Plots of Terence," *Classical Journal*, 62 (April 1967); "The Unity of Elizabethan Multiple-

Acknowledgments

Plot Drama," *Journal of English Literary History,* 34 (December 1967), by permission of The Johns Hopkins Press; "Introduction" to *Michaelmas Term,* Regents Renaissance Drama Series, The University of Nebraska Press, 1967; "The Elizabethan 'Three-Level' Play," *Renaissance Drama,* n.s. 2 (1969), by permission of Northwestern University Press.

I

The Unity of
Multiple-Plot Drama

It takes no great courage today to rise to the defense of the multiple plot, or even to suggest that this very striking feature of English Renaissance drama is worthy of serious study. But that was not always so. Up until some thirty years ago virtually all admirers of this drama were united in deploring its tendency to combine two or more independent lines of action, each with a separate cast of characters and often a distinctly different style and mood, which proceeded side by side in alternating scenes, in defiance of the most elementary and time-honored canons of artistic unity:

> The truth is that, just as in the other imitative arts one imitation is always of one thing, so in poetry the story, as an imitation of action, must represent one action, a complete whole, with its several incidents so closely connected that the transposal or withdrawal of any one of them will disjoin and dislocate the whole.[1]

Although these scholars and critics certainly did not feel bound by classical authority, and were prepared to make an exception for Shakespeare, the pervasive influence of this conception of unity is

---

[1] *Poetics* viii.1451ª30–34 (trans. Ingram Bywater).

apparent in their treatment of the multiple-plot drama of his contemporaries. In their general discussions they approached the subplot as alien matter illegitimately attached to the main action, which
was tacitly assumed to be the *real* play, and which could only be
appreciated after it had been abstracted by the charitable reader from
these distracting and disfiguring excrescences. And such general explanations as they offered for this construction invariably moved
outside the work itself to extra-artistic considerations that might excuse the writer (and their own critical procedure) without condoning
his practice: the tyranny of an arbitrary convention inherited from
the uncouth Mysteries and Moralities, or the problems of collabora-
tive authorship, or the need to provide parts for the company clown,
or to please the groundlings, or to pad out a thin story line, and so on.

This attitude emerged still more clearly in their discussions of
individual plays. Occasionally, it is true, they acknowledged that a
particular subplot was not without merit in its own right if viewed as
a separate entity, but much more often these subordinate actions were
either ignored completely or else condemned out of hand, as in the
following representative reactions to some of the best known double-
and triple-plot dramas of the age:

C. F. Tucker Brooke on Marlowe's *Doctor Faustus:*

> *Doctor Faustus,* though grossly violating the rules of dra-
> matic structure and greatly qualifying its effectiveness by
> the interpolation of comic scenes of unutterable bathos,
> was yet . . . one of the most successful tragedies which the
> age produced.[2]

T. S. Eliot on Heywood's *A Woman Killed with Kindness:*

> This theme [of the underplot] is too grotesque even to hor-
> rify us; but it is too obviously there merely because an
> underplot is required to fill out the play for us to feel
> anything but boredom when it recurs.[3]

John Addington Symonds on Jonson's *Volpone:*

> The slight and meagre under-plot of Sir [Politic] Would-be
> and his wife (which I have omitted in my analysis, except
> in so far as Lady Would-be affects Volpone) is superfluous
> and tolerably tedious.[4]

---

2 *The Tudor Drama* (Boston, 1911), p. 249. Not all of these "comic scenes" are in
the subplot.
3 "Thomas Heywood," *Selected Essays* (New York, 1932), p. 154.
4 *Ben Jonson* (New York, 1886), p. 86.

Émile Legouis on Middleton and Rowley's *The Changeling:*

> *The Changeling* . . . would rank with the Shakespearean
> tragedies were it not disfigured by a coarse and worthless
> secondary plot, without connection with the principal
> story.[5]

Una Ellis-Fermor on Ford's *'Tis Pity She's a Whore:*

> If the comic plot were excised, and we have the evidence
> of Maeterlinck's translation . . . to show us that nothing
> is lost and much is gained by excising it, a play is left
> which . . . is unsurpassed in Jacobean drama.[6]

And a further illustration, perhaps even more revealing, can be found
in the anthology of Elizabethan and Stuart drama that E. H. C.
Oliphant published in 1929 for the college classroom. Following this
approach to the underplot to its logical conclusion, he sought to
assist his readers by printing a line in the margin alongside certain
episodes of the plays he included there. As he explained it,

> what is so marked may be omitted without the value of the
> play being prejudicially affected. This may cover scenes of
> mere foolery having no value in themselves and no bear-
> ing on the story, or it may cover an entire sub-plot. This, it
> is thought, may be useful to both students and instructors,
> and may add greatly to the appreciation of two or three
> plays.[7]

No editor today, of course, would dream of drawing this line,
for our attitude toward the multiple plot has undergone a remarkable
reversal. We have gradually come to realize that the earlier view
betrayed an inadequate understanding of Renaissance dramaturgy,
that in many plays of the period these apparently superfluous subplots
were related to the main action in a variety of significant ways and
were in fact integral parts of a coherent overall structure possessing
a kind of unity not contemplated in the *Poetics*. This revolution in
opinion began, as nearly as such things can be dated, with the
pioneering work of William Empson and Muriel Bradbrook in the

---

[5] *A History of English Literature*, trans. Helen Irvine (New York, 1935), p. 500.
[6] *The Jacobean Drama* (London, 1936), p. 232. Maeterlinck's adaptation, *Annabella*
(or *Annabella et Giovanni*), was produced in 1894.
[7] *Shakespeare and His Fellow Dramatists* (New York, 1929), 1: xvi. He marks off
part or all of the subsidiary plots in *Doctor Faustus*, *Friar Bacon and Friar Bungay*,
A Woman Killed with Kindness, 2 *The Honest Whore*, *Volpone*, and *A Fair
Quarrel*.

1930s,[8] and has been gathering momentum ever since, aided and abetted by several other contemporaneous developments in the study of literature. Certainly the most important of these has been the much broader revolution over these same years in the method of literary criticism itself, which has resulted in a greater emphasis upon a "close-reading" analysis of the individual text and hence upon the explication of the function of each element in the work as a whole. Moreover, the specific kind of explication developed in some of the critical approaches that have lately come into prominence—especially those of the psychoanalytic and "myth and ritual" schools—has focused attention on modes of relationship between plots overlooked by the more literal-minded scholars of the past. And at the same time traditional historical scholarship has also made a valuable contribution to our appreciation of the low-comedy subplot through recent investigations of the drama from which it arose and of the playhouse audience for which it was written—investigations that have revised some of the earlier condescending attitudes. Even the rapidly expanding economy of the academic marketplace has played its part, for the new arrivals who are in ever-increasing numbers seeking the rewards of publication find that it is much easier to place a paper demonstrating the essential unity of some drama previously thought to be disunified than one which merely confirms the original negative judgment. Whatever the reasons, the revolution in opinion is now virtually complete. We have already built up a substantial bibliography of studies defending the multiple plots in a number of plays of the period, including most of the major works; and this new sympathetic view may finally be said to have attained the same canonical status once held by the older antipathetic one. When in 1958 Richard Barker published a book on Middleton in which he expressed the wish that we could simply forget the comic subplot of *The Changeling*, this reassertion of what had been the orthodox position less than three decades earlier struck his reviewers as "particularly imperceptive," if not "simply ludicrous." [9]

Although the campaign on behalf of the subplot has now been won, the fruits of this victory are still largely confined to these isolated studies—in articles, introductions to editions, and passages of books

---

8 Empson's seminal essay, "Double Plots: Heroic and Pastoral in the Main Plot and Sub-Plot," was published in *Some Versions of Pastoral* (London, 1935); but some of this material was included in an earlier lecture which Miss Bradbrook cites as an important influence on her book, *Themes and Conventions of Elizabethan Tragedy* (Cambridge, 1935).

9 Irving Ribner, *RN*, 12 (1959), 180; Calvin Thayer, *Books Abroad*, 34 (1960), 176. (Barker's preface says his book was "written nearly fifteen years ago.")

devoted to other matters—of the integration of individual plays.[10] It should now be possible to attempt a more comprehensive and systematic treatment of the subject which could supply the necessary framework for gathering together and assimilating this scattered body of material, and present a broader picture of the achievement of Renaissance multiple-plot drama. Such an investigation will not lead to many easy generalizations, since the one thing that has emerged most clearly from all of the recent criticism is the remarkable diversity of this drama. The subplots vary in emotional quality from the broadest buffoonery to the most serious themes, and in their internal structure from collections of discrete episodes to complete sequences of action. And in the degree of connection established between the main and subplot, one can discover every gradation from mere contiguity (which reminded Empson of the series of "turns" in a music hall) to extremely complex schemes of interrelationship. The range in the *kinds* of connections employed by the dramatists to integrate their plots is even more impressive and artistically more important, since these are what determine the basic form and effect of the work as a whole, and it is therefore not surprising to find that most of the controversy over the plays has centered here. Some of that controversy, both substantive and methodological, can be clarified if we examine this variable in greater detail by trying to separate out and classify the different senses in which two or more lines of action may be said to be "related" or "unified." And in this undertaking we can refer once more to Aristotle, for while his limited conception of dramatic unity was the source of much of the earlier misunderstanding, the more universal analytic insight embodied in his famous four causes provides a useful tool for organizing a survey of this type in terms of a scale of four possible kinds or modes of inter-plot connection.[11]

I

In the simplest and least significant of these modes, a connection is made between individuals from different plots by means of some conventional relationship which is established in the initial situation and which, since it is independent of their characters or actions, remains unchanged throughout the play. The persons linked in this way may be friends or neighbors, but more frequently they are blood relatives—in play after play of this period someone in the subplot

---

[10] See the lists in the Bibliography. We also have valuable general discussions of the subject in Madeleine Doran's *Endeavors of Art* (Madison, 1954), chaps. 10–11, and Norman Rabkin's "The Double Plot in Elizabethan Drama" (Ph.D. diss., Harvard, 1959).

[11] *Physics* II.iii.194^{b}16–195^{a}25, vii.198^{a}14–25.

is introduced as a sibling or cousin or simply an undefined "kinsman" of someone in the main plot. The utility of this kind of relationship in generating various interactions between the stories is obvious enough; but even if no such actions ensue and the connection is limited to this perfunctory level, it still supplies a ready-made probability for these characters to meet, to comment on each other, and to bring the remaining members of their two plots together in the ensemble scenes which regularly appear at crucial points in these dramas. Thus in *A Woman Killed with Kindness* the titular heroine, Anne Frankford, is the sister of Sir Francis Acton, who belongs to the subplot, and while this fact does not really affect the progress of either story, it helps to justify the presence of Sir Francis and his associates at the two "public" events of the main action that frame the play—Anne's marriage to Frankford in Act I, and her death in Act V. And many other examples could be found, typically in the denouement, where the dramatist is able to assemble the people of the different plots at a formal ceremony because their relationship allows them to meet on such occasions,[12] even though they have not made contact elsewhere. It is easy enough to make fun of this, as Lisideius does in Dryden's *Essay of Dramatic Poesy:*

> From hence likewise it arises, that the one half of our actors are not known to the other. They keep their distances, as if they were Mountagues and Capulets, and seldom begin an acquaintance till the last scene of the fifth act, when they are all to meet upon the stage.[13]

Yet these fifth-act weddings and feasts and funerals, with their still powerful ritual associations, do at least provide a shared activity which unites the separate sets of characters into a kind of community (as they did in real life), and in the better plays also serve to emphasize, through this spectacular visual conjunction, the more significant parallels between them.

Although a connection based on kinship has these advantages, it sometimes conflicts with the general scheme of the play when that requires a differentiation in the mood or tone of the plots in terms of social class. This occurs in *A Woman Killed with Kindness,* where the bourgeois domesticity of Anne's world is contrasted to the more aristocratic preoccupations of her brother's; and there is an even

---

12 E.g., the final wedding festivities in Shakespeare's comedies, the "May-night show" in *May Day,* the funeral in *A Chaste Maid in Cheapside,* the banquet in *The English Traveler,* etc. *The Shoemakers' Holiday* and *The Ball* are named for the closing ceremonies which assemble their separate plots.
13 W. P. Ker (ed.), *Essays of John Dryden* (Oxford, 1926), 1: 57; see also Neander's reply, 1: 69–71.

greater social distance between Russell in the subplot of Middleton and Rowley's *A Fair Quarrel* and his sister, Lady Ager, in the main plot. (Shakespeare avoids this improbability in *The Taming of the Shrew;* the striking difference in the quality of the two actions, which are linked by the fact that Katharina and Bianca are sisters, does not depend on class distinctions but on their opposed personalities, this being established at the outset as the genesis of the comedy.) The same discrepancy can arise when the related persons are friends or neighbors. In some plays we find a very unlikely collection of households set down on the same street simply for the sake of this "geographic" inter-plot connection.[14]

In still another kind of geographic unity the members of the separate plots do not begin as neighbors but come together during the action at a public gathering place which thus becomes the "cause" of the integration of the plots, and usually of the incidents occurring there. Jonson's *Bartholomew Fair* and Shirley's *Hyde Park* are notable examples of this strategy, and there are a few others in the period [15] (there are many modern counterparts, such as those multiplot novels converging on some hotel or ocean liner or doomed bridge). But this is a special case, less common than the relationships among kinsmen, friends, and neighbors.

All three of these relationships are essentially coördinative, implying an equality among the persons involved, which is why they tend to be incompatible with any marked disparity in social status or manner of life. But there are other connections that necessarily subordinate one character or set of characters to another, because they are relations of ruler to ruled—of a master to his servants, a general to his soldiers, a king to his subjects. They are of great historical importance since in such early works as Medwall's *Fulgens and Lucrece,* Preston's *Cambyses,* R. B.'s *Appius and Virginia,* and Pickering's *Horestes* they provide the basis for most of the comic episodes which play a crucial role in the evolution of the subplot convention.[16] And they usually place a much greater "distance" between plots than the

---

[14] As in *Mother Bombie* and *The Captives,* which derive from Roman comedy and may reflect the influence of that theater, where the stage usually represented a street with doors in the permanent back-scene indicating the principal households involved in the action.

[15] Such as *Holland's Leaguer, The Weeding of the Covent Garden, The Sparagus Garden, Tottenham Court,* and *Covent Garden,* all written, along with *Hyde Park,* in 1631–35 when the exploitation of the "sights" of the metropolis became a theatrical vogue (see Theodore Miles, "Place-Realism in a Group of Caroline Plays," *RES,* 18 [1942], 428–40). Compare the forest in *As You Like It.*

[16] David Bevington argues that the clowns in these episodes are descendants of the Morality "vice lieutenants," who have retained a place on the secular stage through this kind of connection (*From "Mankind" to Marlowe* [Cambridge, Mass., 1962], chap. 12).

coördinate relations, although there are exceptions (Gloucester, for instance, is a subject of King Lear, but an especially intimate one, as we infer from his function in the opening ceremony and from the fact that Lear was Edgar's godfather, so that this combination falls somewhere between the two extremes).

Despite their obvious differences, these two kinds of connection must still be located in the same class because they both form part of the *donnée* of the action and remain a constant there. And because they do, this mode of integration can be thought of as corresponding to the Aristotelian "material" cause: it is included in the original matter the playwright begins with prior to the action; it can be used in the manner of a building-block to produce more complicated structural effects; yet, as matter, it itself is static, unaffected by such elaborations or even by the temporal unfolding of the plots. And since it is the material cause, it is the least artistic of the four modes, requiring much less creative effort than the rest.

II

The next mode of integration would be equivalent to Aristotle's "efficient" cause; it is in fact what we ordinarily speak of as a "causal" connection, in which a character or event from one line of action directly affects the other. Although this causation often depends on a material linkage (for persons already related in some way are likely to affect each other), it is more difficult to construct since it cannot merely be added to the antecedent situation but must be built into the plot sequences rendered on the stage. It is also a more meaningful way to combine plots, because their mutual interaction knits them more closely together and makes them, quite literally, part of the same dramatic universe. The great majority of multiple-plot plays include such connnections, although they vary considerably from the most trivial incidents, sometimes obviously inserted for this sole purpose, to entire episodes having the most profound effects upon one or both story lines. And since this mode of connection, unlike the material mode, is necessarily temporal, its location within the larger structure can be another important variable.

In the opening scene of *A Fair Quarrel* the main-plot quarrel of Captain Ager and the Colonel and the subplot romance of Jane and Fitzallen forcefully interact as a result of the family relations that bridge across them; indeed, each plot initiates the other, since Jane's troubles begin when her father makes use of the quarrel to arrest Fitzallen, and Ager's when the Colonel insults him because of this arrest. But after that the plots separate until the final act, and then only come together on the material level in the ensemble scene at

Jane's wedding. In *King Lear,* on the other hand, the plots seem to be independent at the outset but gradually coalesce through a series of events following the arrival of Lear and his daughters at Gloucester's castle in Act II (a consequence of Gloucester's material connection to the royal court established in the first scene), until at the end they are inextricably entangled. A still different structural sequence is adopted in *Volpone* where the Peregrine-Sir Politic Wouldbe subplot starts out separately (II.i), suffers a violent intrusion from the main action when Mosca's ruse to get rid of Lady Wouldbe leads her to attack Peregrine as her husband's "base fricatrice" (IV.ii), and comes to a separate conclusion (V.iv). And the courtship of Beatrice and Benedick in *Much Ado about Nothing* makes contact with the Hero-Claudio action at all three stages: it is instigated by a conspiracy of the main-plot characters in II.i, reaches its turning point in IV.i where Beatrice asks Benedick to kill Claudio, and is resolved through another intervention by Hero and Claudio in the final scene. Nor does this exhaust the number of possibilities, which multiply rapidly when three plots are involved, and when one also takes into account the kind of causal connection and the kind of result it has.

Most of the older critics seem to have regarded this causal mode as the only means of integrating a multiple-plot play, which does much to explain their hostile attitude. When they complained, as they so often did, that two plots were not properly "connected" or "unified," they generally meant nothing more than that one line of action did not significantly affect the other. Such a view is just what one might expect of those who derived their conception of dramatic unity, consciously or not, from the definition in the *Poetics,* since the greater the degree of causal interaction between plots, the more nearly will they "represent one action" and the more extensive will be the dislocation produced by "the transposal or withdrawal of any one of them." This equation of unity with the efficient cause was presumably so obvious to them that they usually did not bother to state it, although sometimes it was made quite explicit. Yet it should be evident that such a formulation is too narrow, not merely because it ignores the two means of plot connection still to be taken up, but because it treats the causal nexus as an end in itself. Clearly unity on this level, as on the level of material relations, is not the ultimate achievement of the multiple-plot play. If it were, it could be attained much more completely and much more easily by eliminating all secondary plots. But if the subplot does make any substantive contribution to the work as a whole, it must be in terms of a broader conception of "unity," encompassing more complex and more important modes of integration. And it would follow that the causal connection, like the material one, is not developed for its own sake but primarily in order to generate and to enhance these other modes.

Before proceeding to them, however, there is one special kind of causation that should be noted, since it seems to occupy an intermediate position between this mode and the next. Whenever two plot lines are connected, materially, by the subordinating personal relations discussed earlier, it is then possible for the major line to influence the minor one without the sort of direct contact usually associated with an efficient cause. Sometimes, for example, we find the subservient characters attempting to imitate the behavior of their "betters" in the main plot; this is the basis of the subplot in *Fulgens and Lucrece,* since the two servants courting Joan are aping their masters' competition for her mistress, and this same device is used to motivate and integrate the comic activity of Wagner and Robin in *Doctor Faustus* and of several Shakespearean clowns. There are also equivalent situations where the protagonist's deeds, particularly if he is a monarch, indirectly affect the lives of his subordinates without any imitation being involved—thus in *Cambyses* the louts of the first subplot scene become soldiers because the king decides to attack Egypt, while those of the second are threatened for condemning his crimes, and similar connections are made in many low-comedy episodes of the Elizabethan history play. Subplots of this general type, whether imitative or not, may be said to be "caused" by the main action in this sense; but the nature of this causation tends to establish them as parallels to or comments upon the main action, and that relationship, which is usually the real point of these plots, properly belongs to the third mode of integration.

III

This third mode, corresponding to Aristotle's "formal" cause, includes all the logical—or more accurately, analogical—relationships obtaining between the plots. Unlike the material mode, it must be rendered through the action itself; but unlike the efficient mode, it is a dramatic constant, no more subject to time or change than a mathematical equation. Not only does the formal relation exist outside of time, but it is also ultimately perceived in this way, for although we infer it from the single sequence of alternating scenes which enact the separate plots, we do not fully comprehend it until we have abstracted these plots from the sequence and compared them as complete wholes placed, as it were, side by side. It is, to continue the figure, a spatial integration of plots, whereas that produced by the efficient mode is temporal.

The formal connection can be much more important to the overall effect than the material or efficient, and it can be much more complicated in its manner of working. It also figures much more prominently than these other modes in recent studies because it has been the primary focus of the whole revolution in defense of the multiple plot, for reasons already suggested. Since this was the mode most seriously neglected by earlier commentators, it is here that one is most likely to discover the unity which they had denied to these plays. Moreover, some formal relationships seem to provide a dramatic counterpart of the ambivalences and ironical tensions savored by the New Critics in their analysis of lyric poetry—particularly the relationship between a very romantic or heroic main action and a subplot that apparently mocks these lofty sentiments in a debased or cynical version of the same experience (Touchstone's antisentimentalism in *As You Like It*, Falstaff's soliloquy on "honor" in *1 Henry IV*, etc.). And the interest of the psychological and anthropological schools of criticism has also centered on certain relations within this mode, such as those between plots dealing with quite different areas of experience which are so combined as to implicate the processes of the subconscious or folk mind. Thus Empson, who devotes part of his essay to this kind of connection, argues that the two lines of action in Greene's *Friar Bacon and Friar Bungay* are unified through the equation of Margaret's beauty with Bacon's magic, and in *Troilus and Cressida* through a similar equation of love (or lust) and war, their respective subject matters. A still more obvious case is the relation of Gondarino's misogyny to Lazarello's gluttony in the separate plots of Beaumont and Fletcher's *The Woman Hater; or, The Hungry Courtier*, which will be examined along with other structures of this type in Chapter 5. Some of these equations, as Empson remarked, may even evoke primitive notions of a hidden causal connection linking the plots—for instance, the suggestion that Cressida's infidelity will bring about Troy's fall. But since this is the causation of homeopathic magic, produced not by the action of cause on effect but by the analogy constructed between them (as when a witch-doctor makes it rain by pouring water on the ground), it belongs to the formal rather than the efficient mode.[17]

Indeed, all the relationships of the formal mode from the most literal to the most "magical" are species of analogy, for they are based on the comparison of two or more persons, events, or concepts in one plot with an equivalent set in the other; and they could therefore be stated as proportions, if it is understood that the symbol ∼ joining

[17] See Angus Fletcher, *Allegory, The Theory of a Symbolic Mode* (Ithaca, 1964), chap. 4, "Allegorical Causation: Magic and Ritual Forms."

the separate ratios (that is, the separate plots) does not denote mathematical equality but only "significant comparability." In these terms the formal integration of *As You Like It* might be expressed as

Orlando : Rosalind ∼ Silvius : Phebe ∼ Touchstone : Audrey

and in the other plays

Hal : honor ∼ Hotspur : honor ∼ Falstaff : honor
Margaret : beauty : suitors ∼ Friar Bacon : magic : familiars
Gondarino : women ∼ Lazarello : food.

While there are many senses of "comparability" involved here, they are all reducible to the two fundamental relations of parallelism and contrast (or positive and negative analogy). But this does not mean all multiple plots can be classified under one of these heads, since their formal connection will always to some extent partake of both. If two plots were completely alike, they would not constitute an analogy but an identity; if they were completely different, there could be no grounds for comparing them. This would seem too obvious to mention were it not for the fact that we have seen recent controversies formulated in terms of whether a particular subplot belonged exclusively to one category or the other. Actually it is much more helpful to think of these not as categories at all, but as tendencies, vectors, possessed by all plot combinations in varying degrees. This truism, however, will not always resolve such controversies, since the relative strength of the two tendencies in a given play can sometimes pose serious problems of interpretation, especially, as will be shown, in so-called parody subplots. But it is not a problem different in kind from that presented by any other multiple-plot drama; we must always take both tendencies into account in order to comprehend the formal structure.

In *King Lear*, for example, everyone has noted how the family configuration of the main plot, Lear : Cordelia : Goneril and Regan, resembles that of the subplot, Gloucester : Edgar : Edmund. But some critics never seem to go beyond the positive aspect of this analogy, and one has even called these plots "precisely similar stories." [18] If that were true, we could justly accuse Shakespeare of sheer redundancy. But it is not, for having set up this basic parallel between his plots, he has then carefully and consistently differentiated them so that the subplot is in all respects less internalized and less serious than the main one. The initial tragic errors of the protagonists are contrasted in these terms, Lear's being self-generated, while Gloucester's

---

18 Wilhelm Creizenach, *The English Drama in the Age of Shakespeare*, trans. Cécile Hugon (London, 1916), p. 254. Those who only see this one aspect usually find that the only function of the subplot is to "universalize" Lear's tragedy.

is imposed upon him by Edmund's machinations; [19] and this also holds for their subsequent sufferings, the emphasis in Lear's case centering on his spiritual torment culminating in his loss of reason, in Gloucester's on the loss of his eyes; and for their regeneration, which Lear attains through a truly miraculous exchange of forgiveness with his wronged daughter, and Gloucester through a fake physical miracle staged by his wronged son; and, finally, for their deaths—Gloucester's heart " 'Twixt two extremes of passion, joy and grief,/ Burst smilingly" during his reunion with Edgar, but Lear's breaks when he is utterly crushed by the loss of Cordelia. This contrast also includes their children since the magnified extremes of pure malignity and self-sacrifice embodied in Lear's daughters are considerably attenuated in the analogous but much more "normal" opposition between Edmund's rational Machiavellianism, motivated by an understandable grievance and directed to an understandable goal, and the naïve innocence of Edgar, which is tempered by a very human instinct for self-preservation. It even determines the choice of scenes to be dramatized: in the main plot we are not shown the deaths of Goneril and Regan (who appropriately destroy themselves) but focus instead on Lear's tragic end, whereas the subplot reports Gloucester's death and represents the defeat of Edmund and triumph of Edgar in an external, non-tragic resolution.

We may need to be reminded that the formal analogy in all effective multiple-plot drama necessarily includes negative as well as positive aspects, because the main thrust of recent criticism tends to emphasize only the latter in refuting the old charges of disunity. In fact, the urgency of the search for relationships in this mode has sometimes driven defenders of the plays into questionable expedients. One of these I call the "atomic" approach to formal unity, the piling up of miscellaneous isolated details of character or incident or diction shared by both plots. This is the method of the "parallel-hunter," and while its application to the separate plots of a single work is a post-Empson phenomenon, it was much used by the older generation of scholars to discover the same sort of resemblance between separate works, in order to prove that one derived from the other or that they

---

[19] Northrop Frye notes that the subplot is a version of "the regular comedy theme of the gullible *senex* swindled by a clever and unprincipled son" (*Anatomy of Criticism* [Princeton, 1957], p. 175). Because of Edmund's trickery his two victims, who have no trouble understanding the main action, are totally confused about their analogical relation to it: Gloucester thinks Edgar's conduct toward him is like Lear's toward Cordelia (I.ii.119–21), and then like Goneril and Regan's toward Lear (III.iv.167–75), and Edgar thinks Lear "childed as I fathered"—i.e., Lear : Goneril and Regan ~ Edgar : Gloucester (III.vi.117). On the two "regeneration scenes" see Alvin Kernan, "Formalism and Realism in Elizabethan Drama: The Miracles in *King Lear*," *RD*, 9 (1966), 59–66.

had a common author. And beyond the scholarly arena it has always had its devotees, of the type Shakespeare parodied in Fluellen's demonstration that King Henry is a second Alexander the Pig, according to "the figures and comparisons of it":

> if you look in the maps of the 'orld, I warrant you sall find,
> in the comparisons between Macedon and Monmouth, that
> the situations, look you, is both alike. There is a river in
> Macedon, and there is also moreover a river at Monmouth.
> It is called Wye at Monmouth, but it is out of my prains
> what is the name of the other river. But 'tis all one, 'tis
> alike as my fingers is to my fingers, and there is salmons in
> both.[20]

Fluellian source and attribution studies are becoming less popular, but our well-founded suspicions of their method should carry over to double-plot analysis as well. It is a method easily abused, since it is without objective controls. Someone with sufficient ingenuity could claim a likeness between any two plots—or any two works or persons —in this manner, simply by taking care to select the right details and state them in such a way as to avoid all inconvenient discrepancies. This easily leads to distortions of fact or emphasis; but even if it did not the method would still be open to objection because the mere accumulation of detailed resemblances, no matter how accurate and numerous, is not in itself meaningful unless they add up to a comprehensive analogy in the structure of each plot and the work as a whole. In some plays we will find that a certain kind of "atomic" parallel—perhaps it should be a "nuclear" parallel—is of real importance in crystallizing this analogy; but the incidents involved will be crucial to their respective actions, usually in initiating the complication, or at the turning point, or the resolution, and their surface similarity will bring out the basic difference between them and between the two plots.[21]

There is another questionable approach to formal unity that goes to the opposite extreme. This method locates the parallel between plots not in a collection of particulars but in a single universal "theme" embodied in both—most commonly in one of those profound dichotomies of the human condition such as "appearance vs.

---

20 *Henry V*, IV.vii.24–35 (compare the recent efforts to connect the assassinations of Lincoln and Kennedy by a list of parallels). The misuse of this method in source studies is discussed by Harold Wilson, "*Philaster* and *Cymbeline*," *English Institute Essays* (New York, 1952), pp. 146–67; and in attribution studies by Ephim Fogel, "Salmons in Both, or Some Caveats for Canonical Scholars," *BNYPL*, 63 (1959), 223–36, 292–308.
21 E.g., the fathers' misjudgment of their children in *Lear*, the fidelity tests and suicides in *The Second Maiden's Tragedy*, the compacts in *Hyde Park*.

reality" or "reason *vs.* imagination" or "natural *vs.* artificial." [22] At its best, it has given us some very valuable criticism which is clearly superior to anything produced by the atomic approach, for it is directed to more interesting and more comprehensive aspects of the work as a whole (and generally attracts more interesting and comprehensive minds). But it is still subject to the same sort of abuse: it is without controls, since these themes could be abstracted from or imposed upon almost any pair of plots; and again, the theme itself will not constitute a meaningful relationship if it is not developed in a concrete structural analogy that orders the separate plots and their combination. And both of these approaches focus on only one side of such an analogy, because by their nature they tend to exaggerate its positive and minimize its negative components.

The overzealous pursuit of inter-plot parallels in the formal mode is also prone to another kind of error; too frequently it proceeds without sufficient regard for the temporal organization of the play. While it is true that this is a mode of atemporal or spatial relations, they must be enacted in and inferred from the single sequence of alternating scenes which we actually experience and which inevitably colors our perception of them. We can expect that the playwright will construct this sequence not only to provide suitable transitions from one plot to another within the larger dramatic movement, but also to invite the relevant comparisons between plots by causal connections and juxtapositions of analogous events. Thus Gloucester's readiness to trust Edmund over Edgar in the second scene of *King Lear* immediately reminds us of Lear's misjudgment of his daughters in the preceding scene, and Edmund's later alliance with Goneril and Regan against his father and theirs reasserts the equivalence of their roles in their respective plots. Any convincing analysis of formal integration, therefore, should produce confirmatory evidence from the arrangement of the action. But the arrangement has a negative role here as well in determining the legitimate limits of this analysis, limits which the critic ignores at his peril. If episodes from separate plots have not been made contiguous, or connected causally, or given comparable functions, it is unlikely that any logical analogy between them would be noticed by an audience, and still less likely that it would significantly affect their response to the work.

IV

The response of the audience is crucial, since it must be the ultimate test and justification of all formal relationships. Yet we find that some

---

[22] For some examples see chap. 2, n. 14; chap. 3, n. 27; chap. 5, n. 9, 34; chap. 6, n. 14.

recent defenders of the multiple plot, while criticizing the failure of the older generation to go beyond the efficient cause, themselves make a similar mistake in stopping short at the formal cause and treating it as an end in itself. Such a procedure, it seems to me, reduces the analysis of these plays to a formalistic game of parallelography, because it leaves out the purpose of their multiplot structure. Just as material connections provided a basis for efficient interactions, and the interactions pointed to the formal analogies, so these analogies subserve a higher level of integration—they relate the separate plots, intellectually and emotionally, in such a way that our reaction to one conditions and is conditioned by our reaction to the other, in order that both sets of responses can be synthesized, if the dramatist is successful, into a coherent overall effect which constitutes the real unity of the play.

This affective relationship between plots, then, is the fourth and last mode of integration, corresponding to Aristotle's "final" cause. It is not coördinate with the other three since it is the result of all of them together, and is in another sense their cause insofar as they are the product of conscious art. It is therefore the most important of the four, "that for the sake of which" the others exist. It is also the most complex because it includes the variables of the first three and others peculiar to itself, and for that reason it is the most difficult to survey in general terms, there being almost as many possibilities here as there are multiple-plot dramas in the period.

The major new variable introduced at this level is the emotional quality of the individual plots, since we must now consider not only how the connections are made but also what is being connected. In the response to a double-plot play it clearly makes all the difference whether the pairing involves two serious actions, or two comic actions, or a combination of both. But even if the plots are of the same genre, we typically find (as in *King Lear*) that each has a distinctive tone appropriate to its own characters and events, and this is also true of most triple-plot drama. In all these plays we are dealing with an effect resembling that of a musical chord, contingent upon the absolute emotional "pitch" of each action as well as the relative emotional "distance" between them. And the priority of the plots can add a further complication, for while the main one is usually the more serious, there are plays such as Middleton's *A Mad World, My Masters* and *A Trick to Catch the Old One* where the reversal of this order creates a special problem.

This differentiation in quality or tone was one of the principal complaints (along with the lack of causal connection) of the older critics in their case against the multiple plot. They were most disturbed, as might be expected, by plays like *The Changeling* with a very serious main plot and very comic subplot, although when the actions were much closer in mood they still protested that the conjunction was inharmonious. It should now be evident that this line of argument is based on an erroneous conception of dramatic unity, since it assumes these plays are integrated only to the extent that their plots are alike. But that is to treat the work of art as a mere aggregation of homogeneous parts, such as is found in the most primitive multicellular organisms and in very few Renaissance dramas.[23] The unity of these plays more nearly approximates that of the higher species in which the components are heterogeneous and complementary, each contributing in its own way to the total living process. And this surely applies to the mood or tone of the plots. It is true that the multiple plot has a simple accumulative effect, as Empson remarks, in encompassing a larger area of life and of our natural impulses,[24] though even this impression of "coverage," which is largely a function of the material cause, requires a differentiation of that matter, and hence of perspective and tone, between the individual actions (and in those plot combinations attempting to "cover" all the relevant possibilities, it also requires an exhaustive formal scheme). Beyond this, however, is the more complex integrative effect of the "final" synthesis, which is not just the sum of these different tones but a composite response produced *because* of their differences when they are brought to bear upon each other in a mutual interplay by means of the system of formal inter-plot relationships.

It might seem possible then to classify the kinds of affective unity in terms of the distinction between positive and negative analogy already noted in the formal mode, yet this is complicated by the need to take into account the mixture of these components in any formal relation, and also the emotional distance separating the plots related in this way. If the distance is not too great and one aspect of the analogy clearly predominates, as in some of the early plays where the didactic impulse is still strong, it is not difficult to generalize about the result. Thus if the compound structure sets up a positive analogy to affirm a universal admonitory lesson (as the title of Lodge and Greene's *A Looking Glass for London and England* promises), the difference in tone can equate the plots as parallel exemplifications of this lesson, accommodated to various levels of society and criminality. And when the purpose is to develop the negative analogy of a moral contrast (for instance, in the two major actions of Edwards's *Damon and Pythias*), a similar differentiation of tone can further separate the plots and reinforce the antithesis by elevating the good characters in

---

[23] A rare example is Yarington's *Two Lamentable Tragedies* which, as its running title acknowledges, is merely "Two Tragedies in One."

[24] "Double Plots," pp. 27, 29, 53–54.

one and debasing their opposites in the other. The homiletic program of *A Looking Glass* rarely reappears in the later drama, but we do find examples of the *Damon and Pythias* pattern of simple, direct moral contrast, which will be examined in Chapter 2.

The emotional and intellectual synthesis sometimes seems much less obvious, however, when the distance between plots is increased—especially, as was suggested, when a serious main action is joined to a so-called parody subplot presenting a low-comic version of that action. In terms of the distinction in the kinds of formal relationship, there are again the two extreme possibilities here. If the positive analogy is stressed, the subplot does function as parody in assimilating the main plot and lowering it to its own level; but if the analogy is essentially negative, the subplot becomes a foil which contrasts with the main plot and so enhances its seriousness, and may also anticipate and abort any potential deflationary response endangering that effect. Although it is easy enough to state this theoretically, the application is another matter; discussions of particular plays of this type have produced such marked disagreements that we can find two critics attributing these diametrically opposite results to the same subplot. Roland Frye claims that in the subplot of *Doctor Faustus* "the conjuring games of the low-life characters point by parallelism to the pettiness of Faustus's accomplishments" and so help "to underscore the dissolution of Faustus's human dignity," while John Crabtree thinks in these scenes "the comedy serves, by way of contrast, to maintain Faustus' dignity." [25] And accounts of the role of Pistol's gang in *Henry V* have divided along these same lines: according to Allan Gilbert they function as a "parody of Henry's heroics," since "by the comedy the bubbles of his glory now and then are pricked and he becomes no nobler than the thievish Pistol"; for Dean Frye they are foils who make the heroic main plot "even more striking and sympathetic by the contrast" and also "draw so much ridicule on to themselves that little will be left for the main characters." [26] I would agree with Roland Frye's view of *Faustus* and Dean Frye's of *Henry V*, although the issues involved in this argument, and the various complications and qualifications that can enter into it, must be reserved for Chapter 4, which will take up the whole question of these "clown" subplots.

The types of affective unity just considered are all the direct (if sometimes disputed) consequence of the formal parallels or contrasts relating the separate plots, but there is another, more indirect way in which these plots can mutually influence each other to produce a final

25 "Marlowe's *Doctor Faustus*: The Repudiation of Humanity," *SAQ*, 55 (1956), 325; "The Comedy in Marlowe's *Dr. Faustus*," *Furman Studies*, 9 (1961), 8.
26 "Patriotism and Satire in *Henry V*," *Studies in Shakespeare* (Coral Gables, 1953), p. 64; "The Question of Shakespearean 'Parody'," *EIC*, 15 (1965), 23–24.

synthesis. In *King Lear*, for instance, it would not be correct to say that the two actions are integrated in this mode either through a simple assimilation of their tones or through a simple repulsion that polarizes them. Rather, it seems that they exist in a kind of balance which helps to clarify the effect of each. The explanation of this, I think, lies in the relativity of the effect of any dramatized action. The seriousness with which one regards it, the attitude one adopts toward its central issues, the judgments made of its characters, and the sympathy they elicit, are all determined, not by an absolute a priori criterion (as is too often assumed in attempts to deduce "what an Elizabethan audience must have felt" from contemporary homiletic essays and the like), but by the context the author supplies. And while that context can be built into the action itself, it can also be extended very effectively beyond the action in a second plot constructed in a different emotional key to provide a further perspective. The tragedy of Lear seems even more extraordinarily moving and meaningful because our reaction to it is continually adjusted, and thereby heightened, in relation to the feeling evoked by Gloucester's fate, which is tragic enough in its own terms and yet is seen to be so much less internalized and less intense than Lear's.

The operation of this indirect affective synthesis, then, involves a tension between the positive and negative aspects of the formal analogy which does not directly equate or oppose the plots but places them in what might be called a hierarchic relationship based on the difference in degree of their relative tones. Such a relationship becomes still clearer when the frame of reference is enlarged by a third sequence (such as the Dogberry scenes in *Much Ado about Nothing,* or the Snuffe scenes in *The Atheist's Tragedy*) subordinated to the second in this same manner, for then the complete structure sets up a gradient of three descending levels of seriousness that defines the emotional and intellectual quality of each action and their integration in this final mode. Chapter 3 will consider a group of dramas making use of this type of hierarchy, where the first level is raised above ordinary life, the second treated more realistically, and the third lowered below the norm in the direction of farce. But this merely describes a very general formula which can encompass a wide range of effects depending upon the specific nature of the three components in any given work. And the formula itself, we will find, can be modified, since in some plays like *A Woman Killed with Kindness* and *The Lady of Pleasure* the first two levels are inverted and the resultant triadic integration is quite different. Moreover, we must remember that these levels are not only juxtaposed but are also joined through various material, efficient, and formal connections, all of which will further qualify the final synthesis to the extent that they participate in organizing our response to the several plots within the total dramatic experience. But detailing their possible contributions to the final mode would require a degree of particularity beyond the scope of this chapter, for the complex network of functional interrelationships is obviously different in each play. At this point in our survey we confront, as every such theoretical excursion must, the uniqueness of the individual work of art.

Nevertheless, if the approach has any validity, the unique configuration of each composite whole should be explicable in terms of permutations and combinations of the kinds of inter-plot connection identified in the four modes, and it therefore can be tested in the following chapters where this scheme is applied to the analysis of the exemplary plays. The chapters themselves, however, are not based on this scheme but on another set of categories located entirely within the formal mode, because it is the one that most directly determines the specific structure and effect of the plays. Thus each of these chapters investigates one of the fundamental relations of this mode, which are derived ultimately from the initial distinction between the positive and negative aspects of the formal analogy. It must be emphasized that this is a classification of plot relationships and not of plays, since any compound plot can employ more than one such relationship, and for that reason it has sometimes been necessary to deal with the same work under two different chapters. Each chapter proceeds from the simpler and clearer examples of its category to the more complicated and subtle, usually ending with an atypical or problematic case. And the chapters are arranged in a similar sequence according to the relative complexity (or difficulty) of the categories involved, from the straightforward contrasts of Chapter 2 to the extremely intricate structures of Chapter 6 which incorporate many of these formal patterns and must be ranked among the most ambitious and most impressive achievements of Renaissance multiple-plot drama.

2

Direct Contrast Plots

There can be little doubt that the simplest, most obvious, and most immediately effective way to integrate separate actions within the formal mode is through the relationship of direct contrast. As evidence we have only to look at the primitive narratives that have come down to us in the form of folktales, fairy tales, nursery stories, and the like, where we find such a connection operating almost every time two or more "plots" are involved. Usually, as students of folklore have pointed out, these structures are triadic: three persons, often siblings, are placed in competition in the same trial situation, in which the failure of the first and second (who are relatively undifferentiated) because of some intellectual or moral deficiency is contrasted with the success of the third (typically the youngest), who is of course their opposite in character. This pattern is repeated again and again in naïve tales on the order of "Cinderella" and "The Three Little Pigs," with their strong appeal to the childhood of the individual and the race, but it also appears in more sophisticated contexts. The episode, clearly of folktale origin, of Portia's three suitors and the three caskets in *The Merchant of Venice* is built upon it, as is the testing of the three wives at the end of *The Taming of the Shrew* and of the three daughters at the beginning of *King Lear* (although here the meaning is altered by the tragic irony inherent in Lear's mistake, so that the older, evil sisters seem to pass the test and the youngest and most virtuous to fail). There is no doubt that the tendency to juxtapose contrasting stories along these lines must be embedded very deeply in the basic narrative impulses of mankind.

Another basic impulse tending to produce this kind of inter-plot connection (which may also have figured in the evolution of the folk-lore pattern) can be seen in those narratives that have been deliberately constructed to teach a lesson by comparing the careers of two characters who exemplify the particular virtue in question and its contrary vice. Many of Christ's parables, for instance, are miniature double "plots" of this type in which the agents are analogized to opposed spiritual conditions—"The House Built on Rock and the House Built on Sand," "The Father and His Two Sons," "The Wise and Foolish Virgins," "The Sheep and the Goats," "The Pharisee and the Publican," "The King and His Servant" (where we have a complete proportion, King : Servant ∼ Servant : Debtor)—and there are even a few, such as "The Good Samaritan" and "The Talents," exhibiting the triple pattern of folklore.[1] A similar recourse to contrasting narrative *exempla,* used either in a literal or analogical sense, is a standard feature of sermons and other kinds of homiletic literature. And it is, of course, characteristic of such fables as "The Tortoise and the Hare" and "The Grasshopper and the Ant."

If we turn to the drama itself we find this formal relationship, involving both folk and didactic elements, in what has been called the earliest English double-plot play, the *Secunda Pastorum* of the Wakefield (or Towneley) mystery cycle. It is divided into two distinct parts —a kind of false nativity wherein Mak attempts to conceal a stolen sheep by pretending it is his newborn child, followed by the true Nativity of the Gospel—which are obviously meant to be contrasted, as a number of critics have shown. The contrast is developed very elaborately by means of a series of detailed parallels in the actions of the three shepherds who observe these events (in both sequences they awake from a sleep, are told of the child's birth through a dream, journey to him, are received by his parents, give him presents, etc.), in order to emphasize the profound differences between the two situations: between Mak's "black magic" used to put the shepherds to sleep so he can steal from them, and the "white magic" of the Angel who wakens them to an infinite blessing; between the two sets of parents, Mak the thief with his shrewish wife Gyll, and the Angel (standing for God the Father) with the Virgin Mary; between the stolen sheep passed off as a child (with its suggestions of heathen animal

---

[1] Matt. 7:24-27, Luke 6:46-49; Matt. 21:28-32; Matt. 25:1-13; Matt. 25:31-46; Luke 18:9-14; Matt. 18:23-35; Luke 10:30-37; Matt. 25:14-30, Luke 19:11-27 (this reverses the folklore sequence; the first two servants succeed and the third fails). Note also the family narratives in Genesis contrasting a favored son and his rejected brother: Abel and Cain, Isaac and Ishmael, Jacob and Esau, Joseph and his brethren.

deities) and the divine Lamb descending into human form. Although other more complex factors are involved in this remarkable juxtaposition, it seems clear that its basic unity, on the formal level, derives from the same kind of direct moral contrast found in the folktales and parables.

However, the structures of these folk and didactic narratives and of the *Secunda Pastorum* are not really multiple plots in our sense, since their components are almost invariably arranged in serial order and are conceived as successive incidents in a single linear progression, rather than as independent lines of action occurring over the same span of time. This is clear enough in the alternative version of the triadic folklore pattern, where instead of three rivals each making one attempt to pass the test, we have one hero making three attempts to pass it, failing wholly or partially on the first two and succeeding on the third. But even when several characters are involved the basic conception remains the same. Thus, for example, the selection of the caskets by the Prince of Morocco, the Prince of Aragon, and Bassanio in *The Merchant of Venice,* II.vii, II.ix, and III.ii (and in the folktale from which it derives), does not give us three separate stories, each with its own claim to our attention, but three episodes of one story, "The Winning of Portia"; [2] and similarly the actions of the Priest, the Levite, and the Samaritan in the parable are significant only as parts of a sequential demonstration of the meaning of "neighbor." And the two nativities in the *Secunda Pastorum* really fall into the alternative pattern of several consecutive attempts by one hero, insofar as they are treated as stages or tests in the enlightenment of the shepherds (a kind of collective protagonist) who earn, by their rejection of the false miracle and punishment of its perpetrator, the right to recognize and adore the true one. (In fact the entire Mystery Cycle itself has been interpreted in this way, with each of the pageants functioning as an event or "plot" in a single great drama portraying the divine plan for man.) This of course does not mean that these works are in any way inferior, for they have their own internal integrity, but that they can only be regarded as a kind of analogue of an actual multiple-plot structure built on the relationship of direct contrast.

A closer approximation to this structure can be seen in the Morality play, which, because of its self-conscious didactic commitment, might be expected to utilize contrasting *exempla* for the reasons already noted. This was not true of the early Moralities, since they were single-

---

[2] In the chief source, Fiorentino's *Il Pecorone,* IV.i, the test to win the Lady of Belmont is taken three times by the same suitor. Northrop Frye suggests an explanation of these triple rhythms in *Anatomy of Criticism* (Princeton, 1957), p. 187.

plot dramatizations of a "Psychomachia" or battle for the soul of a universal protagonist (Humanity, Humanum Genus, Mankind, Everyman), who was led into temptation by the allegorical vices and finally saved by the intervention of the allegorical virtues. But this form subsequently entered upon a process of secularization and specialization, in which the central concern shifted from the ultimate fate of man's soul to his success in this world, and from the whole of man's experience to some particular area of life (the problems of statesmanship, parenthood, education, wealth, etc.). As a result the generic protagonist of the early type tended to disappear, or rather to be narrowed down along various lines. And in one such development his moral and immoral proclivities, with respect to the specific problem of the play, were split off and emerged as two separate persons (or groups) whose simultaneous careers conveyed the lesson—the virtues leading the untempted good example to his reward, and the vices the unregenerate bad example to retribution.

In the third quarter of the sixteenth century we find a number of Morality plays which adopt this kind of double structure in order to show, as one title page puts it, "what punishment followeth those that will rather follow licentious living, than to esteem and follow good counsel; and what great benefits and commodities they receive that apply them unto virtuous living and good exercises." [3] In *Nice Wanton,* for instance, the fate of Barnabas, who was fortunate enough to be chastised in childhood, is contrasted to that of his permissively reared siblings, Ismael and Dalilah; in Wager's *Enough is as Good as a Feast* the two plots portray the lives of the temperate Heavenly Man and the insatiable Worldly Man; in *The Trial of Treasure* they work out the opposition between Just and Lust, and between their matched female consorts, Trust and Treasure; in Fulwell's *Like Will to Like* one plot centers on Virtuous Living and the blessings he earns, but the equivalent role in the second plot is divided among three pairs of knaves whose shared vices and fates illustrate the proverbial title— the profligates Tom Tosspot and Ralph Roister are reduced to beggary, Hans and Fleming, two drunkards, end in the hospital, and the thieves Cutpurse and Pickpurse are finally hanged (all through the unifying agency of Nichol Newfangle, the Vice, who corrupts each pair and promises each a reward, which turns out to be these punishments); and Wapull's *The Tide Tarrieth No Man* has a similar construction, one action depicting the right use of time by Christianity, and the other its misuse by the Courtier, Wantonness, Wastefulness,

---

3 *Like Will to Like.* The same point is made in the Prologue: "Herein, as it were in a glass, see you may/ The advancement of virtue, of vice the decay" (ll. 17–18).

Greediness, and No Good Neighborhood, who are also connected through the intrigues of the Vice.

Although the avowed purpose of this kind of structure would seem to call for a more or less equal development and continuous comparison of the two lines of action in alternating scenes, in actual practice the evil line almost completely takes over these plays, the good line being reduced to a few episodes which are introduced at crucial points (usually the beginning and end) but scarcely add up to a plot. This can be explained by the fact that the virtuous protagonist, since he is never really tempted, is an essentially static character with little more to do than utter pious speeches, and is therefore much less interesting than the villains and fools who are the centers of dramatic activity both in the commission of their crimes and in their subsequent punishment. The increasingly realistic emphasis of the theater, moreover, would tend toward the elaboration of these latter roles at the expense of the more abstract paragons of virtue. And it is also in this plot-line that the playwright could amuse his audience with the slapstick "comedy of evil," particularly through the mischief of the ever-popular Vice. It may even have been felt that the negative example provided by this line was a better incentive to reformation. But whatever the causes, the treatment of the moral opposition in this group of plays did not produce an artistically coherent double plot.

Therefore, while these late Moralities might be called a "source" of the exemplars of multiplot structure based on direct moral contrast which we are about to examine, the connection is at best rather tenuous. It is evident that this special development of the Morality does contain the fundamental idea of such a structure, but it should be equally evident that an idea of this sort does not require any literary source, because it is one of the primitive *données* of the storytelling process itself which can emerge spontaneously in very diverse contexts. The analogous patterns abstracted from various kinds of folk and homiletic narrative were intended to demonstrate this, and these Morality plays are perhaps best thought of in the same terms, as one more analogue or model testifying to the simplicity, obviousness, and effectiveness of the contrast relationship.

I

It must be pointed out, however, that this is not the formal relationship most frequently employed to unify the multiple-plot drama of the Renaissance. Its very simplicity may account for this, since we find that, while many plays incorporate such a connection within more complex structures, there are relatively few which rely primarily upon it. One of the most interesting of these is *The Second Maiden's*

Tragedy, an anonymous play of 1611 that has been ascribed to Middleton; [4] unfortunately, despite some favorable notice in recent years, it is still not very well known, but it can serve as a useful example of the integration of plots through a particularly clear and direct moral contrast.

The entire structure of the play is designed to establish this contrast between its two independent lines of action—a sensationally "romantic" main plot built around a lustful Tyrant, the Lady who becomes his victim, and her betrothed, Govianus, whose throne the Tyrant has usurped; and a much more "realistic" subplot that tells the story of Anselmus, the brother of Govianus, and of his Wife who betrays him with his friend, Votarius. But the relationship was lost on the older critics, who thought the play was not unified because the two plots did not interact and were so strikingly dissimilar in tone. Algernon Swinburne, for instance, complained that "the combination of the plots is . . . pitifully incongruous and formless"; and A. F. Hopkinson argued that their connection "is so slight that they could easily be separated without much injury to either; indeed, in my opinion both would be more effective printed and read separately." Nor have contemporary judgments been very different: according to one recent critic, the play "attempts to dramatize two entirely unconnected plots of revenge"; and another, who has given us our most extended and valuable analysis of the play, says, "It lacks unity of action, the two stories being joined together in a clumsy and arbitrary fashion. . . . The two actions are, indeed, linked through a device that is entirely artless and unconvincing: Govianus is the brother of the over-curious husband, and his Lady, we learn, is the Wife's sister." [5]

On the formal level, however, there is a carefully developed connection between these plots—a connection which does not depend on purely material sibling relations, or on the accumulation of the sort of "atomic" parallels discussed in the preceding chapter, although anyone who cared to hunt for them could find quite a number. Thus

---

4 His case is argued by Richard Barker, "The Authorship of the *Second Maiden's Tragedy* and *The Revenger's Tragedy,*" *SAB,* 20 (1945), 51–62; Harold Stenger (ed.), "The Second Maiden's Tragedy" (Ph.D. diss., Pennsylvania, 1954), pp. 79–197, 377–94; and Samuel Schoenbaum, *Middleton's Tragedies* (New York, 1955), pp. 183–202.

5 Swinburne's introduction to *The Works of George Chapman,* 2 (London, 1875), xxxvi; Hopkinson's introduction to his edition of the play (London, 1892), p. vi; Fredson Bowers, *Elizabethan Revenge Tragedy* (Princeton, 1940), p. 166; Schoenbaum, *Middleton's Tragedies,* pp. 37, 51. Schoenbaum qualifies the first statement in a note: "The two actions may perhaps be regarded as affording a contrast between two kinds of love—the sensuality of the Wife, as opposed to the highly idealized love of the Lady . . . But the two stories are handled so differently that the reader is scarcely aware of the contrast."

each plot centers upon a woman, A (the Lady, the Wife), who is caught in a triangle: she is married or betrothed to one man, B (Govianus, Anselmus), and pursued by another, C (the Tyrant, Votarius), who is aided by a pander, D (the courtier Sophonirus, and Leonela, the Wife's servant); in both plots B suddenly kills D; A commits suicide, using B's sword; A herself is made use of in a scheme to poison C, and so on. But the only essential parallel is the original triangle situation established in the two opening scenes, for once this initial stage is passed we become much more conscious of the differences than of the similarities between these two lines of action, which seem to move in exactly opposite directions.

Each plot begins with an episode that is clearly meant to function as a test of the heroine's virtue, since it requires her to choose between remaining faithful to the man to whom she rightfully belongs, legally and morally, or yielding to another whose desire for her is explicitly characterized as "lust." This test decides her fate, for the remainder of each plot develops the consequences of that crucial choice. The Lady passes her test by rejecting the Tyrant, and the resultant action elevates her through a series of further spiritual victories in the conversion of her father, Helvetius, her noble death, and her posthumous coronation. The Wife fails hers by giving herself to Votarius, and so her life takes an opposite course; because of this illicit affair she sinks deeper and deeper into a morass of suspicion, jealousy, and deception from which she finally attempts to escape by arranging a second, fraudulent fidelity test, but her plan doubles back on itself and destroys her.

These two plots, therefore, have very different emotional forms, since in each this form is determined by the heroine's career. Although they both would be called "tragedies," neither one aims at the kind of effect produced in Shakespearean tragedy by a sympathetic protagonist who, because of some internal flaw, brought on himself a catastrophe that seemed both deserved and undeserved. In the main plot we see, instead, a blameless protagonist whose wholly undeserved catastrophe is caused by the persecution of a villain and is treated as a triumphant martyrdom, so that the response called for by her course of action is not tragic pity and fear, or even pathos, but admiration and wonder. The first scene establishes this in the way it prepares for and focuses on her refusal of the Tyrant. Before her entrance he is shown glorying in his power, and when he announces that he means to make her his queen, everyone in the court, including Govianus, assumes she will accept. Therefore, when she finally appears, dramatically dressed in mourning, and declares, "I am not to be alter'd," the effect is one of general astonishment, stated most explicitly by the

Tyrant himself: "There stands the first/ Of all her kind that ever re-fus'd greatness." The same response is evoked in Act II by her firm resistance to her father's threats and blandishments, and to a still greater degree by her suicide in Act III, since Govianus's weakness then (he had agreed to kill her himself to save her from the Tyrant, but fainted at the last moment) only emphasizes her own strength of will. When he revives and realizes what she has done, his reaction clearly indicates our own:

> why it was more
> Than I was able to perform myself
> With all the courage that I could take to me . . .
> And hast thou, valiant woman, overcome
> Thy honor's enemies with thine own white hand,
> Where Virgin-Victory sits, all without help,
> Eternal praise go with thee!
>
> (III.i.1366–68, 1370–73)

And the Tyrant is also struck with wonder when he sees her corpse:

> And where got'st thou such boldness from the rest
> Of all thy timorous sex, to do a deed here
> Upon thyself, would plunge the world's best soldier
> And make him twice bethink him, and again,
> And yet give over.
>
> (IV.i.1847–51)

This whole movement reaches its climax in the final scene, where the Lady achieves a kind of apotheosis. She has become a secular saint and, like a saint, has the power of transforming those about her. Just as her father was converted by her noble behavior and brought to challenge the Tyrant in terms very like her own,[6] so now Govianus is inspired by her example and the prompting of her ghost to poison the Tyrant and defy the tortures with which his dying victim threatens him:

> Doom me, Tyrant;
> Had I fear'd death I'd never appear'd noble
> To seal this act upon me, which e'en honors me
> Unto my mistress' spirit.
>
> (V.ii.2379–82)

Her martyrdom has had miraculous consequences; it has resulted ul-timately in the cleansing of the entire corrupt court and the restora-tion of the rightful king to his throne. Therefore, Govianus's final

---

6 Compare his phrasing in II.iii.1086–87, 1133 with hers in I.i.130, 136–38.

speech of tribute to her—almost of worship [7]—is a statement of her deserved reward and our own response to her story.

The subplot has a very different emotional form. Here a deeply guilty protagonist is overtaken by a deserved punishment, and the effect is a kind of grim fascination and satisfaction in the workings of this inexorable retribution. During the decisive test in her opening scene when the Wife suddenly feels herself drawn to Votarius, she realizes that to surrender to this temptation is to "run thus violently/ Into the arms of death, and kiss destruction"; and in the climactic episode she cries, "Welcome, ruin," just before she "purposely runs between" the swords of Anselmus and Bellarius to her death. Her real punishment, however, as Schoenbaum observes, is not death itself but the process of internal degeneration leading to it, which can be traced in the gradual coarsening of her character, in her humiliating subservience to her servant Leonela, and in her hypocrisy and increasing reliance on deception, culminating in the second fidelity test where, with appropriate justice, she is "deceiv'd once in her own deceit." The stages in this descent are punctuated by the contemptuous remarks of Leonela, whose commentary on her mistress during or immediately after each meeting with Votarius performs a choric function here roughly analogous to Govianus's reverent tributes to his Lady. And this judgment is also confirmed by the effects of her course of action on those about her, since her example, like the Lady's, has been infectious, but with diametrically opposite consequences. Because of her moral failure she has dragged her husband and lover down with her to degradation and death.

This fundamental contrast defines the formal relationship between the plots when they are abstracted from the play and considered side by side. But it was noted earlier that any such "spatial" analysis must be confirmed in the "temporal" sequence of alternating scenes presented to the audience. When this sequence is examined, it becomes clear that the four scenes of the subplot which enact the Wife's downward movement have been arranged and developed in such a way as to enforce a comparison with the main action. In the beginning of the first subplot scene (I.ii), Votarius, while attempting to dissuade Anselmus from his plan to test his wife, reminds him of the plight of his brother dramatized in I.i—a reminder that serves as a transitional de-

---

[7] The play sharply distinguishes Govianus's reverence for the Lady's ghost (in IV.iv and V.ii) from the Tyrant's sensual adoration of her corpse, which is called "mere idolatry" (V.ii.2237). This ending, and the basic formula for the plot itself, suggest the medieval saint play and later tragedies belonging to that tradition, such as Dekker and Massinger's *The Virgin Martyr* and Marston's *Sophonisba* (whose subtitle, *The Wonder of Women,* could be appropriated for the Lady's story).

vice to link the two plots and also suggests the emotional distance between them. This introduces the crucial episode, Votarius's temptation of the Wife, which we saw parallels in its essential aspects the Tyrant's temptation of the Lady in the preceding scene, thereby establishing the common base from which the stories will diverge.[8] After this the Wife attacks Leonela for acting as Votarius's pander, which both prepares for and contrasts with the situation in the next scene (II.i) where the Lady and Govianus attack her father, Helvetius, as the Tyrant's pander. The Wife is insincere since she is trying to saddle Leonela with her own guilt, and the result of her false accusation, ironically, is to cause Leonela at the end of the scene to undertake this role, while the accusations of the Lady and Govianus are true and quickly bring about the reformation of Helvetius.

This reform is itself utilized to provide the next dramatic contrast between the plots. Because of it the Lady, her betrothed, and her father attain an idyllic harmony based on mutual love and respect, and can end their scene together in the following terms:

HELVETIUS. Be you my king and master still, henceforward
My knee shall know no other earthly lord;
Well may I spend this life to do you service,
That sets my soul in her eternal way.

GOVIANUS. Rise, rise, Helvetius.

HELVETIUS.   I'll see both your hands
Set to my pardon first.

GOVIANUS.   Mine shall bring hers.

LADY. Now, sir, I honor you for your goodness chiefly;
Y'are my most worthy father, you speak like him,
The first voice was not his; my joy and reverence
Strive which should be most seen; let our hands, sir,
Raise you from earth thus high, and may it prove
The first ascent of your immortal rising,
Never to fall again.

HELVETIUS.   A spring of blessings
Keep ever with thee, and the fruit, thy lord's.

GOVIANUS. I ha' lost an enemy and have found a father.

(II.i.801–18)

But immediately afterward Votarius enters to open the next scene with a soliloquy expressing his reaction to his successful seduction of the Wife:

---

8 Note also that the terms in which the Lady refuses the Tyrant: "I come not hither/ To please the eye of glory, but of goodness" (I.i.136–37), are inverted in the argument used by Votarius to seduce the Wife: "You still retain your goodness in yourselves,/ But then you lose your glory, which is all" (I.ii.475–76).

All's gone, there's nothing but the prodigal left;
I have play'd away my soul at one short game
Where e'en the winner loses—
Pursuing sin, how often did I shun thee?
How swift art thou afoot, beyond man's goodness,
Which has a lazy pass; so was I catch'd,
A curse upon the cause! . . .
How I could curse myself! Most business else
Delight in the dispatch, that's the best grace to 't,
Only this work of blind repented lust
Hangs shame and sadness on his master's cheek,
Yet wise men take no warning—nor can I now;
Her very sight strikes my repentance backward,
It cannot stand against her.

(II.ii.821–27, 837–43)

The impact of this speech depends not only on the abrupt, gross change of mood but also on the way this is extended down to particular details and phrases. Votarius's soliloquy matches almost exactly each of the themes in the dialogue that precedes it—repentance is opposed to the inability to repent, blessing to cursing, winning to losing, love to lust, honor to shame. And this elaborate opposition is implicitly related to the basic difference between the two heroines, since it is treated as the consequence of their decisive choices in the first act. The juxtaposition of the plots at this point, therefore, powerfully reinforces the effect of each, and of their combination in the play.

A similar procedure is adopted to introduce the third scene of the subplot (IV.i), which opens upon Votarius's quarrel with the Wife, caused by his groundless suspicions, and thus effectively sets off Govianus's tender eulogy of his Lady at the end of Act III—the quarrel demonstrating the fragility of the relationship built on illicit lust, as the eulogy demonstrates the strength of true love that can even transcend death. It is in the fourth and final subplot scene (V.i), however, that the contrasts with the main action are most fully developed. The two plots actually meet here for the first and only time, when at the close of the scene Govianus comes to his brother's house for aid in recovering the body of the Lady. This action is poorly motivated, to be sure, and has no effect on either plot, but it provides a dramatic transition emphasizing the great distance between them, since he arrives in time to hear the whole sordid tale of intrigue, corruption, and murder that makes up the subplot from Bellarius (who after Leonela's death has taken over her role of sardonic chorus, and further debases the story in his manner of relating it), just before going on in the last

scene of the play to achieve his ultimate victory and the ultimate vin-
dication of his Lady.

Much more important to this conclusion of the subplot is the death
of the Wife, which is deliberately played off against the death of the
Lady in Act III. Although both are technically suicides, they are given
completely different ethical contexts. The Lady's suicide was treated
as a martyrdom, a triumph over the evil forces threatening her sacred
honor,[9] and won for her the admiration of the other characters and
the audience. When the Wife is staging her second test to convince
Anselmus of her fidelity, she vows that to escape Votarius's advances,

> I'll imitate my noble sister's fate,
> Late mistress to the worthy Govianus,
> And cast away my life as she did hers.
>
> (V.i.2079–81)

But this reminder of the Lady's heroic death serves to underscore the
disparity between the situations, since we know the Wife is only saying this to deceive her husband. Her own suicide, following soon after,
does not represent a triumph of any kind; it is a reckless gesture of
utter desperation, part of the punishment for her sin. This essential
contrast between the two deaths—and between the two careers that
culminate in them—is brought home by the epitaphs of these women
and the disposal of their bodies, which constitute the final judgment
of the play upon them. After the Lady's suicide Govianus says:

> Come, thou delicious treasure of mankind,
> To him that knows what virtuous woman is,
> And can discreetly love her, the whole world
> Yields not a jewel like her . . .
> Fountain of weeping honor, I will kiss thee
> After death's marble lip; thou'rt cold enough
> To lie entomb'd now by my father's side;
> Without offense in kindred there I'll place thee
> With one I lov'd the dearest next to thee.
> Help me to mourn, all that love chastity.
>
> (III.1450–53, 1456–61)

And in the last speech of the play he gives orders that her body be
placed on the throne and crowned before it is solemnly borne back to
her tomb.

---

9 The term "honor" has different meanings in the two actions. For the Tyrant
and Helvetius before his change it denoted social status (the Lady calls this
"bastard-honors"—I.i.135); but it is usually applied in the main plot to the
Lady's chastity—her tomb is a "Temple of Honor" and she is the "eternal Maid
of Honor" (IV.iv.1882, 1919). In the subplot after the Wife's seduction it usually
refers to her *reputation* for chastity, and at the end Bellarius calls her "an honorable whore" (V.i.2140). Thus in another sense she also dies defending her "honor."

Over the Wife's body Anselmus, who is himself mortally wounded, pronounces two separate epitaphs. In the first, spoken while he still believes in her, his lament begins, "I ask no more of destiny but to fall/ Close by the chaste side of my virtuous mistress," and echoes some of Govianus's phrasing. But we know he is deluded, and a few moments later when he learns the bitter truth about her his words are very different:

> A whore!
> I fling thee thus from my believing breast
> With all the strength I have; my rage is great,
> Although my veins grow beggars; now I sue
> To die far from thee, may we never meet;
> Were my soul bid to joy's eternal banquet
> And were assur'd to find thee there a guest,
> I'd sup with torments and refuse that feast;
> Oh, thou beguiler of man's easy trust,
> The serpent's wisdom is in women's lust.
>
> (V.i.2188⁷⁻¹⁶)

This marked contrast between the fates of the two women is neatly summed up in a pun that the play seems to insist upon. The Lady, although she nobly refused the title in I.i when it was offered her by the Tyrant, becomes a queen at the end; Govianus addresses her ghost as "thou Queen of spirits" and in the closing speech of the play, during her posthumous coronation, calls her "our Queen" and "Queen of silence." But the Wife, we are reminded, has become a *quean*. This is how Votarius referred to her in that soliloquy following her downfall (II.ii.831). Later, when reproving Leonela for her indiscretion with Bellarius, the Wife calls her "a bold quean," to which her servant retorts, "And are not you, my mistress?" (IV.i.1561–62). And when Anselmus before his disillusionment mourns her death, Bellarius savagely attacks him:

> Thou could'st kill her [Leonela]
> Without repenting, that deserv'd more pity,
> And spend'st thy time and tears upon a quean.
>
> (V.i.2145–47)

This analysis, then, should explain how the playwright integrated his two plots, not through any causal connection (for nothing that happens in either affects the other), but through the formal relationship of direct contrast. An overall analogy has been set up—both in the general conception of the heroines and their fates, and in the details of the dramatic sequence—that establishes a parallel between the actions in order to exploit their differences. Thus the positive aspect of this analogy always subserves and reinforces its negative aspect, since the successive points of comparison increase our sense of the moral distance separating the two women, which, it was seen, continuously widens as they proceed on their divergent careers. And the same is true of the emotional effect of the combination; our grim acquiescence in each new stage of the degeneration and punishment of the Wife tends to enhance, in an inverse proportion, the growing admiration and wonder evoked by each new spiritual victory of the Lady.

The same artistic purpose should also account for the obvious differences of tone or range between the plots that troubled the critics quoted above. Since the main plot is designed to emphasize the Lady's extraordinary heroism, it is rendered in a very elevated (and not very successful) poetic and constructed along quite simple lines, with a slow moving and highly stylized action requiring relatively little complication of incident, and with characters sharply divided into the extremes of virtue and vice. (Even Helvetius is no exception—before his conversion he is wholly evil, and after it wholly good.) In the subplot, on the other hand, both the language and the characters are much closer to the ordinary and more "realistic"—no one is as exalted as the Lady, and no one as depraved as the Tyrant. The action, moreover, is much more complex than in the main plot, since it follows the tangled web of intrigue and counterintrigue produced by the Wife's deviation from the straight path of virtue. The subtle gradations and degradations of personality, as well as the involuted ironies and peripeties, all are appropriate to this drama of moral weakness and retribution; and while this kind of development may well seem the more interesting of the two, especially to the modern sensibility, there can be no doubt that its esthetic function is to provide the debased background that will help to magnify the contrasting drama of pure, triumphant virtue enacted in the main plot.

II

Although most double-plot plays utilizing the relationship of direct moral contrast place the virtuous line of action in the main plot and subordinate the other to it, there are a few where that arrangement is reversed. Certainly the most famous of these is *The Changeling*, by Middleton and Rowley, which has a special importance in this study because Empson's and Bradbrook's defense of its subplot against the universal condemnation of the older critics constituted a major breakthrough in the campaign discussed in the preceding chapter.[10] Since

---

10 A sampling of these earlier attacks on the subplot (by Boas, Ellis-Fermor, Oliphant, Spencer, Swinburne, Symons, etc.) is included in Karl Holzknecht's "The Dramatic Structure of *The Changeling*," *Renaissance Papers* (1954), 77–87.

their time the integration of its two actions has been so thoroughly explored that it should be possible to pass over some points of relatively minor interest (such as the sequential alternation of the scenes) and concentrate on the more significant or unusual aspects of this connection, beginning with those which can be illuminated by a comparison with *The Second Maiden's Tragedy*.

The main plot of this play, set in a citadel governed by Vermandero, centers on his daughter, Beatrice-Joanna, who has been betrothed to Alonzo de Piracquo but falls in love with Alsemero and, in order to marry him, persuades De Flores, her father's attendant, to murder Alonzo, only to find that as a result she must become De Flores's mistress and then his ally in further intrigues (including the murder of her maid, Diaphanta) required to conceal their relationship, until they are finally discovered and destroyed. And the subplot, which is located in an insane asylum run by Alibius, is concerned with the successful efforts of his wife, Isabella, to withstand the advances of Antonio and Franciscus, who have disguised themselves as madmen to gain access to her, and of Lollio, Alibius's assistant, who hopes to take advantage of their suit to get a hold over her himself. The two plots are related on the material level, since Alibius's madhouse is near Vermandero's castle and is apparently dependent upon his patronage, and Antonio and Franciscus are gentlemen of Vermandero's household. Both of these relations also lead to causal connections between the plots in the final scenes, where Alibius is to supply a masque of his patients at the celebration of Beatrice's marriage to Alsemero, and Antonio and Franciscus, because of their unexplained absence from the castle, are suspected of Alonzo's murder. But the principal connection, as recent criticism has demonstrated, is the contrast on the formal level between the two parallel "ratios"—Beatrice : Alonzo : Alsemero : De Flores ∼ Isabella : Alibius : Antonio and Franciscus : Lollio.

This parallelism, while it involves various elements of character, thought, and imagery,[11] is established most clearly in the act of sexual blackmail that is central to both plots. When De Flores sees the secret rendezvous between Beatrice and Alsemero, he decides that if "she transgress; happily/ Then I'll put in for one" (II.ii.59–60), and Lollio, overhearing Antonio woo Isabella, has exactly the same thought: he tells her he will demand his "share" (III.iii.245), and renews his claim

---

11 The parallel imagery is discussed by N. W. Bawcutt (ed.), *The Changeling* (Cambridge, Mass., 1958), pp. lxiv–lxv, and George Williams (ed.), *The Changeling* (Lincoln, 1966), pp. xx–xxii. Christopher Ricks suggests that the density and insistency of sexual double entendre in the subplot alert us to similar but less obvious locutions in the main action ("The Moral and Poetic Structure of *The Changeling*," *EIC*, 10 [1960], 301).

in their next scene, "If I find you minister once and set up the trade, I put in for my thirds" (IV.iii.35–36). The outcomes, however, are completely different. Beatrice is forced by her blackmailer's threats to submit to him, as payment for his killing Alonzo; but Isabella threatens that she will submit to Antonio as payment for his killing her blackmailer:

> Be silent, mute,
> Mute as a statue, or his injunction
> For me enjoying, shall be to cut thy throat
> (III.iii.240–42)

And in IV.iii she manipulates both Antonio and Franciscus in the same way, promising each one her favors if he will dispose of the other for her after the wedding masque (ll. 147–54, 188–99).[12] Thus these repetitions (or rather, inversions) of the turning point of the main plot bring out the basic contrast between the two actions, since Isabella is able to victimize her would-be seducers with the very weapon which Beatrice's victimizer uses to seduce her.

The general development of this contrast closely resembles that found in *The Second Maiden's Tragedy* and can be stated in almost identical terms. In each plot the heroine (Beatrice, Isabella) is tested by being faced with a choice between remaining faithful to her betrothed or husband (Alonzo, Alibius) or betraying him with a rival (Alsemero, Antonio/Franciscus), whose cause is aided, indirectly, by a servant who lusts after her himself (De Flores, Lollio); and again, one woman fails the test and therefore must descend along a path of deception, crime, and degradation to a shameful death, while the other passes and so emerges victorious. Even the consequences for the other characters are similar: as a result of her fatal choice, Beatrice brings death to her betrothed, her maid, and her lover, and dishonor to her father and husband; but Isabella, because she does not succumb, is able to "cure" her husband and suitors of their faults.[13]

This description of Isabella's effect on those around her, however, points to a fundamental difference in the emotional or "final" organization of the two double structures, for while the Beatrice-plot, with its naturalistic portrayal of the deserved and inexorable retribution visited upon a guilty protagonist, can be said to evoke the same gen-

---

12 The language in both incidents echoes that of Beatrice and De Flores—cf. l. 150 with II.ii.144, l. 192 with II.ii.134, and l. 154 with III.iv.97–99.

13 Williams (p. xxi) remarks that this metaphor also functions in the contrast between the women: Beatrice promises De Flores that she will perform "a work of cure" on his complexion (II.ii.85), and Alsemero that his suspicions will be "cur'd" by her (V.iii.18), although she can do neither; but Isabella really "can cure fools and madmen" (IV.iii.32, cf. l. 183).

eral type of response as the Wife-plot in *The Second Maiden's Tragedy*, the Isabella-plot certainly is not aimed at anything like the sense of admiration and wonder produced by the elevated tone and heroic martyrdom of the Lady-plot. Isabella's success entails no sequence of ever more awesome triumphs (in fact there is no clear sequence to her career, since, as will be seen, the plot never reaches its climax), and it depends less on some extraordinary virtue than on her common sense and even her sense of humor.[14] Moreover, this line of action never really threatens any serious harm and terminates, not in the destruction or religious conversion of her antagonists, but in their exposure, deflation, and "cure." It is comedy, and quite low comedy, drawing upon one of the stalest formulas of the period, where an old, jealous, foolish husband married to a young, pretty, clever wife is cuckolded as a result of the very stratagem he adopted to prevent it. But this mode of treatment actually increases our surprise when she remains faithful to him, not only because it establishes the contrary expectation, but also because it provides her with a stronger case for transgressing than Beatrice, to the extent that Alibius is inferior to Alonzo, and has given her, in his jealous tyranny, greater provocation and at the same time greater opportunity. Her victory is therefore as remarkable as the Lady's in its own way and can serve a comparable function in enlarging the distance between the two actions: just as the Wife's complete failure in her much less demanding test in the subplot of the earlier play made the Lady's triumph in her own test seem more astounding, so the kind of miracle represented by Isabella's continued fidelity to Alibius is designed to render even more culpable Beatrice's immediate betrayal of Alonzo in her analogous but weaker temptation.

Although Isabella's success may be a kind of miracle, it is still conceived and enacted on the level of very broad comedy. But this aspect of the subplot, which the older critics found so distressing, also becomes more understandable when compared with the "final" integration of *The Second Maiden's Tragedy*. In both plays the subplot supplies a perspective, a background of contrasting moral coloration, that helps to clarify our judgment of the main plot and to enhance its

---

14 This would place her somewhere between Irving Ribner's Isabella, who is preserved by "the grace of God" so that the two plots can be "united by a common theme" concerning "the nature of evil in the world" (*Jacobean Tragedy* [New York, 1962], pp. 124, 129), and T. B. Tomlinson's Isabella, at the opposite extreme, who must be willing to accommodate her seducers in order to accommodate his quite different "thematic" unification of the play (*A Study of Elizabethan and Jacobean Tragedy* [Cambridge, 1964], pp. 200–3). Those responsible for the 1964 production of the Lincoln Center Repertory Theater apparently agreed with Tomlinson.

significance. And in both this background is subordinated to the foreground of the main action by being pitched in a lower dramatic key. We found that since the Lady-plot of *The Second Maiden's Tragedy* was an exercise in exalted heroics, the Wife-plot appropriately presented a more realistic picture of sordid intrigue and ironic reversal; but since the Beatrice-plot of *The Changeling* aims at approximately this same realistic and ironic tone, the Isabella-plot is with equal appropriateness reduced still lower on the emotional scale. (Even the social status of the characters is defined accordingly: in the first play the domestic world of the subplot was as far below the royal court of the main plot as the inhabitants of Alibius's asylum are below those of Vermandero's castle.) Thus, in order to effect the necessary "final" subordination, these two plays must make use of three distinct levels of sensibility which could be arranged into a single hierarchy of descending seriousness, as will be seen in the group of plays to be examined in the next chapter.

Despite these marked differences of tone, the formal connection between the two plots in *The Changeling* remains essentially the same as in *The Second Maiden's Tragedy*—a negative analogy built on direct moral contrast. *The Changeling*, however, develops further refinements within this basic analogy which are much more subtle and complex than anything in the earlier play. Several critics have shown that the subplot here is constructed not only as an innocent parallel to the serious actions of the main plot but also as a kind of literalization of those actions, particularly in its treatment of disguise and madness. Everything in the subplot depends, of course, on the fact that Antonio and Franciscus (and Isabella in one episode) are actually disguised. And in the main plot everything is made to turn upon a metaphorical disguise which expresses Middleton's brilliant conception of the relationship of his heroine's character to her fate.

It was seen that Beatrice's story, like the Wife's, constitutes a villain-hero or retribution plot; yet it is obvious that neither woman is at all like the gloating Machiavellian "politicians" or bloodthirsty fiends who usually serve as the protagonists of such plots in this period. They are much closer to ordinary humanity; they do not actively seek evil, much less delight in it, but are driven to it by the "push" of circumstances (as opposed to such typical villains as Richard III and Sejanus, who self-consciously undertake a series of crimes because of the "pull" of some long-range vicious goal). This is about all that can be said of the Wife, whose character, while competently drawn, is too thin to provide anything more than a very general probability for the various stages of her dramatic career. But Beatrice has been given a real individuality which is made uniquely appropriate to her original crime, and her downfall, and her punishment. She is, in Una

Ellis-Fermor's phrase, a "spoilt child," [15] who has grown into woman-hood in a castle ruled by her doting father without ever having her desires crossed, without, consequently, ever having to develop an internal discipline. Thus she is not so much immoral as amoral. She literally does not know the difference between right and wrong; all she knows are her wishes. Anything she desires and anyone serving her desires is "good"; anyone standing in the way of these desires (Alonzo in II.ii, De Flores in III.iv, Diaphanta in V.i) is "wicked." And since she has known no other world than the world of her wishes, they become (or rather remain, for they are such in every child) not only her principle of evaluation but also her reality-principle. She has retained the child's ability to refuse to see what she does not want to see, to refuse to admit the existence of whatever might interfere with the fulfillment of her wishes.

But these wishes are themselves determined by another closely related aspect of her personality, her esthetic sensitivity. Beatrice is herself beautiful and is attracted by beauty and repulsed by ugliness in others. She has an innate delicacy of taste, a fine appreciation of the surfaces, particularly the visual surfaces, of life, upon which her responses tend to center. The narrowness of such a focus is correlative to her stunted sense of reality; as Miss Ellis-Fermor says, her "judgements are rather pictures suddenly presented to [her mind] and, once presented, blocking out all other views . . . her limitation is to realize nothing that is not pictured in her mind." But this same quality also is the positive force directing her actions, since it serves as the real basis of all her values, her substitute for a moral consciousness. It is at the heart of her egotism: her awareness of her own loveliness, an awareness which is part of her sensitivity, assures her that she is a special person and that whatever she wants (that is, finds pleasing in her sight) is right, because she, being beautiful, deserves beautiful things. It is also the standard by which she judges others, as becomes very clear in the opening scene where this visual principle is introduced to explain both her love of Alsemero ("Sure, mine eyes were mistaken,/ This was the man was meant me") and her hatred of De Flores ("Such to mine eyes is that same fellow there").[16] This in fact is how these two men are set up as the polar opposites who define her downward movement in the play. And this movement is itself made the direct result of these same traits of character.

For Beatrice brings about her own downfall through the two fatal

---

15 *The Jacobean Drama* (London, 1936), pp. 146–48. Her brief remarks are still, I believe, our most perceptive analysis of Beatrice.
16 Cf. I.i.72–76 and the many other references to sight and appearance in this scene. Later Beatrice often expresses her attitude toward both men in visual terms —e.g., II.i.13–19, 58; II.ii.40–45, 67, 146; III.iv.14–17.

mistakes which determine the sequence of action ending inevitably in her exposure and death—her schemes to kill Alonzo and to deceive Alsemero on their wedding night. Both schemes follow the same pattern, reflecting the special but limited art of the spoilt child, and both backfire for this same reason. In each case, when faced with a problem, Beatrice's immediate impulse is to find someone she can coax into getting her out of it. In each case she succeeds, and is enormously pleased with what she thinks of as her "art." But her blunder, each time, is that of the child who is certain the world revolves around her; she assumes her "servants" will be eager to do what she wants because she wants them to, and content to accept the reward she is willing to bestow—a few kind words and money. She never allows herself to suspect that they might not be grateful for the privilege of serving her, that they might have independent motives of their own. And because of this miscalculation, each of these clever plans becomes a step in her undoing.

In the first and more important of these her esthetic transvaluation of values also plays a crucial role. As she begins to think of Alonzo's murder in II.ii, we quickly realize that her perception of it is visual rather than moral; to her it is merely something ugly. (This is confirmed afterward when De Flores brings her Alonzo's severed finger and she reacts to it, not as the reminder of a horrible crime, but as an unpleasant sight to be disposed of.) Thus while it is beneath the worth of the handsome Alsemero—for he is worthy of *her*—it is perfectly suited to someone as distasteful as the deed. It is in just these terms that her mind lights upon De Flores:

> Blood-guiltiness becomes a fouler visage,
> [*Aside.*]—And now I think on one
> > (II.ii.40–41) [17]

And she comforts herself with the appealing thought that

> the ugliest creature
> Creation fram'd for some use
> > (ll. 43–44)

which in her view of Creation means some use to her. Later in this scene she enlists his aid with all the wiles of the pampered coquette, starting out, typically, at the visual surface by flattering his appear-

---

17 This is the answer to William Archer's complaint, in his famous attack on Renaissance drama (*The Old Drama and the New* [Boston, 1923], p. 97), that she should have found a more appropriate tool, a "needy adventurer" or "moonstruck youth." Middleton deliberately made De Flores ugly (in the source, John Reynolds's *The Triumphs of God's Revenge against ... Murther*, I.iv, he is "a gallant young gentleman"), and made Beatrice the kind of person who will choose him *because* of this, and will ignore the threat he poses.

ance ("What ha' you done/ To your face a-late . . . Hardness becomes the visage of a man well"). But it is also typical that, despite the repeated proofs of his passion for her (a passion she at least subconsciously counts on in her approach), she never even considers that this might present a problem, persuading herself on no evidence at all that his motive is just what she would have it to be—a need for money. Therefore, the stunning impact of the reversal in the great scene where she discovers his real purpose (III.iv) depends on both of her limitations, her inability to realize either that she has made a mistake or committed a crime, the first being responsible for her persistent refusal to comprehend what he wants, and the second for her righteous indignation when she finally does. And the consequence is that she must enter into the liaison that leads inexorably to another crime (to conceal her loss of virginity) and to her eventual destruction.

But she has learned nothing from this, for in the second scheme, the substitution of Diaphanta on her bridal night, she falls into the identical error. The plan comes to her in much the same way as the first; faced with a new difficulty, she needs a new servant and begins to visualize people in terms of their availability for that role ("Seeing that wench now,/ A trick comes in my mind"). Again she ignores inconvenient but obvious facts about this servant (her lusty sexual curiosity and attraction to Alsemero), assuming she has no motives beyond those of easing her mistress' fears and earning the ducats. And again in the ensuing reversal scene (V.i) she is righteously indignant, calling Diaphanta "strumpet" and "whore," not because she is fornicating but because she is committing the worst sin in Beatrice's world: "This strumpet serves her own ends, 'tis apparent now/ . . . And never minds my honour or my peace." Furthermore, as De Flores points out, the result of this scheme would have been as disastrous as the first, since it would have made Diaphanta, too, her master. Such a fate is averted by De Flores's second murder, but the damage has been done, for this makes her still more dependent on him and so more vulnerable to detection, and later adds to Alsemero's suspicions when he realizes Diaphanta's death might have been "the wages of her knowledge." Thus this mistake, like the first, marks another stage in the sequence bringing Beatrice to her catastrophe.

Through this sequence, then, Middleton has succeeded in taking the conception of the criminal hoist with his own petard (which is the basic formula for this type of plot) and building it into the character of his protagonist, so that the very traits responsible for her crimes are at the same time responsible for her downfall. That is itself no mean feat, when one considers the purely mechanical correlations between crime and fall in most of the villain-hero plays of the period; but he has gone beyond this to make these same traits responsible for her punishment. This is not the same as her downfall, which takes place in V.iii when all her crimes are exposed and she is killed. Her punishment is what happens inside her between the time of her first crime and this final exposure, what might be called her "internal" fall, and it is manifested through her increasing attachment to De Flores and alienation from Alsemero, the two constant figures standing at opposite extremes by which we measure her change. It is a process of deterioration somewhat like the Wife's in *The Second Maiden's Tragedy,* but unlike the Wife's, it is uniquely suited to her because it is worked out in esthetic terms. As her attitude toward De Flores evolves from revulsion to condescension, then to reluctant submission, to dependence, and finally to real affection ("I'm forc'd to love thee now"; "Here's a man worth loving"), she joins the world of ugliness from which she was so sharply distinguished at the outset. Her delicacy of taste and fine sense of discrimination are completely corrupted by her habituation to him, so that at the end even he has become "beauteous" in her eyes:

> His face loathes one,
> But look upon his care, who would not love him?
> The east is not more beauteous than his service.
>   (V.i.70–72) [18]

Her punishment therefore is as ironically appropriate as her downfall, since the esthetic sensitivity which first led her to select De Flores for her crime is destroyed by him through the alliance resulting from that crime. And it is also the very worst thing that could happen to her; she has lost the most valuable quality she possessed, the source of her attractiveness and hence of her self-esteem and happiness, the core of her personality. She has lost her equivalent of a soul.

Of course Beatrice is not aware of this loss as it occurs, because of her own limitations; but that only increases the horror of her shock when in the closing scene she is made to understand what she has become. She discovers it in the most painful way, by seeing her reflection in the eyes of Alsemero, who represents the world of beauty she has forfeited forever. And this discovery, with its accompanying reversal, is couched in the same visual terms as Beatrice's change of attitude toward De Flores: just as his loathsomeness finally became "beauteous" in her eyes, so now she learns that in Alsemero's she has undergone the opposite transformation which plunges her from the height to the nadir of her little esthetic world. For now this imagery is adapted to express the contrast between physical and spiritual

---

18 Beatrice unintentionally predicted this in her earlier flattery of De Flores: "When w'are us'd/ To a hard face, 'tis not so unpleasing;/ It mends still in opinion, hourly mends/ . . . How lovely now/ Dost thou appear to me!" (II.ii.87–89, 135–36).

beauty, between the external delicacy which once was hers and the internal ugliness which eventually defiles even that delicacy. Her loveliness is found to be a deceitful mask, a disguise that no longer hides, since it has taken on the nature of, the deformity within. When Alsemero calls her a whore, she replies:

> What a horrid sound it hath!
> It blasts a beauty to deformity;
> Upon what face soever that breath falls,
> It strikes it ugly
>
> (V.iii.31–34)

But he tells her:

> there was a visor
> O'er that cunning face, and that became you:
> Now impudence in triumph rides upon 't
>
> (ll. 46–48)

and after she confesses the murder he exclaims, "Oh, thou art all deform'd!" Then, having extracted from De Flores an admission of their adultery, Alsemero explicitly connects the esthetic and ethical values:

> oh cunning devils!
> How should blind men know you from fair-fac'd saints?
>
> (ll. 108–9)

And in his retrospective speech following the catastrophe he sums up the punishment that has been meted out to Beatrice:

> Here's beauty chang'd
> To ugly whoredom
>
> (ll. 197–98)

It is evident then that the conception of disguise, of the discrepancy between Beatrice's appearance and her inner self, is as important to the main plot as the disguises of Antonio and Franciscus are to the subplot. In fact, the parallel between them is carefully drawn to our attention in the final scene when Vermandero accuses Antonio and Franciscus of Alonzo's murder because

> these two have been disguis'd
> E'er since the deed was done.

and Alsemero adds:

> I have two other
> That were more close disguis'd than your two could be,
> E'er since the deed was done.
>
> (V.iii.126–29)

But the significance of this parallel, again, lies in the crucial distinctions which contribute to the overall negative analogy. The two kinds of disguise are differentiated in terms of the emotional quality of the plots: those of the minor action are literal and therefore comic, for they are external trappings that can be put on and off at will, while Beatrice's is figurative and describes an internal (i.e., "more close"), permanent, and hence tragic alteration. And they are also differentiated in terms of the basic moral contrast since they work in opposite directions: Beatrice conceals a loathsome reality beneath a beautiful "visor," but the normal and attractive subplot characters try to pass as the "wild unshapen" defectives of Alibius's asylum. Just as Beatrice saw her true nature in Alsemero's eyes, which blasted her "beauty to deformity," so Antonio claims that Isabella's eyes can penetrate his diguise to produce the reverse transformation:

> Look you but cheerfully, and in your eyes
> I shall behold mine own deformity,
> And dress myself up fairer; I know this shape
> Becomes me not, but in those bright mirrors
> I shall array me handsomely.
>
> (III.iii.185–89)

Because of this difference in direction, the exposures of these disguises in the denouement of each plot necessarily repeat the same contrast. They are among the "changes" which are listed at the end of the play, and which include all of the characters present except Isabella, who, it was seen, has remained constant and therefore can unmask others instead of suffering Beatrice's tragic unmasking. (Lollio is the only important character not present, since he is not altered.) The roll call begins with the lines just quoted describing this exposure of Beatrice: "Here's beauty chang'd/ To ugly whoredom" (ll. 197–98), and then proceeds to the other changes in the main plot, all resulting from hers. But when it descends to the subplot we are told that the relation of the disguise to the change—here of course only a beneficent comic discomfiture—has been inverted, both in Antonio's confession: "I was chang'd too, from a little ass as I was, to a great fool as I am" (ll. 204–5), and in Franciscus's: "I was chang'd from a little wit to be stark mad" (l. 208). They discover, in other words, that their real selves have taken on the foolishness of their appearance, whereas Beatrice learned that her appearance had taken on the ugliness of her real self.

This list of "changes" reflects back upon the title of the play, which in its various implications also serves to differentiate and integrate the double plot. Although the earlier critics assumed that this title referred only to Antonio, since in the original cast of characters he is designated *"The Changeling,"* we have come to recognize that it is applicable to Beatrice in two related ways. Most obviously, she is "one given to change, a fickle or inconstant person" (*OED,* sb. 1), as demonstrated by the shift of her affections from Alonzo to Alsemero (which is called a "change" by Beatrice in I.i.155 and De Flores in III.iv.143), and then from Alsemero to De Flores. But these changes eventually make her a changeling in another and more profound sense, derived from the folklore notion of a deformed or sickly child substituted by fairies for a beautiful and healthy one (*OED,* sb. 3). Her internal corruption brought about by her association with De Flores can be seen as the equivalent of such an exchange, and her final exposure as the discovery of this substitution which had been concealed beneath her deceptive exterior—the unmasking of the loathsome "changeling" who has replaced Vermandero's real daughter.[19] This metaphor is introduced by De Flores when he tells her:

> Push, fly not to your birth, but settle you
> In what the act has made you, y'are no more now;
> You must forget your parentage to me:
> Y'are the deed's creature; by that name
> You lost your first condition
>
> (III.iv.134–38)

It is later taken up by Alsemero, who calls Beatrice and De Flores "twins of mischief" (V.iii.142), and is given its final expression by Beatrice herself in her dying words to her father:

> Oh come not near me, sir, I shall defile you:
> I am that of your blood was taken from you . . .
>
> (ll. 149–50)

In this sense, then, the conception of the changeling, like that of her disguise, functions as a kind of epitome of Beatrice's fate and therefore of the entire plot which has made her "the deed's creature."

In the subplot Antonio and Franciscus can be considered comic versions of this sort of changeling, since they also become different persons when they don their disguises at the beginning and when they doff them at the end. The nature of these disguises, however, involves a third meaning of changeling, that of "idiot" or "imbecile" (*OED,* sb. 4), which like the disguise itself applies literally to the subplot and

---

19 Compare this rationalization of the folklore with Thomas Fuller's view that "a Changeling . . . is not one child changed for another, but one child on a sudden much changed from itself" (*The Holy State and the Profane State* [1642], III.xii.182). I think Empson is wrong in making De Flores the principal changeling in this sense (p. 50), since he is neither disguised nor altered. He is the agent of Beatrice's transformation, the evil fairy who makes the exchange.

figuratively to the main action.[20] This relationship too has been frequently discussed in recent criticism, yet it requires some qualification because the idiocy or "madness" is not enacted in the subplot characters, who are all quite sane, but in the legitimate inmates of the asylum. These inmates constitute an analytically separable order of reality somewhat similar to the third level of the plays to be studied in the following chapter, except that they have no episodes of their own and are not given the independent elaboration (or even the individuation) necessary to produce another distinct dramatic component. They also resemble the third level of this group of plays in their status as farcical "clowns," which places them below the characters of the subplot proper. But Empson and his successors have shown that they have a much more serious aspect, for they vividly represent the chaotic impulses of man's subrational nature, which finds expression through them as a sinister chorus or background to both of the plots. In the midst of Antonio's wooing they appear, and Isabella says they are "Of fear enough to part us"; she seems to realize intuitively that if she succumbed to his temptation she would be vulnerable to them. But Beatrice, because she lacks Isabella's insight, takes the fatal step that allows them to invade her safe little world—literally, in the plans for her wedding masque, and more significantly in her internal degeneration, which is viewed as a kind of descent into the madhouse:

> rehearse again
> Your scene of lust, that you may be perfect
> When you shall come to act it to the black audience
> Where howls and gnashings shall be music to you
> (V.iii.114–17) [21]

This madness is a foretaste of damnation, and the lunatic's cry, "Catch there, catch the last couple in hell!" (III.iii.165), is echoed in De Flores's dying words, "I coupled with your mate/ At barley-break; now we are left in hell," and in Vermandero's response, "We are all there, it circumscribes here" (V.iii.162–64). The development

---

20 Actually Antonio is disguised as a fool (the *"Changeling"* of the Dramatis Personae) and Franciscus as a madman, and the first subplot scene distinguishes these "two sorts of people in the house" (I.ii.44). But since this has no functional significance, it seems permissible to speak of both disguises and both sorts of inmates as representing a single "madness."

21 Note Vermandero's "An host of enemies enter'd my citadel/ Could not amaze like this" (V.iii.147–48), which recalls the references in I.i to the impregnability of this castle that once protected Beatrice. The masque, rehearsed in IV.iii but never produced, is really an antimasque, as Empson and others have pointed out, standing for the chaos which marriage is supposed to harmonize.

of this parallel, therefore, also bears out the formal relationship of the two plots: on the comic level Isabella, surrounded by literal madness, is able to preserve her sanity and "cure" the insanity of those about her, while on the serious level Beatrice, living in a sane and well-ordered universe, introduces a metaphorical madness which destroys her and others.

But while the conception of the subplot can be justified in terms of this very rich and meaningful formal relationship, even its staunchest defenders have had to admit that its execution leaves much to be desired. The most frequent complaint is that the foolery seems to drag on too long and becomes boring, but I think this is because it all leads to nothing. Had we more of this plot, it might well seem less. For we are missing a major scene, just before or in place of the present V.ii, which was carefully prepared for to bring this action to its climax and into direct contact with the main plot. Presumably it would be set in the castle and would show the wedding masque, rehearsed in IV.iii, that imports "madness" into this world, then the fight between Antonio and Franciscus over Isabella, also arranged in IV.iii to follow after "the masque be past," during which these two counterfeits would give away their identities to the stage audience (including Alibius, who would thereby learn how his jealous imprisonment of Isabella had almost made him a cuckold), and then their arrest for Alonzo's murder. This would provide not only the much needed comic deflations of Antonio, Franciscus, and Alibius, the absence of which leaves us perplexed and frustrated (the perfunctory confession of their "changes" in the closing lines of the play is certainly no substitute for the dramatization of them, and in fact seems to look back to such a dramatization), but also a much better discovery scene for this plot than V.ii now gives us, since there is no reason why Isabella should have told Alibius about her suitors before the masque. And this scene might also have affected the main plot as well. The public arrest of Antonio and Franciscus could make Beatrice and De Flores feel more secure (in our version they are not even aware that these men are suspected of their crime), and so more careless, thus increasing the probability of Alsemero's coming upon them in the incident reported at the beginning of V.iii. Of course there is no way of knowing whether the scene I am suggesting was actually composed by the authors and then lost in the thirty years that elapsed before the publication of the quarto, or whether, as appears more likely, they only planned the scene and for some reason failed to write it. But whatever the explanation, the present V.ii seems a clumsy piece of patchwork covering up a missed opportunity to bring the two plots together on the stage in a climactic interaction, at the "efficient" level, that would have reinforced the moral contrast basic to their formal integration.[22]

III

The Second Maiden's Tragedy and *The Changeling* have been selected for extended analysis because they so clearly exemplify the inter-plot unity produced by means of a direct contrast. Yet it should be remembered that this kind of connection is usually not encountered in such a relatively pure state but in a subordinate role within more complex dramatic structures. Thus among the three-level plays to be considered in the following chapter, there are a number which develop a similar moral contrast between the two major plots; but in these works that relationship is accommodated to the presence of a third level of action under the larger formal principle of "hierarchy."

Before turning to this group of plays, however, we ought to glance briefly at some other kinds of direct contrast used to combine two plots. Although, as might be expected, the simple opposition between good and evil, embodied in the protagonists of the respective actions, is by far the most common type in the period, there is certainly no reason why the principle of "contrast" itself need be limited in this way, and so we should also expect to find dramatists employing it along somewhat modified or even quite different lines to integrate their main and subplot. Only a few of these possibilities can be illustrated here.

An interesting borderline case is Davenport's *The City Nightcap*, where each action portrays a sexual triangle composed of a husband, his wife, and his trusted friend. Each action begins with an attempt by the friend to seduce the wife, setting up an obvious comparison of the two women through their responses to these parallel fidelity tests: in the main plot Abstemia remains true to her husband and eventually meets her deserved reward, while Dorothea in the subplot commits adultery and so must be exposed and punished. This is practically the same formal pattern seen in *The Second Maiden's Tragedy*,[23] although there is a reduction in the relative seriousness

---

22 There are other reasons to suspect V.ii. Vermandero tells Tomazo, Alonzo's brother, that Antonio and Franciscus "both feign'd a journey/ To Briamata" (ll. 80–81), but in IV.ii.7–8 he learned one was "intending to Briamata, th' other for Valencia." And Tomazo's sudden attack on De Flores is completely unmotivated and leads nowhere. (Perhaps in the missing scene he too had a role in discovering the suspects.) For a contrary view see Bawcutt, pp. xvi–xvii.

23 In both the Wife's trial and Abstemia's, the husband forces his reluctant friend to cooperate; but the results are completely different (they have different sources, the former coming from "The Novel of the Curious Impertinent" in *Don Quixote*, the latter from Greene's *Philomela*). And Dorothea, like the Wife, stages a second test to deceive her husband, but this is taken from the *Decameron*, VII.vii.

of the plots, the first to the level of tragicomedy, the second to comedy. However, Davenport adds a direct contrast between the two husbands in terms of their attitude toward their wives' fidelity: Lorenzo in the main plot is consumed with jealousy, and Lodovico in the subplot is completely trustful. But this contrast, while also based on moral character, is of a very different order since it does not oppose a virtue and vice but two undesirable extremes, emphasized by their equidistance from the truth, Lorenzo's obsessive suspicions of the chaste Abstemia being just as wrong as Lodovico's complacent faith in the wanton Dorothea. The relation of the men, therefore, imparts a neat logical symmetry to the plot combination, as is explicitly pointed out many times,[24] and also helps to differentiate these plots in emotional value, for the credulous cuckold is much more absurd than the jealous oppressor and requires a much less serious reformation. But its principal function is to enhance the contrast of the wives. Because of Lorenzo's vicious accusations, Abstemia's continued loyalty to him seems even more impressive and her suffering at his hands even more pitiful, especially when juxtaposed to Dorothea's callous betrayal of the doting Lodovico, which she brazens out with impunity. And because Abstemia has been slandered and Dorothea honored by the complementary mistakes of their husbands, the discoveries and attendant reversals of their fortunes in the resolution produce a sharper sense of the opposition between the ultimate fates of these women, and of its justice:

> Vice for a time may shine, and virtue sigh;
> But truth, like heaven's sun, plainly doth reveal,
> And scourge or crown what darkness did conceal.
>
> (IV.ii.p.164)

But even though the male contrast of extremes subserves the female contrast of good and evil, the combination creates problems. Since the women represent moral absolutes, Dorothea's punishment must be as serious as Abstemia's reward (she is condemned to "the monastery for matrons," and her lover and pander are handled with like severity), which violates the comic mood of the subplot. And it throws the paired denouements off balance, for after the husbands are cured of their equivalent aberrations, Lorenzo is reunited with his paragon of purity (though he must first undergo some trials of his own to deserve her), while Lodovico is left with nothing. These are no doubt minor faults in a play replete with all the major ones, yet they suggest the incompatibility of the two kinds of direct contrast. Further evidence of this incompatibility can be seen in *Patient*

---

[24] I.ii.p.101, II.ii.p.115, III.i.p.128, etc.

Grissil, a joint venture of Dekker, Chettle, and Haughton. Here again a comparison is built around two married couples: Grissil's "patience" is contrasted to the shrewishness of Gwenthyan, her counterpart in the subplot; and the tyranny of the Marquis Gwalter, Grissil's husband (and a relative of Gwenthyan), to the docility of Gwenthyan's husband, Sir Owen ap Meredith. If these were both contrasts of extreme deviations from the mean, like that of Lorenzo and Lodovico, the scheme would be perfectly coherent.[25] But the values of the folk-tale source of the main plot dictate that Grissil's utter self-abnegation be treated as the wifely ideal. This places Gwalter in an ambiguous position, for while his persecution of Grissil (like Lorenzo's of Abstemia) is defined by the double structure as a gross distortion of proper husbandly behavior at the opposite pole from Sir Owen, the folk doctrine would have us accept it as the prerogative of his sex (and rank), as well as a justifiable subterfuge designed to demonstrate her worthiness. On the other hand, although Grissil's "patience" is meant to win our whole-hearted sympathy, the contrary trait in Gwenthyan is not judged in ethical terms at all but simply as a comic extreme or "humor." And because of this mixture of the two kinds of contrast, the comedy of the subplot actually works at cross-purposes with the idealization of the main-plot heroine, whose claim to perfection is undercut both by its *reductio ad absurdum* in the henpecked Sir Owen and by Gwenthyan's spirited refusal to emulate "such ninny pobby fool as Grissil." [26]

The inconsistency becomes even more apparent, as in Davenport's play, at the conclusion, where both of the aggressors, Gwalter and Gwenthyan, reveal that they were only "trying" their mates and will now be reconciled. These are presented as parallel denouements, which they would be if the contrast relationships between the plots really had been made equivalent, but since they have not, the analogies asserted in this final scene are only verbal. We are told there that "as her cousin has tried Grissil, so Gwenthyan has Sir Owen," yet the meekness for which Owen was tested, unlike Grissil's, is not a virtue of his sex and is abandoned as soon as he earns his passing grade. And while Gwenthyan, as a result of the test, announces that she "shall no more be call'd Gwenthyan but patient Grissil" and that

---

25 As it is in William Rowley's *A New Wonder, A Woman Never Vexed,* which sets up a similar contrast between the never-vexed Widow of Cornhill in the main plot and the ever-vexed Mistress Foster of the subplot, but avoids a moral problem by treating both traits as comic extremes (though the first is certainly made more amiable).

26 III.ii.202; cf. III.ii.140, V.ii.19–20. Note also the parallel between IV.i, where Gwalter dresses Grissil in her old rags to humiliate her, and IV.iii, where Gwenthyan dresses herself in rags to humiliate Sir Owen and revenge Grissil ("pecause Grissil is made fool and turn away, Gwenthyan mag fool of Sir Owen").

"Sir Owen shall be her head," in the main plot Grissil herself does not change after her restoration to favor, and her husband remains in complete control. Thus we are not convinced by the Fluellian logic (and accent) of Owen's desperate attempt to impose a common pattern upon the two actions in the last speech of the play:

> marg that well: if Sir Owen was not patient, her lady had not been pridled; if Grissil had not been patient, her cousin Marquis had not been pridled

(V.ii.301–3)

for Gwalter is certainly not "pridled" in the same sense as Gwenthyan, and Grissil's "patience" was not adopted for the sake of converting her spouse, but was supposed to be her characteristic excellence. The archaic morality of the folktale cannot be assimilated to the contrast of extremes posited by this double-plot formula.[27]

That same morality also interferes with yet a third kind of direct contrast between these plots which is based simply on gender, since if the special value attached to female obedience could be ignored, the two couples would present a balanced opposition in the relative "power" of husband and wife, Gwalter ruling Grissil as Gwenthyan rules Owen. This relation is coördinate with the contrasts of character, to be sure, but it is logically separable from them and can be considered as another scheme of formal integration in its own right. While not as common as the other two types of contrast, it is still of some importance because it lends itself so readily to a combination of plots dealing with the battle of the sexes (even the activity of Patient Grissil is summed up in the closing scene as "the war of marriage," notwithstanding the fact that the titular protagonist is a conscientious objector). And for this reason it is usually restricted to non-serious drama.

One of the clearest examples of such a structure appears in one of John Fletcher's most successful comedies, Rule a Wife and Have a Wife. In the main plot, which probably owes something to The Taming of the Shrew, Leon tricks the Lady Margarita into marriage and then subdues her, and in the subplot Margarita's former maid, Estefania, does the same to Michael Perez, the "Copper Captain." The contrast between these couples obviously depends on the inversion of sexual roles, which are defined here partly, as in Patient Grissil, by the marital "rule" indicated in the title, but primarily by the relation of wit to dupe established through a contest of intrigue. The losers of the two contests, the main-plot heroine and the subplot hero, are

---

[27] Perhaps this morality was always "archaic," as Chaucer's Envoy to the Clerk's "Tale of Grisilde" would suggest. Compare the Sly Epilogue to The Taming of a Shrew.

equated in terms of both of these variables. At the outset they both are shown to be completely confident of their own cleverness and their ability to manage the other sex. Both are convinced that they have found the perfect mates who can be exploited to serve their needs—for Margarita, a foolish wittol willing to cloak her amours; for Perez, a rich gentlewoman willing to support him. But after the weddings they both discover, in parallel and consecutive scenes (III.iv and III.v), that they have been caught in their own nooses (as Perez puts it), since the persons they married turn out to be exactly the opposite of these expectations—Margarita's husband is actually a valorous gentleman who will permit no trifling with his honor, and Perez's wife a servant-girl as poor as he and much more bellicose. Finally, also in consecutive scenes (V.iii and V.iv), they both submit to their spouses and to their fates. And the other equation links the two victors, the main-plot hero and subplot heroine, along the same lines: they both succeed in duping their prospective mates by misrepresenting themselves, outface them when the deception is revealed, force them to surrender, and then relent somewhat for a harmonious resolution.

This arrangement, of course, also requires contrasts between the two men and between the two women. However, that does not entail an ethical judgment (for Margarita is not more evil than Estefania, nor Perez than Leon), but only the same qualities of intelligence and mastery which are at issue in this comedy, and which thus take the place of the moral virtues in serious drama. Even in these terms, the contrasts of character are much less significant here than in *The City Nightcap* or *Patient Grissil*, because they do not present direct opposites (Margarita and Perez are neither stupid nor docile, but only relatively inferior to their mates), and because the *positive* analogy between the actions as equivalent "wars of marriage" is so pronounced that we are much more aware of the parallel roles of the two wits and of their two victims. The main weight of the *negative* analogy, therefore, falls less on the traits of the contenders than on the sexual reversal itself. And this effect is reciprocal, since the juxtaposition of two comparable plots in which the most striking difference is the relation of male to female tends to accentuate the battle of the sexes, in itself, as the central phenomenon of each action and of the play as a whole. It also serves to equalize the two sides of this battle, so that we get a sense of logical balance in the work of art, and in the design of nature which engineers these antagonisms to unite and propagate the species. It is presumably for these reasons that this kind of inter-plot contrast seems especially appropriate for this kind of comedy.

Although the characters and events of the two plots are not brought into direct opposition, then, except through the transposal of sex, they are distinguished on an emotional scale. As in every other play examined so far, the subplot is markedly less serious than the main one. And as in most of those plays, this depends not only on the social rank of the characters but also on the dramatic treatment they are given. Leon's role in his intrigue is more dignified or "straight" than Estefania's: he is never fooled himself and is always one jump ahead of Margarita, while Estefania is for a time taken in by Perez's pose as a man of wealth, so that she more nearly approaches his comic situation, and their mutual recriminations, once the truth is discovered, descend closer to the level of a farcical and almost slapstick brawl. But the treatment of these roles reflects a more basic mode of differentiation that was also found in *The Changeling*—a differentiation in the relative internality of the two lines of action, which again can be seen very clearly in the schemes adopted by the wits. Their schemes are parallel, we noted, in that they both must misrepresent themselves in order to win their mates; but Leon has to invent a false *personality,* as a servile coward, whereas Estefania need only falsify her external *identity,* with respect to class status and the ownership of Margarita's house. (Thus the misrepresentations also point in opposite directions, like the disguisings in *The Changeling:* Leon pretends to be worse than he really is, and Estefania better.) And that is itself a consequence of the way the principal issues of the plots have been defined. Both of them turn on money and "honor," which here means chastity for the woman and the avoidance of cuckoldom for the man. The main action, however, focuses our attention and serious concern upon the continual efforts of Margarita to acquire a lover and of Leon to prevent this, and the significance of money is minimized by making her wealthy enough to ignore it (she in fact deliberately seeks a poor husband since he will be more submissive) and by passing over his own motivation; but in the subplot the external financial problem (centering on the title to the house) is obviously paramount, and the lies told about Estefania's "lewdness" (in III.iv–v) are simply a clever stratagem planned by her to get revenge on Perez and, presumably, prepare him to accept more readily the truth about her poverty.[28]

It is not merely the double standard of the time, therefore, which determines that Margarita's desire for a life of promiscuity be regarded more seriously than Perez's desire for a life of luxury, and that it call for a more elaborate and more internalized purgation, almost a change of character, while he has only to reconcile himself (with the aid of a thousand ducats procured by Estefania) to the loss of an

---

28 Her purpose is not as clear as it might be, but see IV.i.107–17 and V.v.152–57. (This play and *Patient Grissil* contain tertiary plots not relevant to the subject of this chapter.)

imaginary fortune. Yet one is always aware that this emotional separation of the two dupes is just a difference in degree within the overall comic framework, which strictly limits any tendency to moralize and insures that both of their aberrations remain fundamentally ridiculous rather than vicious. It is thus not at all like the direct moral opposition established between the Lady and Wife in *The Second Maiden's Tragedy,* or Beatrice and Isabella, or Abstemia and Dorothea, or (inconsistently, as was seen) Grissil and Gwenthyan. And because it is not, these two versions of the "war of marriage" can be integrated by this sexual contrast, on the formal level, to produce a coherent and enhanced comic effect.

3

Three-Level Hierarchies

It is surprising to see how many of the works of this period which we have grown accustomed to calling "double-plot" plays are actually "two-and-one-half-plot" plays. These are the works that include in addition to the standard main plot and subplot a third distinct set of characters, usually of the clownish sort, who may be loosely attached to one of these major actions but who are also elaborated independently to create a kind of effect quite different from either. However, since this elaboration typically occurs in more or less isolated episodes rather than in a sequential line of action, it would be more accurate to speak of it not as another plot, or fraction thereof, but as another level of emotional tone or sensibility. And since in most of these plays the main and subplot are differentiated from each other, similarly, in terms of the modes of sensibility they embody —in the characters themselves and in the response these characters evoke in the audience—the result is a structure that can with some precision be defined as "three-level" drama. Such a conception of emotional levels, implying as it does a vertically articulated relationship, seems to be particularly fruitful here, for while the three components vary considerably from play to play, they are very frequently ordered into a hierarchy of descending magnitude and seriousness which is reducible to the formula seen in our comparison of *The Second Maiden's Tragedy* with *The Changeling:* a main plot consisting of characters deliberately elevated above the others, usually in heroic or romantic terms; a subplot of more ordinary people viewed from a more realistic and often ironic or satiric perspective; and a third group debased to the level of low comedy.

Although the effect of this formula will of course depend on the specific nature of the levels and of their combination in each play, the basic purpose underlying it can be seen as an extension of some of the general principles outlined in the introductory chapter. Empson's notion of material "coverage," for instance, would seem even more applicable to this triple structure than to his double plots, since the addition of another action with a different kind of character and point of view will widen still further the area of life encompassed by the play and the range of the audience's impulses that it satisfies. And this increase in the number of actions will obviously increase the possibilities for causal connections and formal parallels and contrasts among them. But much more important is the enlargement and refinement of the kind of indirect affective synthesis discussed in Chapter 1 in terms of the dramatic "context." Since this formula is not a mere aggregation but an organic composite, integrated by all of these material, efficient, and formal relationships, our response to each action will necessarily be conditioned by its position in the hierarchy. And this will hold true regardless of the genre involved, because the emotional quality of the levels is not determined by some external standard but by the particular scale of values built into the play. (Thus, to anticipate, the first plot of *The Family of Love* is still comic, even though it is more serious than the second, which in turn is also comic but more serious than the third.) This theory of relativity is really the whole point here. In all of these plays each level, with its distinctive tonality, helps to "place" those above and below it in the scheme, and so both reinforces and circumscribes their significance. Or, reverting to the original language, the articulation of all three levels operates in the manner of a contextual definition or frame of reference to specify the mood and meaning of each of them.

The terms of this explanation may seem too abstract, but the formula itself is only a general strategy for "final" integration which can produce the greatest variety of effects and therefore cannot take on much substance until seen in actual examples. For the rationale behind this strategy—the idea of "hierarchy"—is after all quite simple. It is so simple, and so relatively easy to work out in dramatic form, that there is not much more point in searching for a particular literary source of this kind of plot combination than there was for the combinations based on the equally primitive notion of "contrast." But, as with the contrast plots, one can hypothesize a model genesis in the native dramatic tradition, provided that no historical claim is made for it. Such a model might be discovered in the conception of the Psychomachia in the early Morality plays. These were all single-plot constructs, it was noted, but the very nature of this plot required agents of three completely different orders of reality: the allegorical virtues necessary for salvation; below them the protagonist, representative man, who by definition occupied an intermediate place in this hierarchy; and below him the vices who tempted him to damnation and also indulged in their own semi-independent episodes of slapstick buffoonery. It is not difficult to see how with the secularization of the drama these theological categories could reappear as the characters "better than us," "like us," and "worse than us" (to adopt the Aristotelian terminology [1]) who figure, respectively, in the heroic, realistic, and farcical levels of the formula. The analogy could be pressed even further, since in these plays the virtues and vices usually were presented in alternating scenes,[2] much like the separate components of the three-level structure; yet it breaks down at one crucial point—the "real" man on the middle level of the Psychomachia did not act in a sequence of his own, but only in conjunction with those forces above and below him contending for his soul. For this reason it might be argued that there is an even closer analogue to the formula in the late Moralities of the *Nice Wanton* type, where the good and evil aspects of the universal hero bifurcated into two separate men, one allied to the virtues and the other to the vices. In the previous chapter that pattern was related to the direct contrast plots; but one has only to carry the process of separation a step further, isolating the comic aspect of the vices from the more serious career of the man they destroy (or, again using Aristotle's terms, subdividing the agents "worse than us" into the vicious and the ridiculous [3]), in order to envisage a possible model of the three-level formula.

It is almost a paradigm of one of the earliest examples of this formula, Richard Edwards's *Damon and Pythias*, which may actually have preceded some of these Moralities in time. The first plot here portrays the testing and eventual triumph of the true friendship of the legendary pair named in the title; the second, the testing and downfall of two false friends, Aristippus and Carisophus; and the third, the ludicrous escapades of their friendly servants, Will and Jack.[4] This does seem to be a simple extension of the kind of double structure

---

1 *Poetics* ii.1448ª1–6.
2 David Bevington relates this alternation to the "doubling" of roles required in small repertory companies (*From "Mankind" to Marlowe* [Cambridge, Mass., 1962], chap. 8).
3 *Poetics* v.1449ª31–36. In the Morality itself these categories were combined, particularly through the Vice, in the "comedy of evil."
4 Plots one and two derive from the distinction between "friendships of virtue" and "friendships of utility" in the *Nicomachean Ethics*, Bk. VIII. Perhaps the relationship of Will and Jack is meant to exemplify Aristotle's third type, "friendships of pleasure."

examined in Chapter 2, with the main and subplot developing the opposition between moral and immoral protagonists in comparable situations, and a new level added to present a comically amoral version of the same activity. But while this ethical contrast will be found in *The Family of Love* and similar three-level dramas, it is by no means essential to the formula itself. In other plays based on that formula, such as *A Fair Quarrel,* both the first and second levels center on virtuous characters, although those of the second are less noble and less serious; and in *The Atheist's Tragedy* and other tragedies of this sort they both have villain-heroes who are also distinguished in equivalent terms. Even the "amorality" of the third-level comedians introduces another variable, since they can cover a broad range from Vice-like rogues to innocent fools, and can qualify the values of the major plots in significant ways which will require separate consideration in the following chapter. It seems, therefore, that what is most constant in this formula is not the ethical differentiation of the three levels but their relative emotional tones.

The regularity with which this same emotional scale reappears may suggest another kind of source of three-level drama in the society itself rather than in any theatrical or literary tradition. One might reasonably suppose that during the evolution of the secular stage the theological hierarchy of the Morality would be translated into the class hierarchy of Renaissance England, especially since it seems so appropriate to relate the idealized, heroic main plot to aristocratic characters and sentiments, the realistic subplot to the bourgeoisie, and the farcical sub-subplot to the urban or rural proletariat. But such an equation is not at all common. Usually, when the third-level characters are social inferiors, as in *The Atheist's Tragedy,* the agents of the two major actions belong to a single higher class, and where a social distinction is made between main and subplot, in such plays as *A Fair Quarrel,* the third level is not differentiated in the same manner. We even find works like *The Family of Love* where the social structure is partially inverted by the dramatic structure. Apparently this class division of their society speaks more insistently to us, with our post-Marxist perspective, than it did to the dramatists; when they wished to present a systematic cross section of their nation, it was more likely to emerge as a survey, not of classes, but of various vocations or "estates" that do not readily arrange themselves into three descending levels of sensibility.[5]

---

5 See Alan Dessen, "The 'Estates' Morality Play," *SP,* 62 (1965), 121–36; he includes *A Looking Glass for London and England* in this category, along with *The Three Ladies of London, The Cobbler's Prophecy, A Knack to Know a Knave,* and *Nobody and Somebody.* Probably the most common formulation of class divisions was the triad of "court" aristocracy, "country" gentry, and "city" bourgeoisie (e.g.,

There are, however, a few plays that define these levels in terms of the class hierarchy for some special purpose. An early example is Lodge and Greene's *A Looking Glass for London and England*, which very methodically sets about to cover the representative vices of the entire social scene. The main plot concentrates on the court of King Rasni, where the sins—adultery, incest, murder, and blasphemy—are most heinous and require the miraculous intervention of an avenging God; the subplot of the Usurer and his two victims, a young gentleman and an old farmer, is limited to the more venial economic offenses— usury, bribery, and theft—and has a substantial comic element (which is also differentiated by social status, the farmer being much funnier than the gentleman); and on the third level a servant, called the Clown, reënacts some of the crimes of the royal court in a broad, drunken burlesque placed outside of the moral scheme. (Above all three is another level, represented not by a fourth plot but by the choric prophets Oseas and Jonas, who speak for the Deity.) And a roughly similar division is used in Dekker's *The Shoemakers' Holiday*, although his treatment of all three classes is sympathetic: the first action deals with the sentimentalized romance of young Lacy, a nobleman, and his beloved Rose; the second with the rise of Simon Eyre, the shoemaker, to the height of "citizen" aspiration, the mayoralty of London; and the third with the trials of Eyre's journeyman, Ralph Damport, and his wife Jane, which mirror the Lacy-Rose plot. (Again a higher level is included, not in a separate plot but in the person of King Henry, whose appearance in Act V caps the three-class hierarchy.) But this is also a very special case, since the class system is not merely the frame of the triple structure but the actual subject matter of the play, the primary issue at stake in all three actions and in their combination. In most of the other three-level dramas to be examined, class status makes some contribution, as does moral character, to the differentiation of one plot from another, but neither variable seems to be essential to the formulaic hierarchy of tone or sensibility underlying the entire group.

I

The three plays selected for analysis here should illustrate most of the possible permutations of these social and ethical distinctions among the separate levels, as well as the adaptation of the formula as a whole to the principal genres of the period—comedy, tragicomedy, and tragedy. It seems appropriate to begin with *The Family of Love*, one of the earliest of Middleton's "city comedies," for while it

---

As You Like It, II.i.59), which omits the lower orders. Cf. *The Antiquary*, II.i.p.453: "a country gentleman among courtiers . . . a clown [i.e., peasant] among citizens."

is an inferior work it possesses much the same advantage as *The Second Maiden's Tragedy* in its particularly clear and straightforward application of the structural principle we wish to investigate. And it has the further, incidental advantage of casting light on the evolution of Middleton's multiple-plot technique that was to culminate in *A Chaste Maid in Cheapside,* which will be seen to build on the same elements as this play and on its imperfectly realized design.

That design was overlooked by the older critics, many of whom, misled perhaps by the title (although it will turn out, like the title of *The Changeling,* to have a larger significance than they supposed), treated the entire work as "a satirical exposure of a religious sect." [6] But there are three separate components to be accounted for: a main plot concerned with the efforts of Gerardine to marry Maria over the opposition of Doctor Glister, her uncle and guardian; a subplot which includes the so-called "exposure" of the Family of Love, but centers not so much on the sect itself as on Rebecca Purge, an "elder in the Family" and Doctor Glister's mistress, and also involves Glister, his wife, and Rebecca's husband, Peter Purge the apothecary; and finally, a series of adventures (not quite forming a connected plot) of two gallants, Lawrence Lipsalve and Gregory Gudgeon.

The entire action is limited to a very small world in which all the major characters are well known to each other: Gerardine is a distant relative of the Purges and is in love with Glister's niece; Glister is one of Purge's best customers as well as his cuckolder; and Lipsalve and Gudgeon are acquaintances of Gerardine and the Glisters and Purges, and, at the outset, rival suitors of Mistress Purge. Because of the material relationships, Gerardine, the chief manipulator of the play, is able to bring almost everyone together in the two ensemble scenes which enclose the action—the farewell dinner he gives at Purge's house in I.iii, where he sets his plan in motion, and the trial he stages in V.iii at the home of Dryfat, his accomplice, where that plan is successfully completed. These relations are also drawn upon to establish a network of inter-plot causal connections, most of which operate through Doctor Glister in his roles as the adversary of Gerardine and Maria in the first plot, the lover of Rebecca Purge in the second, and the tormentor of the gallants in the third. Glister's liaison with Rebecca is used by Gerardine to awaken Mistress Glister's suspicions of her husband and prepare her to accuse him of impregnating Maria at the trial. And the trick Glister plays on Lipsalve and Gudgeon,

---

6 Ashley Thorndike, *English Comedy* (New York, 1929), p. 260; cf. C. S. Alden (ed.), *Bartholomew Fair* (New York, 1904), p. xxx; Algernon Swinburne, *The Age of Shakespeare* (London, 1908), p. 156; and Felix Schelling, *Elizabethan Playwrights* (New York, 1925), p. 197.

when they come for help in getting Mistress Purge, leads them to seek revenge by determining to seduce his wife and to testify against Mistress Purge at this trial. Finally, the trial itself juxtaposes these actions and so emphasizes the parallels between them, primarily through the comments of Dryfat who, in his disguise as Poppin the lawyer, has been hired by Purge to prosecute his wife for adultery and by Glister to defend him against his wife's suit on the same charge:

> Master doctor Glister hath a cradleful and a bellyful, you see, thrust upon him; and master Purge a headful.—Your wife is an angry honeyless wasp, whose sting, I hope, you need not fear,—and yours carries honey in her mouth, but her sting makes your forehead swell;—your wife makes you deaf with the shrill treble of her tongue,—and yours makes you horn-mad with the tenor of her tale.
>
> (V.iii.390–97) [7]

It is this system of relationships that combines these three lines of action and organizes them into the hierarchy of the formula, where the relative importance of each action within the triple structure also corresponds to the relative seriousness of its distinctive emotional mood. Gerardine and Maria are "straight" characters, the only ones in the play (and the only ones without comic names); their plot is the conventional romantic comedy of young lovers who overcome the efforts of the older, mercenary generation to separate them, and it expresses, particularly in the early scenes, an exalted sentimentality that is deliberately marked off from the much more realistic perspective of the subplot. This subplot is not at all romantic but domestic and social in its emphasis, being concerned with the marital relations in the Purge and Glister households and with the sect to which Mistress Purge belongs; its tone is satirical, although the satire is not directed at any specific tenet of the Family (which disturbed some critics), but at Puritanism in general and certain middle-class attitudes associated with it.[8] And the third plot is still less serious in its farcical treatment of the antics of Lipsalve and Gudgeon, which frequently descend to the level of sheer slapstick.

This arrangement is confirmed by an intellectual pecking-order among the three plots: Glister makes fools of the gallants when he tricks them into whipping each other in order to win Mistress Purge

---

[7] See the similar comparisons in ll. 60–62, 126–30, 154–59.
[8] On this see Bertil Johansson, *Religion and Superstition in the Plays of Ben Jonson and Thomas Middleton* (Upsala, 1950), pp. 102, 157.

(III.iv–vi), and again when he doses them with a drastic "purge" after they come to his home as patients to seduce his wife (V.i); but Gerardine and Maria make a fool of Glister at the very end by implicating him in her pregnancy and so forcing him to consent to their marriage and to pay Gerardine an extra thousand pounds; and in III.ii they also make a fool of Lipsalve, who has come, disguised as her beloved, to court Maria. To underscore the point, this scene is constructed in parallel to the whipping episode; Gerardine, like Glister, "enters above" and remains concealed there, laughing at the folly below which seems to be presented for his amusement, the staging itself serving as a visual demonstration of the relation between wit and butt. One of the principal effects of this scale of trickery is to establish Gerardine as the master-wit of the play. His complete control of the situation and brilliant versatility are further emphasized in the sequence of three disguises he adopts in rapid succession in the last stage of his scheme (moving up the social ladder from Nicholas the porter to Placket the apparitor to Stickler the judge), which enable him to manipulate the Glisters, the Purges, and Lipsalve and Gudgeon as he wishes and to sit in judgment on all three plots, in the final scene, and determine their outcomes. And these successes appear even more impressive when contrasted to the utter failure of the disguises attempted by the bungling gallants at the opposite end of the continuum.

This hierarchic arrangement of the characters reflects not only their relative importance and seriousness and cleverness, but also their morality—specifically their sexual morality, since "love" is the principal issue here. The bottom of this scale is again occupied by Lipsalve and Gudgeon, the two "libertines" who are compulsively preoccupied with satisfying their lust. They think of little else, and it matters little to them who their victim may be, for they manage to pursue at one time or other every woman in the play. They are also prepared to go to any lengths for this purpose; they traffic with a demon (as Glister leads them to believe) to win Mistress Purge, then try to leap her in a house of worship, and then submit to Glister's medication in order to get at his wife. The disguises they require for these campaigns may even suggest a moral vacuum, an absence of any fixed character, as if they were themselves as undifferentiated as their sexual objects; thus when Lipsalve dresses as Gerardine in III.ii, and when they claim to be Familists in IV.i, they seem to be trying to assimilate to the other two levels. They have no real identities beyond the physical drive that impels them (hence the appropriateness of their physical punishments —the whipping and "purge"). But they are entirely open about their attitude, which is frankly acknowledged by Lipsalve, among other occasions, when his page asks if he is not weary of "this chase of love":

> Indefatigable, boy, indefatigable. . . . 'Tis my vocation,
> boy; we must never be weary of well-doing: love's as proper
> to a courtier as preciseness to a puritan.
>
> (III.ii.21, 25–27) [9]

This comparison points to the ethical basis of the second plot as
well as the third, for while the two courtiers are reduced to simple,
lustful animals, the middle-class world of the Glisters and Purges is
characterized by a hypocritical "preciseness." Rebecca Purge is the
most obvious example: she insists that the true believer "must never
hereafter frequent taverns nor tap-houses, no masques nor mummeries,
no pastimes nor playhouses," is unwilling to admit her body has "or-
gans," professes to fear the dangers of the senses, and always "speaks
pure devotion"; [10] but she is Glister's secret mistress and uses the meetings of the Family for further sexual adventures. The Family of Love
itself is made a symbol of this hypocrisy, for the sect's lofty spiritual
pretensions (as well as its finicky obsession with the minutiae of conduct) only serve to camouflage the promiscuity of its members, who
are aptly summed up in Dryfat's comment on the discrepancy between
their appearance and reality: "narrow-ruffed, strait-laced, yet loose-
bodied."

However, this discrepancy is not limited to religion. Mistress Glister
is no Familist but she ostentatiously displays a fastidiousness in her
housekeeping which is the secular equivalent of Mistress Purge's "preciseness," [11] and which again stands in marked contrast to her real
character, as we learn from her acceptance of the gallants' propositions
in V.i, and even more clearly from her advice to Maria in II.iv, where
the juxtaposition of the external and internal values clinches the
point:

> I pray, let's have no polluted feet nor rheumatic chaps en-
> ter the house; I shall have my floor look more greasy shortly
> than one of your inn-of-court dining-tables.—And now to
> you, good niece, I bend my speech. Let me tell you plainly,
> you are a fool to be love-sick for any man longer than he
> is in your company: are you so ignorant in the rules of
> courtship, to think any one man to bear all the prick and
> praise? I tell thee, be he never so proper, there is another
> to second him.
>
> (ll. 1–9)

---

[9] His page glosses, "Love, *subaudi* lust." W. J. Olive noted the similarity of
Lipsalve's response to Falstaff's in *1 Henry IV*, I.ii.116 ("Imitation of Shakespeare
in Middleton's *The Family of Love*," *PQ*, 29 [1950], 77).
[10] See I.iii.110–13, II.iii.68–76, III.iii.21–51, IV.i.91–95.
[11] Mistress Purge is also fastidious about her dress when she goes to a meeting of
the Family—see I.iii.56, III.iii.1–3.

Let them come in if their feet be clean.—So, then, your
best-beloved is gone; fair weather after him! all thy passions
go with him! recomfort thyself, wench, in a better choice.

(ll. 44–47)

Peter Purge is also portrayed as a hypocrite, for while he immediately
goes to court when he uncovers his wife's activities at the Family, he
reveals in his speech in II.i—the unnoticed ancestor of Allwit's famous
soliloquy in *A Chaste Maid in Cheapside* in praise of wittoldom—that
he was perfectly happy to exploit her charms to attract business, especially Doctor Glister's; and he has apparently accepted their relationship (though we are not certain he knows how far it has gone)
because of the money it brings in.[12] And Glister himself shows his
hypocrisy in his argument with Maria in the opening scene, where this
unscrupulous adulterer conceals his real objections to Gerardine's suit
(which are also economic) beneath pious warnings against the "libidi-
nous humour" of love and the fickleness of gallants.

The opposition between the values of the young couple and those of
the other characters emerges very sharply in Maria's reply to her aunt's
advice:

Let rules of courtship be authentic still
To such as do pursue variety;
But unto those whose modest thoughts do tend
To honour'd nuptials and a regular life,
As far from show of niceness as from that
Of impure thoughts, all other objects seem
Of no proportion, balanc'd with esteem
Of what their souls affect.

(II.iv.10–17)

This speech, like many others given to Maria and Gerardine, is meant
to raise their love far above the sordid emotions of plots two and three
through the obvious elevation of verse and diction. But more specifically, its key terms are chosen to dissociate them from Lipsalve's and
Gudgeon's pursuit of sexual "variety," as well as from the "show of

---

12 This is the implication of Gerardine's remark in I.iii.166–69 and of the conversation reported by Purge's apprentice in IV.i.61–66. When Purge sees his wife
with Dryfat on her way to the meetinghouse, he says:

What, so close at it? I thought this was one end of your exercise:
byrlady, I think there is small profit in this. I'll wink no more; for
I am now tickled with a conceit that it is a scurvy thing to be a
cuckold.

(III.iii.57–60)

which suggests that her infidelity with Glister did not bother him, and that this
does only because it will not pay.

niceness" of Mistress Purge and Mistress Glister, which was only a cloak for "impure thoughts."[13] Their love is pure, but it is not at all puritanical, as we are shown by Maria's glowing description of the "amorous folds" of marriage in II.iv and of course by her premarital pregnancy. That is just the point, since the assumption behind this scheme is that those who claim, on the ground of their "niceness" or "preciseness," to be better than normal humanity ("a regular life") are actually worse. Genuine love then is neither the frankly animalistic lust of the third plot nor the superhuman (and hypocritical) spirituality of the second, but an intermediate state attained by the couple of the main plot.

This moral scale, like the other aspects of the hierarchy to which it corresponds, is designed to structure the comic effect by determining the kind of response appropriate to each level of action. Thus the chief function of the contrasts developed among these three attitudes would be to lower the false lovers of the second and third plots and to raise the true lovers of the main plot, whose relationship thereby becomes the only real "family of love" in a hostile world incapable of achieving or even appreciating it. The arrangement of the opening scenes clearly works to this end, the first presenting Maria's defense of that relationship against the sanctimonious "niceness" of Glister and his wife, and the second Gerardine's analogous defense against the hedonistic cynicism of Lipsalve and Gudgeon, so that before Maria speaks to Gerardine from her balcony their love has been defined and validated in confrontation with the antiromantic objections advanced from the opposite extremes of the other plots. And during their ensuing dialogue it is again contrasted to, and elevated by, the bawdy commentary of the gallants, who serve much the same purpose here as Mercutio in the more famous balcony scene from which this derives.

Although the exploitation of these contrasts is most obvious in the initial sequence, similar effects are produced throughout the play—in Lipsalve's debased version of this same balcony scene in III.ii, for instance, or the juxtaposition of Glister's "spirit" and Gerardine's "apparition" in II.iv, or the combination of all three resolutions in the final trial. Even the imagery, unimpressive as it is, continually turns on the oppositions of external to internal and physical to spiritual which differentiate the ethical positions of the plots. And other details of the play can also be shown to contribute to the organization and unification of these three complementary treatments of love in terms of the romantic, realistic, and farcical levels of the formula.

The weakness of the play, then, does not lie in this coherent design but in its inadequate execution. The subplot fails to realize the pos-

---

[13] See III.iv.4 on Lipsalve's "variety in love" and I.iii.172 on Mistress Glister's "niceness."

sibilities inherent in the Purge-Glister triangle—possibilities that will become clear by hindsight when we see what Middleton was able to make of a similar situation in *A Chaste Maid in Cheapside*. Still more damaging is the awkward handling of romantic sentiment in the early stages of the main action, particularly in the frigid set pieces given the lovers, of which Maria's speech quoted above is a fair sample. This Middleton was not to try again. Whether he recognized it as a limitation in himself or one imposed by his form, in his other city comedies he never concentrates so exclusively on love, or attempts to render the emotion itself so directly. And when he returns to this triadic formula in *A Fair Quarrel*, the love interest is reduced to the realistic subplot and the idealized main action is devoted to honor, which he can deal with more comfortably at this level, although it requires a readjustment of the whole structure to the more serious genre of tragicomedy.

II

In proceeding to *A Fair Quarrel,* which Middleton wrote in collaboration with Rowley, we move not only into another genre but also into another league, for since the time of Charles Lamb's enthusiastic rediscovery of the play it has been recognized by many critics as one of the best tragicomedies of the period. Their admiration, however, is directed entirely to the main plot, the story of Captain Ager, his mother, and his estranged friend, the Colonel, while the subplot of Jane Russell, her father, and Fitzallen, her betrothed, and the independent "roaring" episodes of her suitor, Chough, are either ignored or else condemned on the usual grounds that they do not connect to the main action or harmonize with its mood.[14] Yet we will find that a formal integration of these separate actions has been achieved here, and a final synthesis of their varied tones, through the playwrights' relatively complex and sophisticated deployment of the triadic formula.

The most obvious connection, in formal terms, is that each action leads to a "quarrel" of the same sort—a threatened duel over a woman's honor that fails to come off. The Colonel calls Captain Ager "son of a whore," and Ager is prepared to fight him until his mother says it is true. In the subplot Chough draws his sword on the Physician when he claims Jane is a whore, and then Russell, her father, almost challenges Chough when he repeats this. And the third-level roaring scenes include two of these quarrels, first at the School (IV.i) where the tutors in their exhibition use the same insult translated into the "Londonian roar" ("I say thy sister is a bronstrops"; "I say thy mother is a callicut"), and again on the street (IV.iv) where Chough and his

---

14 E.g., Swinburne, p. 164, and Arthur Symons, "Middleton and Rowley," *CHEL*, 6 (Cambridge, 1932), 75. Lamb's remarks are included in his *Specimens of English Dramatic Poets* (London, 1835), 1: 148–49.

servant Trimtram apply these terms to Meg and Priss and so almost cross swords with their pimp, Captain Albo.[15] But a "nuclear" parallel of this sort (like the sexual blackmail in *The Changeling*) underscores the differences in treatment on the separate levels, which seem to exhaust the possible variations of the basic situation. One such variable is the relation of the women to the insulting epithet: Lady Ager is an absolutely chaste widow who belies herself in order to prevent Captain Ager from fighting for her honor; but this is reversed in IV.iv where Priss, a real whore, insists that Captain Albo defend her "good name"; and Jane is in an ambiguous position between them, for, thanks to the contemporary attitude toward betrothals (which proved so useful to so many of the dramatists), she is both innocent and guilty of fornication. Another variable is the men's relationship to the dueling code: in the main plot they are professional soldiers to whom dueling is a sacred obligation, in the subplot peaceable citizens, and in the third swashbuckling bullies who teach roaring or protect prostitutes for a living.

Even more significant is the change in the focus of these treatments. Each action emphasizes a different role in the encounter: in the first the protagonist is Ager, the defender; in the second Jane, the insulted woman, and in the third Chough, the insulter. And each centers on a different aspect of the situation, subordinating everything else to it. The real issue of the main plot is the "fair quarrel" itself. The Colonel hurls his insult at Ager, not because he believes his mother is a whore or is at all concerned about her, but simply to provoke a duel; and it is her desire to stop this duel, rather than any doubt about her chastity, that prompts Lady Ager to admit to the charge. Both of these incidents are aimed at placing Ager in the difficult position which is brought to a head and resolved in the duel, the crucial episode of this plot and the one that gives the play its name. In the subplot, however, the problem is Jane's plight as an unwed mother, and the abortive duels at the end exist for its sake—as a result of her difficulties and a means of solving them. The Physician does not call her a whore to provoke another man but to injure her, for he knows it is in a sense true; and the ensuing quarrels are quickly passed over as subsidiary incidents leading to her marriage to Fitzallen. Finally, the chief interest of the roaring scenes lies neither in duels nor women's reputations, but in the insults themselves, which are savored and bandied about by Chough and Trimtram and their tutors without any regard for their accuracy or any expectation that they will result in actual fights.

---

15 IV.iv was added in the second issue of Q1 (1617) and so presumably was not in the original production, though it must have been written soon after and simply expands on material already found there.

These changes in focus are the consequence of a more fundamental distinction in the nature of the actions and their presentation, through which they are ordered into a hierarchy that is at once social, ethical, and emotional in its determinants. At the most serious level is the main plot, a study in extraordinary virtue that marks Middleton's closest approach to the Fletcherian school of heroic drama. The principal value here, in the characters' own motivation and our judgment of them, is honor. Although it is one conception, designated throughout by one set of interchangeable terms ("honour," "fame," "good name," "reputation," "nobleness," "worth"), its application is differentiated according to sex: a man's honor inheres in his courage (specifically the courage displayed in wars and duels—the "field of honour"), a woman's in her chastity.[16] The equivalence of the two is indicated at the outset when Ager is said to have

> an anger more inclin'd to courage
> And moderation than the colonel;
> A virtue as rare as chastity in youth
> (I.i.44–46)

and again in the analogy drawn by the Captain between "manhood" and virginity (ll. 86–89), and is further emphasized in his celebrated interview with his mother in II.i. But it becomes most meaningful in the duel scene when Ager, who cannot fight to defend his mother's virtue, finally seizes upon a "just cause" in the insult to his courage, producing the startled reaction of his second that states the shift from female to male honor: "Impossible! coward do more than bastard?"

This shift is essential since, as was pointed out, the function of the Colonel's original insult and Lady Ager's lie is to precipitate a crisis within the Captain, which must, given the values of this plot, be posed in terms of his honor. It is a crisis for him only because his ideal of honor includes something more than courage, as he explains:

> I am too full of conscience,
> Knowledge, and patience, to give justice to't;
> So careful of my eternity, which consists
> Of upright actions, that unless I knew
> It were a truth I stood for, any coward
> Might make my breast his foot-pace.
> (II.i.9–14)

---

[16] Courage is often called "manhood" (I.i.77; II.i.208, 235; III.i.7, 48; etc.) and chastity is "thou glorious woman's virtue" (III.iii.27). The idea is common; see *The Spectator*, No. 99: "The great Point of Honour in Men is Courage, and in Women Chastity" (ed. G. Gregory Smith, 1 [London, 1945], 306).

Because of this scruple, Ager finds himself in an excruciating dilemma on the dueling field, for he must choose between appearing a coward in the eyes of his world or risking his soul in an unjust cause. His anguish arouses our pity, but it also arouses our admiration since, like the dilemmas of the typical Beaumont and Fletcher heroes,[17] it results directly from his moral commitment, in the refinement of his principles and his steadfast devotion to them under the most agonizing pressure, which sets him above even the noble code (the "fellowship of honour") of his associates, as the embodiment of male perfection. It is appropriate, then, that his ideal have the sanction not only of religion (as in the preceding quotation) but also of a higher and truer "manhood," so that when the Colonel finally is converted to it he can express his new insight in the language of the "field of honour":

> This is the only war we should provide for!
> Where he that forgives largest, and sighs strongest,
> Is a tried soldier, a true man indeed,
> And wins the best field.
>
> (IV.ii.53–56)

The action of the subplot is at once more realistic and less intense. Honor is no longer an important consideration. It is true that Jane speaks of it as the reason for concealing her pregnancy, but she is only thinking of her reputation—the appearance of chastity—and not the "glorious woman's virtue" itself, which she has already lost. She is quite explicit about this when she thanks the Physician:

> Your secrecy keeps me in the state of woman;
> For else what husband would choose me his wife,
> Knowing the honour of a bride were lost!
> I cannot number half the good you do me
> In the conceal'd retention of my sin.
>
> (III.ii.59–63) [18]

That "sin" does not render her at all unsympathetic within her world, however, since the chief value here, which determines our standard of

---

17 Such as Amintor in *The Maid's Tragedy*, Leucippus in *Cupid's Revenge*, Thierry in *Thierry and Theodoret*, Virolet in *The Double Marriage*, and Valerio in *A Wife for a Month*, who also face a conflict between honor and a higher principle (usually the divine right of king or parent). The Colonel's role then is analogous to the villain in these plays, whose main function is to force the hero into his dilemma.

18 And see ll. 162–68 where the Physician's sister tells her that "reputation" or "good name" is "more esteemed than our actions,/ By which we should deserve it." Compare the distinction between the Lady's and Wife's "honor" in *The Second Maiden's Tragedy*.

judgment, is not a highly specialized code that elevates its adherents far above the mass of mankind but ordinary romantic love; and with this descent from the rarefied moral atmosphere of the main plot, there is a corresponding decline in the sensitivity of the characters and the seriousness of the action. This demonstrates the law of relativity of the three-level formula, for the Jane-Fitzallen plot is built on the same convention of young love triumphing over parental opposition that was employed to place Gerardine and Maria at the most serious and most sensitive level of *The Family of Love;* but now its effect is greatly reduced because of the change in context provided by another hierarchy.

One significant element in that context is the role of money, the conventional cause of the parental opposition, which becomes a second major value in the action and separates it further from the heroic mode of the main plot. Although Russell is Lady Ager's brother, he inhabits an entirely different society—the bourgeois society of the city—with entirely different attitudes toward the questions of honor that dominate the lives of his sister and nephew. The imagery of his opening soliloquy, for example, reveals that he regards his daughter's chastity as a piece of troublesome merchandise:

> 'Tis such
> A brittle niceness, a mere cupboard of glasses,
> The least shake breaks or cracks 'em. All my aim is
> To cast her upon riches.
> (I.i.8–11)

We soon get a similar insight into his view of male honor when he sees the duel between the Captain's friend and the Colonel's:

> Here's noble youths! belike some wench has cross'd 'em,
> And now they know not what to do with their blood.
> (ll. 52–53)

And the kind of honor he does appreciate is stated in the concluding couplet of Act I, in which he sums up for Jane his whole philosophy of life:

> Honour and attendance, these will bring thee health;
> And the way to 'em is to climb by wealth.

This philosophy is the real enemy of love, since it is what leads him to imprison Fitzallen and hurry Jane into marriage with Chough, that "rich simplicity." A second and less conventional adversary later emerges when the Physician attempts to seduce Jane; but this is another manifestation of the same attitude that reduces love to a commodity, and that assumes her submission is the "price" due him for helping her (III.ii.73–119). We sympathize with Jane in her predicament; yet our feelings are never as deeply engaged as in the main plot because her struggles are against external obstacles and so seem less serious than Ager's spiritual crises. The action is not completely external, however, for these obstacles also function as trials of Jane's constancy, demonstrating her possession of this virtue (the appropriate one in a plot where love is the chief value) which raises her above the cynical commercialism of her world, much as Ager's scruples raise him above the code of his. In the terms given us by the subplot she is the most admirable person there, although these terms, and consequently our admiration, are on a significantly lower level than in the main action.

At a still lower level stand the farcical Chough episodes, which are wholly external and rely heavily on visual and verbal humor. While he shares the mercenary attitudes of the subplot, Chough's real interests, as they emerge on his first appearance, are even cruder, centering on the pleasures of sheer physical activity—eating, drinking, and wrestling. Love, too, is simplified down to the sexual act, which itself becomes a form of wrestling:

> I will not catch beneath the waist, believe it;
> I know fair play . . .
> the hug and the lock between man and woman, with
> a fair fall, is as sweet an exercise for the body as you'll
> desire in a summer's evening.
>
> (II.ii.168–69, 171–74)

This is more than just another double entendre, since it brings together, from Chough's reductive viewpoint, the primary concerns of all three plots, equating his favorite sport with romance and also, in the phrases "fair play" and "fair fall," with the "fair quarrel" of the titular action.[19] This latter connection is more important, for although Chough has a minor role in the subplot and is never allowed any contact with Ager or the Colonel (which would be as fatal to their refined heroics as the introduction of financial problems), his independent development as a distinct component of the hierarchy turns entirely upon his education in roaring, which sets up an obvious parallel to the dueling cult of the main plot.

The roaring "profession," we soon realize, is nothing more than a fantastically exaggerated imitation of the outward forms of this cult of honor, without the essential basis of a "just cause" to give it mean-

---

[19] In his roaring contest with Albo the phrases "foul play" and "fair fall" also occur (IV.iv.103–6). On the technical significance of "fair" in this context see Fredson Bowers, "Middleton's *Fair Quarrel* and the Duelling Code," *JEGP*, 36 (1937), 40–41.

ing. But that was just what distinguished Ager's ideal of honor from the Colonel's. Therefore, the elaborate rules taught at the Roaring School (which is run by the Colonel's friend) are to be seen as an ironic comment on the mechanical and irrational application of a noble code by the Colonel in Act I and III.i, where he insists on creating and maintaining a quarrel out of nothing, and perversely twists each of Ager's sincere attempts at reconciliation into a further aggravation of the dispute. Even the insults of the roarers ("I say thy mother is a callicut, a panagron, a duplar, and a sindicus") are no more nonsensical or outrageous than the Colonel's "son of a whore," the ritual challenge flung out in his rage without any sense of its meaning or justice. And this "profession" is made still more ridiculous, and so still more telling a comment on the Colonel's behavior, when it is passed down from the tutors to Chough—partly because of his buffoonery and the comic discrepancy between his bravado and cowardice, but also because of his gross earthy perspective, which manages to debase even this debased version of the honorable duel. Just as Russell and the Physician reduced honor and love, the values of the main and subplot, to commercial transactions, so Chough reduces them both to a wrestling match at a country fair. And this process of corporealization reaches its nadir when his servant Trimtram defeats Captain Albo in their "duel" by a scatological anticipation of gas warfare, deflating the verbal flatulence of roaring with the more pungent thing itself.

Although the integration of these levels of soldier, lover, and clown is achieved primarily through the "spatial" hierarchy based on their formal and final relationships, an important contribution is also made by the temporal arrangement of the action at the beginning and end of the play. Act I is particularly noteworthy because of the skill with which the material connections linking the first two levels—the fact that Russell is Lady Ager's brother, and Fitzallen the Colonel's kinsman—are exploited to introduce the principal characters and issues of both plots in a single sequence of causal interaction that establishes the fundamental analogy between them. Immediately after Russell's opening soliloquy in which he determines to cast Jane "upon riches," Lady Ager tells him she will beg her son, who has just returned from the wars, never to leave England again, and Russell comments:

> Affectionate sister! she has no daughter now;
> It follows all the love must come to him,
> And he has a worth deserves it, were it dearer.
>
> (ll. 35–37)

This at once suggests the equivalence of Russell's concern for his daughter and his sister's concern for her son, focusing our interest on the two young people who become the protagonists of their separate plots, and informs us that the problems of these plots will involve marriage and the profession of arms, respectively. The parallel can be extended, for each parent's solicitude is misdirected in the same way in that it places an inferior good above the real value at stake: Russell wants Jane to substitute money for love, as Lady Ager wants her son to substitute safety for honor; and these twin errors bring about the two complications, causing Russell to arrest Fitzallen and so leave Jane vulnerable to the Physician's blackmail, and his sister to tell the lie that creates Ager's dilemma.

No sooner has Russell mentioned his nephew's "worth," however, than the Captain's friend and the Colonel's enter disputing this very question ("His worth for me!" "This gentleman/ Parallel'd captain Ager's worth with yours"), and the two principals then take this up in an interchange that defines male honor as the chief issue of the main plot (it being the virtue tested in "quarreling," as well as the subject of their particular quarrel), and also displays in action the crucial difference between the two men's conceptions of this honor. They are interrupted by the appearance of Jane and Fitzallen, which pacifies the Colonel, since he would not injure his kinsman's prospects of marrying Ager's cousin. Consequently, all four join in urging Russell to consent to the match, producing a series of analogies that emphasize the parallel significance of the "fair quarrel" and romantic love in these two plots:

> Here enters now a scene of loving arms;
> This couple will not quarrel so.
>
> (ll. 134–35)

> We'll have no arms here now but lovers' arms.
>
> (l. 183)

> He [Russell] took your hand from your enraged blood,
> And gave it freely to your opposite,
> My cousin Ager: methinks you should claim from him,
> In the less quality of calmer blood,
> To join the hands of two divided friends,
> Even these two that would offer willingly
> Their own embrace.
>
> (ll. 200–6)

> you shall do a lover's part
> Worth one brave act of valour.
>
> (ll. 208–9)

But this truce does not last long, since Russell takes advantage of it to secure the men's weapons so they cannot resist when he has Fitzallen arrested, and this blow to the lovers causes the Colonel to attack Ager more violently than before, in his fury changing the ground from the Captain's "manhood" to his mother's chastity, which leads directly to their duel.

This pattern of causal interaction does not continue beyond Act I, for thereafter the main and subplot go their own ways and do not meet again before Act V. (The same is true of the roaring sequence, which proceeds separately until Chough reënters the subplot at the conclusion to try his technique on the Physician and Russell.) Even in Act V they are combined, like the two suits at the trial ending *The Family of Love,* only through their material connection (the family ties that bring the Agers to Jane's wedding), since the problems of the subplot are all settled before the main-plot characters arrive to wind up their affairs, without affecting or being affected by the other action. Nevertheless the juxtaposition of the denouements makes possible a vivid dramatization of the analogical and emotional relationships developed between these plots throughout the play. They are both happy endings, but the nature of this happiness and the way it is attained reflect back upon and reinforce the difference in the two value systems. Since the complication of the main plot involved a profound moral conflict, its resolution must be equally serious and internalized, requiring nothing less than a spiritual conversion on the part of the Colonel which raises him to Ager's level and so brings about a reconciliation of the two on an even nobler basis than their original friendship. The complication of the subplot, however, consisted of attacks on the lovers by their two enemies, and it is therefore resolved by another action equally external to them, an unexpected turn of events that hoists these enemies with their own petards: the Physician's attempt to ruin Jane by revealing her secret actually helps her, as she reminds him ("I am much bound unto your malice, sir"); and Russell, who prided himself on his cleverness in imprisoning Fitzallen and then in getting him to father Jane's child, also learns he has suffered the usual fate of the comic villain ("By my troth, the old man has gulled himself finely!").

Both these resolutions reward the protagonists with love, honor, and money, the three values of the play, but with essential differences. In the subplot the triumph of love, in the marriage of Jane and Fitzallen, is primary, yet money is also very prominent, because that triumph turns on a battle of wits in which Fitzallen tricks Russell into adding another thousand to Jane's dowry to compensate for her "shame." By this marriage Jane also recovers a somewhat tarnished honor, or what passes for honor according to the relaxed, pragmatic standards of her plot—although we are reminded again that this is all relative to the specific context, since practically the same ending seemed entirely appropriate for the most serious level in *The Family of Love*. It certainly would not seem so in this hierarchy; one cannot imagine Captain Ager ever responding to such a revelation about his mother as Russell does to his daughter's admission that she has had an illegitimate child:

> Hast thou?
> Well, wipe thine eyes; I'm a grandfather then.
> If all bastards were banish'd, the city would be thin
> In the thickest term-time.
>
> (ll. 255–58)

Nor would there be any way of redeeming her within the much more exacting code of the main plot, which requires a radical reordering of these values for a satisfactory conclusion. Most important is the attainment of the loftiest ideal of honor in the new "brotherhood" of Ager and the Colonel. Money also figures in their reconciliation, for the Colonel wills his property to Ager as part of his sister's dowry and even adds another manor at the last minute (it is called "a fair increase," just as Russell calls his extra thousand "a fair proffer"), but there the resemblance to the subplot ends. In that denouement money was the prize in a gulling contest between adversaries, while here it is an unvalued counter passed back and forth between friends, each striving to outdo the other in a contest of magnanimity. Ager also wins the love of the Colonel's sister, but she is actually just another counter in their contest, carefully subordinated, like the property, to the central issue of male honor; the real equivalent in the main action to the final embrace of Jane and Fitzallen is not Ager's betrothal to this woman (which is disposed of in IV.iii), but the climactic moment at the very end when he falls into the Colonel's waiting arms. And the obvious contrasts between these parallel embraces, and between the parallel contests immediately preceding them, with all the ramifications of meaning and value those contrasts have been seen to imply, provide the definitive statement of the relationship of the two plots within this hierarchy.

III

In Cyril Tourneur's *The Atheist's Tragedy; or, The Honest Man's Revenge* we find again the three levels of the formula—the first portraying the conflict between the "atheist," Baron D'Amville, and his antagonists, Charlemont, the "honest man," and his beloved Castabella; the second, the adulterous affair of Levidulcia and Sebastian; and the third, Languebeau Snuffe's attempted seduction of Soquette. And again we find that the critical commentary, which has grown considerably over the past thirty years, deals almost exclusively with the first level. This is quite understandable, for the most striking feature of the play (as the double title suggests) is its development of general theses opposing atheism and private vengeance through the careers of D'Amville and Charlemont, respectively. Yet even in these didactic terms it can be shown that the second action and, to a lesser degree, the third contribute to the formulation of the "doctrine" of the main plot, as a necessary consequence of their integration into the hierarchic structure of the work as a whole. And this structure will turn out to be the most elaborate yet encountered, since it in itself necessarily reflects the highly self-conscious and systematic program entailed in the play's ethical commitment.

The first two levels are related through their common form; they are both villain-hero or retribution plots, focusing on the criminality of D'Amville and Levidulcia and their deserved punishments (indeed, D'Amville's atheistic Machiavellianism makes him a much more typical protagonist of this genre than those discussed earlier). But while this is an essential aspect of the analogy between these levels, the detailed dramatic and conceptual scheme in which that analogy is worked out takes as its basic components not the plots themselves but their major characters—D'Amville, Charlemont and Castabella (who, it will be seen, are treated as a single unit), Levidulcia, and Sebastian—and the moral positions represented by them. In material terms the plots are linked by the family relationships of these people: Levidulcia is the stepmother of Castabella, and Sebastian the son of D'Amville, and hence Charlemont's cousin. And these relationships produce a series of causal connections in which the subplot characters directly affect those of the main plot—at the outset, when they intervene in D'Amville's plan to marry his son Rousard to Castabella, Levidulcia attempting to promote the match and Sebastian to prevent it (I.iv); in the middle, when Sebastian defends D'Amville against Charlemont and then uses the money, given him by his grateful father, to free Charlemont from prison (III.ii–iii); and at the end, where the death of Sebastian in his duel with Levidulcia's husband, Baron Belforest, becomes part of D'Amville's punishment (by destroying his hopes to found a dynasty), and Levidulcia's suicide, following her husband's death in this duel, brings Charlemont and Castabella the Belforest inheritance, which is named in the closing lines as part of their reward. It is also through these material relations that the main plot affects the subplot; in fact it initiates the subplot, because the sight of Castabella's preparations for her bridal bed (II.iii) fires Levidulcia's passion and leads her to accept an assignation with Sebastian, which he makes ostensibly to enlist her aid in healing the breach with his father caused by his protest against the marriage. And their affair comes to its bloody close when Belforest's suspicions are confirmed by

Fresco (IV.iv), whom he questions because on the night of this wedding he was discovered in Levidulcia's room (II.v), where she had lured him to satisfy the desires it aroused in her.

In bringing the plots into contact at these crucial junctures, this pattern of causal connections also helps to establish the more significant formal relationships, both positive and negative, between the two sets of characters, which are manifested on the occasions when their separate stories intersect. The most obvious example of this is the opposition (implicit in their names) of Castabella's chastity and Levidulcia's lust in the nuptial chamber scene just referred to (II.iii), where, as several critics have noted, the bride's relief on learning of the groom's impotence is played off against her stepmother's mounting sexual excitement. Actually the opposition begins with two earlier encounters of the women leading up to this scene. The first of these, in I.ii, is our introduction to Levidulcia, which is timed to occur while Charlemont is kissing Castabella good-bye, so that Snuffe's warning to the lovers—completely inapplicable, as we realize, to them—becomes her entrance cue: "Fie, fie, fie, these carnal kisses do stir up the concupiscences of the flesh"; and her immediate reaction to Charlemont's reassurance that their kiss "was but a parting one" clinches the point: "A lusty blood! Now, by the lip of Love,/ Were I to choose, your joining one for me." And in the second such encounter, in I.iv, she urges Castabella, with the same blunt argument used by Juliet's nurse, to abandon "th' imaginary joy/ Of an unsatisfy'd affection to/ An absent man" for "the sweet possession of a man" whose body is available.

The contrast set up by this opening sequence is elaborated in the subsequent action, which contrives a certain artificial symmetry by confronting each woman with three actual or potential sexual partners: her unwanted husband (Rousard, Belforest), her "true love" (Charlemont, Sebastian), and another man who nearly enjoys her (D'Amville, Fresco). The parallelism of course emphasizes the difference between them. This is clear enough in the case of the third man, for D'Amville's approach to Castabella is an attempted rape, while Levidulcia tries to seduce Fresco; but in their marital and romantic relations the contrast is still more impressive. Although Castabella was forced to marry Rousard against her will (which is also called "a rape" —I.iv.128–31), and is so devoted to Charlemont that she eagerly joins him on the scaffold, she is never tempted to commit adultery with him, even when the maximum opportunity presents itself in the churchyard scene (IV.iii), where their mutual restraint in going to sleep chastely side by side is magnified by our knowledge that at this same time Levidulcia is in bed with Sebastian, and that this same place was chosen by D'Amville and Snuffe for their own sexual adventures. (When they are later found by these same two men and accused of fornication because "The time, the place,/ All circumstances argue" for it, this again underscores their innocence.) On the other hand, Levidulcia's professed love for Sebastian seeks immediate physical gratification in violation of her marriage vows; and when he is not accessible we are shown, in the Fresco episode, that she eagerly solicits a substitute. The basis of this opposition is stated for us by the women themselves in their explanations of the source and power of their love. Castabella attributes her affection for Charlemont to her God-given free will:

> O thou that know'st me justly Charlemont's,
> Though in the forc'd possession of another,
> Since from thine own free spirit we receive it
> That our affections cannot be compell'd
>
> (III.i.53–56)

But Levidulcia locates her affection for Sebastian in a physiological determinism that reduces her to the animal world:

> My strange affection to this man! 'Tis like
> The natural sympathy which e'en among
> The senseless creatures of the earth commands
> A mutual inclination and consent.
> For though it seems to be the free effect
> Of mine own voluntary love, yet I
> Can neither restrain it, nor give reason for 't.
>
> (IV.v.16–22)

Levidulcia's appeal to "natural" principles here, as well as in the counsel she gives Castabella in I.iv, not only distinguishes her view of love from the idealized, religious conception of her stepdaughter but also links her to D'Amville, who derives his creed from "Nature and her large philosophy" in the dialogue with his servant Borachio which opens the play,[20] and relies upon the same reductive analogy between "man and beast," both in this introductory dialogue and later in the churchyard when he tries to overcome Castabella's horror of incest by arguing that "Nature allows a gen'ral liberty/ Of generation to all

---

20 This is one of the catechisms in "policy" where the typical Machiavellian expounds his evil principles to his accomplice and the audience—cf. *The Jew of Malta*, II.iii; *Alphonsus, Emperor of Germany*, I.i, II.ii; *Antonio's Revenge*, I.i; *Sejanus*, II; *The Devil's Charter*, I.iv. D'Amville's motive for seducing Castabella conforms strictly to this type; see Richard on his proposal to Lady Anne (*Richard III*, I.i.157–59) and Sejanus on his courtship of Livia: "Prosper it, Pallas, thou that better'st wit,/ For Venus hath the smallest share in it" (*Sejanus*, I.373–74).

creatures else." This important parallel between the villain-heroes of the two plots has been pointed out by the critics, but they have usually overlooked the equally important difference.[21] The "Nature" that Levidulcia celebrates is the physical world of instinct—primarily sexual instinct—which she opposes to and elevates above human reason. In I.iv she begins her advice to Castabella by rebuking Snuffe (who was also promoting the Rousard marriage) for his use of the wrong rhetoric:

> Tush, you mistake the way into a woman;
> The passage lies not through her reason but her blood
>
> (ll. 65–66)

And in her following speech she insists on the superiority of the "fruitful body" to the "barren mind":

> If reason were
> Our counsellor, we would neglect the work
> Of generation for the prodigal
> Expense it draws us to of that which is
> The wealth of life. Wise Nature, therefore, hath
> Reserv'd for an inducement to our sense
> Our greatest pleasure in that greatest work
>
> (ll. 86–92)

D'Amville's naturalism, however, is nothing if not rationalistic. In that expository catechism in I.i he and Borachio agree that while man does not differ in kind from the beasts, he excels them by virtue of his natural reason, which informs him that his goal in life should not be the instinctive indulgence of the senses, since it is "improvident" to "spend our substance on a minute's pleasure," but the calculated pursuit of wealth, the "lord/ Of all felicity." This reverses the values of Levidulcia, who placed sensual pleasure over wealth (figuratively in the speech just quoted, and literally in II.v.9–13). Even his one sexual action in the play, his attempt on Castabella in IV.iii, does not spring from passion, as some commentators have thought, but from "policy" —from his long-range plan to found a dynasty. His whole approach to Castabella during this scene, in marked contrast to Levidulcia's in I.iv, is aggressively intellectual; and while we saw that Levidulcia could not "give reason for" her love, he assures Castabella:

---

[21] Two notable exceptions are Muriel Bradbrook in *Themes and Conventions of Elizabethan Tragedy* (Cambridge, 1952), pp. 180–81, and Peter Murray in *A Study of Cyril Tourneur* (Philadelphia, 1964), pp. 91–94.

> I love
> Thee with the freedom of my reason. I
> Can give thee reason for my love.
>   (IV.iii.86–88)

Even in the closing scene at the trial, after all his hopes are destroyed, he still maintains this position to the judges:

> I can give you sense
> And solid reason for the very least
> Distinguishable syllable I speak.
>   (V.ii.85–87)

The schematism of the play, then, aligns Levidulcia and D'Amville as the two representatives of naturalism—thus pitting them both against Charlemont and Castabella, who believe in a supernatural providence—and at the same time differentiates them in terms of this opposition between instinct and reason.

Levidulcia's paramour, Sebastian, is similarly related to D'Amville's principal adversary, Charlemont. Like Charlemont he is presented sympathetically; he is a generous, good-natured, brave, and honest young man, whose fundamental decency emerges very clearly in his two interventions in the main plot where he defies his father, at the risk of his own livelihood, by protesting the enforced marriage of Castabella and later by freeing Charlemont from prison. In both instances, however, he acts not on reasoned conviction but on an emotional impulse of the sort that characterizes his behavior throughout the play, whereas Charlemont's actions are based upon a rational understanding and acceptance of Christian principles which typically restrain his impulses (to avenge his father, to defend himself against D'Amville, to make love to Castabella).[22] This major difference is brought out effectively in the second of these episodes through the juxtaposition of Sebastian's soliloquy at the end of III.ii, where he determines to aid Charlemont, with Charlemont's soliloquy on divine justice that begins III.iii. Each man is dealing with a moral question and each arrives at the right answer, which makes the contrast even more striking. Sebastian faces a practical problem requiring immediate action, grapples with it in abrupt fits and starts, and is finally impelled to his decision by the convergence of various emotions—his feeling of obligation to Charlemont, his admiration of him, and his outraged sense of fair play ("He fought bravely, but the officers dragged him villainously"); but Charlemont is examining a difficult

---

[22] Murray argues (pp. 100–4) that Charlemont gradually progresses toward this position, and does not fully attain it until his prison soliloquy in III.iii.

theoretical problem of universal import in an organized argument deduced from a logically articulated religious philosophy. The styles of their soliloquies make the same point, Sebastian's earthy language and colloquial prose rhythms being contrasted to the abstract diction and measured periods of Charlemont's blank verse. And the distinction between these two moral states is confirmed by the outcomes of the two plots, since Charlemont's ultimate victory depends on his adherence to his ethical and theological principles, while Sebastian's impetuous, manly good nature is responsible for his ignominious death: it is what first attracts Levidulcia to him (II.iii.57–59), and leads him to approach her, and, at the end, to fight her husband—an action which, like his clash with Charlemont in III.ii, is not premeditated and certainly not malicious, but a spontaneous response of his mistaken sense of honor that has engaged him in an unworthy cause.

Therefore, it appears that the major characters of these plots have been placed on a moral scale deriving from one of the classical analyses of the soul. Charlemont and Castabella (who are not differentiated in this respect) belong at the highest point since their conduct is grounded in true goodness or wisdom, an intellectual apprehension of the divine ideal. Below them is Sebastian, ruled by what Plato calls the "spirited" part of the soul,[23] which tends toward noble action but can, when not joined with reason, produce the opposite. Levidulcia, driven by sheer physical "appetite," is still lower. And at the bottom stands D'Amville, the man of perverted reason who, unlike all the others, deliberately takes evil for his good, both in his Machiavellian philosophy and in his career of crime. These four positions could be located along a single line, but in terms of the system of parallels and contrasts found in the play, they arrange themselves into a more complex structure that resembles the well-known "square of opposition" of traditional logic.[24] If for the purposes of the analogy we substitute characters (or more strictly, kinds of "character") for the four types of propositions, using ethical instead of logical distinctions as differentiae, then the scheme might be diagramed as follows:

---

23 It is the seat of the emotions (anger, shame, etc.) that are the natural allies of reason and are associated with courage and honor—see *Republic* 439E–441C and *Phaedrus* 246A–256D (the white horse represents this part). William Elton lists a number of Renaissance restatements of this division in *"King Lear" and the Gods* (San Marino, 1966), pp. 267–69. Although Tourneur does not use the scheme with philosophic precision, the term "spirit" is applied to Sebastian in this sense in II.iii.58, III.ii.54, and IV.ii.38, and "appetite" to Levidulcia in IV.iv.9. See also Castabella's distinction between the mercy based on natural impulse and that based on reason—defined, in good Platonic fashion, as "the impression in your soul/ Of goodness" (III.iv.4–24).

24 See Thomas Wilson, *The Rule of Reason* (1552), sig. F8ʳ, and Walter Ong, *Ramus, Method, and the Decay of Dialogue* (Cambridge, Mass., 1958), pls. VI, X.

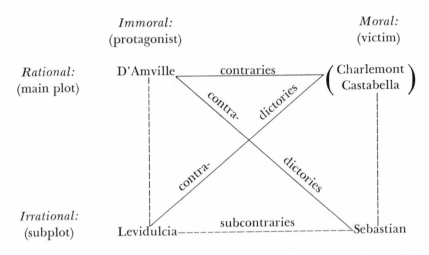

The relationships obtaining among these ethical states are analogous to those of the logical square. The two "contraries," like the universal affirmative and universal negative propositions, are diametrically opposed, the conflict between the piety of Charlemont and Castabella and the atheism of D'Amville being of course the basic issue of the main plot. Each diagonal indicates a "contradiction" equivalent to the relation between universal and particular propositions of different quality, since Levidulcia's lust is contrasted to Castabella's chastity, as was shown, and D'Amville's cold-blooded malice to Sebastian's impulsive good nature. The vertical lines stand for a relation roughly similar to the "subalteration" of particular to universal propositions of the same quality, if we regard Sebastian's good nature and Levidulcia's lust as attenuated forms of the absolute virtue and vice portrayed in the main action. Finally, the "subcontraries," like particular affirmatives and negatives, are not in opposition and even show a mutual affinity (as noted in IV.iv.9–14). And the causal interactions of these characters correspond to the formal relationships of the positions they represent: Charlemont and Castabella are D'Amville's chief antagonists and intended victims, and eventually his conquerors; Levidulcia's intervention in the main plot allies her with D'Amville against his victims (thus we saw that Castabella must withstand the attacks of both "naturalist" positions—Levidulcia's in I.iv and D'Amville's in IV.iii), while Sebastian's interventions have the opposite effect; and in the subplot itself Sebastian is certainly not Levidulcia's antagonist and can only be called her victim in the limited, "objective" sense that she unintentionally becomes the agent of his destruction.

Although this scheme would seem to explain the formal integration of the main plot and subplot, it does not account for the third level of action, which must be included as another distinct component of the total structure. Belforest's Puritan chaplain, Languebeau Snuffe, is used as an instrument by the protagonists of both plots—in I.ii D'Amville bribes him to betray Charlemont and Castabella, and in IV.i Levidulcia brings him along to cover up her rendezvous with Sebastian in Cataplasma's house; but in this second venture he strikes out on his own by attempting the seduction of Cataplasma's not un-willing servant, Soquette. His efforts come to nothing, since he is in-terrupted in the churchyard by Charlemont and again back at the house by Belforest, yet this brief episode makes some interesting con-nections to the subplot and, through it, to the main action. It is motivated entirely by lust, as is the subplot; and it is a direct out-growth of that plot, for Snuffe finds himself in Cataplasma's home as a result of Levidulcia's liaison, and the sight of her going upstairs with her lover, he says, "makes the spirit of the flesh begin to wriggle in my blood," which prompts him to try Soquette. This causal nexus also establishes an analogy between the two plots because it parallels the situation in II.iii where the sight of Castabella preparing for her bridal night set Levidulcia's own "blood a-boiling," leading to her af-fair with Sebastian; and Snuffe's exit speech here:

> The flesh is humble till the spirit move it,
> But when 'tis raised it will command above it
>
> (IV.i.92–93)

echoes Levidulcia's last words in the bridal scene:

> Lust is a spirit which whosoe'er doth raise,
> The next man that encounters boldly lays.
>
> (II.iii.65–66)

(The parallel is reinforced later, in IV.v, when Soquette agrees to join Snuffe "so soon as my mistress shall be in bed," just before Levidulcia decides to spend the night with Sebastian if Fresco "brings word/ My husband is i' bed"—ll. 10–14.)

These efficient and formal connections link Snuffe and Soquette to Sebastian and Levidulcia in such a way that they appear to serve as the "belowstairs" representatives of this couple in the churchyard scene (IV.iii) where the various plot strands are brought together, and consequently their actions in that scene are interpreted as a com-mentary upon the subplot. It is certainly not a flattering commentary. The lust of Levidulcia and Sebastian at least had a forthright, natural vitality; but this is completely lost in Snuffe's hypocritical cant and Soquette's vulgar protests, in the nasty, mechanistic view of sex re-vealed by their own imagery (the analogy to drawing water from a well in IV.iii.44–48, and that "wriggle" in the blood, which sounds so much worse than Levidulcia's "boiling"), and in the sheer clumsiness of their physical encounter, reduced by Snuffe's struggles with his false beard to a very broad and bawdy slapstick. The effect of the third-level episode is therefore quite clear; Sebastian's affair with Levidulcia, when reflected in this grotesque mirror, is made to seem more reprehensible, and by contrast the chaste love of Charlemont and Castabella seems more admirable. Even the protagonist of the main action is glanced at indirectly in this mirror, since Snuffe's religious hypocrisy had earlier confirmed D'Amville's atheism (I.ii.206–15), and his fiasco with Soquette is immediately followed by D'Amville's own attempt to seduce Castabella, which is also thwarted in the same way by the unexpected appearance of Charlemont.

The inter-plot causal sequence in which each action initiates the one below it is an unusual feature of this play, but it simply reaffirms the order of decreasing importance and seriousness of the standard three-level formula. The main plot is elevated above the others since its characters embody the absolutes of good and evil (much like the main plot of *The Second Maiden's Tragedy*, except that protagonist and antagonist have been reversed), and their conflict raises and resolves the most basic questions of man's existence. The characters of the subplot represent a scaling down of this polar opposition, and its issues, accordingly, are posed in subrational terms rather than in an explicit philosophic formulation; it even admits a comic element (in the scenes where Fresco appears) and, while it ends grimly enough, the mood throughout is closer to realistic satire than tragedy. And the third action, it was seen, is given an obviously farcical treatment. Thus the hierarchic arrangement serves the general purpose of the formula by providing a context that "places" the three components and our responses to them, but it also takes on a more specific function within the particular ethical orientation of this play. The intermediate characters of the second level and their burlesque counterparts of the third fill in the continuum between the extremes of the main action, which seems to force these extremes still further apart and thereby sharpens and clarifies the personal and ideological contest enacted there. At the same time, they enhance the sense of "coverage" (implicit in the formula itself) by exhausting all of the possibilities defined by the moral scheme, and so tend to universalize the villain-hero "retribution" plot that reappears in all three actions (for the Snuffe episode is a comic version of this plot, terminating in his comic discomfiture). The repetition of that plot pattern constitutes the formal parallel relating these separate levels, while the differentiations among them insure that the gravity of the crime and punishment at each level is commensurate with its place in the emotional hierarchy. Therefore the combination of the positive and negative aspects of the fundamental analogy suggests a comprehensive demonstration of the "wages of sin" and of the omnipresence of a punitive providence throughout all the various manifestations of human depravity and frailty. (A similar effect was noted in *A Looking Glass for London and England,* which is even more openly didactic.) And it also has the complementary result of isolating and emphasizing by contrast the virtue of Charlemont and Castabella and the beneficent power of this same providence that protects and rewards them.

IV

The extensive influence and remarkable flexibility of the three-level formula can be further illustrated by a brief look at some other adaptations of it in important tragedies and comedies of the period. One of the best known of these is Ford's *'Tis Pity She's a Whore,* which resembles *The Atheist's Tragedy* in its arrangement of three "punitive" actions, the first centering on Giovanni's incestuous liaison with Annabella and her marriage to Soranzo, the second on the vengeance of Hippolita, Soranzo's cast-off mistress, and of her own husband Richardetto, and the third on Bergetto's courtship of Annabella and Philotis, Richardetto's niece, and his murder at the hands of Grimaldi. These plots are brought together in a sequence of causal interactions turning on the competition for Annabella. Formally, they are related through the series of changes rung upon a single triangular pattern, Giovanni : Annabella : Soranzo $\sim$ Richardetto : Hippolita : Soranzo $\sim$ Annabella : Bergetto : Philotis. And in "final" terms, the intensity and extraordinary nature of Giovanni's passion and the ideological dimension it introduces (again like Tourneur's play) in his direct confrontation with divine law, represented by Friar Bonaventura, serve to place his action above the subplot, where the same ingredients of illicit love and jealousy appear in the more mundane and sordid form of a conventional revenge intrigue, and this subplot is in turn raised above the ludicrous wooing of Bergetto, assisted by his servant Poggio, who together are developed along much the same lines as Chough and Trimtram up to the moment of Bergetto's pathetically accidental death.

A few critics have argued that because these subordinate actions degrade all of Annabella's available suitors (Soranzo, Grimaldi, Bergetto), they work to justify her preference for her brother. The focus of the main plot, however, is not on Annabella's search for the right mate but on Giovanni's dominant role in initiating and continuing their incest, which is condemned by almost every other character in the play (including Annabella herself after her conversion in III.vi) and by its terrible consequences, since it destroys him, his sister, their father, her husband, and her maid, and is indirectly responsible for the deaths in the underplots as well, the line of causation proceeding from his impregnation of Annabella to her hasty betrothal to Soranzo and then to the two parallel attempts on Soranzo's life by those opposing the marriage, with their unintended results (in III.vii, immediately after the betrothal, Bergetto is stabbed by Grimaldi, who mistakes him for his hated rival; and during the wedding banquet in IV.i Hippolita is given the poisoned wine she had prepared for her former lover). One must be careful, therefore, not to confuse the inter-plot relationship of "hierarchy" here with that of "contrast." Giovanni's criminal course, for the reasons just noted, is more moving, even more "elevated" than Hippolita's, but this heightening does not make it any less criminal, as we are shown by the decided stress on the positive rather than the negative aspect of the analogy between them in the climaxes of their respective plots. They both bring about their own ruin through their vengeful attacks on Soranzo. They are both killed by Soranzo's servant Vasques, acting in his master's behalf. They both go down without a sign of repentance, and their deaths evoke identical judgments from the spectators: Hippolita's is called "Wonderful justice!" (IV.i.88), and Giovanni's a "Strange miracle of justice!" (V.vi.109); and Richardetto, who has taken on a choric role, explains the first as "the end/ Of lust and pride" (IV.i.101–2) and the second as "the effect of pride and lust at once/ Brought both to shameful ends" (V.vi.153–54).

Perhaps this point can be clarified in a comparison with *Love's Sacrifice*, where Ford uses the same general pattern of a main action devoted to the "illicit" romance of Fernando and the Duke's wife, Bianca; a less serious subplot of fornication and revenge in which the wanton Ferentes is killed by Colona, Julia, and Morona, the women he has wronged; and a third level that presents, in Mauruccio and Giacopo, another comically ineffectual suitor and his servant-critic. But here Fernando and Bianca, because of their heroic self-restraint, are supposed to achieve a spiritual union superior to marital legality, so that in their ensuing tragedy they are not regarded as malefactors responsible for their own deserved punishment but as innocent victims of the Duke's unjust jealousy (inflamed by the evil machinations of his sister, Fiormonda, and her creature D'Avolos, who plays Iago to the Duke's Othello); and the final verdict of this plot, rendered by the repentant Duke before his suicide and by his successor, Roseilli, rewards them with something very like a posthumous apotheosis, while severely condemning their enemies.[25] This resolution, therefore, definitely places their love in a direct moral contrast to Ferentes's gross promiscuity in the second plot and to Mauruccio's inane courtship in

---

25 For a less sympathetic view of their relationship see Robert Ornstein, *The Moral Vision of Jacobean Tragedy* (Madison, 1965), pp. 218–20.

the third, both of which receive punitive treatment (the latter, of course, in a comic mode). The histrionic posturing of Fernando and Bianca may not be as impressive as the passion of Giovanni and Annabella or even, ultimately, as credible, but it is certainly meant to be more admirable, and to take on increased value in the predominantly negative analogies that define it in relation to the two debased versions of "love" on the lower levels of the hierarchy.

Fletcher's *Rule a Wife and Have a Wife* was one of the comedies discussed in the preceding chapter in terms of the contrast between the battles of the sexes in its main and subplot; but it also contains another line of action that puts it in the category of three-level drama, a sequence devoted to the efforts of the wealthy fool Cacafogo to purchase the favors of Margarita, the main-plot heroine. This broad farce supplies the third emotional tone of the standard formula, pitched well below that of the Estefania-Perez subplot, which was seen to be distinctly less serious than the contest of Leon and Margarita; and it also supplies (along with Margarita's house) one of the principal causal links connecting these two major actions, since Estefania capitalizes on Cacafogo's interest in Margarita to mulct him of a thousand ducats in exchange for Perez's "copper" jewelry (IV.i), and then turns him over to Leon, her fellow wit in the other plot, for further "sport or profit" (V.i). More unusual, however, is the manner in which this third level affects the two couples and our attitude toward them. In each plot it contributes to their reconciliation: Perez's resentment of his marriage is weakened considerably by those thousand ducats his wife acquires from Cacafogo, and even more by his admiration of her cleverness in managing it ("She has taken half mine anger off with this trick"); and Margarita's reformation is confirmed when she obediently joins her husband in his scheme to shut up this poor fool in their wine cellar, in order that his drunken cries will frighten off her much more formidable suitor, the Duke of Medina.

Both of these ruses depend on Cacafogo's complete gullibility, which thus comes to have a special significance in this comedy of intrigue, where the characters divide into wits and dupes. It was pointed out previously that, although the sexual contrast between the main and subplot couples turns primarily upon this division, the two parallel dupes, Margarita and Perez, are only relatively inferior to their mates in intellect rather than direct opposites. Therefore the Cacafogo episodes, coming after these dupes have been tricked by their mates in their own plots, can work toward a reduction of that inferiority by allowing them to take a part, albeit a secondary one (Margarita by following her husband's instructions, Perez by sharing the proceeds with his wife), in tricking this universal "fall guy," so that at the end they seem to have ascended the scale of wit to a point more nearly equal to Leon and Estefania.[26] As a result, the character of the third-level fool helps not only to reconcile each of these couples but also to make us feel they are suitably matched. Finally, Cacafogo's other notable trait, his completely mercenary approach to love, also functions to mitigate, by comparison, the financial motives of both couples and enhance the credibility of the emotional attachments achieved in the resolution.

Eastward Ho, the joint effort of Jonson, Chapman, and Marston, represents a more complicated comic development of the formula, although its basic structure seems simple enough. In the main plot we are shown the deserved reward of a model parent, child, and apprentice—Master Touchstone the goldsmith, Mildred, and Golding, who becomes her husband; in the subplot, the deserved punishment, repentance, and salvation of their erring counterparts, Touchstone's wife, their daughter Gertrude, and Quicksilver, Golding's fellow apprentice, along with Gertrude's runaway husband, Sir Petronel Flash; and in a low-comedy episode connected to the subplot, the trick by which Flash steals Winifred, the wife of the old usurer Security. It is in fact a structure that goes all the way back to *Damon and Pythias* (and possibly, as we surmised, to the double-plot Moralities of the *Nice Wanton* type) with its hierarchy of moral, immoral, and amoral actions presented in the three modes of decreasing seriousness. It even follows this early tradition in emphasizing the subplot "vices" at the expense of the less dramatic "virtues" of the main plot, and in generating the third sequence through an elaboration of the purely comic aspect of those "vices." And like the Moralities and early three-level dramas using this structure, it is aggressively didactic in pressing home the lesson to be learned from the direct moral contrasts in the two major actions between the foolish and wise parent, the haughty and humble sister, and the idle and industrious apprentice (*alias* the grasshopper and ant, *alias* the Prodigal Son and his brother):

Now, London, look about,
And in this moral, see thy glass run out:
Behold the careful father, thrifty son,
The solemn deeds, which each of us have done;
The usurer punish'd, and from fall so steep
The prodigal child reclaim'd, and the lost sheep.
(V.v.205–10)

---

26 A similar strategy is adopted in the closing scenes of *Love's Labor's Lost* and *A Midsummer Night's Dream* where the male lovers who made fools of themselves in the main-plot courtships can demonstrate their superiority, alongside the non-comic women, to the even greater fools of the subplot—not by gulling them, but by laughing condescendingly at their absurd theatrics.

The difference is that here the authors are having some fun with this convention. They have exaggerated to the point of burlesque many aspects of the main plot, such as Touchstone's repetition of his "good wholesome thrifty sentences," the self-righteous practicality displayed by Mildred and Golding in their courtship (II.i.53–83) and in their wedding feast, limited to "the superfluity and cold meat" left over from Gertrude's (ll. 151–61), and Golding's meteoric rise up the "city" ladder of success ("Ta'en into the livery of his Company, the first day of his freedom? Now, not a week married, chosen Commoner? And Alderman's Deputy in a day? Note but the reward of a thrifty course. The wonder of his time!"); and this is also true of the equally rapid downfall of Gertrude, Quicksilver, and Flash in the subplot, and of the effusive repentance of these two men, epitomized in the hideous piece of doggerel that Quicksilver composes on the subject and the raptures it evokes. The effect of this obviously ironic inflation is quite complex. It severely qualifies the commendation of the "citizen" virtues (honesty, frugality, industry, family and class loyalty, etc.) exemplified by the paragons of the first level and the reformed prodigals at the end of the second, while leaving intact the condemnation of the vices of profligacy and social climbing in that second level up to the reversal. But since these vices are the direct opposite of the virtues, having been defined as violations of the same bourgeois standard, the authors seem to be playing it both ways, and the result is a kind of double vision—an ironic perspective superimposed upon but not completely replacing the conventionally moralistic one—which retains the basic contrast between two distinct levels of sensibility, even though neither now turns out to be the norm.

Within such a context the third level of the regular formula might be expected to take on a somewhat altered significance. The story of the young wife and her lover who manipulate her old, jealous husband into presiding over his own cuckoldom belongs to a stock repertory of bawdy intrigue (already seen in the subplots of *The Changeling* and *The City Nightcap*), which is related to the contests of wit between *adulescens* and *senex* in Plautus and Terence. The audience would immediately recognize the situation and the mode of treatment: it is perfectly "straight" comedy, without either the sermonizing or the burlesque inflation of the other two levels. Thus while it can scarcely be claimed as a norm for the play, it does provide a very familiar and unambiguous base to underpin the larger structure, a fixed point of reference for gauging the more uncertain tones of the major plots. Moreover, the comic tradition embodied in it assumes a value system wholly different from those major plots and the Moralities from which they derive, because it enlists us on the side of youth and cleverness and sexuality against age and credulity and moneygrubbing, on the side of the impecunious wastrel against the wealthy miser. To the extent that we desire Flash's victory and Security's defeat, therefore, this episode tends to undercut the lesson inculcated in the "didactic" contrast between the main and subplot (which teaches that the young achieve success by respecting their elders, restraining their impulses, saving their money, and working hard) and so reinforces the "ironic" subversion of that lesson. This effect should not be overestimated, since it is soon lost when these characters are swept along by the storm and shipwreck to the edifying jailhouse resolution of the subplot, although it reappears even there, amid all the lachrymose reconciliations, in Security's brief "lamentable tune" on cuckoldom, which seems to strike a jarring note as a kind of coda to Quicksilver's ravishing masterpiece of repentance and hence becomes part of the complex balance of attitudes underlying this comic conception. It is quite a sophisticated conception, but one that for this very reason is necessarily posterior to and dependent upon the original straightforward version of the three-level formula.

Certainly the most famous comedy of this period, or any other, to make use of that formula is Shakespeare's *Much Ado about Nothing*. Its hierarchy of three distinct emotional tones is unmistakable: the solemn romance of Hero and Claudio, which is brought to the brink of tragedy by the villainous Don John and his tool, Borachio; the contest of wits between Hero's cousin Beatrice and Benedick, the friend of Claudio; and at the bottom the buffoonery of Dogberry, Verges, and the Watch. The causal interactions connecting the couples on the first and second level were noted in the introductory chapter— Hero and Claudio help to initiate and to resolve the courtship of Beatrice and Benedick, who in turn intervene to avenge Claudio's repudiation of Hero; and the third level also makes contact with the first when Dogberry and his cohorts uncover Don John's treachery. The formal integration is based primarily on the parallelism of the three eavesdropping episodes that play such a crucial role in each sequence. Claudio breaks off his wedding after witnessing what he takes to be Hero's tryst with her lover, following III.ii; the relationship of Beatrice and Benedick is drastically altered in II.iii and III.i (which constitute a single formal unit), where each listens in on a report that the other loves him; and Dogberry's moment of greatness is thrust upon him because his Watch overhears Borachio boasting, in III.iii, of his part in the defamation of Hero. (In addition to these, Don Pedro's proxy wooing of Hero led to three earlier eavesdroppings in I.ii–II.i which—like Iago's subterfuge in Act I of *Othello*—do not affect the ensuing action but indicate what to expect there.[27])

27 On this point see Bertrand Evans's detailed analysis in *Shakespeare's Comedies* (Oxford, 1960), chap. 3. Some critics have sought the formal integration of the

As in other "nuclear" parallels of this type, the surface similarity of the incidents calls attention to their much more significant differences, and through them to the "final" differentiation of the levels where they appear. The first two are contrasted with the third since they are not accidental but deliberately staged in order to deceive the auditor, and they are themselves directly opposed in their purposes and results, the first being a malicious conspiracy to separate people already in love, and the second a benevolent one to join those who are not in love (or at least not aware of it); the third is a chance encounter and hence without motive, but it completes the scheme of possible consequences by joining lovers who have been separated. And the possibilities are similarly exhausted with respect to the reliability of the information conveyed to the eavesdropper: in the first episode it is false, in the third true, and in the second somewhere between, a kind of "honest slander" that is false to the facts but not to a deeper reality in the hearts of Beatrice and Benedick. It is easy to see how this series of permutations of the one common situation is related to the specific quality of each level. The initial serious moral commitment of the two lovers in the main plot can only be shaken by the outright calumny of an equally serious enemy as vicious as they are virtuous. The subplot, however, begins as "a kind of merry war" between two mockers of love which does not seem to present any moral problems; therefore they are converted by an equally merry deception devised by their friends so that "the time shall not go dully by," although it can succeed only if it is potentially true. And the ponderous clowns of the third plot, the antitheses of the subplot wits, can only discover the evidence exonerating Hero if they stumble upon it inadvertently and uncomprehendingly, and can only cope with it in the bumbling fashion appropriate to their characters and the farcical tone of their sequence.

These parallel incidents are also related to each other, by means of the inter-plot causal connections, in a pattern of ironic reversals, both serious and comic, which underlie the final integration of this triple structure. The subplot couple, who pride themselves on their wit and antisentimentality, are tricked into falling in love by the very people they have felt so superior to—the pair of romantics in the main plot. Those main-plot lovers, after bringing the subplot couple together, and thus demonstrating their superiority to them, through the eaves-

---

play in an abstract "theme" exemplified on all three levels, but most of those proposed have either been so narrow that they cannot encompass Dogberry without considerable stretching (e.g., by making him another kind of "lover"), or so broad that they encompass almost everything, such as my favorite candidate for all-purpose thematics which unifies the plots around "the study of a common human frailty—the inability to observe, judge, and act sensibly."

dropping conspiracy, are themselves torn apart through the same kind of stratagem. And they are finally reunited by yet a third eavesdropping, where the combination of blind chance and blind stupidity, at the bottom of the hierarchy, proves superior to the crafty villain and his baffled victims at the top, and to their clever friends of the subplot as well: "What your wisdoms could not discover, these shallow fools have brought to light."

There is another inter-plot reversal of this sort that involves an unusual and very successful exploitation of the tonal distinction between the first two levels of the formula. All the critics have admired the way in which the separation of Hero and Claudio is made to bind Beatrice and Benedick more closely together at the end of IV.i, when she asks him to kill Claudio for dishonoring her cousin.[28] As things work out, this has absolutely no effect on the main plot, but it has a very profound one on their own. It is the turning point that both tests and intensifies their feeling for each other. They had been maneuvered into this romance as the passive dupes of a joke contrived by the characters of the main plot; now, even though they are again responding to an event in that plot, their actions arise out of the attachment between them—out of her readiness to rely completely on him in this crisis, and his to risk everything for her—which thereby generates a dynamic of its own independent of its derivative, comic origin. It will require one more intervention from the main plot at the very end, but that is only to stamp the seal of public confirmation on a love which has, in this crucial scene, achieved and demonstrated its autonomous validity. Moreover, the nature of the issue raised by this scene breaks through the comic bounds of the subplot. Here Beatrice and Benedick do not merely adandon their "skirmish of wit" and the protective masks it furnishes them, they commit themselves to a course leading to the same threatened possibility that defined the emotions of the main action—the threat of death itself. It is true that all danger is soon eliminated by Dogberry's revelation, and that they then revert to their earlier bantering style, but their relationship has been permanently altered. Because it has carried them to this point, it has acquired something of the serious tone established initially at the first level. In this remarkable episode the "efficient" connection of these two levels has been used to modify the "final" synthesis.

That result, however, is attained at a certain cost,˙ since it tends to make the second plot more interesting than the first. There are other reasons for this as well—one being the sheer brilliance of those

---

28 See Denzell Smith's concise analysis, "The Command 'Kill Claudio' in *Much Ado*," *ELN*, 4 (1967), 181–83. The French King's death at the end of *Love's Labor's Lost* has a comparable function.

"skirmishes of wit"—but I think the chief source of the difficulty lies in a major departure from the standard triadic formula. In the comparable plays examined so far, the more serious and sentimental main action was also more internalized than the comic, realistic subplot. But in *Much Ado,* although the lines of causation all proceed "down" from the serious to the comic level, even in this climactic subplot scene, it catalyzes a genuine internal development within the romance of Beatrice and Benedick, whereas that of Hero and Claudio merely responds to external forces which pull them apart and then together again. As a consequence it fails to maintain the affective primacy required by the structure. Nor is this only a modern, post-romantic reaction, since from its early days *Much Ado* seems to have been admired mainly for its subplot.[29] One might infer from this that Shakespeare's own feeling for these two types of action did not coincide with the evaluation implicit in the formula itself. At any rate, we are about to see that in his most successful three-level plays he reversed their places.

V

Shakespeare, however, was not the only one to alter the formula in this way, and before turning to him again we will look at a few of the other works which also transpose these levels, for such a rearrangement yields a kind of subspecies qualifying the general conception of "hierarchy." At first glance Thomas Heywood's *A Woman Killed with Kindness* may appear quite unexceptional: the main-plot triangle of John Frankford, his wife Anne, and her lover Wendoll ends in tragedy; the subplot conflict between Sir Francis Acton (Anne's brother) and Sir Charles Mountford, with his sister Susan, is tragicomedy; and the episodes of Frankford's servants make up the low-comic third level. Yet the social scheme is not what one would expect; despite the fact that the members of both major plots technically belong to the same country gentry (and that the Acton family relationship cuts across them), the story of Frankford and Anne is saturated with bourgeois domesticity, while that of Sir Francis and Sir Charles is located in a higher stratum, defined not only by their knighthood but also by their typical activities and preoccupations, as is shown in the treatment of the sporting wager in scene i, the duel in iii ("How, knight?—So, knight? You will not swagger, sir?"), and the Mountford ancestral estate in vii. Even the servants of the third level contribute to this distinction because they are made an integral part of Frankford's world

---

29 It was called *Benedicte and Betteris* in the Chamber Account of 1612–13, and Charles I added their names to the title of the play in his copy of the second Folio. In Leonard Digges's commendatory verses to Shakespeare's *Poems* (1640), they are the only characters mentioned from *Much Ado.*

and anchor it firmly in the intimate everyday details of a bustling household that itself becomes a felt presence in the drama, whereas Mountford's home remains a mere abstraction whose only function is to keep his name in "the bead-roll of gentility."

This reversal of the class hierarchy corresponds to a reversal in the scale of sensibility of these two levels that differentiates their versions of the basic parallel between them, the gratuitous act of "kindness." Both levels are built on causal sequences of such acts and their effects on the recipients; but here the sequence in the main plot with its characters "like ourselves" is more realistic, proceeding from Frankford's generous befriending of Wendoll to Wendoll's seduction of Anne to Frankford's generous forbearance toward Anne to her repentance and death, while the subplot sequence is an escalation of heroic exchanges between the two enemies, turning on a thoroughly patrician obsession with debts of honor and terminating in a contest of magnanimity—first Acton decides to win Susan by freeing her brother from prison, since this "will fasten such a kindness on her/ As shall o'ercome her hate" (ix.66–67); then Mountford, concerned that Acton's "kindness like a burden hath surcharged me," sends Susan to him in recompense (xiv.63); Acton tells him, "You overcome me in your love," and offers to marry her (xiv.133); and Susan in accepting acknowledges that "You still exceed us" (xiv.147).[30] The servants, again, enhance the realistic emphasis of the main line of action with their two interventions in it: Nicholas reveals to Frankford the affair between Wendoll and Anne that resulted from his first kindness, and Sisly by preventing him from killing Wendoll makes possible his second.

The rationale of this reordering of the formula can be found in the avowedly naturalistic program of "Our Poet's dull and earthy Muse" announced by the Prologue:

> Look for no glorious state, our Muse is bent
> Upon a barren subject, a bare scene . . .

The structure has deliberately subordinated the conventional extravagances of the "glorious" contest of the two knightly foes to the humbler verisimilitude of the Frankfords' domestic "bare scene." But it has done more than that, for it also necessarily affects our view of the value systems embodied in these two plots and in their two social classes. Sir Francis makes the distinction between them very clear in

---

30 On the parallel between the plots, see the studies of Townsend, Ure, and Van Fossen in the Bibliography, and on their emotional relationship, the article by Coursen. The resemblance of Heywood's subplot to the main action of *A Fair Quarrel*, noted by Muriel Bradbrook in *The Growth and Structure of Elizabethan Comedy* (London, 1955), p. 232, indicates the extent of his departure from the standard formula.

the concluding scene, where he explains how he would have acted in Frankford's situation:

> My brother Frankford show'd too mild a spirit
> In the revenge of such a loathed crime;
> Less than he did, no man of spirit could do.
> I am so far from blaming his revenge
> That I commend it; had it been my case,
> Their souls at once had from their breasts been freed;
> Death to such deeds of shame is the due meed.
>
> (xvii.16–22)

And earlier the values of the third-level servants were distinguished in the same way, by having Nicholas contrast Frankford's scrupulous self-control in apprehending his wife and Wendoll with the precipitate course he would have followed:

> Here's a circumstance!
> A man may be made cuckold in the time
> That he's about it. And the case were mine
> As 'tis my master's—'sblood, that he makes me swear—
> I would have plac'd his action, ent'red there;
> I would, I would.
>
> (xiii.34–39)

Each man, in telling us what he would have done if the "case were his," is speaking for his level of the social and dramatic hierarchy, so that we are asked to judge among the three different standards of conduct presented by the play. Although the aristocrat and the plebian both espouse violence, their motivations are directly opposed, the former acting on an artificial code of private honor and vengeance, the latter on a simple and spontaneous natural impulse. Yet they are both opposed to Frankford's middle-class morality, with its restraint, prudence, and respect for religious and legal sanctions, which led him to treat his adulterous wife with "kindness." And since we are shown that this kindness resulted in Anne's repentance and salvation, we must recognize the superiority of his standard to the other two. This judgment is confirmed in Sir Francis's closing speech when, after witnessing his sister's edifying death, he admits that he was wrong:

> Brother, had you with threats and usage bad
> Punish'd her sin, the grief of her offence
> Had not with such true sorrow touch'd her heart.
>
> (xvii.133–35)

And even Nicholas is won over in this final scene (although in characteristic clown fashion he declines to join the others in their wish to share Anne's fate: "I'll sigh and sob, but, by my faith, not die"). The inversion of the first two levels of this play, therefore, serves an important ethical as well as esthetic purpose, in contributing to the crucial transvaluation of values which celebrates the code of Franklin and his class, and would seem to be in large part responsible for the impression, recorded in the literary histories, that it is the foremost "domestic" or "bourgeois" tragedy of the period.

Since James Shirley's *The Ball, Hyde Park,* and *The Lady of Pleasure* also reverse the first two levels of the standard formula, these "comedies of manners," as they are often called, can be considered members of the same subspecies as *A Woman Killed with Kindness,* although the result of their reversal is very different. In all three plays the main plot and subplot are battles of the sexes, related in the two formal patterns discussed at the end of the previous chapter—a contrast of gender, and a contrast of comic extremes between the defeated parties in each conflict. The primary action of *The Ball* opposes Winfield and several other suitors to Lucina, a "scornful lady" who was an enemy of love but eventually succumbs to him, while the secondary action is a mirror image of that situation, in which two women, Honoria and Rosamond, woo and reform Lord Rainbow, who was too free with his love. This symmetrical scheme reappears in *Hyde Park,* where a man converts a lady who is too "cruel to mankind" in the first plot (Fairfield and Carol), and a lady converts a man who is too "tenderhearted" to too many women in the second (Julietta and Lord Bonville). And in *The Lady of Pleasure* the defects of the losers are interchanged: the main-plot hero cures a philandering female (Sir Thomas and Lady Bornwell), and the subplot heroine cures a male misogamist (Celestina and the unnamed Lord).

Each play develops these contrasting plots and another "half-plot" in three distinct comic modes, but their arrangement is obviously not on a scale of descending seriousness: the first level takes the form of a sophisticated contest of wits, observed realistically and satirically, and appealing chiefly to the intellect; the second is a less clever and more elevated sentimental comedy directed to our ethical feelings; and the third, as usual, introduces a separate character or set of characters (Freshwater and Gudgeon, the Bonavents and Lacy, and Frederick, respectively) in a sequence of farcical episodes, to which might be added the antics of the clownish suitors of the main-plot heroine (Lamont, Travers, and Bostock; Venture and Rider; Kickshaw and Littleworth), to the extent that they are elaborated independently of her contest with the hero. (A roughly similar pattern is found in another Shirley comedy of manners, *The Gamester,* although it uses different material and doubles the couples in the major actions: Wilding and his wife, and Hazard and Penelope are combined in a main plot of trickery, here much bawdier, where the worst thing threatened is adultery; Delamore and Leonora, and Beaumont and Violante make up a second plot of exalted romantic sentiment that narrowly averts death; and Barnacle and his nephew a third of low-comic buffoonery ending in a slapstick beating.)

This inversion of the emotional scale is again accompanied by an inversion of the social hierarchy, since in all three subplots the male lead is a Lord, the only one present; yet the greater elevation and moral earnestness of his line of action prove that Shirley does not share Heywood's "revolutionary" perspective. In fact social distinctions are much less sharp and much less significant in these plays than in *A Woman Killed with Kindness.* The characters of the main plot are only slightly inferior to the Lord in status (the citizens, where they appear, being relegated to the third level), and follow the same round of activities. In *The Ball* and *Hyde Park* they are not differentiated from the subplot by a competing code of conduct, and even in *The Lady of Pleasure,* where they are, the opposition is not defined primarily in class terms.

Although all three works adhere to this common pattern, they do not produce the same effect. It is difficult to talk about any coherent effect in *The Ball,* because of the fatuity of its topical subplot, but the other two comedies provide an illuminating contrast, not only to Heywood's tragedy but also to each other, in the nature and purpose of their inverted structures. *Hyde Park* distinguishes the three levels and integrates them through a series of changes rung on a "nuclear" parallel initiating each action—a formal agreement in which a man surrenders his claim on the woman he loves. Fairfield's compact binding Carol "never to desire my company" is really a ruse to awaken her interest and ultimately succeeds in winning her. Trier's compact with Julietta that requires her "to entertain" Lord Bonville is also a trick, designed to test her fidelity, but because of it he loses her to his rival. The compact Bonavent made with his wife before putting to sea, allowing her to remarry after "a seven years' expectation," was not a trick but also seems to be the cause of his losing her, since on the day it expires she marries Lacy; yet when he arrives on this same day we realize it has preserved her for him.

Unlike the others, however, Bonavent's victory turns on sheer coincidence (in the timing of his return, as the name indicates) and does not require any alteration in the characters or their affections— as soon as he doffs his disguise his wife automatically reverts to her original marital status, and Lacy has no choice but to acquiesce. Hence this plot is the least internal and least serious. The resolutions of the two major plots do produce such an alteration, since in both one person reforms another's attitude toward love; but the relation of these reformations to the respective compacts places them in different orders of experience. Carol's change of heart is the final result of the agreement Fairfield exacts from her to trick her into submission, which in turn leads her to react with countermeasures of the same sort, so that their plot becomes a battle between adversaries trying to manipulate each other by external devices, a kind of game that engages their feelings but without raising any real moral issue. Trier's equivalent agreement, however, merely brings Julietta and Bonville together and then ceases to operate, by removing him from the scene; and her victory over Bonville is achieved without trickery since she confronts him not in the intellectual but the ethical arena, where it is her ingenuous adherence to the principles of "honor," rather than any skill at intrigue, that eventually cures him.

The differentiation of these tones is reflected in the ordering of the incidents within each plot. The four interviews between Fairfield and Carol form an oscillating pattern appropriate to their contest: in I.ii she defeats him, in II.iv he defeats her, in III.ii he seems to have won, until she unexpectedly turns the tables, and in V.i they fight to a draw and make peace. This sequence adopts the terminology of tactical maneuver against a foe—" 'twas a poor trick in him," "there is some trick in it," "You work by stratagem and ambuscado," "do not triumph in your conquest, sir,/ Be modest in your victory," "Observe but how I'll triumph"—ending in the recognition that they are "Each other's now by conquest." The subplot's three major episodes (II.iii, III.i, V.i) proceed in a straight line described by the increasing importunacy of Bonville's advances and Julietta's respectful attempts to parry them, up to the moment when she delivers her impassioned appeal to honor and conscience that brings about his crucial change, which is expressed not in the language of war but of religion: "You may in time convert him," "I'll be a convertite," "If I do turn Carthusian, and renounce/ Flesh," and in his last speech,

> By thy cure
> I am now myself, yet dare call nothing mine
> Till I be perfect blest in being thine.

Finally, the two big scenes of the third plot are arranged, much like the first, in terms of the alternating success of the adversaries, who here are the two men (since Mistress Bonavent's affections are not involved): in II.ii Lacy forces Bonavent to dance against his will, and then in IV.iii. Bonavent reciprocates. Thus their conflict does not turn on wit, still less on ethical principle, but on the sheer physical slapstick appropriate to this simpler comedy of disguise, coincidence, and external situation. And unlike the other contests it does not lead to the resolution of their plot, which has no necessary connection to the preceding action and is correctly attributed by Lacy, not to anyone's defeat or conversion, but to "fortune" and "providence."

The effect of this reversal of the first two levels, then, is quite different from Heywood's, for while the main plot presents a more exciting version of the battle of the sexes (which is pitched at about the same tone as the subplot of *Much Ado about Nothing*—another clear sign of Shirley's departure from the standard formula), it is certainly not meant to present a superior set of values. Fairfield and Carol subscribe to essentially the same social code as Julietta and Bonville, and the specific comic quality of their battle depends on its avoidance of the questions of chastity and honor confronted by the subplot. This suggests that the subplot serves a structural purpose roughly analogous to the Dampit scenes of *A Trick to Catch the Old One*, which will be examined at greater length in the following chapter: it tends to drain off any potentially serious response to the principal characters by separating them from the area of genuine moral concern, and so leaves us free to enjoy the amoral play of wit between them, while at the same time reassuring us, in the background, of this other aspect of courtship that underlies all their clever maneuvering and validates their happy union at the end. Such a function would require this reordering of the three-level formula, and seems to explain the psychology of its final synthesis.

It would also provide a partial explanation of the reversal of the formula in *The Lady of Pleasure*, where the more realistic and bellicose contest of the main plot, in which Bornwell outwits and reforms his wife Aretina, is again set off in this way by the more courtly and romantic subplot contest of Celestina and the Lord whom she reforms. Another dimension has been added here, however, since Aretina is not only contrasted to the Lord (as Carol was to Lord Bonville, and Lucina to Lord Rainbow) through their parallel roles as losers of the two contests, but also to Celestina through their parallel programs to become "the lady of pleasure." And this contrast, unlike the others, is not between equally undesirable extremes. In her pursuit of "pleasure," Celestina is able to maintain the proper mean that constitutes the code of manners recommended by the play, while the alternative course of Aretina leads to vicious excesses (primarily financial and sexual) which are emphatically condemned by the action of her own plot and the comparison with her rival. (Their names also confirm this, Celestina being "heavenly," and Aretina the feminine form of Aretino, the Italian pornographer.) Therefore they establish a direct moral contrast of the sort already seen in *The Second Maiden's Tragedy* and *The Changeling*.

This contrast between the two women is more important than the contests themselves, because these are not given the same structural weight here as in *Hyde Park:* on the second level Celestina does not even meet the Lord until the end of Act IV, and on the third Frederick does not engage in another battle of the sexes that would have accentuated this situation in the main and subplot. The formal analogy unifying all three actions is not based on a common situation at all but on a common concern with "manners" as such, which connects Frederick directly to Aretina and defines her opposition to Celestina. This opposition is set up in the two expository scenes of Act I where Aretina and then Celestina are introduced defending their respective ways of life or "manners" against the remonstrances of their stewards; and it is expanded in the next pair of scenes in Act II where we find Aretina trying to impose her type of sophistication upon her nephew Frederick, and then Celestina teaching her kinswomen, Isabella and Mariana, a lesson in the standards of the true sophisticate, from which Lady Bornwell's vulgar distortion is to be measured:

> It takes not from the freedom of our mirth,
> But seems to advance it, when we can possess
> Our pleasures with security of our honor;
> And, that preserv'd, I welcome all the joys
> My fancy can let in.
>
> (II.ii.74–78)

The following scene (III.i) introduces the Lord and relates him to the two ladies in contrasting terms: he indignantly refuses the offer of Madame Decoy, the procuress, to arrange an assignation with Aretina, and accepts the challenge of the gallants, Scentlove and Kickshaw, to test his imperviousness to love by visiting Celestina. Then, in III.ii, the women finally meet in a hostile confrontation that enables Celestina to demonstrate her superiority in both morals and manners to her malicious rival, and in the process to expose the "coarse woolen-witted fellows," Kickshaw and Littlewit, whom Aretina so admired, just as the Lord showed up the gallants' false wit in the preceding episode.

It is evident then that throughout the first three acts the parallel evolution of the main plot and subplot focuses on this contrast. Even the two causal connections between these plots, weak as they are, point to it. In II.ii Bornwell propositions Celestina, as part of his campaign to cure his wife by outdoing her, and in the next scene the Lord writes to Aretina, who is his relative, warning her of Madame Decoy's profession. But the women's responses are exactly the opposite; Celestina cleverly fends off Bornwell, while Aretina, when she receives the letter in III.ii, decides to use Decoy to initiate her affair with Kickshaw, and also reveals during the same episode that she welcomes her husband's courtship of Celestina because it justifies this affair. Thus in both of these plot interactions the effect on her is the reverse of the man's intention and further emphasizes her licentiousness.

Acts IV and V develop the opposition between the two battles of the sexes, but we have been conditioned to look upon it as an outgrowth and an extension of the opposition between the two ladies: the "court Platonic" spirituality of Celestina's "trial" wooing of the Lord in IV.iii contrasts with the gruesome carnality of Aretina's seduction of Kickshaw in IV.i, and her honorable triumph over him with Aretina's wretched surrender to Bornwell in the paired resolutions of the closing scene. This final contrast is reinforced by the intervention of the third plot, which serves as a kind of object lesson proving the inferiority of Aretina to her rival. It has actually operated in this way from its inception in II.i, since the sequence of episodes portraying poor Frederick's degeneration is a debased parallel of his aunt's career, showing up on its comic level the perniciousness of the code of manners she has espoused and forced on him under the tutelage of her gallants. Therefore when he staggers in at the end with these gallants, after a drunken debauch, and tries to court her, she must recognize this as a consequence of, and a judgment upon, her own behavior, which becomes one of the causes of her conversion, along with Kickshaw's reaction to their rendezvous, and her husband's scheme that also led him to imitate her example—although in his case this was a clever pretense designed to reform her, while in Frederick's it was the result of her obtuse plan to reform him.

The purpose of Shirley's inversion of the three-level formula is thus very clear; the emotional quality of the two subordinate actions is determined by their function in enhancing the satirical exposure of the "lady of pleasure" of the main plot—the second providing the serious and elevated ideal that she has perverted, and the third a low-comic burlesque of her perversion. But this dimension of the structure presents the same sort of problem found in *The City Nightcap* and *Patient Grissil,* because the severe reprehension of Aretina elicited by the direct moral contrast with Celestina undercuts the happy resolution of the main plot and its symmetrical relationship to the subplot established through the parallel contests with their contrast of defective extremes. This may be in part a problem of the double standard, for the "defect" of promiscuity seems more serious in a woman than it did in the men who were given the equivalent roles in the contrasts of *The Ball* and *Hyde Park;* but Shirley goes much further here by having her actually commit adultery (whereas the sexual ventures of Lord Rainbow and Lord Bonville in the two earlier plays never got beyond the conversational stage). It is true that the tragic consequences of this act are averted by Aretina's timely repentance, and the promised reformations of Kickshaw, Decoy, and Frederick; yet we can scarcely forget it and so have some difficulty in accepting the apparently unqualified triumph of Bornwell at the end, or the parallel between this triumph and Celestina's which the formal integration requires.

Another kind of triadic effect, based on a more consistent inter-plot contrast, is produced by the inversion of the formula in two plays of Shakespeare that many regard as his greatest achievements in the genres of romantic comedy and history. The romance in *As You Like It* (leaving aside Oliver's marriage to Celia, which is handled quite perfunctorily and does not add another significant element to the scheme) inheres in three couples who represent very different conceptions of love, in terms of which they are arranged on an emotional scale quite similar to Shirley's, ascending from the earthy burlesque of Touchstone and Audrey to the sentimental idealism of Silvius's love for Phebe to the more ironical and witty tone of the Orlando-Rosalind sequence. Here, however, the direct contrast is constructed not between the main and subplot but the two subordinate actions. The ritualized Petrarchanism of the second courtship and the forthright carnality of the third stand at polar extremes of the "romantic" spectrum, and the characters and their relationship are similarly opposed: in the former the haughty lady from her pedestal rules her pining adorer, and in the latter the cynical male looks down condescendingly upon his passive and humble "ill-favored thing."

In this context, as several critics have noted,[31] the main-plot romance is able to synthesize and transcend the opposition between the other two, primarily through the role of Rosalind, who dominates it (although even in that respect there is a synthesis, since her dominance depends on her disguise as a man, and Orlando is given the opportunity, at the beginning with the wrestler and at the end with the lioness, to assert his masculinity). With her clear vision and buoyant sense of humor, she can comprehend, and see through, the more limited perspectives of both the second and the third couples, so that her own love seems to maintain a precarious but precious balance between them. She knows all that Touchstone could tell her about the absurdity of romantic illusions:

> The poor world is almost six thousand years old, and in all this time there was not any man died in his own person, videlicet, in a love cause
>
> (IV.i.94–97)

and about the physical drives they conceal:

---

[31] See especially Harold Jenkins in *ShS*, 8 (1955), 40–51, and C. L. Barber in *Shakespeare's Festive Comedy* (Princeton, 1959), chap. 9.

in these degrees have they made a pair of stairs to marriage which they will climb incontinent, or else be incontinent before marriage.

(V.ii.40–42)

(In III.iii Touchstone informed Audrey, "We must be married or we must live in bawdry.") Yet Rosalind never really identifies with his position, as we are shown, for instance, in III.ii when his attempt to reduce Orlando's love poem (which she can laugh at herself) to the level of animal sexuality is at once rebuked: "Peace, you dull fool! . . . you'll be rotten ere you be half ripe." And conversely, although she vehemently censures Silvius's agonized worship of Phebe ("he deserves no pity . . . for I see love hath made thee a tame snake"— IV.iii.66–70), on his first appearance she immediately recognizes her affinity to him:

> Alas, poor shepherd! Searching of thy wound,
> I have by hard adventure found mine own . . .
> Jove, Jove! This shepherd's passion
> Is much upon my fashion.

(II.iv.44–45, 61–62)

For despite—or rather because of—her awareness of this entire spectrum of attitudes, she can admit, at the end of the same scene where she had insisted no one ever died of love, that her own love for Orlando is so deep "it cannot be sounded."

The effect of this scheme, therefore, is to impart a special value to that love, to guarantee its genuineness and its superiority over the two inadequate, antithetical extremes which are compared to it and help to define it. The scheme itself could have just as easily been worked out within the standard three-level formula—in fact we found something very like it in *The Family of Love*, where the relationship of Gerardine and Maria was presented as a mean between the two minor actions. But a reversal of the first and second levels is required to accommodate the formula to this complex vision of true love, which is earned by acknowledging and assimilating the claims of the antisentimental point of view. Such a dimension was completely missing in the "straight" romanticism of Gerardine and Maria, and also, we saw, of Claudio and Hero, who seemed in this respect more simplistic than Benedick and Beatrice. But here the places of the couples in *Much Ado* have been transposed, as it were, and the resultant hierarchy is much more convincing, since its ranking now coincides with our own judgment—and surely the author's—of the relative value of the sensibilities embodied in its three components.

This hierarchy involves still another mode of differentiation that might be called a class angle. The Forest of Arden, despite its egalitarian associations with the "merry men" of "old Robin Hood of England" and "the golden world" of ancient mythology (I.i.120–25), is a very rigidly stratified society of three distinct groups which, before the arrival of Rosalind, Orlando, and their companions, were not even aware of each other's existence (an indication that they represent not so much "real" social classes as artistic orders of "reality"): the exiled Duke with Amiens, Jaques, and the rest of his court; the idealized shepherds of pastoral convention, Phebe, Silvius, and Corin; and the actual peasants, Audrey, William, and Oliver Martext. Each group has its own nomenclature (French names for the first, classical for the second, English for the third) and its own animal "totem" (deer, sheep, goat), and together they seem to recapitulate the progress—or more likely the degeneration, for the movement proceeds downward—of man from a hunting to a herding to a farming economy, where Audrey and William become contemporaries of the original audience (who could also relate this to the competition of the deer park, the sheep enclosure, and the farm in their own countryside).[32] And since these groups correspond to the three pairs of lovers and the three versions of love (although Rosalind, unlike Orlando, does not join her father's party at first, and the presence of Jaques in this party introduces further complications which cannot be dealt with here), they work to reinforce the scale of values established by the triple-plot structure.

Class divisions also have an important role in the differentiation of emotional levels in *Henry IV, Part 1*, but they are the divisions of an historical society. Empson and a number of others have shown that this play is organized around the three worlds of the royal court, the rebel nobility, and the tavern, represented by Prince Hal, Hotspur, and Falstaff. They dramatize a range of perspectives which are analogous to those in *As You Like It*, and are ordered into the same sort of inverted hierarchy with the same basic interrelations. A direct contrast is again developed between the secondary and tertiary levels, now opposed in terms of their conceptions of honor rather than love. The Falstaffian attitude can be seen as the equivalent of Touchstone's antiromantic stance:

> Honor pricks me on. Yea, but how if honor prick me off
> when I come on? How then? Can honor set to a leg? No.
> Or an arm? No. Or take away the grief of a wound? No.

---

32 The economic definition of the third level is anticipated by Touchstone's account of his earlier love, Jane Smile the milkmaid, in II.iv. Jonson's *The Sad Shepherd* has these same three classes, each with its own habitat and totem: the deer-hunters of Sherwood Forest, the shepherds of the Vale of Belvoir, and the family in Witch's Dingle who keep swine.

Honor hath no skill in surgery, then? No. What is honor? A word. What is in that word honor? What is that honor? Air. A trim reckoning! Who hath it? He that died o' Wednesday. Doth he feel it? No. Doth he hear it? No. 'Tis insensible, then? Yea, to the dead. But will it not live with the living? No. Why? Detraction will not suffer it. Therefore I'll none of it. Honor is a mere scutcheon. And so ends my catechism.

(V.i.131–43)

Hotspur's enraptured worship of honor resembles Silvius's infatuation with Phebe and with the idea of love itself:

> By Heaven, methinks it were an easy leap,
> To pluck bright honor from the pale-faced moon,
> Or dive into the bottom of the deep,
> Where fathom line could never touch the ground,
> And pluck up drowned honor by the locks,
> So he that doth redeem her thence might wear
> Without corrival all her dignities.

(I.iii.201–7)

And Hal, like Rosalind, encompasses both of these extremes in the kind of honor he ultimately earns at Shrewsbury where, in an emblematic rendering of this synthesis, he stands triumphant over their prostrate bodies and pronounces the two epitaphs that pass a final, balanced judgment of praise and blame on each man and on the principle he lived by.

Because of the nature of the virtue at stake here, this triadic scheme has a political dimension not found in *As You Like It*. Although there is an absolute opposition between Falstaff's and Hotspur's views on the value of honor and even on its mode of being (which goes back to the medieval controversy between nominalism and realism), there is also a significant agreement: they are both completely individualistic and anarchic, in that they ignore the social context. Since Falstaff, the "nominalist," believes honor is just a word, he is always led to seek his own safety and comfort—as we see first at Gadshill and finally at Shrewsbury—regardless of the consequences to others; and since Hotspur, the "realist," believes it is an objective entity, good in itself, which can be acquired as a personal possession, he is always led to seek more of it for himself, regardless of the issues involved—thus fighting alongside the Scots against his King at the end seems just as honorable to him as fighting for his King against the Scots at the outset. In this respect, then, Hal directly opposes both men, for the honor he aims at and attains is defined politically, as a function of his special responsibilities to the state. His honor becomes inseparable from the welfare of England, and therefore proves to be a real virtue, in contrast to Falstaff's conception, even though, in contrast to Hotspur's, it has no real existence independent of its social causes and effects.

This aspect of the hierarchy is determined by the specific political problem of the history play, but it can be translated into more general terms also applicable to *As You Like It*. Because the positions of Falstaff and Hotspur, like those of Touchstone and Silvius, are absolutes, unqualified by circumstances, they are by their very nature inflexible. In every situation these characters must behave in the same repetitive pattern, even when it is self-defeating. During the rebel council in III.i, for example, Hotspur deliberately and needlessly provokes his own ally, Glendower, in a stubborn display of will which his uncle Worcester reproves for its untimeliness:

> You must needs learn, lord, to amend this fault,
> Though sometimes it show greatness, courage, blood—
> And that's the dearest grace it renders you—
> Yet oftentimes it doth present harsh rage,
> Defect of manners, want of government . . .

And Falstaff exhibits the equivalent "fault" at Shrewsbury (V.ii) where in the heat of battle he responds to Hal's urgent plea for a weapon with a bottle of sack and a pun on "sacking" a city, drawing from the Prince a bitter remonstrance based on the same temporal discrimination as Worcester's:

> What, is it a time to jest and dally now?

The question is placed to emphasize Falstaff's characteristic defect, since it is the last thing Hal says to him before the epitaph (just as his first question to him in Act I was, "What a devil hast thou to do with the time of the day?"), but it also emphasizes Hal's characteristic virtue, which distinguishes him in this respect from Hotspur as well. For he has Rosalind's ability to adapt to the "time"; he knows when to act like Falstaff and when to act like Hotspur, and he can defeat them both in their own arenas, outwitting the one in the tavern and outfighting the other on the battlefield. That is why we feel he has transcended the opposition between them. And this transcendence involves yet another temporal dimension: Hal is so adaptable because he is always oriented toward the future, when "time" will make him king (that being the meaning of his position as heir apparent), whereas Falstaff never sees beyond the gratifications of the immediate present, and Hotspur constantly looks back to the fossilized ideals of the feudal past.

Finally, the general relationship of these three levels can be understood in psychological terms. Freudian critics have pointed out that Falstaff, Hotspur, and Hal seem to correspond, respectively, to the id, the superego, and the ego that mediates between these two conflicting forces in adjusting to the external world. They also might be said to correspond to the Platonic taxonomy which was found in *The Atheist's Tragedy* (and which some have seen as an anticipation of Freud), Falstaff representing the appetitive part of the soul, Hotspur the spirited, Hal the rational. But there is a crucial difference between this scheme and Tourneur's (as there was between *As You Like It* and *The Family of Love*), resulting from Shakespeare's inversion of the hierarchy, for Hal's rationalism, unlike Charlemont's, is not at all Platonic. Here it is Hotspur, on the second level, who treats honor as a kind of Platonic Idea, while Hal's view is much more pragmatic and circumstantial, and hence closer to the Freudian ego. But the scheme fits neither psychology exactly. If we must find a theoretical basis for it, Hegel's would seem to be the most promising, since the transposition of the first two levels makes it possible for the antithetical perspectives of Falstaff and Hotspur to cancel each other out, as it were, to generate and validate Hal's synthesis. Or translating back into dramatic terms, Falstaff's antiheroic critique is deflected from Hal because it is absorbed by Hotspur, at the opposite pole. Hal in fact joins in this critique since he himself is fully aware of the absurdity of

> the Hotspur of the North, he that kills me some six or
> seven dozen of Scots at a breakfast, washes his hands, and
> says to his wife, "Fie upon this quiet life! I want work."
>
> (II.iv.114–17)

Yet despite this knowledge he can, like Rosalind, commit himself completely to the true ideal and become its truest embodiment.

Although Hal is thus placed in a role analogous to Rosalind's by the inversion of the standard formula, I think most critics would agree that this role is not as successfully realized. For one thing, his synthesis of the two extremes depends on a very cold-blooded calculation (as he reveals in his soliloquy at the end of I.ii), which makes it less persuasive and attractive than hers. No doubt this reflects the difference between politics and love, yet it also reflects a relative failure to internalize the synthesis, which is announced and displayed but does not really develop within his character, and so seems just as contrived and "schematic" on the author's part as on his. It must be acknowledged, however, that Rosalind has a much less difficult time convincing us of her achievement because the lovers in the subordinate actions offer her so much less competition. Shakespeare took a greater risk in *1 Henry IV* by pitting Hal against such formidable rivals that they continually threaten his hold on our attention and affection—which can be related to the preceding point, since an important reason why Falstaff and Hotspur are so sympathetic, despite their faults, is that they are never calculating but always gloriously themselves (though this response to Falstaff introduces other considerations, also associated with his "timelessness," that must be reserved for the next chapter). Hal's structural and emotional primacy in this hierarchy could have been assured by diminishing these rivals on the two lower levels, but that is a price few of us would be willing to pay.

4

Clown Subplots: Foil, Parody, Magic

In the introduction it was pointed out that the farcical sequence which presents a debased version of the main action seems to pose a special problem in multiple-plot analysis. It is a problem that can, at least in certain of its aspects, be examined apart from any single mode of formal integration, for although these sequences were found at the third level of most of the "hierarchy" plays, they also figure in other quite different structural relationships in a wide variety of works of all genres. They are in fact one of the most common features of English Renaissance drama and one of the most misunderstood. Their presence, especially in combination with a serious main plot, has been the target of a more or less continuous attack beginning with Sidney's famous complaint,

> all their plays be neither right tragedies nor right comedies, mingling kings and clowns, not because the matter so carrieth it, but thrust in the clown by the head and shoulders to play a part in majestical matters, with neither decency nor discretion, so as neither the admiration and commiseration nor the right sportfulness is by their mongrel tragicomedy obtained [1]

[1] *The Defense of Poesy,* ed. Albert Feuillerat, *The Prose Works of Sir Philip Sidney* (Cambridge, 1962), III, 39.

and persisting on down, as was seen, practically to our own day. Even now that this attitude has changed and many critics are prepared to defend them, there still appears to be considerable disagreement on their function in general and in particular plays.

For convenience I have called all sequences of this sort "clown subplots," although they are often series of loosely connected episodes rather than true plots, and are not limited to what Sidney would recognize as clowns, or to any one social or psychological type. Their personnel range in intellect from the stupid to the shrewd, in morals from the innocent to the petty criminal, and while the early plays almost invariably drew them from the lowest class—peasants, domestics, and the like—there is a later tendency to give this role to a foolish gentleman, sometimes with a more practical and critical servant, a combination already encountered in *The Family of Love, A Fair Quarrel, 'Tis Pity She's a Whore,* and *Love's Sacrifice.*[2] These subplots are best identified, therefore, not by a specific kind of character but by his status in the play. The "clown" in this functional sense is someone who occupies a world and embodies a level of sensibility so far below the major plot (or plots) that his fate does not really matter to the other characters or the audience (or ultimately, it will be shown, to himself). This is actually just another way of saying that his line of action is "farcical." It is a very relative definition which will not settle all borderline cases, but it allows us to study under this category a number of subplots with similar attributes. And since the principal role in them was always taken by the company clown, the label is at least precise in that respect.

The source of these plots has already been indicated. Although their development may have been subject to other influences, they descend directly from the independent elaborations of various minor comic figures, both human and allegorical (the "vice lieutenants"), associated with the Vice in the late Moralities. We can even see the missing link of this evolution in the clowns of certain transitional works—Huff, Ruff, Snuff, Meretrix, and Lob, Hob, and Marian in *Cambyses,* Mansipulus, Mansipula, and Subservus in *Appius and Virginia,* Hodge

---

2 This change is described in Ola Winslow's *Low Comedy as a Structural Element in English Drama* (Menasha, 1926), chap. 5. Other master-servant clowns include Sir Gregory Fop and Pompey Doodle in *Wit at Several Weapons,* Tim Yellowhammer and his Tutor in *A Chaste Maid in Cheapside,* Lapet and Galoshio in *The Nice Valor,* the Ward and Sordido in *Women Beware Women,* Sancho and Soto in *The Spanish Gypsy,* Freshwater and Gudgeon in *The Ball,* and Young Barnacle and Dwindle in *The Gamester.* The combination was influenced by Cervantes's Don Quixote and Sancho Panza, as well as by the braggart warrior and his parasite in Roman comedy and the *capitano* and *zanni* of the *commedia dell'arte,* from which are descended Ralph and Matthew Merrygreek in *Ralph Roister Doister,* Don Armado and Moth in *Love's Labor's Lost,* Pistol and his Boy in *Henry V,* etc.

and Rusticus in *Horestes*—whose scenes are connected to the main plot by the presence of the Vice. This ancestry points to a major difficulty in interpretation, for the so-called comedy of evil in the Morality episodes (and in the analogous material in some of the Mystery pageants) must have arisen in response to deeply felt folk attitudes which were accommodated within the context of the medieval "naïve" drama, but which survive in the clown subplot long after the secularization and sophistication of the stage. This kind of subplot, therefore, represents an archaic—I would say the most archaic—element in the later drama, one whose significance cannot be fully understood from the literal perspective of the preceding chapters. But since its origin did not prevent the playwrights from adapting this plot to the needs of their literal structure, we will deal with that aspect of it first, in the terms of analysis already developed, before turning to its more primitive or "magical" undertones.

The most obvious effect of these subplots is the immediate pleasure provided by this brand of humor in its own right ("scurrility unworthy of any chaste ears," Sidney calls it, "or some extreme show of doltishness, indeed fit to lift up a loud laughter and nothing else"), which was exploited by such clowns as Tarlton, Kempe, and Armin, sometimes with extempore flourishes, to establish what must have been a very direct and personal rapport with their audiences. And because this comic milieu usually stood at a considerable social as well as emotional distance from the main action, it also contributed significantly to the "coverage" of the play in both dimensions. But these are merely additive effects, like that of a jig between acts, which are independent of the larger scheme of the drama (and may even conflict with it, as Hamlet complained in his advice to the players [3]). In relation to that larger scheme the structural function of the clown material is not different in kind from any other subplot; it sets up the same sort of formal analogy with the major plot (or plots), which can develop either the contrast or the parallel between them, or some combination of the two. But since the clown operates at a level so much lower than the ordinary subplot, there will be a corresponding difference of degree in the effect that calls for a distinct pair of terms. If the negative aspect of the analogy is stressed, it seems more appropriate to speak of this plot as a "foil" rather than just another direct contrast, in the strict sense that it is a devalued background added to bring out the superior qualities of "centerpiece" characters belonging to a very different order of being—to repel them from its level and so

---

[3] *Hamlet*, III.ii.42–50. In Q1 he also says that some clowns had their own private set pieces ("one suit of jests"), like "stand-up" comics today, which would be repeated from play to play and strengthen the impression of an extradramatic personality appealing directly to his fans.

reinforce our sense of their elevation above the everyday world. And if there is a positive emphasis on the similarity between the two actions, the result is not just parallelism but "parody," because the clown matter will assimilate the main plot and draw it down to its own level.

When these theoretical possibilities were outlined in the preliminary chapter it was acknowledged that their application would not always be easy, as evidenced by the fact that two intelligent readers could come to opposite conclusions about the effect of the same clown plot. That depends in large part on the "set" or predisposition one brings to it, which can vary not only with individuals but also with the times. While the earlier critics seemed to discover foils everywhere, those of the present generation are much more likely to assume that any analogy between a low character and a noble one must imply some kind of parody.[4] Parody-hunting has become as popular as (and sometimes synonymous with) parallel-hunting, and we even hear terms like "parody plot" employed generically to include all clown episodes. This tendency naturally follows from changes in the modern sensibility, which is no longer willing to accept at face value the heroic or romantic ideals of so many Renaissance main plots, and from the closely related change in modern criticism, with its focus on ironic ambivalences of attitude in the work of art. We are led to find in these subplots what we want to find, what we feel is needed to rescue the play from sentimentality, naïveté, directness, univocality, and the other moral and esthetic sins of our day. But since serious misreadings are bound to occur if we approach all the clown plots with an a priori commitment to one of their two extreme possibilities (to say nothing of the intermediate variations), it seems advisable to restore a sense of balance, before proceeding to the plays, by rising to the defense of the forsaken foil.

Although the conception of the foil was applied too indiscriminately in the older interpretation of these episodes (the same could be said of "comic relief," which also postulates the contrast relationship), it is still a valid explanation of one of their most important and most frequent uses. The dramatists themselves were perfectly aware of the function of the clown-foil and speak of it explicitly. Jonson notes that his antimasque in *The Masque of Queens* will "have the place of a foil" because it portrays "the opposites" of his main theme (ll. 10–22), and has Dauphine refer to the lesser Ladies Collegiates in *Epicene* as "mere foils" to their president, Madame

---

4 As Dean Frye points out in "The Question of Shakespearean 'Parody'," *EIC*, 15 (1965), 22–26. (In an outline of Shakespeare's plots published in 1935, no less than 35 characters are designated in the Dramatis Personae as "foils"—few, however, in the clown category.)

Haughty (V.ii.15). Shakespeare makes the point in Berowne's argument persuading the King to allow Costard and his fellow clowns in *Love's Labor's Lost* to stage their performance:

> We are shameproof, my lord, and 'tis some policy
> To have one show worse than the King's and his company.
>
> (V.ii.513–14)

and again in Prince Hal's justification of his association with Falstaff in the comic third level of *1 Henry IV*:

> And like bright metal on a sullen ground,
> My reformation, glittering o'er my fault,
> Shall show more goodly and attract more eyes
> Than that which hath no foil to set it off.
>
> (I.ii.235–38)

At the wedding festivities in Dekker's *The Welsh Ambassador,* the Clown is permitted to read his "strange chronicle" because

> 'Twill be a foil to the night's brighter glories,
> As a blackamoor by a Venus.
>
> (V.iii.26–27)

And in *Hengist, King of Kent* Middleton has the protagonist of his farcical subplot explain the general purpose of the role:

> there's nothing in a play to a clown's part, if he
> Have the grace to hit on't, that's the thing indeed:
> The king shows well, but he sets off the king.
>
> (V.i.135–37) [5]

This kind of foil relationship should be equally familiar to us since it turns up far more frequently in our practice than our theory (or bias) would suggest. It may be easier to see this in a simplified and isolated form of the problem, posed by a common type of humor which gives to some "low" person or activity or thing the name of a "high" analogue. When the Elizabethans called a whorehouse a "nunnery," was the laugh at the expense of the whores or the nuns? Was it a positive "parody" analogy deflating the high term ("Beneath their pious façade nuns are really no better than whores"), or a negative "foil" analogy used as a comic euphemism for the low term ("Whores are so obviously inferior to nuns that the comparison itself makes them seem ludicrous")? I suspect most of us would opt for the first alternative without pausing to consider that it is intrinsically no more probable than the other, and that our own jokes of this sort—calling the

---

[5] Quoted in Empson's "Double Plots." Cf. *Hamlet,* V.ii.266–68; *The Winter's Tale,* III.ii.171–73; *The City Nightcap,* III.i.p.132, III.iii.p.142.

stupidest boy in a group "genius," or the scrawniest "Hercules," or dishwashing "pearl-diving"—almost always assume the second alternative. (There are of course a few exceptions: in World War I the doughboys relieved themselves in "the Berlin.")

It is also significant that low comedy usually functions as a foil in what are probably our two closest approaches to the indigenous popular drama of the Renaissance—the Hollywood western and the Broadway musical. The good guy of the western film in its original folk form, before it went adult, is accompanied by a clownish sidekick (a role perfected by the gravel-voiced Andy Devine) who is notably deficient in all the cowboy virtues: he is chubby, slovenly, inept with horses and guns, easily scared, and easily hoodwinked by the villain. Although he does not have his own plot, he continuously invites comparison with the epic hero, often by attempting to imitate his style; yet no one so far has claimed him as a parodist since it is clear that he is introduced to make this hero seem even more heroic (in addition to supplying, like the earlier clown-foils, a good deal of incidental humor in his own right). The protagonists of a number of minor Hollywood and television genres are given equivalent companions for much the same reason—the brilliant private eye has his obtuse friend on the police force (compare Holmes's Dr. Watson), the football star his rotund or skinny hanger-on (typically a bespectacled grind in the pre-Sputnik era), Superman his Clark Kent, Tarzan his chimp, and so on. The clown material is frequently expanded into a subplot in Broadway musicals, many of which are constructed on a formula that calls for two parallel courtships, the first bringing together a more or less idealized "straight" couple who find true love, and the second a much more comical and much less virginal cynic and his female counterpart, who explains that she "cain't say no" or "has been faithful in my fashion" in a husky contralto setting off the lyric soprano of the ingénue. Here too it does not seem to have occurred to anyone that these antiromantics are parodying the lovers of the main action. They may turn out (again like their Morality antecedents [6]) to be more interesting than the main action, but there can be little doubt that they are meant to enhance its sentiments by contrast.

All of this does not prove that any particular clown subplot in the Renaissance drama must be a foil. It would be just as illogical to begin with that assumption as the opposite, although in practice this would more often bring us closer to the truth. But it should prove that we must come to each plot of this kind with an open mind to determine its actual effect, without being influenced by the prevailing

---

6 And like Beatrice and Benedick, who are more serious and moral but share some of their traits. See also Appendix A on Terence's subplot couples.

fashionable preference for parodic readings. Fashions change, and "parody" may well be destined to the same fate as "foil" or "comic relief," now that it seems to be degenerating into another catch-all label applied to widely different situations as a convenient means to avoid thinking about them.

There is another current explanation of the clown plot that should be noted, since it appears to offer an easy way out of any problem. We sometimes hear that these sequences function simultaneously in both directions, as foil and parody. It is also evident how this idea would naturally arise from recent critical trends which have encouraged the search for "plurisignification" in the work of art and for interpretations "embracing as many meanings as possible"; [7] but we should not be less suspicious of it on that account. If it means that one spectator, at one moment, and on one level of consciousness, is supposed to feel that any one character is being both elevated and mocked, then I find it very difficult to believe. When the idea is spelled out in detail, however, some sort of division is usually made. The critic may locate it in the audience, claiming that two classes or factions would take the clowning in opposite senses. But while this might occur in a performance, to attribute it to the author's intention reduces his play to a rhetorical grab bag (like too many political speeches and platforms) with no possibility of esthetic unity. The separation, on the other hand, may be in the analogue to the clown episodes, which seems much more reasonable since we shall see that they often do relate as a foil to one character or plot and at the same time as parody to another. And finally, it may be within the spectator himself, if the episodes work in these two opposite ways upon two different levels of his reaction. This again is a real possibility that must be considered, although it will take us beyond the bounds of "literal" analysis.

These additional complications, however, like the basic alternatives outlined earlier, cannot be dealt with in the abstract but only in terms of a specific dramatic context. That context itself defines the emotional thrust of the clown plot, since this should be in harmony with all the other devices by which the values of the play are established. The point would not seem worth mentioning were it not sometimes overlooked by parody-hunters who want to impose an ironic function upon clown sequences even when the entire development of the main action is clearly aimed at a serious, sympathetic response. Actually the significance of any of the functions described here will necessarily be qualified by the total design of the drama, which is always the ultimate determinant. But this can be said of every component in it. The

---

[7] Robert Graves and Laura Riding, *A Survey of Modernist Poetry* (London, 1927), p. 74.

clown sequence is just one of those components and must be approached in the same spirit as the others, with no preconceptions that might interfere with our understanding of its particular modes of operation in that particular composite.

I

It seems best to begin with a comparison of two clown subplots, both in double-plot plays, which are relatively simple examples of the foil and the parody. But since this simplicity has not prevented each of these subplots from being interpreted in the opposite direction by some contemporary critics, we should examine them in enough detail to demonstrate their effect and the essential difference between them, even though that will require a certain amount of belaboring of the obvious. For this illustrative purpose it would be hard to find a better set of clown-foils than Pistol and his cronies in Shakespeare's *Henry V*. One can appreciate why a modern audience might wish they acted as a "parody of Henry's heroics" to prick "the bubbles of his glory," [8] since the kind of heroics and glory exhibited in the main plot now sound so hollow; but while we are free to criticize the main plot on those grounds, we are not free to read that criticism into the subplot. For everything in the subplot points unambiguously to its function as a foil employed to contrast with, and so render still more admirable, the exploits of the "mirror of all Christian kings."

This can be seen in each of the modes connecting the two plots. Pistol's gang is related to the main action on the material level as part of the army Henry brings to France; but they are not like the other parts. Shakespeare shows us the complete table of organization of this army—from the commander-in-chief to his generals and staff (the dukes of the royal family and the earls), to the captains, Gower, Fluellen, Macmorris, and Jamy, representing the four nations of the British Isles, down to the common soldiers, Bates, Court, and Williams. And he shows it as an organic unity, where every rank is properly subordinated to the one above, and all are bound together by an unquestioned loyalty to the King and his reciprocal loyalty to them, emphasized in his direct contacts with each group of men from the highest to the lowest, and in his speech before Agincourt:

> We few, we happy few, we band of brothers,
> For he today that sheds his blood with me
> Shall be my brother.
>
> (IV.iii.60–62)

---

8 See the remarks of Allan Gilbert quoted in chap. 1, p. 18, and also Harold Goddard, *The Meaning of Shakespeare* (Chicago, 1951), pp. 227–66, and Roy Battenhouse, "*Henry V* as Heroic Comedy," *Essays on Shakespeare and Elizabethan Drama in Honor of Hardin Craig* (Columbia, 1962), pp. 169–80.

This sense of brotherhood does not eliminate martial or social ranks within the army (Williams cannot duel with Henry as an equal, much less marry his sister), but it establishes the importance and value of the charismatic leader who is able to weld them all into a harmonious fighting body. However, the three clowns of the subplot are outside this body. They serve under no company commander, and although they have somehow acquired military titles—Ancient Pistol, Lieutenant Bardolph, Corporal Nym—no one but the Boy serves under them. Nor, despite Pistol's ferocious bluster and bragging, will they ever bloody their swords. They do not operate in the army but only at its edges (or rear), as "counterfeits" or camp followers despised by any real soldier who recognizes them. Even the "brotherhood" they form at the outset, as "three sworn brothers to France" and "yokefellows in arms," separates them from the rest, since we soon learn that they are just "sworn brothers in filching." [9]

The causal connections of these plots also widen the distance between them at the expense of the subplot, because each interaction works downward and each works against the clowns—Fluellen (who acts as their comic Nemesis) forces all three into battle in III.ii, rebuffs Pistol in III.vi, and beats him in V.i, and we are told in IV.iv that Bardolph and Nym were hanged under Henry's martial law. But it is on the formal level that this foil relationship is most fully developed through a number of negative analogies. There is a general analogy of this kind between the two lines of action as complete wholes, for while the clown material is treated episodically, it makes up a coherent sequence which contrasts directly with the main plot. It is a sequence of continuous decline, both in the characters' fortunes and in our estimation of them. At the beginning (II.i, iii) they are presented at their highest point, patching up their quarrel and setting off hopefully for France, and also at their most sympathetic, because of their association with Falstaff and the Hostess, and with the heroic expedition itself. But in their next scene at the siege of Harfleur (III.ii), which presumably typifies their behavior throughout the campaign, we discover they are such cowards that Fluellen has to drive them forward, and such thieves that their Boy deserts them. By III.vi they have sunk still lower; Bardolph has been condemned to death for stealing a "pax of little price" from a church and Fluellen rejects Pistol's plea to intercede, which initiates their quarrel. The scene at Agincourt (IV.iv) where Pistol captures Monsieur le Fer seems to be included more as a stock comic routine than as part of this downward sequence,[10] although it ends with the news that Nym as well as Bar-

9 II.i.13, 114; II.iii.56; III.ii.46.
10 Compare Falstaff's encounter with Sir John Colevile in 2 *Henry IV*, IV.iii, and Derick's with the Frenchman in *The Famous Victories of Henry V*, xvii.

dolph has been hanged. And the last episode (V.i) brings Pistol, the sole survivor, to the nadir of his fortunes. He loses what remains of his bogus reputation in his ignominious surrender to Fluellen without resistance (the opposite of his bloodless victory at Agincourt), loses his source of livelihood in his wife's death "of malady of France," and must sneak back to England friendless, penniless, and utterly defeated. It is a very grim conclusion for a clown subplot, but it is necessary if this sequence is to complete the contrast with the unbroken chain of successes in the main action, which ends by sending Henry back to England in triumph, with a new wife, a new kingdom, and a new heroic stature that commands the respect and admiration of his countrymen, his foes, and the audience.

The formal opposition between the plots is also worked out on a more particular level, each of the clowns' major scenes serving as a foil to a comparable main-plot scene with which it is juxtaposed. Their decision to go to France follows right after the King's, but the motive is entirely different; he is the aroused lion fighting to claim his rightful throne and avenge the Dauphin's insult, while Pistol's rallying cry is

> Let us to France, like horseleeches, my boys,
> To suck, to suck, the very blood to suck!
>
> (II.iii.57–58)

The contrast at Harfleur (III.i–ii) is especially striking: immediately after Henry leads the army into battle with his impassioned speech that begins "Once more unto the breach, dear friends," Bardolph enters to repeat, "On, on, on, on, on! To the breach, to the breach!"; but of course he and his fellows do not budge until Fluellen descends on them and curses, "Up to the breach, you dogs!" In Pistol's noncombat with le Fer at Agincourt (IV.iv), his absurdly easy (and wholly verbal) terrorization of the even more cowardly Frenchman is contrasted with Henry's astounding victory over the vastly superior French army (IV.v–vii), and his eagerness to pocket a ransom with Henry's steadfast refusal to name one for himself (IV.iii). But the most elaborate parallel is reserved for the end, between Pistol's confrontation with Fluellen and Henry's with Williams in the preceding scene. Both meetings are the upshot of an earlier challenge signified here by a gage worn in the hat, the leek in V.i being the comic equivalent of the gloves in IV.viii; both Henry and Pistol back out of this challenge, the King because the honor of his rank demands it, the Ancient because he has no honor; as a result both quarrels are resolved without a fight, the first in an amicable understanding which preserves the mutual respect of both parties and the second in Pistol's abject submission to a beating; the gage itself figures in this resolution, for Henry returns the glove to Williams filled with crowns while Pistol must eat Fluellen's leek; and Henry's magnanimity to Williams is inverted when Fluellen, as a final insult, forces Pistol to accept "a groat to heal your pate." (A further link is provided by Fluellen in the first episode; he wears the glove for Henry and so receives Williams's blow, and after Williams accepts the crowns he tries to give him a shilling "to mend your shoes," but is indignantly refused.)

Therefore in all these subplot episodes, as in the sequence itself, the negative analogies have been consistently deployed to augment the seriousness and elevation of the main action. And to underscore this contrast every episode following the introductory scenes in England ends with a commentary emphatically depreciating the clowns. The Boy, in his role as their servant-critic, takes on this choric function in a soliloquy closing each battle scene: at Harfleur he reveals the petty crimes of his "three swashers" just shown aping Henry's heroic style, and at Agincourt he exposes the cowardice of his braggart warrior just seen lording it over le Fer. And Gower, the English and hence most sensible captain, does the same after Pistol's two encounters with Fluellen: in III.vi he explains Pistol's real nature to the Welshman, and in V.i the significance of his "Welsh correction" to Pistol. These comments then are an additional device to guide us in responding to the episodes correctly, as debased foils rather than debasing parody—to make doubly sure that we understand the "clown's part . . . sets off the king."

Equally clear examples of the opposite parodic extreme, it was suggested, are much more difficult to come by in the clown plots of the period. One of the most obvious is the series of scenes in Marlowe's *Doctor Faustus* built around Wagner, Robin, and Dick. It would be temptingly paradoxical to claim that is the reason why this parody is overlooked by some parody-hunters, since the same complex of attitudes which might lead modern readers to reject the main plot's glorification of Henry, and so to believe he is deflated by Pistol when the reverse is intended, would also lead them to reject the main plot's condemnation of Faustus, so that they will not believe he is deflated by Wagner even though it is intended. But this antiorthodox view of the play involves other factors as well, going back to the nineteenth-century "romantic" identification of Faustus with the playwright's alleged atheism and with the aspirations or tensions of Renaissance Man. Whatever the cause, the more one sympathized (or thought Marlowe sympathized, which usually amounted to the same thing) with Faustus's rebellion, the more anxious one would be to explain away the parody in the subplot, either by denying Marlowe's authorship of these scenes or by finding that they serve as a foil "by way of contrast, to maintain Faustus' dignity." [11] But that is now a minority view; most critics today, following the reaction against the romantic misinterpretation, would probably agree on the reductive purpose of the clown material, and several illuminating studies along those lines have already appeared.

The clown episodes form much less of a sequence here than in *Henry V*. They are strung together on a very thin causal and temporal thread—in I.ii Faustus's servant, Wagner, bandies words with two scholars looking for his master; in I.iv he forces Robin (called the "Clown") to serve him by raising two devils and promising to teach him "this conjuring occupation"; in II.iii Robin persuades Dick the ostler to come to a tavern to "conjure" some free wine; in III.iii, after stealing a cup from the tavern, they are chased by the Vintner and call up Mephostophilis, who transforms them into an ape and a dog; in IV.vi they meet Faustus's comic victims, the Carter and Horse-courser, and determine to "go seek out the Doctor"; and in the second half of IV.vii all four break in on him at the Duke of Vanholt's castle, only to be "charmed dumb." But the series as a whole shows no real development or sense of direction. It is essentially static, even repetitive (in the farcical use of magic at the end of I.iv, III.iii, and IV.vii), and leaves the clowns in about the same state we found them.

Actually the connections linking these scenes together (except for the two sequential pairs, II.iii and III.iii, and IV.vi and vii) are much weaker than those linking them to the main action. Each of the first four clown episodes is presented as an effect of, and an analogue to, the preceding episode in Faustus's career. Wagner has to cope with the visiting scholars in I.ii because Faustus is too busy with his consultant magicians to see them, and his logic-chopping answers to their questions mimic his master's syllogistic reasoning in I.i. His conjuring up of Banio and Belcher in I.iv must have been learned from Faustus and parallels Faustus's encounter with Mephostophilis in I.iii, as does his seven-year compact with Robin. Robin at the beginning of II.iii has "gotten one of Doctor Faustus's conjuring books" given him by Lucifer at the end of II.ii (a connection lost in the "A" text where the scene is misplaced), and on the strength of it promises to satisfy all of Dick's desires, as Lucifer had just promised Faustus. Their theft of the cup and raising of Mephostophilis in III.iii (another employ-

---

11 See John Crabtree's statement quoted in chap. 1, p. 18, and Max Bluestone's summary of the controversy over this subplot in *Reinterpretations of Elizabethan Drama,* ed. Norman Rabkin (New York, 1969), pp. 53–55. In the following analysis I use the "B" (1616) text, now generally regarded as the more authoritative, in which the relation of the plots is much clearer, and draw upon the articles by Ornstein and Hunter cited in the Bibliography.

ment of Faustus's book) correspond to the theft of the Pope's meat and wine by Faustus and Mephostophilis in III.ii. After this the pattern changes, because the two plot lines which began in parallel are converging. Robin and Dick's dialogue with the Horse-courser in IV.vi is the result of the preceding scene where he was cheated by Faustus; however, since that event is recounted here in detail, instead of an analogy there is an identity of material. And in IV.vii not only the formal but also the efficient relationship coalesces, for the two clowns are themselves directly victimized by Faustus,[12] in an episode which parallels his earlier silencing of Benvolio (who also sought revenge for a trick played on him), and which now joins the main-plot cause and the subplot effect together in a single action.

It is necessary therefore to determine the final significance of these inter-plot connections, and the crucial question here is the relative strength of the positive and negative thrusts in the series of formal analogies. In the first pairing we cannot be sure: if Faustus's refutation of "Divinity" in I.i is meant to betray his own fallacious reasoning (in proceeding from "The reward of sin is death" through "If we say that we have no sin/ We deceive ourselves" to "We must all die an everlasting death," and so to the conclusion, "What doctrine call you this?", without touching on the central role in that doctrine of Christ's sacrifice), then Wagner's pseudological defeat of the scholars in I.ii ("That follows not by force of argument . . . therefore acknowledge your error") is a *reductio ad absurdum* of this kind of sophistical elench; but if we are to agree with Faustus's refutation, then Wagner's comic imitation would make *him* seem more absurd and his master more brilliant by contrast. The isolated analogy, like the "nunnery" joke, does not supply its own interpretation. That is supplied by the context of the action to follow, which establishes with increasing clarity in each succeeding episode both the error of Faustus's original decision and the positive aspect of the subplot parallel.

The effect of the next analogy is less questionable, since the ease with which Wagner raises his devils has to undercut his master's elaborately erudite conjuration, and the terms of his negotiation with Robin:

> WAGNER. I know he would give his soul to the devil for a shoulder of mutton, though it were blood raw.
> ROBIN. Not so, neither; I had need to have it well roasted, and good sauce to it, if I pay so dear, I can tell you.
>
> (I.iv.348–53)

---

[12] In this scene (ll. 1759–65) they also blame Faustus directly for their animal transformation in III.iii.

are not really so very different from Faustus's own satanic bargain (although this too only becomes apparent by hindsight). In the third parallel the comic disproportion between the infinite possibilities that Robin's magic holds out to Dick ("Do but speak what thou't have me do, and I'll do't"—II.iii.769) and their trivial goals ("white wine, red wine, claret wine, sack, muscadine, malmsey, and whippincrust, hold belly hold, and we'll not pay one penny for it") seems an even closer approximation of the discrepancy between what Faustus thought he had gained by his bargain and what we are coming to realize (from the frustration of his inquiry in II.ii, which the devils put off by the "pastime" of the seven deadly sins) he must settle for. The positive thrust is still more obvious in the next analogy between stealing a tavern cup and the Pope's food. And the final subplot scenes bring Faustus's magic into direct contact with the clowns in what amounts to a self-parody of his original grandiose aspirations.

The subplot's parodic effect, therefore, is ultimately established by its gradual assimilation of the main action; or putting it another way (since we saw the subplot remains more or less static), by the gradual descent of the main plot into it. For the most notable fact about Faustus's career after the compact is the inexorable degeneration of his sphere of operations and of the use to which he puts his powers: from universal speculations in theology and cosmology, to playing politics and practical jokes at the Papal Court, to satisfying the Emperor's historical curiosity, to indulging the pregnant whim of a minor duchess, and swindling a Horse-courser and Carter. And at the lower limit he enters the subplot itself as if to confirm the deflationary function of the clowns whose adventures in necromancy have all along been a mocking echo of the increasing futility and pettiness of his own.

Although the differences between these two extreme examples of the clown subplot are easily seen, it is not so easy to derive from them any general criteria for distinguishing foil from parody. The unity of the sequence itself is not very significant since there are foil plots just as disjointed as Marlowe's; but the converse is rarer because of the tendency of comic parody to operate through a series of ad hoc attacks on "targets of opportunity" as they present themselves in the main plot, rather than through a coherent line of action of its own. A more promising guide seems to be the kind or degree of causal connection between main and subplot, for this influences our attitude toward their formal and final relationship with respect to the protagonist's "responsibility" for the clowns. It is no accident that there is such a loose connection of this sort joining Pistol, Bardolph, and Nym to King Henry. He is responsible for them only to the extent that they are part of his army—and not a very integral part, it was shown; he does not cause them to do anything either directly or by his example (even when they do imitate his language summoning the army "To the breach," they have no intention of following him there), and so is never tainted by their exhibitions of cowardice, braggadocio, and venality, which are diametrically opposed to his own behavior. But the situation is very different in Marlowe's play, where Faustus, through his agency or example or books, affects every episode involving Wagner, Robin, and Dick. Consequently their clowning reflects directly upon him, since this causal nexus, by making him responsible for their actions, points up the essential similarity between them which is the basis of the parody.

I believe there is another aspect of Faustus's responsibility for the subplot clowns that contributes to their reductive effect, although it is never stated in the play. Because he is a "learned doctor" and Wagner's master, he should be a model worthy of their emulation, so that whatever guilt they incur in following his example seems to attach less to them than to him as their corrupter; therefore their traffic with the devil not only burlesques his own but also renders it more culpable. This would probably be clearer to a society more stable and stratified than ours, where the lower classes were expected to learn from "their betters," and their betters were expected to "know better." The idea is expressed in the Moralities and homiletic literature of the time and is exploited in other clown parodies of this general type. The brawling of the Montague and Capulet servants in *Romeo and Juliet,* for instance, although not part of a separate plot, is presented at the outset as the direct consequence of their masters' feud in order to make that feud seem even more senseless and pernicious. In *The Atheist's Tragedy* we saw that Languebeau Snuffe's abortive seduction of Soquette constituted an especially telling comment on Levidulcia's affair with Sebastian because he was consciously imitating the example of his patroness. The same sort of effect was produced by Frederick's relationship to Aretina in *The Lady of Pleasure* (though she was his "better" in age and position within the family, rather than in class status). And it is even more explicit in the anonymous *Lady Alimony,* where the six Alimony Ladies are ridiculed in and censured for the attempt of Christabel, the Country Boor's wife, to ape their behavior by getting a divorce for "Ale-money." She herself explains the connection to the main action:

> I have been neither so long nor ill taught by my betters,
> but I know the meaning of ale-money well enough. My
> land'slady Joculette, God bless her! is matched to as hand-
> some a frolic youngster as one can see on a summer's day;
> yet she dislikes him, and has recovered a good stock of ale-
> money. I love to follow the example of my betters.
>
> (V.iii.p.358)

And when she appeals to the Duke for judgment, he places the blame squarely on the Alimony Ladies in the same terms:

> See what examples, ladies, you have given
> To simple women!
>
> (V.vi.p.363)

Thus this special kind of causal relation between the clowns' activity and the bad example given them by the more serious characters, with the criticism of those characters that it implies, can be used as a criterion to identify the parody plot.

However, the identification will hold only if the example set for the clown is a bad one, since if it is good, then his inept imitation of it (as in the Andy Devine role) will have the opposite effect of a foil. And this brings us back exactly to where we began—to the recognition that the thrust of any clown sequence can only be determined by the total dramatic context. Even these relatively "pure" examples of foil and parody contain no infallible sign within the sequence itself which tells us how to regard it.

II

Other literal uses of the clown subplot necessarily complicate this simple distinction between foil and parody, but I do not think they undermine it. For one thing, it is possible for a single subplot to affect the main action in both directions, if the main action is built on an opposition to which the clowns can relate. This is what we found in *A Fair Quarrel*: the fantastic external ritualization of the code of honor taught in the Roaring School to Chough and Trimtram debases the misapplication of that code by the Colonel (who is indirectly "responsible" for the school since his friend runs it), and at the same time elevates the true ideal of honor upheld by Captain Ager. Pistol in *Henry V* does the same, to the extent that his cowardly boasting not only provides a foil to Henry but also a parody of Henry's opposite number, the Dauphin. In situations of this sort the clown helps to differentiate the two conflicting forces in the main plot and our judgments of them. And if he is on the third level of a "hierarchy," he can be similarly used to differentiate the two major plots when they are in direct contrast. Such a function is more or less implicit in the double-plot Moralities of the *Nice Wanton* type, for the "comedy of evil" assimilates the vicious exemplar of the subplot and repels the virtuous exemplar in the main action. In *Damon and Pythias*, which adopted their pattern, the expansion of this comic role in the mischievous lackies, Will and Jack, relates them in these two opposite ways to the false friendship of their masters (who are thus accountable for them) on the second level and to the true friendship of the titular heroes on the first. We also encountered this kind of dual-action clown sequence in *The Atheist's Tragedy,* since Snuffe's tryst with Soquette sets up a positive analogy with the relationship of Levidulcia and Sebastian and a negative analogy with that of Casta-bella and Charlemont, and again in *The Lady of Pleasure* where the comic misadventures of Frederick become a parody of his aunt's code of manners (that corrupts him) and at the same time a foil to Celes-tina's. Another example is the third-level clowning of *The Insatiate Countess,* which degrades the "insatiate" lust of the main plot while it enhances the chaste love of the subplot. Touchstone and Falstaff could be thought of as operating in a roughly analogous manner, puncturing the inflated romanticism or heroics of the subplot char-acters (Silvius and Hotspur) and emphasizing the real virtue of the protagonists, but since that virtue is defined as a synthesis of the second and third levels, the clown's function in relation to it is itself doubled in a different sense.

To explain this it is necessary to add another dimension to the analysis. In the earlier examples the two opposing thrusts of the clown sequence were separated "objectively," because they acted on two opposing characters or plots; but sometimes both of them can be aimed at a single main character through a "subjective" distinction in the levels of our response. Typically, this strategy is designed to ensure the elevation of the protagonist. Some years ago Robert Penn Warren showed how this worked in the balcony scene of *Romeo and Juliet,* where the bawdy, cynical humor of Mercutio serves as an ob-vious foil to Romeo's passion, yet also serves, on a subordinate and presumably less conscious level, as enough of a parody to anticipate and so cancel out our own potential skepticism.[13] The secondary parody, in other words, does not contradict the primary foil reaction but actually augments it. This must have been how Middleton under-stood the episode, for we saw that in his imitation of it in *The Family of Love,* I.ii, he tried for the same effect in a more heavy-handed fashion by having Gerardine defend his love against the antisenti-mental attack of the clown-foils Lipsalve and Gudgeon, just before Maria (who passed an equivalent test in the previous scene) appears on the balcony, and then went on to extend the clowning into a third level of action which performs this same function throughout the play. Mak's fraudulent nativity in the *Secunda Pastorum* is another example, although the shepherds are not clowns in the strictest sense since there are no "normal" people between them and the sacred char-acters (unless they are implicit in the frame of reference supplied by the cycle as a whole). And this would account for the special roles of

---

[13] "Pure and Impure Poetry," *Kenyon Review,* 5 (1943), 231–33.

Touchstone and Falstaff, who not only provide a contrast to the values of love and heroism in their respective main plots but also deliberately question those values in such a way as to place them beyond question. In these and similar cases it seems that the clown subplot works directly to set off, as a foil, a main plot intended to evoke a serious and sympathetic response, while it also works indirectly as a sort of lightning rod attracting to itself and draining away some undesired negative feeling which might endanger that response.

This kind of effect has been a central concern of various New Critics in their study of lyric poetry (the principal subject of Warren's essay), since it was often seen as a device to guarantee the reliability of the poet or "speaker" by proving his awareness of attitudes opposed to his own, and thus making his own attitude less vulnerable to the charge of sentimentality which they found so threatening. In the drama, at least in this period, we are usually less conscious of a particular personality behind all the action whose sophistication certificate must be validated, but if we make the necessary translation from the "speaker" to the audience's emotions, I think this does describe the secondary effect of these dual-purpose clowns. It is probably what some modern commentators have in mind when they speak loosely of "parody plots," although it would help if they found a better name because the result is the reverse of parody; it is rather an inoculation against parody, or in the language of Empson, who also deals with this point, "pseudo-parody to disarm criticism." [14]

As a consequence of this complex function, these clown subplots also differ from the preceding examples of foil and parody in the nature of their causal connection to the main action. In those simpler forms the parallelism, positive or negative, between the two plots was brought about either by external circumstances or by the clown's attempt to imitate his betters. But in these subplots the connection is more emphatic, since the clowns not only imitate but deliberately mock the protagonist and his values. (There is none of this in *Henry V*; Pistol is never given Falstaff's ability to challenge the ideal of honor, and we may suspect that Henry's honor is now too exposed for such a challenge, since he no longer has a Hotspur to deflect it, and has himself lost the ability, which was seen in the Hal of *1 Henry IV* and in Rosalind, to incorporate the negative clown view within his own synthesis.) Presumably to appease our potential skepticism it is important to have this attitude explicitly stated, rather than merely

---

14 "Double Plots," pp. 30, 51, 57. Among the many recent examples we find a critic stating that the comic scenes in *Doctor Faustus* afford "by their contrasting parody, a kind of second accentuation" of the main theme; and another that, when Jerome "parodies" the protagonist of *Hoffman*, "the parody, of course, works to the disadvantage of Jerome."

implied in a debased analogue, and so we are faced with the apparent parodox that the antiparodic and not the parodic clowns are themselves the conscious parodists. The full explanation of this paradox, however, includes certain "magical" associations of the clown-as-mocker to be examined in the following section.

Throughout this discussion we have more or less assumed a combination in which the main action was much more serious than the clown material; but while this is by far the most common arrangement it is not the only one found in the period. In some plays the emotional distance between these two levels is considerably foreshortened, and in *A Trick to Catch the Old One,* probably the best known of Thomas Middleton's early city comedies, their relationship is actually reversed. This treatment of the clown is unique, so far as I know, yet for that very reason it should warrant extended analysis, since as an extreme or limiting case it will provide a useful test of the applicability of the conceptions of foil and parody outlined here, and also of the adaptability of the clown role (or perhaps our definition of it) to a serious purpose.

This drama has been frequently praised for the skillful construction of its plot based on the ingenious "trick"—the passing off of his mistress as a rich widow betrothed to him—that Witgood plays on his uncle, Pecunius Lucre, and his uncle's enemy, Walkadine Hoard, in order to repay his creditors, recover the property he lost to Lucre, and marry Hoard's wealthy niece; but into this plot are inserted three isolated scenes portraying a corrupt and drunken lawyer named Harry Dampit, which have nothing to do with Witgood's scheme and consequently are either ignored by the critics or else condemned as irrelevant clowning.[15] A few have even fallen back on what used to be the standard last-ditch maneuvers for surmounting difficulties of this type in Renaissance plays, claiming that the part was "written in" to accommodate a particular actor of the company or satirize a particular person familiar to the audience,[16] though no evidence has

---

[15] "Dampit seems to be introduced for no particular reason except to fill up the time with mediocre fun" (A. H. Cruickshank, *Philip Massinger* [Oxford, 1920], p. 206); "seems intended to relieve the tension of the interest in the intrigue of the main action by the insertion of boisterously humorous scenes" (Wilbur Dunkel, *The Dramatic Technique of Thomas Middleton in His Comedies of London Life* [Chicago, 1925], p. 18); "a soliloquizing drunken lawyer in *A Trick to Catch the Old One,* who replaces the clown" (Muriel Bradbrook, *The Growth and Structure of Elizabethan Comedy* [London, 1955], p. 157). He has one soliloquy of five lines.

[16] Hazleton Spencer, *Elizabethan Plays* (Boston, 1933), p. 982; Martin Sampson, *Thomas Middleton* (New York, 1915), pp. 17, 387–88, 391. A third and more modern alternative is proposed by R. B. Parker, who finds an unresolved tension in Middleton "between satiric observation and determined moralizing" which required him to add these scenes "as a safety-valve" for his own disgust ("Middleton's Experiments with Comedy and Judgement," *Jacobean Theatre* [London, 1960], pp. 179, 188).

been produced for either hypothesis. Yet even if both turned out to be true, it would not preclude the possibility that Dampit had an artistic function within the larger unity of the play. To understand this function we must first see how his three scenes themselves are unified, for while they can scarcely be called a plot or a line of action (indeed they are almost devoid of action in the usual sense), they are designed, like the Pistol scenes of *Henry V*, to form a meaningful sequence of their own. And although this sequence is full of buffoonery it has a serious dimension as well, since it attempts to render in a sort of dramatic shorthand the significance of Dampit's physical and spiritual destruction.

In the first of these episodes (I.iv) we are given a glimpse of Dampit at the very top of his world, sauntering down the streets of London in exuberant good humor, with his "fellow-caterpillar," young Gulf, subserviently trailing along. Although Witgood prepares us to meet "the most notorious, usuring, blasphemous, atheistical, brothel-vomiting rascal, that we have in these latter times," Dampit seems to be enormously pleased with his life and reputation, even eager to brag of the sordid means by which he amassed his fortune. This bragging has a euphoric, almost compulsively clownish tone, as if he enjoyed presenting himself in the exaggerated role of a bumptious comedian— "a mad old Harry," in Witgood's words—and the bold colors of this portrayal accentuate the contrast with the second scene in the sequence (III.iv), where we see what lies behind his public, daytime façade.

In this somewhat longer episode Dampit is shown in the privacy of his own house in the dead of night, alone except for his servant Audrey, whom he holds in such contempt that he does not bother to preserve appearances before her. It is a remarkable scene of self-exposure which uncovers the other side of the isolation he boasted of in I.iv, entirely through the objective depiction of his drunkenness. The stages of his alcoholic descent are demarcated with shrewd precision of detail in his treatment of Audrey: he begins on a quite reasonable, bantering note, then bids for her sympathy as he wallows briefly in self-pity, and then grows increasingly truculent, first adopting the quasilogical stance of a debater ("I answer you"; "are you answered"), which is soon dropped as his abuse becomes more and more vicious and pointless, until he is overcome by his hallucination of an "abominable stink." But beneath this realistic and still comic sketch of the stage-drunk we can sense the torment within Dampit which is responsible for the interminable drinking itself, his inability to sleep, and his need to drive off the one person who offers some sort of human contact. And beneath this a more sinister level, a vaguely satanic presence, begins to emerge in the incantatory quality of his last curses, with their fantastic vocabulary and marked triadic rhythms ("thou base drudge of infortunity, thou kitchen-stuff-drab of beggary, roguery, and coxcombry, thou cavernesed quean of foolery, knavery, and bawdreaminy"), and in his grim suggestion at the end that the odor comes from burning horns.

That satanic association becomes more insistent in the third and longest of the Dampit episodes (IV.v), which opens with Audrey's song explaining his name ("There's pits enow to damn him, before he comes to hell") and includes a number of statements by the others linking him to the devil. This climactic scene draws upon and rearranges in a new and startling way the chief elements of the preceding two. It takes place in daytime, but within his house. Dampit is on his deathbed, facing the most "private" experience of his life, yet his visitors come and go, greet each other, jest and argue, as if they were on the city streets. The situation is much more serious than III.iv, since Dampit is brought up to the moment of death, accompanied by the piously sententious condemnations of the onlookers; but the practical jokes and final slapstick brawl are also more farcical than anything in I.iv. It is just this peculiar combination of the private and public, the serious and comic, that seems to account for the special impact of the scene. Although the room is crowded with his visitors, Dampit is completely isolated; he cares nothing for any of them (he even fails to recognize and insults Sir Launcelot, whom he called "the only friend that I honour and respect"), and Launcelot and the rest alternate between making fun of him and heaping abuse upon him.

This isolation, however, does not cause Dampit to withdraw into himself, since he does not really have a private "self"; instead he brashly attempts to dominate the scene once more, parading his wealth and cynical dishonesty as in I.iv and cursing Audrey as in III.iv. But his coarse clowning falls flat here, for he is at the very bottom of this world, the butt of everyone's scorn—even young Gulf, who in Act I literally stooped beside him, now swaggers over him and threatens a beating. The others stop Gulf, though not out of any feeling for Dampit; only the despised Audrey shows sympathy at the end, and her last speech, "Sleep in my bosom, sleep"—an unexpected but very fine touch—emphasizes their indifference as they leave him to die, having already forgotten him. Yet Dampit has forgotten himself too, not only in his loss of memory that furnishes the occasion for their sport, but also in his loss of any sense of the solemnity of this moment. He descends to his death as a nasty, drunken buffoon, too disgusting to arouse even the minimal pathos we feel at the death of an animal and too ridiculous to evoke the serious punitive emotion that attends the death of a villain. It is an unusual effect and one not easy to describe, a kind of subdued horror that is nowhere actually expressed but implicit in this stark portrayal of an utterly empty life ludicrously trailing off, without a trace of dignity or even a decent privacy, into an utterly meaningless death. It must be admitted that Middleton does not altogether succeed in fusing these comic and serious elements, but the conception itself was certainly very daring.

What these three Dampit scenes add up to then, beneath their clown surface, is a grimly Hogarthian "Usurer's Progress," a series of separate vignettes carefully ordered to give us increasing insight into this kind of character even as we observe the stages of his deterioration from apparent success to absolute failure. Clearly Dampit is to be regarded as a type of "the usurer"; this identification is established by Witgood's remarks preceding his entrance in I.iv, by his own closing speech in III.iv ("If ever I smelt such an abominable stink, usury forsake me"), by the first line of Audrey's song that begins IV.v ("Let the usurer cram him, in interest that excel"), and most pointedly in the choric pronouncements made by his visitors in this final episode (which are not properly assimilated to the other aspects of the scene and are in part to blame for its imperfect success), hammering home the significance of his death: "Note but the misery of this usuring slave"; "Here may a usurer behold his end"; "here's a just judgement shown upon usury"; "Is this the end of cut-throat usury . . . now mayst thou see what race a usurer runs."

But "usury," as typified in Dampit, means something more than the charging of excessive interest; it represents an entire philosophy and way of life. The usurer here is really a domesticated version (reduced from affairs of "state" to the "city" financial arena) of that familiar stage-villain of the period, the Machiavellian—the man who has rejected all the personal and social ties of the older order and is out for himself alone. This is why the first Dampit scene emphasizes the fact that he is a wholly self-made man who has fought his own way up to riches in a permanent war with society. But he is just as isolated in his private as in his public life; he seems to be without family,[17] and has no human feelings for anyone else—not for his confederate Gulf, or his supposed friend Sir Launcelot, or even Audrey. Dampit's atheism is intimately related to his "usury," not so much through the attitude of the medieval church toward the begetting of money by money as through the attitude of the usurer, who rejects the obligations of religion along with those of family, friendship, law, morality, and the rest, when they cannot be manipulated to his advantage (as he reveals in his remarks on prayer in III.iv.1–5). Even his drink-

---

17 Audrey once refers to others living in the house (III.iv.7) and once mentions "my mistress" (IV.v.58), perhaps the landlady. But even if a family exists it cannot mean anything to him.

ing conforms to this character configuration because it is a completely voracious, ingestive activity and completely solitary, not requiring any relationship, even a vicious one, with another person. Finally, the loss of memory accompanying his drunkenness is peculiarly appropriate, since the climber cuts himself off from his own past as well as from society, so that his world narrows down and fragments into the succession of discrete moments immediately present to him. Without a sense of the past, however, there can be no sense of one's identity, which also disintegrates (as in the chronic alcoholic) into an agglomeration of desires and gratifications. Therefore the man who lives only for himself is left at the end with no self to live for.

The sequence of this "Progress" from sin to retribution is developed with considerable restraint, through the kind of implicative understatement that was to become Middleton's characteristic technique. Dampit does not indulge in long soliloquies telling us how evil he is and reciting his Machiavellian credo, nor does his punishment take the usual form of some catastrophic stroke designed to demonstrate the avenging hand of providence.[18] There is no last-minute conversion, not even the shrill defiance of the world with which some of this type meet their fate; instead we are simply given this low-keyed report of the miserable death that is made to follow inexorably from the miserable life of the usurer.

The function of these three episodes in the play can be accounted for in terms of this idea of the "Usurer's Progress," since through it we make a formal connection to the two professed usurers of the main action, Lucre and Hoard. But the connection is not an equation. Although we are told repeatedly that Lucre and Hoard are usurers, they are not at all like Dampit; in fact compared to him they seem quite human. They are very much part of their society, they have families and friends, and beneath their crusty exteriors can be discerned, in somewhat attenuated form, the standard emotional equipment of our race, including even a rudimentary good nature. Moreover, for reputedly sharp businessmen they appear singularly inept and credulous in the way they are taken in—as Dampit with his pervasive cynicism never would have been—by Witgood's imposture. Yet they cannot be any more shrewd or vicious if Witgood is to succeed as readily as he does in attaining his goals and bringing the action to a close on a note of general reconciliation. (It might be objected that the play would be improved by increasing his difficulties,

---

18 These creeds, influenced by Innocent Gentillet's *Contre Nicholas Machiavel*, became a standard feature of the villain-hero plays which had such a vogue in this period (cf. chap. 3, n. 20). Some of the villains die still faithful to their vicious doctrine, as in *The Jew of Malta* and *Lust's Dominion*, while others, as in *The Atheist's Tragedy* and *The False One*, renounce it at the very end.

but this could have been arranged without changing Lucre and Hoard, if Sam Freedom and Moneylove carried out their intention to intervene in the widow-hunt, which would give Witgood more balls to juggle and so complicate the intrigue in the direction of Jonson's much more brilliant *Alchemist*.) The detached, almost "pure" comic effect of the main plot requires that the action establish an overall confidence in Witgood's scheme without deeply engaging our moral feelings, and this in turn requires that Lucre and Hoard be too ineffectual and innocuous to arouse any great fear or antagonism.

This conception of Lucre and Hoard suggests the principal reason for Dampit's presence, since it was seen that the positive analogy relating him to them as fellow usurers is subordinated to the negative analogy accentuating their differences. Therefore he can draw off to himself the audience's detestation of usury, and its apprehensions (for he would be dangerous if he were Witgood's adversary). The Dampit sequence acknowledges, as it were, the existence of a more serious world of real crime and retributive justice, while at the same time separating it from the world of the main plot, which leaves us freer to regard Lucre and Hoard simply as ridiculous butts who represent no moral threat and so can be let off at the end with relatively mild comic discomfitures. The separation of these two worlds, however, cannot be absolute because the positive aspect of the analogy, even though it is subordinate, places all three usurers in a common class and, with respect to the values of the play, in a common opposition to Witgood (who admits in I.iv that he was once "nibbled" by Dampit too). Therefore Dampit's downfall not only affects our attitude toward Lucre and Hoard but also serves much the same purpose as Pistol's in setting off by contrast the triumphant upward movement of the hero. These functions are confirmed by the location of his three scenes, for they are placed at strategic points in order to exploit both their positive and negative relations to the main action. Each one comes at the end of an act and of a definite stage in Witgood's master plan, so that Dampit's career is made to seem exactly the reverse of Witgood's and to parallel on its grimmer level the careers of Lucre and Hoard, the scenes of his descent punctuating the steps in Witgood's ascent, which coincide necessarily with the steps in the comic defeat of his two victims.

The first of these episodes (I.iv) terminates the expository section of the main plot that showed the inception of Witgood's "trick" (I.i–ii) and the feud between Lucre and Hoard (I.iii) on which his success will depend. Because Dampit appears immediately after this introduction of Lucre and Hoard, we tend to associate both usurers with him, but also perceive the striking difference between their petulant, senseless bickering and his self-assured dominance of Gulf, his fellow usurer. The following scene of the main plot (II.i), with its second view of Lucre, again suggests a comparison back to Dampit and a difference, since here Lucre is shown foolishly rising to the bait set for him. And although these juxtapositions connect Dampit to the two comic butts, in I.iv it is Witgood he confronts, just when he seems at the top of his fortunes and Witgood at the bottom of his.

The second Dampit episode marks the transitional point in his career and in Witgood's. At this juncture Witgood has completed the preliminary phase of his plan by establishing his mistress as a rich widow and capitalizing on this to inveigle small loans from his creditors and his uncle, so that he closes the preceding scene on a very hopeful note which contrasts sharply with Dampit's dark mood at the opening of III.iv. Once more Dampit's appearance is bracketed by two views of the main-plot usurers—III.iii ends with Lucre in a rage because Hoard has stolen the widow, and IV.i begins with Hoard's joyful celebration of his marriage. Both men are utterly mistaken, and their gullibility as well as their intense emotional involvement separate them still further from the distrustful misanthrope revealed in III.iv.

In the third episode of the sequence the complex functions of Dampit's role are most fully realized. Here, as in I.iv, his position is diametrically opposed to Witgood's, but now he is losing everything while Witgood has just achieved total success by recovering his mortgage from Lucre, forcing Hoard to pay off his debts, and eloping with Joyce—and from her promise ("our happiness attends us") at the conclusion of IV.iv we measure the abrupt descent to IV.v, which opens with Audrey's song of damnation. And whereas the first Dampit scene made contact with the main action through the meeting with Witgood just before he began his ascent, in this final one the contact is provided by the visit of Hoard just prior to his downfall. That visit associates Hoard with Dampit as members of the same social circle, but it more emphatically differentiates them since his connubial happiness and friendly invitation are contrasted to Dampit's bitter, unprovoked attack, and his easy credulity to Dampit's immediate, and equally unprovoked, suspicion of the "Dutch widow." Thus in the crucial death scene Dampit is again used to assimilate Hoard—and through him Lucre—to himself in the class of usurer and at the same time to underscore in this dramatic confrontation their more comic and human qualities, in preparation for the reconciliations to follow in Act V.

It should be evident then that even though Dampit's formal connections to the main action are complicated by his more serious dimension, they can be understood in terms of the functions defined earlier in the general analysis of the clown subplot, and so provide a further confirmation of them. His relation to Witgood presents no problem since it is least affected by this dimension; it is that of the clown-foil already seen in *Henry V*. The relation to Lucre and Hoard may be harder to recognize, but it also fits into the original definitions, for we have a secondary positive analogy between them that is developed only enough to set up the primary negative analogy separating them. It is therefore another example of what was called the "pseudoparody" or "lightning rod" function of the clown plot which enables it to drain off a potentially undesirable response to the main action and to heighten by contrast the desired response. The difference is that here the heightened effect is comic, because the tones of the two levels are reversed.

Similar reversals are found in two other city comedies of Middleton, although neither involves a clown: the Country Wench's father in the subplot of *Michaelmas Term* is treated more seriously than anyone in the main action, and the subplot of *A Mad World, My Masters* breaks right out of the comic framework in Act IV when a succubus suddenly appears and brings about the religious conversion of Penitent Brothel. In *A Trick* Middleton also introduces an infernal presence into his comic world, in a much less incongruous form, through the cumulative suggestions connecting Dampit with the devil. There is no supernatural intervention, yet the suggestions are justified because the subplot shows that the self-regarding, self-isolating life of the usurer is demonic and damned; this in fact is how Dampit is related indirectly to the title of the play. The title is a proverbial expression, "the old one" being a common euphemism for the devil, viewed as the shrewd adversary of man, and since the old ones caught by Witgood's trick are Lucre and Hoard, its primary reference must be to them as equivalents of the proverbial victim.[19] Yet their devilish traits are greatly attenuated by the requirements of the plot, and these traits are emphasized instead in Dampit, who thus becomes in another sense the "old one." Therefore, in their different relationships to the title we again see how Dampit is both associated with and distinguished from the usurers of the main plot.

The complex function of the Dampit sequence can be further illustrated in a comparison with Massinger's *A New Way to Pay Old*

---

19 See Morris Tilley, *A Dictionary of the Proverbs in England in the Sixteenth and Seventeenth Centuries* (Ann Arbor, 1950), W149. In other plays the phrase is applied in this way to a character (usually old, shrewd, or evil) who is "caught" during the action—see Tilley's citations and also *A Match at Midnight*, IV.i.p.80, *The Maid in the Mill*, V.ii.p.72. But here the diabolic references accumulate around Dampit in his final scene; even in I.iv Witgood explicitly links him to the devil (ll. 29–31, 39), and may be implying this by addressing him three times as "old Harry," though the *OED* and Partridge's *Dictionary of Slang* record no examples of this nickname for Satan before the Restoration.

Debts, which takes over the basic elements of *A Trick* but drastically alters their significance by reshaping the double-plot structure. Lucre and Hoard are combined into a single figure, Sir Giles Overreach, while the role of Witgood is divided between Frank Wellborn, the nephew of Overreach, who gets his land back from the usurer, along with the money to satisfy his creditors, and his friend Tom Allworth, who gets the usurer's daughter, Margaret. Thus Middleton's main action bifurcates into two "tricking" plots which are entirely separate but parallel, in that they employ the same strategy (enlisting a confederate, like Witgood's Courtesan, to take part in a pretended courtship or betrothal), and are directed against the same man:

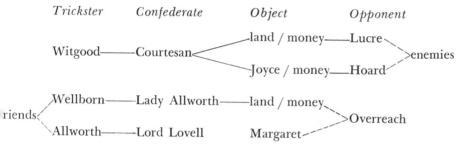

This change has radical consequences in itself. It enables Massinger to expand and sentimentalize Middleton's trivial romance by segregating it from all the financial chicanery (and also to develop a secondary romance, if that is the word, between the two confederates). But, more important, it shifts the center of attention from the trickster to his opponent, Overreach, who becomes the protagonist of both plots, completely dominating the play. And since he is not rendered vulnerable by a foolish feud with another of his kind, he also becomes much more powerful and threatening as well as more antipathetic, for his intended victims are now all noncomic sympathetic characters, whereas Lucre and Hoard were primarily interested in victimizing each other.

This shift is greatly magnified by a second structural change; Massinger eliminates the Dampit sequence and adds his sinister dimension to the Lucre-Hoard combination. The result is most instructive because this brings the audience's moral condemnation, which Dampit had deflected from Lucre and Hoard, into the center of the play and transforms the comedy into melodrama. Since the man who is given the whole evil aura of "usury" is now the usurer who acts against the persons we admire, he arouses very painful emotions and so cannot be disposed of, like the inactive Dampit, by a squalid fade-out, nor, like the innocuous Lucre and Hoard, by a comic embarrassment, but requires a fully elaborated and emphasized punishment, his final madness registering just how seriously he and we took his villainous plans. This does not mean that Overreach is characterized in the same way as Dampit; the clowning is gone (it is relegated to his accomplice, Greedy, and to the low-comic third level of Tapwell and Froth), and so is the understatement, for he is presented as a monstrous stage-Machiavel with all of the standard embellishments so notably lacking in Dampit: he keeps boasting of his devilish creed (to Marrall, Wellborn, Margaret, and Lovell), delights in tormenting his victims, gloats over his forthcoming triumphs, and reacts to his defeat with impenitent fury, like Barabas, while simultaneously suffering the pangs of conscience in the manner of D'Amville and similar last-minute converts (his insanity giving the playwright license to try for both of these conventional but contradictory endings). And the portrait is further exaggerated by a really venomous class-hatred (Overreach's and Massinger's) which is not found in *A Trick*. But even if Massinger had exercised more restraint his play would still have moved in the direction of melodrama, since this seems to be the inevitable result of joining the perspective of the Dampit scenes to the action of Lucre and Hoard. (That is why it needs the "comic relief" of Greedy and the Tapwell-Froth sequence, whereas *A Trick* needed the "serious relief" of Dampit.)

Middleton, by detaching Dampit from the main plot, is able to preserve the comic effect, although the isolation of his sequence tends to leave it relatively inert in the dramatic composite. This in fact is true of most clown subplots, almost by definition, for they do not "matter" in the same sense as the major actions; however, since Dampit is relied upon to contribute so much more to the overall meaning than the ordinary clown, it becomes a special problem in *A Trick*. One proof of this is the number of critics who have complained of the play's immorality.[20] Because they either ignore Dampit or dismiss him as a mere buffoon, they fail to recognize that his scenes provide an ethical ground for the Witgood plot, but it must be admitted that these two components (like the farcical and serious aspects of Dampit's death) are imperfectly assimilated. Massinger's structure, on the other hand, focuses on the morality at the expense of the comedy, and while the effect may be more unified than Middleton's, it is not the kind of unity that he was seeking here, and that he finally did achieve, as we will see, some six years later in *A Chaste Maid in Cheapside* through a successful integration of these moral and comic perspectives. But in that play Dampit's function is taken over by a

---

20 These are mostly of the earlier generation which took the moral function of literature very literally, but a more modern and sophisticated attack on this front appears in L. C. Knights's *Drama and Society in the Age of Jonson* (London, 1937), pp. 256–69, 274.

more serious character, Sir Walter Whorehound, and the clown, Tim Yellowhammer, is a simple comic foil. Presumably Middleton came to realize that in Dampit he had put the clowning under too great a strain by assigning it a task which exceeded its inherent limitations, for he did not attempt the same thing again, nor, I believe, did any other dramatist of the period. But it was still an extraordinary attempt that should not pass unnoticed in any study of the clown subplot.

III

This study has so far been restricted to what might be called the "literal" functions of that subplot, in the sense that they all assume the clown's identity as an individual personality who is as "real" as those in the main plot and enters into overt relationships with them, in both the causal interactions and formal analogies, which obey the laws of dramatic probability and logic, and which we ourselves are conscious of as we watch or read the play, or at least could easily bring to consciousness upon a moment's reflection. But the work of Empson and others has taught us to look for more in the clown plot than meets the eye of reason, since as an archaic survival it may mobilize and "act out" certain attitudes or impulses, embedded in folk belief and ritual and in our own subconscious, that will color our dramatic experience whether or not we are aware of them. These are the functions or undertones I have termed "magical." They can only be surveyed briefly here, and for that purpose it seems most convenient to group them under a few quite general metaphorical *roles* which may lie beneath the clown's literal identity, and upon which his "magic" depends.

We must realize, however, that these roles admit of no precise classification, since they operate through the prelogical laws of association and so will tend to overlap and merge. Nor should we expect them to be equally applicable to all clowns, after having seen such a range of variation in these characters and their treatment. The roles usually appear in their most naïve and isolated form in the early plays, many of which simply carry them over, undigested, from the Morality tradition; and they gradually diminish in importance toward the end of the period as the clown loses his folk roots and rises up the social scale to the status of gentleman-fool or fop, although they never entirely disappear because they are grounded in the universal processes of the mind as well as in their particular historical origin. It is during the two or three decades between these stages, while the metaphorical roles still retained their vitality but the dramatists had learned to adapt them to the literal multiplot structure, that we find the most memorable and effective clowns, including the greatest of them all, who because of his rich complexity can be used to exemplify each of the roles and its magical powers—the Falstaff of the two parts of *Henry IV*.

A significant clue to these roles and powers is the fate meted out to the clown in the resolutions of most of the plays, since this proves he is not held accountable for his actions in the same way as the other characters. Although he is often guilty of transgressions that are (or would be) punished with the utmost severity in the major plots, he very rarely has to pay any real penalty for them. Falstaff's cowardice at Gadshill and at Shrewsbury directly violates the ideal of honor presented in *1 Henry IV*, yet he gets away with it on both occasions, and on the second is even rewarded by being allowed to claim the honor of killing Hotspur. Costard, similarly, escapes the consequences of his violation of the romantic ideal in *Love's Labor's Lost* by successfully foisting off his bastard (*in utero*) upon Don Armado. The clowns in *Doctor Faustus* suffer no permanent damage from the necromancy which brings the protagonist to damnation, nor does Scumbroth in *If It Be Not Good, the Devil Is in It,* the only person in all three plots whose traffic with the devils requires no expiation. The same discrepancy appeared in many "hierarchy" dramas employing the *Damon and Pythias* pattern, where the main and subplot are differentiated on moral terms that are never applied to the clowns of the third level. That is why we called it the "amoral" level, which is another way of saying the clown's fate does not really matter to the other characters or the audience.

The clown's fate does not even matter to him in those plays where he is given an apparently serious punishment, for he does not take it seriously, and consequently neither do we.[21] In *Friar Bacon and Friar Bungay,* for example, Miles mounts the devil's back for his journey to hell in the very best of humor, and a number of others—such as Adam the Clown in *A Looking Glass for London and England,* William Murley in *Sir John Oldcastle,* and Timothy Stilt in *Hoffman*—go right on with their joking while they are being led off to execution. This kind of exit derives from the Vices and Vice lieutenants of the Morality tradition and remains a common feature of the transitional semi-Moralities (as can be seen in the fates of Haphazard in *Appius and Virginia* or Simplicity in *The Three Ladies of London*). But long after that tradition died out the clown continues blithely on his way, as if he had been granted a special exemption from the demands and penalties of the "real" dramatic world in which he finds

---

21 We saw two exceptions: the murder of Bergetto in *'Tis Pity She's a Whore* and the hanging of Bardolph and Nym in *Henry V* (which is not dramatized). Although the citizen and gentleman clowns are seldom harmed they are sometimes taught a lesson—cf. the reform of Claridiana and Rogero in *The Insatiate Countess,* Young Barnacle in *The Gamester,* Frederick in *The Lady of Pleasure,* etc.

himself. It is easy to understand then why the older critics would complain that his presence contradicted the ethical basis of the play.

The answer to their objection, it was suggested, lies in the recognition that the clown, whatever his individual identity, can embody more generic roles existing on another level of reality and appealing to another level of the audience's reactions. Probably the most obvious such role implied in his fate and his attitude toward it is that of the child, who is not yet expected to adjust to adult standards or to be judged by them. Although there are many sorts of clowns, most of them share some of the other characteristics belonging to the universal state of childhood, or rather, to the adult's nostalgic vision of that state—the concentration on bodily functions (especially those at both ends of the digestive tract) and on their gratification, the natural energy and spontaneity, the complete absorption in the present and happy-go-lucky approach to life. The more foolish ones have the innocence of children; and even the shrewd rogues are childishly amoral, without scruples but without sinister motives, mischievous rather than malicious, and incapable of the long-range scheming of the ambitious or vengeful villain. Like the child, the clown is dependent upon an indulgent providence or paternal figure to protect him from doing or suffering any serious harm. And in the same way he also seems to place himself under the protection of the audience, which is one reason why we acquiesce in his escapades and his escape from punishment.

Our response, however, goes well beyond mere acquiescence because we positively enjoy these escapades, and this can be explained by our subconscious tendency to identify the clown not only with a child of ours but also with the child in us, which through him is permitted to throw off the repressions of maturity and civilization and to enact some of its milder fantasies. In this sense, therefore, the old-fashioned term "comic relief" might be said to describe one of the clown's magical effects, although I prefer to call it "comic release." This is not a verbal quibble since the connotations suggest a choice between two psychologies—between seeing the mind as a passive mechanism that suffers strain, like a muscle, if it is forced to move in the same way for too long, and so requires the "relief" of another form of exercise; or seeing it as an active dynamism of drives and impulses that build up pressure, like a steam boiler, if they are too long confined and therefore demand "release" in real or imagined action. The very notion of clown "magic" assumes this second view, as did the earlier discussion of his "lightning rod" function, which would make no sense if there were no self-generating impulses in the audience to be coped with. To the extent that these impulses find release in the "childhood" of the clown, we will take a vicarious satisfaction in the ability this role gives him to ignore or even flout the serious rules governing both the main action and our own consciences—provided that he is kept within proper bounds so as not to threaten either.

Such a role is an important aspect of Falstaff's magical function, for we noted in the previous chapter that the triadic scheme of *1 Henry IV* associates him with the "id" or "appetite"—the infantile component of the mind. His childish traits are consistently emphasized in the action and dialogue, and in the disparity between his psychological and physical ages, which he himself insists upon ("They hate us youth . . . Young men must live"). And he finds in Hal the benevolent father who tolerates his irresponsible behavior and protects him from its consequences, by preventing his arrest for the robbery at Gadshill and paying off the victims, and by agreeing to "gild" his lie about killing Hotspur at Shrewsbury. This generic role also encompasses the crucial flaw attributed to him in the earlier discussion of the play—his inability to adapt to noncomic situations. He is the eternal, unregenerate child for whom time and change do not exist, for whom every occasion is an invitation to "jest and dally." So long as he remains within this role he can claim our indulgence as well as Hal's, and our gratitude for the pleasure it affords; but when he steps out of it at the end of Part II to reveal a very unchildlike ambition and vindictiveness posing a real threat to the adult world ("Let us take any man's horses, the laws of England are at my commandment. Blessed are they that have been my friends, and woe to my Lord Chief Justice!"), we and Hal both demand his expulsion.[22]

Robin and Dick take on this role of clown-child in the subplot "conjuring" scenes of *Doctor Faustus,* as is demonstrated by the marked contrast between their simple oral desires ("white wine, red wine . . . and whippincrust") and Faustus's infinite aspirations, and therefore they too can claim the "benefit of childhood" exempting them from his terrible punishment, or indeed from any significant alteration, which is why their subplot seemed so static and repetitive. But in this context I think they also serve another magical purpose that is perhaps just a specialization of the general effect of comic release implicit in the role: their ridiculous and essentially harmless dealings with the devil manage to make him a little less fearsome, to domesticate him as it were, while furnishing an excuse for our protective laughter, which here protects *us* as well as them. Scumbroth

---

[22] Many people are troubled by this expulsion scene, but I think they object not so much to the necessity of curbing Falstaff (though some have certainly oversentimentalized him) as to the hypocrisy and cruelty of Hal—or in terms of our analysis, to his failure to acknowledge and assimilate the Falstaff-in-him (unlike the ending of Part I). See Jonas Barish's able discussion of this problem in "The Turning Away of Prince Hal," *ShakS,* 1 (1965), 9–17.

is used to a similar end in *If It Be Not Good, the Devil Is in It,* as is Miles in *Friar Bacon and Friar Bungay,* the Clown in *The Birth of Merlin,* and even the Clown in *A Looking Glass for London and England,* though his demon turns out to be a fraud. In *The Witch of Edmonton* (another "hierarchy" play) Cuddy Banks's meeting with the devil-dog Tom provides further reassurance by suggesting that his childlike innocence renders him impervious to temptation and thus transforms the familiar, whose malign influence proves fatal to Frank Thorney and Mother Sawyer on the first and second levels, into a friendly pet.

This same tendency to reduce the power and frightfulness of evil —especially supernatural evil—by treating it in comic terms presumably underlies much of the clowning in the Mystery cycles, which usually centers around Satan and the great ogres of the biblical story (Pharaoh, Herod, etc.), and also the "comedy of evil" in the Moralities, so it is not surprising to find vestiges of it in these later works. In fact a modern version can be seen in many of our horror movies where a clownish character blunders into the monster and, being too stupid to fear him, engages in some slapstick buffoonery—a situation not unlike the encounter of Stephano and Trinculo with Caliban in *The Tempest,* although that is complicated by the contrast with Prospero's "white magic." Even in *A Midsummer Night's Dream* where the supernatural is relatively benign, it is comforting as well as amusing to observe Bottom's imperturbable preoccupation with eating and scratching (the pregenital gratifications of the child) in his wonderful love scene with Titania; and the shepherds of the *Secunda Pastorum* seem to perform an analogous function, to the extent that they take on the clown's childishness, in confronting both the black magic of Mak and the white magic of the Nativity.

The association of the clown with childhood was said to be metaphorical because he is usually an adult (though there are young servant or page clowns in such plays as *Fulgens and Lucrece* and *Mother Bombie*); yet this generic role draws upon and exploits some of the actual beliefs and practices of the time. Real-life simpletons like Cuddy Banks, who would have been at least as common then as our "village idiot" of a few generations back, were in fact regarded both as permanent children and as "innocents" or "naturals" (two standard names for them) uncontaminated by civilization, and were treated with some indulgence for these reasons—and also, no doubt, in deference to the very ancient superstition that they enjoyed divine protection. Most stage clowns are not "children of nature" in this special sense, but in the early drama they are almost all members of the lower economic classes, typically the country yokelry (this being the original meaning of "clown"), which amounts to much the same thing because these people were generally thought to be more child-ish than their betters and closer to nature, ignorant of the moral and intellectual restraints that inhibit the higher levels of the mind and of society, and therefore prone to a certain amount of "natural" license—mainly drinking, wenching, and brawling—that was looked upon with a condescending tolerance so long as it was confined to their own kind. This view has had a very obvious appeal in stratified cultures (it appears, for example, in the scheme of Plato's *Republic* which relates the artisan class to the appetitive part of the soul, in the treatment of the "prols" of Orwell's *1984*, and in our modern stereo-types of the Negro and the "native"), and its bearing on the magical use of the clown is equally obvious, for it allows us to take a vicarious pleasure in his freedom while feeling superior to it. We can have our release and our reassurance simultaneously.

In these two instances the attributes and privileges of childhood were conceded permanently by contemporary custom to specified groups of adults, the stupid and the servile, but there was another sort of custom which extended this same concession temporarily to all adults. That was the saturnalian holiday, still a vital tradition in Renaissance England, when for a specified period everyone was sup-posed to become a "clown"; and its characteristic rituals completely reversed the normal order of things by vesting authority in those elements of the population—and hence those components of our nature—represented by the clown's metaphorical roles: the boy ruled over the man (most strikingly in the institution of the Boy Bishop), the servant or laborer over his master, the carefree fool, real or pre-tended,[23] over the wise and sober, and, symbolically, the instinctive "id" over reason and conscience. We should therefore expect to find something of the atmosphere and significance of this holiday under-lying many clown subplots. In fact the dramatist does not even have to go out of his way to suggest such a connection because it is implicit in the very nature of these plots, whose alternating episodes were shown to offer a kind of emotional vacation from the more serious business of the main action.

Shakespeare, however, deliberately emphasizes Falstaff's saturnalian role [24] by giving him a separate little world in the Boar's Head Tavern which he dominates in the manner of a festival Lord of Misrule, enforcing a comic antidiscipline upon all who enter there,

---

23 In England and France one version of this festival was the Feast of Fools (Fête des Fous), and the ceremonial ruler was given such titles as King of Fools, Precentor Stultorum, Prince des Sots, and Mère-Folle.
24 On this point see C. L. Barber, *Shakespeare's Festive Comedy* (Princeton, 1959), chap. 8.

including the Prince. This has important consequences for the dramatic structure; it means that his magical function of providing a licensed release for the drives and fantasies of childhood will apply not only to the audience but also to Hal himself, since Falstaff stands in the same double metaphorical relationship to him as to us: he is both Hal's child and the child-in-Hal (or from the theological perspective of the Archbishop of Canterbury in *Henry V*, "the offending Adam" in him). Thus in both the anthropological and psychological senses Hal's sojourn in the tavern world becomes his saturnalia. He is always aware, however, that it *is* a holiday and so must come to an end, as we learn in his first soliloquy when he explains his association with Falstaff in these terms ("If all the year were playing holidays . . ."). But Falstaff does want to make all the year one continuous saturnalia, this being the ritual corollary of his perennial childishness and obliviousness of time which is brought out most forcefully in his parallel attempts to extend his misrule into the serious climaxes of both parts of *Henry IV*, and in the Prince's parallel rebukes. During the Battle of Shrewsbury at the end of Part I, we noted earlier, Hal must warn him:

What, is it a time to jest and dally now?

and during the coronation procession at the end of Part II:

Reply not to me with a fool-born jest.

The crucial point here is not so much the temporary duration of the saturnalia as its permanent effect on society. Hal, unlike Falstaff, realizes that this holiday does not subvert the inhibitions of "everyday" but actually conserves them. It releases the natural impulses pent up by social control and at the same time demonstrates through its wild excesses the necessity for such control, so that we return to normality purged of these impulses, with renewed faith in the existing order which has been able to allow this purgation, contain it, and survive it. There is then a close analogy between the social purpose of saturnalian ritual and Hal's justification of his personal saturnalia in that first soliloquy, where he claims he will "show more goodly" in the everyday world "when this loose behavior I throw off." And there is a closer analogy to what was called the "foil" function of the clown subplot, which enhances by contrast the seriousness of the main action. In this sense the saturnalia itself can be thought of as a low-comic foil to the serious business of life, and we saw that Hal speaks of his holidaying as a "foil to set off" his princeliness. The analogy can even be extended to the clown's "comedy of evil" which helps the audience to master their fear of the demonic forces appearing in *Doctor Faustus* and the other "devil" plays, just as the festival clowning helps the participants to master their internal demons—the frightening "id" instincts—that it brings to the surface.

One of the most common features of saturnalian revelry seems to have a special bearing on the clown subplot—the so-called ritual abuse vented by the mock-king and his court upon the real rulers of the group and its sacred beliefs.[25] This ceremony may seem dangerously subversive to modern man, whose orthodoxies are so much more vulnerable, but in its original form it has the same purpose as the larger ritual to which it belongs: it provides another opportunity for "licensed license," another safety-valve to purge antisocial tendencies and prove society's imperviousness to them, and so strengthens rather than weakens the very officials and institutions it attacks (indeed in some primitive cultures it was supposed to bring "good luck" to them). It finds a dramatic counterpart in those clowns who openly ridicule the main characters and their heroic or romantic ideals, since this ridicule was usually seen to function as a means of anticipating and so canceling out our own skepticism—or in Empson's formulation, as a kind of "pseudo-parody to disarm criticism." That is why we could say the antiparodic rather than the parodic clown was the deliberate parodist, for this is confirmed by the magical power of his role as ritual mocker.

This does not mean, however, that the opinions and attitudes of the clown need be ignored, for we must remember that all three of the real personalities associated with his metaphorical roles—the child, the idiot, and the proletarian—were traditionally believed to possess an intuitive wisdom by virtue of their special affinity to nature (or the deity) which could yield insights denied to the more intelligent and mature.[26] Many of the clowns demonstrate this ability, although it does not always emerge in the form of mockery and sometimes, especially in the early plays, does not even attain the level of speech. To take a simple example: each of the clown episodes in *Cambyses* ends with a woman, Meretrix in the first and Marian in the second, beating

---

25 This ritual is discussed by Enid Welsford, *The Fool* (London, 1935), chap. 9, and Robert Elliott, *The Power of Satire* (Princeton, 1960), chap. 2. Compare the games of "vapors" and "jeering" in *Bartholomew Fair* and *The Staple of News*.
26 Different kinds of insight were attributed to children and to the lower classes—contrast the implications of "out of the mouths of babes" and "common sense" (or its fancier modernization, "folk wisdom"). "Fool wisdom" might be nothing more than the child's alleged ability to see, or blurt out, truths concealed by the hypocrisies or reticences of the adult world ("The Emperor has no clothes!"), but it was complicated by two related traditions: the "sacred innocent" speaking from divine inspiration, and the clever impostor ("crazy like a fox") adopting the mask of imbecility to say things that would otherwise endanger him—e.g., Saxo's and Shakespeare's Hamlet, and the professional Fool (who often shares some of the clown's traits but poses special problems that cannot be dealt with here).

off the Vice Ambidexter who has easily managed to trick the men there, as well as those in the more serious action. Neither woman utters any profundities, yet they are the only ones in the play to get the better of Ambidexter because they are the champions of a healthy life force (of a comic Earth Goddess, perhaps, divided into her sexual and maternal aspects) that makes them superior to their menfolk, engrossed in the "higher" pursuits of war (in II.i) and politics (in IV.iii), and even in this limited sense to the "higher" characters of the main plot.[27] The shepherds of the *Secunda Pastorum* exhibit a similarly inarticulate folk wisdom when they finally catch on to Mak's imposture and toss him in a blanket; and so do Dogberry and his Watch in *Much Ado about Nothing* when they stumble upon the information that defeats Don John's scheme, after it had deceived all the other characters ("What your wisdoms could not discover, these shallow fools have brought to light"). In *A Woman Killed with Kindness* Nicholas immediately perceives the true nature of Wendoll, which his master is blind to, but this is again subrational ("I do not like this fellow by no means . . . yet know not the reason why"). And as Empson notes, we feel that Miles is right to disobey Friar Bacon's orders and allow the Brazen Head to be destroyed, although he does not have the least idea of what he is doing. Here the clown's intuitive capacity can be seen in its purest and most magical form, operating without any conscious intent, yet proving wiser than the wisest magician in Christendom.

The clown-mocker is of course much more verbal, but the ideas he voices typically spring from the same "earthy" or "folk" source, asserting the claims of common sense and the natural instincts (of hunger, sex, and self-preservation) against the high-flown sentiments of his betters. Shakespeare is particularly fond of this character and often permits him to state his case with considerable force in a terse, almost epigrammatic prose. In the romantic comedies, for instance, Costard informs the lords who have just contracted themselves to a three-year abstinence from female company that "it is the manner of a man to speak to a woman" and "Such is the simplicity of man to hearken after the flesh"; when Bottom (with his ass head) hears Titania swear she has fallen in love with "thy note," "thy shape," and "thy fair virtue," he remarks,

> Methinks, mistress, you should have little reason for that.
> And yet, to say the truth, reason and love keep little company together nowadays;

---

27 Compare the mothers in the Digby *Slaughter of the Innocents* who beat off Herod's courtier, and also Noah's Wife in the various cycles, although her earthy common sense is pitted against divine wisdom.

and Touchstone tells Rosalind, "As all is mortal in nature, so is all nature in love mortal in folly" (to which she replies, "Thou speakest wiser than thou art ware of"), and he later imparts to Jaques the "natural" explanation of marriage:

> As the ox hath his bow, sir, the horse his curb, and the falcon her bells, so man hath his desires; and as pigeons bill, so wedlock will be nibbling.

Another obvious example, quoted in the previous chapter, is Falstaff's "catechism" on the ideal of honor in *1 Henry IV*. Mockery of this sort certainly contains a part of the truth, as it must have in the saturnalia itself, but it is not the whole truth or even the most important part. (It does seem to be in *Troilus and Cressida,* but we will find that this is a very unusual play and that Thersites and Pandarus are very unusual clowns, whose wisdom comes not from the good earth but from the brothel and spital.) In the earlier and cruder works the mocking remains relatively isolated since it never really confronts the more serious action; in the better ones, where these confrontations occur, it becomes an element of the final synthesis; but in either case it is subordinated to the values of the main plot and usually serves to ensure and to enhance them.

I think we are justified in concluding, therefore, that these magical functions of the clown subplot do not contradict the preceding literal analysis, and in many ways reinforce it. For one thing, they help to explain our initial impression that the clown belongs to a different order of being, to a timeless, static world of his own, and so does not "matter" in the same sense as the other characters. They also help to explain the special delight we take in him, which we have now seen depends on his capacity to act out and satisfy, through his metaphorical roles, some of the most deeply rooted needs of man's nature. But more significant for our purposes, the various magical functions deriving from these roles turn out to correspond (and thus would contribute) to one of the literal functions of his subplot described earlier—that of the "lightning rod" which works directly as a foil to set off an elevated main action, while also working indirectly to attract and drain away those potential reactions hostile to that elevation. For the clown's roles as child-idiot-lout, as saturnalian ruler, and as ritual mocker all seem to operate in this manner by sanctioning the release through the subplot of our anarchic impulses and feelings, under controls which prevent them from threatening the adult, civilized norms of the main plot, even as they are prevented from threatening these norms in the spectator himself and in society at large. This should not be surprising, given the inherent conservatism of folk culture and the effect of its attitudes and rituals in promoting conformity to the communal ideals and neutralizing anticonformist tendencies within the individual or group. Therefore, to the extent that these subplots retain the "magical" powers of their primitive origin, we would expect that they will not undercut the social and ethical standards of the main action but confirm them—that they will function, in other words, as foil rather than parody, except in plays like *Doctor Faustus* or *The Insatiate Countess* where the protagonist himself violates those standards, and even then the protagonist and not the standard is the target of the parody. All this of course does not preclude the possibility of another kind of parodic clown plot, but it may account for our difficulty in finding any in the drama of the period.

5

Equivalence Plots

In almost all the plays seen so far the formal analogy joins two or more actions concerned with the same area of human experience. For some analogies this area could be defined only in general terms— love, marriage, friendship, manners, war, class conflict, and the like— but for others built around what we called a "nuclear parallel," it can be narrowed down to a specific situation: two fathers misjudging their children, two wives tempted to commit adultery, two threatened with sexual blackmail, pairs of lovers thwarted by parental opposition, a servant imitating his master's ventures in black magic. In either case the basis of the connection is immediately apparent in the common subject matter. But while this is true of most multiple-plot dramas of the period, there are a number whose actions are drawn from very different aspects of life that must in some sense be equated on the formal level. And because relationships of this sort, to which I have given the name "equivalence plots," are more easily overlooked and raise unique problems of their own, they have been reserved for special consideration.

It must be acknowledged at the outset that this classification, like all the others, is necessarily relative, since no matter how widely separated the subjects of the plots may be it is always possible to find a more inclusive term that subsumes them both as members of the same category of experience. Thus the combination in Medwall's *Fulgens and Lucrece,* where the main action portrays the extended debate between Cornelius and Flaminius over their qualifications to marry Lucrece, and the clown subplot a singing and wrestling contest between their servants for the favor of her maid, might be regarded either as an equation of "debate" and "wrestling" or as two versions of "courtship competition." The determination in each play will have to depend on the felt distance between the activities as well as the emphasis of the structure itself, and there will be plenty of borderline cases. For this chapter I have tried to limit the discussion to some of the more extreme examples in which we are clearly meant to understand that two distinctly different subject matters have been made equivalent by the inter-plot parallel.

The search for a literary source of this kind of combination is not very fruitful. It does not appear in classical drama, and cannot in the double-plot Moralities since their actions always exemplify the virtue and corresponding vice of a given area of behavior. As with the direct contrast plots, the really significant source is not to be found in art but in a universal impulse—here the impulse to construct or discover satisfying connections among the disparate aspects of our experience by the sort of analogical reasoning that underlies so much primitive myth and ritual (for instance, in the continual appeal to correspondences between external nature and human events), and folk and proverbial lore ("All's fair in love and war"), and of course the metaphorical language of everyday life and of poetry. As a matter of fact these same equivalences can also be established within a single-plot drama as a pervasive motif (the state and the body in *Coriolanus*) or within each of several plots as a means of relating them (courtship and gambling in all three levels of *Hyde Park*). What we are dealing with now is simply a particular application of this universal tendency, in which the equation bridges two separate plots, each centering on one of the two terms.

The special problem posed by structures of this type turns upon the emotional meaning of the equation, since the analogy asks us to compare not only two sets of characters and events, as in the other plays, but two kinds of human activity, and that in itself will involve some judgment of their relative value. This judgment cannot be deduced from contemporary attitudes toward the two activities, however, for while the mere juxtaposition of the plots would not suggest an equivalence between their subject matters unless some basis for it already existed in the predispositions of the audience (by virtue of the general tendency just described), the playwright may exploit those predispositions in many different ways. Therefore the equivalence relationship does not really constitute another independent mode of formal integration, since it can be used in any of them—to connect two contrast plots, or two levels of a hierarchy, or a clown subplot to a main plot, as foil or as parody. It only sets up the inter-plot analogy but does not itself determine which aspect is to be stressed or to what purpose. The failure to appreciate this can lead to misinterpretations of these plays, similar to the parody-hunting noted earlier. If the equation joins a "low" area of experience to a "high" one, as many of them do, we may be too ready to assume that the effect must be parodic ("rational argument is no better than wrestling"), although the preceding chapter showed that it could be exactly the reverse when the contrast between the two is accentuated to elevate the higher at the expense of the lower. In this respect the interpretative problem is not essentially different from that already encountered in the clown subplot.

The problem, however, and the temptation to assume a deflationary effect can become more acute in this group of plays where the analogy equates different kinds of activity, because the character of this equation will often seem to imply a causal connection between the two activities as such (as distinct from the causal interactions between the two plot lines), in terms of certain magical or psychological or social relationships. It is here that the Freudian theory of causation, which explains the more civilized pursuits and ideals of man as sublimations of his primitive instinctual nature, turns out to be both a valuable tool of analysis and a potential source of difficulty. This difficulty does not lie in the anachronism of applying Freud to pre-Freudian literature, since very similar ideas (whether conscious or not) are found in some of these plays and in the folk psychology of the time. It is rather that the theory, or its popular distortion, tends to debase the sublimated effect to its instinctive cause. For if we read the equivalence that way ("rational argument really *is* a disguised form of wrestling"), then of course the result will be a still more devastating parody. But there is no reason why this same connection cannot function in the opposite direction if the thrust of the analogy points up the superiority of the effect to the cause ("how much nobler to restrain the impulse to wrestle by settling disputes through rational argument"). Therefore, although the Freudian account of human behavior will provide very useful insights into many of these equivalence plots, it must never be used automatically to justify a reductive interpretation. (This would not even be good Freud, since he was fully aware of the beneficent as well as the pathogenic role of sublimation.) And the same should be said of Marxism, the other great reductive philosophy of our day, which will contribute to our understanding of those combinations—found, for instance, in some of Middleton's city comedies —where one plot deals with economic intrigue, provided that we do not assume the second plot must necessarily be translated down to its terms (which also would not be good Marx but what used to be called the "vulgarization" of his doctrine). Neither of these modern "anachronistic" approaches, any more than an historically oriented reconstruction of "the Elizabethan world picture," can determine the relative values attached to the two aspects of experience brought together in this format. Only the play can do that.

I

Empson's pioneering essay, which opened up so many other areas of multiple-plot analysis, also explored this kind of connection, primarily in *Friar Bacon and Friar Bungay* and *Troilus and Cressida*. But we will begin, again, with a simpler example where the nature of the equivalence seems unmistakable, an early Beaumont and Fletcher comedy named *The Woman Hater; or, The Hungry Courtier* (the alternate title was not added until the second issue of the second quarto, published in 1649). The main plot depicts the efforts of Gondarino, the woman hater, to avoid all females, and the subplot the efforts of the courtier Lazarello to hunt down a choice morsel of fish. The stories never make contact on the causal level, and I have never seen any explanation of their combination. Yet the continuous juxtaposition of these two activities suggests a relationship between them, as does the language itself, for alimentary terms like "appetite," "stomach," "taste," "meat," and "flesh" are frequently used in a sexual sense (which is certainly not unique to this play, but here takes on a special significance), and Lazarello consistently speaks of the fish as a desirable woman to be possessed:

> Thither must I
> To see my love's face, the chaste virgin head
> Of a dear fish, yet pure and undeflower'd,
> Not known of man, no rough bred country hand
> Hath once touch'd thee, no pander's withered paw . . .
> O let it be thought lawful then for me
> To crop the flower of thy virginity.
>> (I.iii.216–20, 227–28)

> Show me but any lady in the court,
> That hath so full an eye, so sweet a breath,
> So soft and white a flesh.
>> (III.ii.65–67)

> The looks of my sweet love are fair,
> Fresh and feeding as the air . . .
> Was never seen so rare a head
> Of any fish alive or dead.
>> (IV.ii.151–52, 154–55)

This connection is reinforced by the parallel treatment of the men, for although Gondarino's line of action is more serious than Lazarello's, they are both made ridiculous in the fantastic lengths to which they will go for their absurd ends, and are given homologous roles in the comic structure, each being deliberately manipulated to provide "sport" for one of the two wits of the drama, the first for Oriana and the second for her brother, Count Valore.[1] And it is confirmed by their discomfitures in the resolution; Gondarino is punished by a kind of forced sexual feeling when he is tied to a chair and has to endure the caresses of the court ladies, and Lazarello at the end of the trail learns he must marry a whore to get his fish. Clearly we are to feel that sex is somehow equivalent to food, and the rationale of this equation is supplied by Lazarello himself:

> Hunger, valor, love, ambition are alike pleasing, and let our philosophers say what they will, are one kind of heat, only hunger is the safest . . .

> (III.iii.74–76)

In these terms, therefore, the comic aberrations of the protagonists of the two plots are exactly balanced in that they represent opposite distorted responses to this "heat," the one going too far to avoid, the other too far to pursue. Thus the combination is unified through a direct contrast of extremes of the type discussed at the end of Chapter 2.

Perhaps this is as far as we are justified in proceeding, but if we go on to ask whether there is a causal relation between these two varieties of "heat," I think the play has an answer. It is significant that while Lazarello keeps confusing food with females, Gondarino never does the reverse. It is more significant that Lazarello, as the quotations indicate, not only equates eating to coitus but actually *prefers* it. And in one revealing passage, he argues that it is even preferable to sodomy:

> O 'tis far above the good of women, the pathic cannot yield more pleasing titillation.

> (III.ii.83–84)

It appears then that we are to regard his gourmandizing as a flight from sex, so that the opposite extremes of the two protagonists turn out to be different roads to the same goal; Lazarello, just as surely as Gondarino, is rejecting women, only he tries to accomplish this indirectly through the substitution of oral gratification ("hunger is the safest"). This is the point of the dual resolutions, since each man must

---

[1] I.iii.74, 229–36; II.i.220, 299, 397–99; III.i.216; V.iv.175.

finally surrender to the aggressive female (Oriana, and the prostitute Julia), who emerges victorious in her erotic aspect (and it also seems to be the point of the third-level sequence, in which a mercer with scholarly pretensions ends up married to another whore). Therefore the universal "heat" is basically sexual and man's other drives are reduced to it, or rather to mechanisms to escape from it, which is why the efforts of Lazarello, taking the form of an infantile regression that harms no one but himself and provides innocent amusement for Valore, are less serious than those of the avowed woman hater who confronts his enemy directly and fights back by trying to destroy Oriana. I do not mean to suggest that anything very profound is involved in what is after all a quite perfunctory comedy of humors, but the formal integration and final effect of these humors depend on a perception of their common departure from the natural sexual norm posited by the play.

We have already come upon two more sophisticated combinations of this type in the group of three-level dramas examined in Chapter 3. The analogy between the main and subplot of *A Fair Quarrel* centers on male and female "honor"—courage and chastity—and so equates the "field of honor" and the field of sex. We saw how this equivalence was expressed in the diction of the play by the application of the various terms for the central concept ("honor," "fame," "good name," "worth," etc.) to both of these virtues, and by the many figures of speech, especially in the opening scene, which associate loving with fighting.[2] It is also embedded in the dramatic structure—in the causal and formal connections between Ager's quarrel and Jane's romance developed in Act I; in the duel itself, which shifts its ground from the chastity of Ager's mother to his own courage; in the resolution where each plot crosses over into the other's area, the marriage of Jane and Fitzallen being hastened by an abortive duel, and the reconciliation of Ager and the Colonel by a betrothal (of Ager to the Colonel's sister); and in the final moment when the analogy between this marriage and this reconciliation is vividly rendered in the parallel embraces of the two lovers of the subplot and the two friends of the main action. We saw too that Chough, the third-level clown, adds another component to this equation in his comparisons of copulation and dueling (in its debased form of "roaring") to each other and to his favorite sport:

> I am to marry shortly; but I will defer it a while till I can roar perfectly, that I may get the upper hand of my wife on the wedding-day
>
> (IV.i.201–3)

---

2 See I.i.44–46, 86–89, 134–35, 183, 200–6, 208–9, quoted in chap. 3.

the hug and the lock between man and woman, with a fair
fall, is as sweet an exercise for the body as you'll desire in
a summer's evening

(II.ii.171–74)

wrestling and roaring are as like as can be
(IV.i.154)

The effect of these equations, however, is the opposite of that in
The Woman Hater. We certainly are not supposed to feel that the
cult of "manhood" affirmed in the embrace of Captain Ager and the
Colonel is being reduced to a form of latent homosexuality—still less
to Chough's wrestling match, or Trimtram's flatulent duel in IV.iv—
because the entire strategy of the hierarchic structure was shown to
elevate it above the erotic attachments of the subplot in moral value,
so that even the Colonel's sister is not regarded as a love object but
as another gift in the contest of magnanimity between the two friends,
who have heroically dedicated themselves to a "mistress" in the martial rather than the much less exacting marital arena.[3] And wrestling,
far from becoming the ultimate causal "reality" behind love and
honor, is separated still further from them. Therefore the difference
between these two uses of the equivalence pattern can be translated
into our earlier distinction: in Beaumont's comedy the positive aspect
of the equation was emphasized for a reductive or parodic purpose,
in this case directed at both plots (since both protagonists deviated
from the standard), but in Middleton's tragicomedy, because the negative aspect is paramount, the lower levels of the equation serve as foils
to the higher—the third to the second and first, and the second to the
first. Or in Freudian terms we might say that Gondarino's and Lazarello's humors were treated as obsessive repressions of sexuality which
made them inferior to the adult norm represented by Oriana and
Valore, whereas the "fellowship of honor" achieved by Captain Ager
and the Colonel is a noble sublimation of their libidinal energies resulting in a more exalted fulfillment than the normal marriage of
Jane and Fitzallen.

The Atheist's Tragedy sets up a still more complex equivalence of
this sort including both positive and negative dimensions, through
which its three levels of criminality are integrated and contrasted to
the virtuous union of Charlemont and Castabella. It was shown in
Chapter 3 that the analogical relationship of these levels depends
on their common form as villain-hero plots; but this form must in-

[3] Ager refers to "victory, our mistress" in III.i.56 and the Colonel calls war "my
mistress" in V.i.441.

here in some specific "matter" or area of experience. The area of the second and third plots is sexual, of course, and in the first it might appear to be financial, since D'Amville's immediate goal is the accumulation of wealth. However, relatively little is seen of this (except for a brief episode in V.i where he worships gold in the manner of Volpone), nor is that surprising in an age when such a motive was usually regarded as comic material. Instead his villainy is made more serious by subordinating the avarice to his master plan to found a dynasty (thus associating him with the ambitious "politicians" of the more typical dramas of this genre), by treating that plan as the outgrowth of his atheism, and by having it lead him very quickly to kill his brother, Montferrers. This act is decisive in that it irrevocably commits the plot early in its course to a tragic denouement and at the same time precipitates the central conflict with Charlemont that will bring it about. And because of this it is established as the "matter" of the first level, which can therefore be related to the other two by the equation of lust and murder.

That equation is built into the action itself, for each of the major plots assimilates the material of the other: D'Amville's ambitious plan leads to his attempted rape of Castabella, but this is motivated by calculated "policy" rather than by the lust that impels Levidulcia; and her lustful liaison ends in the killing of Sebastian and Belforest, although this is not premeditated like D'Amville's murder of Montferrers but is a crime of passion. It also appears in the language—for example, in such key terms as "the deed," which is used interchangeably for copulation and killing,[4] or "blood," which becomes either the seat of sexual energy or the emblem of violent death, as can be seen in the parallel between Levidulcia's advice to Snuffe:

> Tush, you mistake the way into a woman;
> The passage lies not through her reason but her blood
> (I.iv.65–66)

and Belforest's challenge to Sebastian:

> Villain, give me way,
> Or I will make my passage through thy blood
> (IV.v.56–57) [5]

Still more striking is the metaphorical conjunction of the two subject matters at moments of great emotional pressure, especially in D'Amville's exultant peroration to his crime:

---

[4] E.g., II.v.152; IV.ii.24; IV.iii.222; IV.v.6, 83.
[5] See also IV.v.64–65, 90–91, and V.ii.24–25 on the causal connection between "lust" and the "blood" of murder.

> Now farewell black night,
> Thou beauteous mistress of a murderer
> (II.iv.178–79)

and in his much admired soliloquy in the churchyard where he recalls that earlier scene:

> And that bawd,
> The sky there, she could shut the windows and
> The doors of this great chamber of the world,
> And draw the curtains of the clouds between
> Those lights and me about this bed of earth,
> When that same strumpet, Murder, and myself
> Committed sin together. Then she could
> Leave us i' the dark till the close deed
> Was done, but now that I begin to feel
> The loathsome horror of my sin and, like
> A lecher empty'd of his lust, desire
> To bury my face under my eyebrows and
> Would steal from my shame unseen, she meets me
> I' the face with all her light corrupted eyes
> To challenge payment o' me.
> (IV.iii.215–29)

and in his dying words after that "payment" has been exacted:

> The lust of death commits a rape upon me,
> As I would ha' done on Castabella.
> (V.ii.267–68)

Levidulcia's own death speech confirms this equation, in very similar language, when she blames the murder of Sebastian and Belforest on "my shame," "my deed" of "light lust," and acknowledges that her suicide will be "As full of horror as my life of sin" (IV.v.62–86). Only now the situation is reversed: D'Amville's "shame" or "deed" or "sin" was his fratricide, which he figuratively relates to illicit sex, while she uses these terms to denote her adultery, which has literally caused the deaths of her husband and lover.

The equivalence of lust and murder is also asserted in what might be called the "visual imagery" of the action, most notably in the sequence of alternations and transitions from one plot to another leading up to and through the churchyard scene (IV.iii). The sequence begins with the episode in Cataplasma's house of assignation (IV.i), which opens upon the grisly iconography of Soquette's embroidery (suggesting the lethal aspect of sexuality and so preparing for the subplot catastrophe) and closes by sending Snuffe and Soquette out to the graveyard as the surrogates for Sebastian and Levidulcia. In IV.ii we return to the main action to find D'Amville planning the seduction of Castabella and murder of Charlemont, which again couples the two subject matters. Then in the following scene in the graveyard these different levels and their materials are brought together on the stage in a dramatic fusion of the carnal and the charnel. The locale is itself significant, not only because it is the abode of death, but also because it is regarded as especially suitable for both kinds of crime: D'Amville persuades Borachio to kill Charlemont there since "The place is unfrequented" and will be "favour'd by the darkness of the night" (IV.ii.21, 25); Snuffe overcomes Soquette's objections by assuring her it is "verily a convenient unfrequented place . . . under the close curtains of the night" (IV.iii.53–54); and later D'Amville tells Castabella "The dead men's bones" invite them to copulate (ll. 155–57). And the action here consists of a series of rapid oscillations between sex and death. First Borachio tries to kill Charlemont and is killed by him. Next Soquette is led in by Snuffe, who to avoid detection disguises himself as the ghost of the slain Montferrers (providing some comic interference with his lovemaking, and another connection of lust and murder); but before he can complete his business they are frightened off by Charlemont holding a drawn sword. Then D'Amville attempts to rape Castabella and is routed by Charlemont, who now appears in the disguise abandoned by Snuffe, as the ghost of the man D'Amville killed. And the most macabre junction occurs when Snuffe, returning to find Soquette, mistakes Borachio's corpse for her and addresses it:

> Verily thou liest in a fine premeditate readiness for the purpose. Come, kiss me, sweet Soquette.
>
> (ll. 206–7)

At the end of the scene Charlemont and Castabella are discovered asleep side by side in the graveyard and arrested for committing adultery and killing Borachio. It was pointed out in Chapter 3 that this false accusation, in the particular context, actually emphasizes their innocence (it also prepares us by analogy for Belforest's true accusation of his wife and Sebastian in the next scene); but the episode has an additional function—it marks the penultimate stage in the identification of this couple with another very different version of the love-death equation in which the love is completely chaste and the death completely honorable. This version of the basic equivalence has also developed out of the action of their plot and becomes a major element in the idealization of their relationship. It was introduced in I.iv where Castabella defended Charlemont's going to war, at the "hazard of his blood and life" (as Snuffe complained), by insisting that this increased her love for him, and reappeared in her speech in III.i at the monument erected to him upon the report of his death. The churchyard scene presents it still more vividly, because their sleeping together among the skulls suggests at once a symbolic (and asexual) marriage and a symbolic death. But the definitive connection is made in the closing scene when they leap on the scaffold and prepare to meet death there "hand in hand"—a fate which is now viewed as a welcome culmination of their love that preserves its purity:

> Our lives cut off
> In our young prime of years are like green herbs
> Wherewith we strew the hearses of our friends,
> For as their virtue gather'd when th' are green,
> Before they wither or corrupt, is best,
> So we in virtue are the best for death
> While yet we have not liv'd to such an age
> That the increasing canker of our sins
> Hath spread too far upon us.
>
> (V.ii.132–40)

This conception of a heroic love fulfilled in a heroic death draws upon the metaphorical association, common enough in the period, of copulating with dying. Here the metaphor is certainly not exploited for its usual bawdy connotations (which are reserved for the criminal form of the equation), yet the sexual undertone is not to be dismissed; it is essential to the validation of their sacrifice, since value in this context, as in the main plot of *A Fair Quarrel,* is earned by the sublimation of erotic instinct to a higher end. The final turn of the action, to be sure, converts their virginal *Liebestod* into a conventional marriage with the conventional rewards—the inheritance of the D'Amville, Montferrers, and Belforest estates; but this means that there are really two alternative endings so that Tourneur can have it both ways, giving Charlemont and Castabella a normal sexual consummation and yet elevating them far above this norm through the ultimate transcendence of love-in-death, just as D'Amville, Levidulcia, and Snuffe are debased far below it—and related to each other—by the lust-murder version of the same equation.

So far as I know this kind of equivalence plot is unique in Renaissance drama, but the equation of love and honor (or chastity and courage) figures in a number of plays, two of which provide instructive contrasts to *A Fair Quarrel.* Both actions of Heywood's *A Challenge for Beauty* are triangular situations built around a contest or "challenge": in the main plot between Queen Isabella and Hellena, with the life of Hellena's betrothed, Bonavida, at stake; in the subplot between Valladaura and Ferrers, Hellena's brother, with the hand of Petrocella as the prize. During these contests Hellena and Ferrers (who represent England in this Iberian setting) are severely oppressed by Isabella and Valladaura, but they eventually prove their worth and emerge triumphant to reap identical rewards—the capitulation of their admiring rival and marriage to their beloved, Bonavida and Petrocella. The formal analogy integrating the two actions (which also includes parallels between Isabella and Petrocella in I.i–ii,[6] and between Petrocella's father and Hellena's mother in I.ii–II.i) thus equates the values at issue in them, which are differentiated by sex along the same lines as *A Fair Quarrel*. The female contest of the main plot centers on "virtue" or chastity (it is also supposed to be a contest of beauty, as the title promises, but no action comes of that); to win it the Queen has a courtier swear he slept with Hellena, and on the strength of this orders the execution of Bonavida, who challenged her own preëminence in this arena, but Hellena arrives in time to refute her accuser, rescue her champion, and receive her opponent's surrender. The male contest of the subplot, variously defined in terms of "fidelity," "gratitude," "noble courtesies," "noble passages of honor," and the "unmatch'd courtesies/ In honor's duel,"[7] begins on a question of "valor" (since Ferrers defeated Valladaura in battle and their courtship of Petrocella at first seems to turn on this), but is soon transformed, when Valladaura ransoms Ferrers from slavery and befriends him, into a series of "trials" of Ferrers's ability to fulfill his obligation to this friendship at the expense of his love for Petrocella: he must trick her into marrying Valladaura, perform the ceremony himself, and then spend the wedding night with her without engaging "so much as in a kiss," after which Valladaura grants him the victory and the girl. And the equivalence of the values of these plots is established not only by their parallel structures but also by the double resolution, for Ferrers's final test involves his own chastity, and when his sister's pretended admission of the charge against her leads him to call her a strumpet, he is challenged to a duel by Valladaura, who has found him "so noble" that he cannot believe "any of thy line,/ Can ever stand polluted," which convinces him to accept Hellena's chastity solely on the ground of Valladaura's friendship.

More obviously than in *A Fair Quarrel*, masculine honor here requires the sublimation of sexuality, since this is the whole point of the tests Ferrers must undergo. On first agreeing to win Petrocella for Valladaura, who appealed to him in "the name of friend," he affirms that "Honor should still precede love"; Valladaura warns him that the second trial, the wedding ceremony, will "shake thine honor";

---

[6] See Freda Townsend, "The Artistry of Thomas Heywood's Double Plots," *PQ*, 25 (1946), 106–8.
[7] IV.i.p.50; IV.iii.p.57; V.i.p.61.

and in the third he goes off to Petrocella's bed with a punning statement of the inverse relationship between sex and honor: "How e'er
I set, I'll rise bright honor's son." Therefore in Valladaura's fervent
praise of Ferrers his suppression of normal male instinct is seen as an
extraordinary kind of "valor" which is "beyond the strength/ Of man
to act," and makes him something "more than man" who has done
"far more than ever was in man" and has "more deity/ Than man
within him." Unlike *A Fair Quarrel,* however, this cult of friendship
and honor is not raised above romantic love by the inter-plot equation. Even within the honor plot Petrocella has a much more significant role than the Colonel's nameless, faceless sister, because she is
the source and goal of the opposition between the men, whose love
for her gives meaning to their contest and to their special virtue. And
Hellena is a much more exalted figure than Jane; her chastity is supposed to be as absolute as her brother's valor and as wonderful in
her sex, making her the match for a queen, and it is placed in the
main plot that begins and ends the play (whereas Jane's chastity, such
as it was, was relegated to the subplot), although there is very little
distance between the two actions either in their dramatic importance
or in their bombastic and preposterously "heroic" tone.[8] This near
equality of the plots is in fact further evidence of the coördinate
elevation of the virtues which are exemplified by these two English
paragons and equated by the double structure, as the summary at the
end tells us:

> Spain, show thy justice; now where, or from whence,
> Canst thou desire so rare a precedent:
> Wouldst thou see beauty? look upon that face;
> Or virtue? here, see thy true innocence;
> Valor in him, true nobleness in them all;
> And happy them, that naked of all these,
> Hath sent thee hither foreign precedents,
> For instruction and example.

(V.ii.p.77)

Although Shakespeare's *Troilus and Cressida* is of course an infi-
nitely superior work, it can be compared to *A Challenge for Beauty*
because it constructs the same love-honor equation between plots
which are, again, practically equal in importance and tone (so that
we will not even try to determine which is primary). Empson and a
number of other critics have shown that the play sets up a connection
between the subject matters of the "love" plot of Troilus and Cressida
and the "war" plot of the Greek and Trojan forces, but their explana-

---

[8] Swinburne, one of the play's few admirers, says "they can hardly be described as
plot and underplot" (*The Age of Shakespeare* [London, 1908], p. 230).

tions of this connection have usually settled upon the fact that the war itself was initiated by another "love" action, Paris's abduction of Helen from Menelaus, which parallels the Diomedes-Cressida-Troilus triangle.[9] This does not seem adequate, however, for while Helen's status is continually alluded to and even debated at length in the Trojan council scene, it is not what the war plot is about. Paris, Helen, and Menelaus are minor and essentially static characters whose relationship undergoes change only before the play begins and after it ends. Their story therefore is not really a plot at all but what might be called, to borrow a term used by Harry Levin in a somewhat different sense, an "overplot," [10] a kind of "unmoved mover" that generates the activity of the drama and serves as a fixed point of reference for it.

The actual war plot focuses not on Paris and Menelaus but on Hector and Achilles, the greatest warriors of the opposing armies; it begins in I.iii with Hector's challenge to the Greeks and the scheme of the Greek generals to make use of this opportunity to goad Achilles into battle, and reaches its climax when these two finally clash in V.viii. Thus the equation of war and love must depend on an analogy between their conflict and that of Troilus and Diomedes. It may not be immediately apparent since there is no one equivalent to Cressida in this conflict, but that is because Hector and Achilles are contending for the value itself at issue here—martial honor—which is not embodied in a person yet plays the same role in their action as the love-object in Troilus's. The overplot then would parallel *both* of these actions, for in it the honor of two nations has been invested in the possession of a woman who is loved by two men. The complete structure combines three oppositions between Trojan and Greek, which can be transcribed in the usual manner into a series of ratios indicating the relations of the principal characters in the inter-plot analogy and of the values in the inter-plot equation.

Overplot   Paris (Troy) : Helen (love/honor) : Menelaus (Greece) ∼
War plot   Hector : honor : Achilles ∼
Love plot   Troilus : Cressida (love) : Diomedes

And this scheme is confirmed by the final battle, where we are shown in rapid succession the encounters between Troilus and Dio-

9 "Double Plots," pp. 34–42. For some recent attempts to explain the plot combination in terms of an abstract theme see Una Ellis-Fermor, " 'Discord in the Spheres': The Universe of *Troilus and Cressida*," *The Frontiers of Drama* (London, 1945); L. C. Knights, "The Theme of Appearance and Reality in *Troilus and Cressida*," *Some Shakespearean Themes* (London, 1959); and Norman Rabkin, "Self Against Self," *Shakespeare and the Common Understanding* (New York, 1967).
10 "The Shakespearean Overplot," *RD*, 8 (1965), 63–71. He locates the overplot of *Troilus and Cressida* in "those principles of social and cosmic order which Ulysses enunciates."

medes (V.iv, vi), Paris and Menelaus (V.vii), and Hector and Achilles (V.vi, viii).

As in the other equivalence plots, each of the two actions appropriates the subject matter of the other to its own purposes. The war enters into every stage of the love story: when we first see Troilus he is holding back from battle because of his unrequited passion for Cressida (I.i); her interest in him is related to his military prowess (I.ii); they are separated by the exchange of prisoners (III.iii); he learns of her infidelity when Hector's duel brings him to the Greek camp (V.ii); and he reacts to it, in a direct reversal of his conduct in the opening scene, by dedicating himself to carry on the war with still greater fury (V.ii–iv). Love is almost as important in the war plot: Hector sends his challenge "To rouse a Grecian that is true in love" to defend his mistress (I.iii); Achilles withdraws from combat because of his love for Priam's daughter, Polyxena, and for his tent-mate Patroclus (the two attachments are pointedly juxtaposed at III.iii.191–225 and again at V.i.17–49); and he is finally impelled into battle to avenge the death of his "masculine whore" at Hector's hands (V.v). Moreover, we are constantly reminded that this entire conflict and the honor at stake in it hinge upon the sexual triangle of the overplot.

The principal means of establishing the equation, however, is the detailed parallel worked out between the two lines of action, particularly between the two Trojans. Hector is the oldest and Troilus the youngest of King Priam's sons, and they share a special prominence within the royal family. During the council scene (II.ii) they lead the two sides of the debate, each seconded by one of his brothers (Hector by Helenus, Troilus by Paris). The main function of the brief interchange between the Greeks and Trojans preceding the duel in IV.v is to place them in the same category, for immediately after Aeneas's speech in praise of Hector, Ulysses reports his words in praise of Troilus, which conclude with an explicit comparison of the two (and another equation of love and honor):

> Manly as Hector, but more dangerous,
> For Hector in his blaze of wrath subscribes
> To tender objects, but he in heat of action
> Is more vindicative than jealous love.
> They call him Troilus, and on him erect
> A second hope, as fairly built as Hector.
> Thus says Aeneas . . .
>
> (IV.v.104–10)

And this is borne out in the last scene following Hector's death, when Troilus, inflamed by "vindicative" rage at the infidelity of his beloved, seems to be taking over his brother's role as head of the Trojan forces.

It is in their relationship to the specific virtue implicated in their respective plots that the parallel between the brothers is most significant, since this is the focus of each plot and the basis of the equation. They are the idealists of the play, Troilus the true lover and Hector the true knight of honor, and in the end their ideals are shattered by the actions of their Greek adversaries, Diomedes and Achilles. This equivalence is demonstrated very effectively in the aftermath of the duel, for Hector and Troilus are the only Trojans invited to the Greek camp, and while there they come into contact with these adversaries in terms of these values. Hector is entertained by Achilles, in what looks like a display of chivalric courtesy, and after accompanying his brother to the entrance of Achilles' tent, Troilus in the following scene goes to seek Cressida in the tent of her father. But the "honor" to be found in the first visit is as false as the "love" found in the second. Achilles, who before the visit insolently boasted to Hector that he would kill him in battle (IV.v.242–46), prepares to feast him with the explanation:

> I'll heat his blood with Grecian wine tonight,
> Which with my scimitar I'll cool tomorrow.
> (V.i.1–2)

And Troilus sees Cressida give his love-token to Diomedes, whom he likewise swears to kill in battle the next day (V.ii.163–76). During the final conflict in V.iv–ix he does not achieve his purpose, but Achilles does by having the Myrmidons attack his disarmed foe, so that this betrayal of Hector and the ideal of honor is made the counterpart in the war plot of the preceding betrayal of Troilus and the romantic ideal in the other action. The parallel also includes the two Greeks responsible for these betrayals, who both succeed because of their cynical rejection of the values in question, Diomedes by his brutally direct courtship and calculated show of indifference which win him Cressida's "love," Achilles by his equally brutal and direct pursuit of his goal, in which he makes use of the most dishonorable expedients to win the "honor" (in his own words, "reputation" or "fame") of conquering Hector. In each plot, therefore, Greek opportunism defeats Trojan idealism and its champion. "All's fair in love and war."

This opposition between the two attitudes is extended to characterize the nations themselves, particularly in the contrasting council-of-war scenes. In I.iii the Greek generals argue exclusively about the *means* of gaining victory, without discussing the justice of their cause, while this moral problem of the *end* of the war, rather than the means of attaining it, is the subject of the Trojan debate in II.ii. It is also

significant that the Greek camp is rent by dissension and outright dis-
loyalty, motivated not by any concern for the issues at stake but by
the leaders' petty egotism, whereas the Trojans, despite their disagreement on these issues, are all loyal to their side and each other. Yet
this scheme must not be oversimplified. Although the two Trojan
protagonists represent the "ideal" pole of the opposition, their ideals
are tainted from the start. We are quickly convinced—by Pandarus's
sordid manipulations in the first two scenes and Cressida's own admission, at the end of I.ii, of her courtship strategy (a strategy Diomedes later uses against her)—that Troilus's love is bestowed upon an
unworthy object. And Hector has engaged his honor in a war fought
for another unfaithful woman, despite his realization that "she is not
worth what she doth cost/ The holding," and that the "moral laws/
Of nature and of nations speak aloud/ To have her back returned"
(II.ii.51–52, 184–86). So our feeling that both men have been mistaken
in the commitment of their ideals is reinforced by the obvious parallel
between Cressida's infidelity and Helen's, which is one of the principal contributions of the overplot.

A similar qualification must be made with respect to the Greek
side of the opposition, on the basis of the very interesting and almost
self-contained sequence centering on the duel of Hector and Ajax.
Hector's original challenge, conveyed by Aeneas, is a direct appeal
to the ideal of honor and the ideal of love:

> If there be one among the fair'st of Greece
> That holds his honor higher than his ease,
> That seeks his praise more than he fears his peril,
> That knows his valor and knows not his fear,
> That loves his mistress more than in confession
> With truant vows to her own lips he loves,
> And dare avow her beauty and her worth
> In other arms than hers—to him this challenge . . .
> To rouse a Grecian that is true in love.
> If any come, Hector shall honor him.
> (I.iii.265–72, 279–80) [11]

And it is answered by Agamemnon in the same spirit:

> This shall be told our lovers, Lord Aeneas.
> If none of them have soul in such a kind,
> We left them all at home. But we are soldiers,
> And may that soldier a mere recreant prove
> That means not, hath not, or is not in love!
> (ll. 284–88)

---

[11] The same play on the two senses of "arms" was found in *A Fair Quarrel*, I.i.134–
35, 183, where it also connected the honor and the love plots.

What we have here is a temporary assimilation not only of the two values of the double-plot equation, which are fused in this single code of knighthood, but also of the two contending armies who find a common ground in their mutual acceptance of that code. It is true that Ulysses then proceeds to exploit the situation by his politic scheme to play off Ajax against Achilles; but the duel itself (in IV.v), ending in Hector's "embracement" of Ajax and their "loving interview," is a model of knightly conduct, as is the elaborate exchange of compliments and courtesies between Greeks and Trojans just before the event and after it.

Except for providing Troilus with the opportunity to eavesdrop on Cressida and Diomedes, which could easily have been managed in another way, the duel has little effect on the subsequent action; its primary function is not to further the plot but to produce this brief flowering of the chivalric ideal so that we can respond properly when we see it destroyed by Achilles' cowardly murder in Act V (hence the one sour note in the episode is sounded by his threatening speech referred to above). And it is Agamemnon again who serves as the Greek spokesman for the ideal in his very moving evocation of the preciousness and the ephemerality of its fulfillment in this meeting:

> What's past and what's to come is strewed with husks
> And formless ruin of oblivion.
> But in this extant moment, faith and troth,
> Strained purely from all hollow bias-drawing,
> Bids thee, with most divine integrity,
> From heart of very heart, great Hector, welcome.
>
> (IV.v.166–71)

The equivalent high point in the other plot is the lovers' exchange of vows in III.ii and their parting the next morning in IV.iv, which immediately precedes the duel (and also represents a conjunction of the two values, since Troilus must surrender his love for the sake of Trojan honor). Thus Troilus's discovery of his betrayal in V.ii marks an abrupt descent from the ideal moments of both plots, and prepares us by analogy for Hector's betrayal in the battle that follows.

Although the languages of honor and of love come together on the ideal level in the sequence leading from Hector's challenge to the duel, throughout the rest of the play the verbal connections between these areas more often point to the deflation which is enacted in the two plots. They are compared as two forms of "sport," Troilus's courtship of Cressida is called a "war" or "fight," the anticipated consummation brings to his mind a "battle," and so on.[12] The most emphatic and most debasing statements of this kind are found in Thersites'

---

[12] I.i.116–18; III.ii.27–30, 54, 178–79.

running commentary on the action, which continually reduces both values to the lowest sexual terms. That is the obvious effect of his re- actions to the individual encounters of Troilus and Diomedes and of Menelaus and Paris during the final conflict—the first he sees as a squabble over a "dissembling luxurious drab" between two "wenching rogues" whom he cheers on impartially: "Hold thy whore, Grecian! Now for thy whore, Trojan!"; and the second elicits a parallel re- sponse: "The cuckold and the cuckold-maker are at it. Now, bull! Now, dog!" In his eyes the entire war is simply the same thing on a larger scale, two armies who "fight for a whore" or "war for a placket," since "All the argument is a cuckold and a whore," and he twice sums up from this perspective the equivalence that integrates the double plot: "war and lechery confound all!"; "Lechery, lechery! Still wars and lechery! Nothing else holds fashion." [13]

These comments of Thersites not only contribute to the equation of the two values and to their common degradation, but also imply a causal connection between them proceeding from "lechery" to "war," or in non-Thersitean terms, from love to honor. This implication is borne out by the sexual motivation which lies behind most of the fighting—behind the war itself, and Hector's challenge, and the in- volvement of Achilles, Troilus, Diomedes, Menelaus, and Paris in the battle of Act V. Indeed the savagery of Achilles' assault on Hector in V.viii may be explained in part by the loss of his beloved Patroclus, just as the loss of Cressida can account for Troilus's vehement criti- cism of Hector's chivalry as "a vice of mercy" (V.iii.37–49). The ar- rangement of the last act is also relevant here; the love plot really comes to an end with Troilus's disillusionment in V.ii, but that leads directly to his threat to kill Diomedes, bringing us back into the war, and it is only at this juncture that the war plot, which has remained more or less dormant so far (even the duel, we saw, was only an inter- lude that did not affect its course), suddenly is activated and takes over the remainder of the play. Thus the general momentum of this movement into the final combat, as well as the particular motives of so many of the combatants, suggests that the fighting itself is a kind of acting out of sexual frustrations. And this impression is strength- ened at the end when, immediately after his bitter denunciation of the "coward" Achilles for the act that destroyed the ideal of the honor-plot, Troilus turns to attack the "broker" Pandarus for his role in destroying the ideal of the love-plot, and then leaves him alone on stage to equate once more the degenerate forms of these two values ("O traitors and bawds") and bequeath us the disease in which both seem to terminate.

---

[13] II.iii.23, 79, 82; V.ii.196–97; V.vii.21.

Finally, we might go on to ask whether there is another dimension to this causal relationship, whether the equation not only makes war the result of love, but also makes the outcome of the war plot the result of the love plot. In a literal sense the opposite is true, for the lovers are separated by the exigencies of war; yet the "magical" associations implicit in the combination of these two lines of action reverse the literal cause and effect. Cressida's submission to Diomedes in V.ii marked the turning point from the love to the war plot, as was seen, but it is at the same time the turning point in the fortunes of the two nations. Before this the Trojans were winning, or at least holding their own—Hector seemed invincible on the battlefield and Achilles sulked in his tent; after it Achilles reënters the war, Hector falls, and Troy is doomed. Therefore, we conclude, her infidelity has something to do with Troy's destruction.[14] The inference is obviously unjustified, based as it is upon the *post hoc, ergo propter hoc* fallacy, yet that is how the logic of luck works, and in this context it takes on an added plausibility because the "Freudian" reductionism within the equation itself has prepared us to understand warfare in sexual terms. Thus we tend to feel that Troy's original military advantage was related to Paris's amatory triumph over Menelaus, who as a scorned cuckold brings bad luck to the Greek side, so that with Troilus's defeat this advantage is lost. The Trojan "love" hero has now been cuckolded by a Greek in one arena, and the magical consequence is that the Trojan "war" hero is killed by a Greek in the other arena, and that Troy will succumb to the invaders.

The causal connection then is not used to elevate one term of the equation above the other, as in *A Fair Quarrel;* their relationship, rather, is like that of *A Challenge for Beauty* insofar as they are placed on an equal footing, although here this equality is realized not in an idealization but a degradation of both to the lowest possible level. Therefore these plays can be seen as three radically different developments of the same love-honor equation, and I would argue that in each one the analysis of that equation goes to the heart of our dramatic experience. In the case of *Troilus and Cressida,* especially, this analysis has omitted many important aspects of the work, which is one of Shakespeare's most difficult,[15] but if it is valid these

14 Empson saw this connection as well as the simple equivalence: "The two parts make a mutual comparison that illuminates both parties ('love and war are alike') and their large-scale indefinite juxtaposition seems to encourage primitive ways of thought ('Cressida will bring Troy bad luck because she is bad')." I think the point is not so much Cressida's badness as the resulting horns—"Troy will be conquered because Troilus is cuckolded."

15 He uses this equation again in *Cymbeline,* in the parallel between Cymbeline's condemnation of Belarius, on the basis of perjured testimony, for treason with the Romans, and Leonatus's condemnation of Imogen on the same basis for adultery with Iachimo, although little is done with the relation of the two arenas.

should also be explicable in terms of the basic double-plot structure. And it can at least claim a certain uniqueness in the critical literature devoted to this play, in that it has not once mentioned Ulysses' speech on Degree.

II

Another interesting type of equivalence plot is found in *A Mad World, My Masters* and *Michaelmas Term,* the two plays which are usually ranked along with *A Trick to Catch the Old One* as the best of Middleton's early city comedies. They have similar structures: the main action in both is a "cony-catching" tale of a shrewd operator who relieves a gull of his property—in *A Mad World* Richard Folly-wit cheats his grandfather, Sir Bounteous Progress, and in *Michaelmas Term* the merchant Ephestian Quomodo cheats Richard Easy—while the subplot is concerned with a carnal affair, between Penitent Brothel and Mistress Harebrain in the first work and Andrew Lethe and the unnamed Country Wench in the second. In each case these two plots are linked by a few relatively unimpressive and unconvincing causal interactions, but the most significant relationship between them is the formal analogy that equates their respective subject matters—money and sex. As with so many of the other plays, this equation can be discerned in the absorption of the material of one action into the resolution of the other, for both main-plot cozeners after their economic victories over the gulls ultimately lose out to them in the sexual arena. Although he succeeds in three clever schemes to fleece his grandfather, Follywit suffers his comic discomfiture at last when he marries a supposedly "perfect maid," Frank Gullman, only to discover she is Sir Bounteous's mistress; and the estate Quomodo acquires by his brilliant entrapment of Easy must be returned because his wife, Thomasine, marries Easy immediately after his own supposed death.

Both comedies also follow the practice of the other plays in spelling out the inter-plot equation through the speeches and their imagery. Quomodo (like Lazarello with his fish) thinks of the property he hopes to steal from Easy as equivalent or even preferable to an attractive female:

> Oh, that sweet, neat, comely, proper, delicate parcel of land, like a fine gentlewoman i' th' waist, not so great as pretty, pretty . . .
>
> (II.iii.82–84)

He tells his accomplice, Shortyard, that he has just been to Essex (the site of Easy's estate), "where I have seen what I desire"; and when Shortyard asks if he means a woman, he retorts,

> Puh, a woman! Yet beneath her,
> That which she often treads on, yet commands her:
> Land, fair neat land.
>
> (I.i.99–101)

Later he reveals that

> I am as jealous of this land as of my wife.
>
> (IV.i.110–11)

And after learning she has slept with Easy, he comforts himself:

> He does devise all means to make me mad,
> That I may no more lie with my wife
> In perfect memory; I know't, but yet
> The lands will maintain me in my wits;
> The land will do so much for me.
>
> (V.iii.64–68)

But the jealous husband of Mistress Harebrain reverses this personification; he thinks of her chastity as one of his household possessions that must be protected from burglars, and even hires watchmen to stand guard over his home for this purpose:

> The truth is, there is a cunning plot laid, but happily discovered, to rob my house . . . Let me not be purloin'd— [*aside*] purloin'd indeed; the merry Greeks conceive me.— There is a gem I would not lose, kept by the Italian under lock and key . . .
>
> (I.ii.8–9, 19–21)

And Brothel later adapts this image to his description of a prostitute:

> He that kept open house now keeps a quean.
> He will keep open still that he commends,
> And there he keeps a table for his friends;
> And she consumes more than his sire could hoard,
> Being more common than his house or board.
>
> (IV.iv.65–69)

We will see that these opposing conceptions of the equivalence of women and property take on a special significance in the main plot of *Michaelmas Term* and the subplot of *A Mad World,* but both plays also include many incidental figures which simply point to a general relationship between the two areas of experience. In *A Mad World* sexual and financial indulgence are metaphorically connected in IV.i.4–5 and IV.iii.83–91, and again in Follywit's bawdy joke about the money he has just stolen from Sir Bounteous:

It came somewhat hard from him at first, for indeed nothing comes stiff from an old man but money; and he may
well stand upon that when he has nothing else to stand
upon.

(II.iv.59–64)

In *Michaelmas Term,* which has still more of this, bankruptcy is
compared to a virgin's defloration (I.ii.41–44), keeping a mistress to
leasing property (III.i.146–47), poverty to syphilis (III.i.257–58), de-
faulted debts to "the offsprings of stol'n lust" (III.iv.152–56), and a
man envying Quomodo's wealth to

an old lecher, girt in a fur'd gown,
Whose mind stands stiff, but his performance down.

(III.iv.10–11)

We are even given a riddle to this same effect:

Porters' backs and women's bellies bear up the world.—
'Tis true, i' faith; they bear men and money, and that's
the world.

(II.iii.320–22)

and a proverb:

being the world's beaten word, what's got over the devil's
back (that's by knavery) must be spent under his belly
(that's by lechery).

(IV.i.86–88)

It must be acknowledged again that locutions of this sort, like those
linking sex and food or sex and war, are quite common in the dramatic dialogue of the period and in everyday speech ("Not for love
or money"). In these two plays, however, they are drawing attention
to an equation that has been built into the structure itself through
the formal analogy integrating the separate plots.

This analogy is more obvious in *A Mad World, My Masters* because
the subplot belongs to the same genre as the main action; it is also (at
least up to the denouement) a straightforward comedy of intrigue
pitting a wit against a gull, Penitent Brothel against Master Harebrain, only here the wit seeks the gull's wife instead of his wealth,
thereby equating these two prizes. The parallel between the wits is set
forth in the opening scene, where Follywit plans his robbery of
Bounteous with his accomplices, Mawworm and Hoboy, and then is
greeted by Brothel, who proceeds to plan the cuckolding of Harebrain with his accomplice, Frank Gullman, after first comparing his
own immoral designs to Follywit's comic "pranks." And it is then

developed in the details of their two careers: they both work out complicated schemes to deceive their victims, requiring the use of disguises; both manage by means of these schemes to fool the victims so successfully that they participate in their own deception and even reward the wits for it; as a result both attain their goals; and at the end they both suffer abrupt reversals which undercut their earlier triumphs and bring about a reconciliation with their victims—Follywit when he is told his new bride is Bounteous's mistress, and Brothel in a much more serious vein when he is converted by an encounter with a succubus and breaks off his affair with Mistress Harebrain.

The relationship between the two gull-victims, consequently, will follow from the fact that the theft of Bounteous's money and goods has been made equivalent to the seduction of Harebrain's wife, and since it was shown in the above quotation that Harebrain regards his wife's chastity as a piece of property threatened by thieves, we are invited to compare them in this respect. Their attitudes toward these objects sought by the two wits constitute their comic flaws, but the flaws are exactly opposite in nature, as we are led to expect by the parallel expository speeches of the wits in I.i in which they characterize their intended victims. Follywit reveals that his grandfather "keeps a house like his name, bounteous, open for all comers . . . and thinks himself never happier than when some stiff lord or great countess alights to make light his dishes," whereas Brothel describes Harebrain as a "sick husband" who "With a fantastic but deserv'd suspect,/ Bestows his serious time in watch and ward" over his wife.

This contrast is confirmed by our introductions to the gulls in the next two scenes, also clearly parallel, where each in turn is seen exhibiting and even boasting of his flaw. In I.ii Harebrain hires the watchmen to protect his home and, after welcoming what he takes to be a virtuous maiden come to lecture his wife on the horrors of adultery, he congratulates himself on the wisdom of his stand against visitors, adapting the idiom of finance to express his jealous inhospitality as a form of thrift:

> I'll teach the married man
> A new selected strain. I admit none
> But this pure virgin to her company;
> Puh, that's enough. I'll keep her to her stint,
> I'll put her to her pension;
> She gets but her allowance, that's a bare one.
>
> (ll. 56–61)

Then in the following scene (II.i) we find Bounteous welcoming a supposed lord and rejoicing in his hospitable talent for attracting and entertaining guests:

there's not a lord will miss me, I thank their good honors;
'tis a fortune laid upon me, they can scent out their best
entertainment; I have a kind of complimental gift given me
above ordinary country knights . . . There's a kind of
grace belongs to't, a kind of art which naturally slips from
me.

(ll. 49–56)

And it is through the exploitation of these traits that the wits succeed
in their figurative or literal burglary of the gulls' houses—as we
learn, again, from the plans of the former in the initial exposition,
and then from the actions of the latter on their first appearances. For
the "pure virgin" admitted into Harebrain's home in I.ii is Frank
Gullman, who is thus able to help Brothel "purloin" Mistress Harebrain by using the very restrictions her husband imposed upon her
(or in Brothel's words, by "Making his jealousy more than half a
wittol,/ Before his face plotting his own abuse,/ To which himself
gives aim"); and the lord admitted into Bounteous's home in II.i is
really Follywit, who in this way takes advantage of his grandfather's
opposite flaw in order to rob him—a strategy he repeats in the two
later schemes which also bring him to the house disguised as a welcome visitor (as Gullman in IV.iii and an actor in V.ii) for the same
purpose.

It is evident, therefore, that the relation between Bounteous and
Harebrain within the sex-money equation is meant to set up a contrast
of comic extremes, much like that between Gondarino and Lazarello
in *The Woman Hater,* where the two gulls, each in his own sphere,
represent antithetical but equally ludicrous departures from a common norm that has been established through the translation of one
term of the equivalence into the other. Here the translation is from
the erotic to the economic arena: Harebrain is obsessively hoarding
his property by locking up his wife's sexual "house" from the world,
while Bounteous is just as obsessive in his generosity with the pro-
visions of his "open house." And this corresponds to the social differentiation of the plots, Harebrain being a prudent, parsimonious
city Puritan of the new breed and Bounteous one of the easygoing
country gentry maintaining the ancient traditions of "housekeeping."
But in this play there is no one to represent the norm. We would
ordinarily expect to find it (as we did in *The Woman Hater* and other
comedies of intrigue) in the cleverness of the successful wits, against
which we have measured the gulls' absurdity during the course of the
action, yet the reversals at the end destroy their authority without
creating an acceptable alternative. Follywit's improbable marriage
to Frank Gullman reduces him to the level of Harebrain, who had

also mistaken her for a "pure virgin" and had also suffered cuckoldom as a result (since he placed her in a position to assist Brothel); and the standard proposed by Penitent Brothel's reformation is much too sternly moralistic to be applied retroactively to either plot, for our enjoyment of his deception of Harebrain had assumed the same sort of amoral detachment as had Follywit's trickery.[16] The problems raised by this resolution do not alter the equation itself, but they certainly qualify its effectiveness.

The formal integration of the two plots in *Michaelmas Term* is more complex and in some respects less satisfactory. Because the sub-plot is not an intrigue of wit against butt like the main action, the inter-plot analogy does not focus on that situation but on another which is not really central to either. It is developed around two sexual triangles: the contest between Quomodo and Easy for Quomodo's wife, Thomasine, in the main plot, and in the subplot between Lethe and Rearage for Quomodo's daughter, Susan. Although the actions generated by these triangles are quite different, there is a certain parallel in their outcomes; in each the woman rejects the man to whom she was originally attached (legally or emotionally) and marries the other. And this parallel is related to the structure of the play since the two men who lose out, Quomodo and Lethe, have analogous roles as the comic villain-heroes of their respective plots, so that their defeat in love constitutes part of their punishment. The same parallel is also related to the play's sociological scheme, for both Quomodo and Lethe are presented as social climbers, whereas their successful rivals, Easy and Rearage, are gentlemen born, and that distinction seems to be a crucial factor determining the attitudes of these characters and their relationships—it explains Quomodo's hostility to Easy and Rearage and his preference for Lethe as a son-in-law; it aligns Easy and Rearage on the same side; and it also figures significantly in the choices of the two women. This would suggest that these triangles are to be viewed, at least in part, as expressions of the class conflict, and because that conflict is built into the action of each plot it becomes much more important to the formal analogy connecting them, and so to the sex-money equation, than in *A Mad World* where the classes were segregated in separate plots.

The conflict had of course taken on a special urgency in Middleton's day, as a result of the economic revolution that was gradually transforming a feudal into a capitalistic society through the transfer

---

16 This reformation was anticipated by his self-castigation in I.i.80–110 (and by his name), but he and we soon forget this. (See Standish Henning's introduction to his edition of the play [Lincoln, 1965], pp. xii–xiv.) There is also some talk of a "mean" or "measure" (e.g., I.i.22, 101; III.i.14–16; IV.iv.64) which could provide a standard, but nothing comes of it.

of wealth and power from the landed gentry to the rising urban middle class.[17] In the play Easy, Rearage, and his friend Salewood are representatives of the decaying older order, as their names imply; they are country gentlemen who have abandoned their ancestral estates to become London "gallants," squandering their time and money in a way of life which is epitomized by a series of vivid genre scenes depicting three of their typical diversions—parading about the middle aisle of St. Paul's Cathedral (I.i), gambling in a tavern (II.i), and courting a harlot (III.i). Just as clearly their opponents, Quomodo and Lethe, represent the newly emerging order, although they have different places in it. Quomodo is the ambitious "citizen" entrepreneur engaged in accumulating capital at the expense of the gentry and clambering up the social ladder by making his son a lawyer, marrying his daughter to Lethe to secure a "friend at Court," and most important, acquiring Easy's country estate that will establish him in his new station. He is quite explicit about all this, especially in the sharply etched domestic scene at the beginning of II.iii which conveys the intensity of bourgeois aspirations (in contrast to the studied hedonism of the gallants), and in the soliloquies at III.iv.2–18 and IV.i.64–77 where these aspirations reappear in fantasy form.

Lethe is also distinguished from the gallants, through the tension evoked by his presence in the three episodes just mentioned which focus on them, but his presence there distinguishes him as well from the middle-class merchant. He is the "adventurer" or "upstart," of humbler birth than Quomodo, who because of the dislocations of the time has been able to rise higher than him, not by economic enterprise but by the more rapid route of sycophancy and influence-peddling. His assumed name suggests this, for while it may involve a pun on the Scotch river Leith,[18] its primary reference is to the river of forgetfulness and hence to the tendency of the social upstart to deny his origins. And it points beyond that to a more profound forgetfulness which is revealed in Lethe's explanation of his failure to recognize the gallants he dined with the night before:

> Oh, cry you mercy, 'tis so long ago,
> I had quite forgot you; I must be forgiven.
> Acquaintance, dear society, suits, and things
> Do so flow to me,

---

17 See Laurence Stone, *The Crisis of the Aristocracy, 1558–1641* (Oxford, 1965), and Brian Gibbons's account of the general relation of this change to the drama in *Jacobean City Comedy* (London, 1968), which supplies a useful corrective to L. C. Knights's *Drama and Society in the Age of Jonson* (London, 1937).

18 Baldwin Maxwell shows that Lethe is a caricature of the Scots who followed James I to England to make their fortunes ("Middleton's *Michaelmas Term*," *PQ*, 22 [1943], 33–35).

That had I not the better memory,
'Twould be a wonder I should know myself.

(I.i.166–71) [19]

and again later in the reply of his mistress, the Country Wench (who is also trying to rise above her station by a more literal form of prostitution), when she is told her own father would not know her now:

Why, I think no less. How can he know me, when I scarce know myself?

(III.i.30–31)

This is a comic version of the idea, expressed in the Dampit scenes of *A Trick to Catch the Old One,* that the loss of one's social roots leads to a loss of identity; and it further differentiates Lethe's mode of climbing from Quomodo's, with his strong ties to class and family. But it remains undeveloped here, as does the opposition between Lethe and the gallants, which never comes into sharp focus because no meaningful code of manners is given us to separate the pretender from the gentleman.[20]

We noted that this "class angle" of the triangles affects their outcome, since it influences the decisions of both women. In the competition for them the two victors, Easy and Rearage, turn out to have a definite advantage by virtue of their social position. Thomasine makes it very clear that she prefers Rearage to Lethe as a husband for her daughter because "first, he is a gentleman" (II.iii.50); this is also a reason why she prefers Easy to Quomodo as a husband for herself. Her affection for Easy has other more important sources, but the class distinction is one of the things she has in mind when, after her marriage to him, she remarks on his superiority to Quomodo:

What difference there is in husbands, not only in one thing, but in all.

(V.i.50–51)

And it is the one thing her daughter emphasizes, at an equivalent point in the subplot, when she acknowledges Rearage's superiority to Lethe:

---

[19] Cf. I.i.266. R. C. Bald ("The Sources of Middleton's City Comedies," *JEGP,* 33 [1934], 377) suggests this is borrowed from Sir John Davies's thirty-first epigram, *In Priscum;* but the notion may be proverbial—see *A Tale of a Tub,* V.iv.24; *The Case is Altered,* V.vi.47; *What You Will,* III.i.p.260; *The Great Duke of Florence,* III.i.p.259.
[20] See Kathleen Lynch, *The Social Mode of Restoration Comedy* (New York, 1926), chap. 2. One has only to compare Lethe to his descendants, the Fopling Flutters, Sparkishes, and Tattles of the Restoration stage, to appreciate the importance of such a code in defining this character type.

For now the difference appears too plain
Between a base slave and a true gentleman.
(V.ii.9–10)

This is not the determining factor in either resolution, however, for the change in the feelings of both women is precipitated less by their attraction to the winners than by their alienation from the losers, which is not attributed primarily to the class status of the losers but to their involvement in another activity: it is Quomodo's scheme to steal Easy's land that first estranges Thomasine (and his feigned death, resulting from this scheme, finally frees her to marry his rival), and it is Lethe's liaison with the Country Wench that leads to his arrest and Susan's disillusionment. Therefore the analogy between the plots must be extended:

Easy : Thomasine : Quomodo : land ~
Rearage : Susan : Lethe : Country Wench

But even this formulation distorts the actual structure of the play, since the relationships indicated by these added terms, rather than the triangles, are the principal concerns of the two plots; and this means that while the triangles can provide a kind of symmetrical frame for the plot combination they cannot themselves integrate it. That integration depends upon a connection between the characteristic preoccupations of the two villain-heroes, which is not worked out in parallel actions, as in *A Mad World,* but is established through the same sex-money equation.

The equivalence of the areas is announced in the Induction, where we are told the coming Term will be devoted to legal skulduggery (the basis of Quomodo's intrigue) and whoring, and again in the brief interchange between Rearage and Salewood that opens Act I by linking these subjects, and we found it embedded in the language and imagery of the play, most significantly in the passages quoted earlier revealing Quomodo's tendency to think of the estate he yearns for as a sexual object or substitute—a metaphorical identification which is borne out very literally in the denouement of the main plot itself, for Quomodo's financial success in winning Easy's land is completely canceled out by Easy's romantic success in winning Quomodo's wife. The nature of these connections would indicate that this equation also resolves one of its terms into the other, in the same manner as *A Mad World* but in the opposite direction, translating with Quomodo from "land" into "woman," instead of with Harebrain from "wife" into "property." The result is to relate the protagonists of the two plots through another contrast of extreme deviations from a common norm which, since it is based on this translation, will be in the sexual arena, where Lethe's flaw is seen as an excess (evinced not only in his affair with the Country Wench but also in his advances to Thomasine), and Quomodo's as a deficiency. And these flaws, so defined, explain the failure of these men in their respective triangles: Susan rejects Lethe because she "loath[es] the sin he follows" (V.iii.117), and her mother finds the most compelling "difference . . . in husbands" in the fact that Quomodo

> ne'er us'd me so well as a woman might have been us'd,
> that's certain; in troth, 't'as been our greatest falling out.
>   (IV.iii.54–56) [21]

In this play, unlike *A Mad World,* there are characters to represent the norm—the two gallants who, because they strike a happy mean between lust and debility, are able to defeat their opponents in the romantic contests and consequently in the other sphere as well, Rearage by getting the dowry and Easy by recovering his lands. However, this economic victory of Easy's poses some serious problems. There is no adequate preparation for Quomodo's sudden decision in IV.i to stage his own death (à la Volpone), which brings about his downfall, or for his sudden attack of stupidity in signing the "memorandum" in V.i, or for the sudden surrender of his accomplice, Shortyard, earlier in that scene, or for Easy's sudden acquisition of the strength and acumen necessary to outmaneuver the two of them. But the difficulty goes beyond this lack of probability to the emotional basis of the action. We are expected to side with Easy and enjoy his triumph, that being the response called for by the inter-plot equation, and by the convention on which this plot is formed, where the central conflict is between an improvident youth and a wealthy older man. Yet the long complication has given us such a vivid sense of Quomodo's and Shortyard's brilliant mastery of the situation, and of Easy's passive gullibility, that our sympathies tend to reverse. An attempt is made to rectify this at the end by insisting that Quomodo is justly caught in his own trap ("Thou art thine own affliction, Quomodo") and by rehabilitating his victim ("But for Easy,/ Only good confidence did make him foolish,/ And not the lack of sense, that was not it"), but we are never wholly persuaded that we should be pleased by the defeat of the man whose cleverness has been the chief source of our pleasure, or by the victory of one of the weakest and least interesting characters of the play. It was seen that the main plot of *A Mad World* ran into the same problem, but with the age scheme inverted, for Follywit successfully cheats his grandfather

---

21 Compare her earlier complaint, "Why am I wife to him that is no man?" (II.iii.206), where the primary reference is to Quomodo's inhumanity in the financial realm but the sexual meaning is also implied.

throughout the complication and then abruptly succumbs because of a blunder that again violates our sense of probability and our emotional set. *A Trick to Catch the Old One* also follows the formula of a battle of wits between generations, wherein the crafty deceiver ironically brings about his own downfall, but avoids this difficulty by having Lucre's cozening of Witgood take place before the play begins, so that the representation is given over entirely to the shrewd countertrick by which Witgood turns the tables on his uncle, who becomes his "own affliction," like Quomodo, when he is made to outsmart himself. This is surely the best arrangement of the three, since if Lucre's original swindle had been depicted at length and Witgood's retaliatory scheme relegated to the final scenes, we would have had the same disconcerting shift in sympathy and credibility that is experienced in *Michaelmas Term*.

Although the resolutions of the two plays thus suffer from similar structural defects, the treatment of the equivalence itself in the relationship between Quomodo's financial success and sexual failure at the close of *Michaelmas Term* involves something more fundamental than the simple translation found in *A Mad World*. There appears to be a causal connection here, for while Quomodo's inferiority to Easy in bed may reflect his age, it is also presented as a consequence of his exclusive concentration on business. The speeches quoted above in which he viewed the land as an alternative to a woman suggest that these are competitive and incompatible interests. Indeed, the play seems to assume the existence of a law of inverse proportion governing man's moneymaking and lovemaking, a law given a universal application in the Induction:

> I think it be a curse both here and foreign,
> Where bags are fruitful'st, there the womb's most barren;
> The poor has all our children, we their wealth.
>
> (ll. 21–23)

and still more explicitly in the words of Shortyard, speaking in the guise of a wealthy alderman's deputy:

> We could not stand about it, sir; to get riches and children
> too, 'tis more than one man can do. And I am of those
> citizens' minds that say, let our wives make shift for chil-
> dren and they will, they get none of us; and I cannot think
> but he that has both much wealth and many children, has
> had more helps coming in than himself.
>
> (IV.i.33–38)

If this is true, it would explain why the outcome of the main-plot triangle could be attributed both to Quomodo's economic excess and to his sexual deficiency, since one implies the other. And the same law would explain why Easy, who is no match for his rival in the ability to "get riches," towers over him in the ability to "stand."

This law of inverse proportion is related to several primitive ideas which were widely held at the time and are still very much with us. One is the belief in some principle of "compensation" that operates through heredity to ensure an equitable distribution of natural endowments and handicaps (seen in various fairy tales and in our own stereotypes of the dumb athlete or blonde, and of the scrawny male or ugly female intellectual), or in later life through some supernatural agency ("lucky in cards, unlucky in love")—both possibilities are assumed by Rosalind and Celia in their discussion of the benefits the "good housewife Fortune" bestows on women:

> CEL. 'Tis true, for those that she makes fair she scarce makes honest, and those that she makes honest she makes very ill-favoredly.
>
> ROS. Nay, now thou goest from Fortune's office to Nature's. Fortune reigns in gifts of the world, not in the lineaments of Nature.
>
> (*As You Like It,* I.ii.40–45)

Another such belief, more relevant to this equation, is that we possess an initially undefined but limited store of life energy, so that if we expend too much of it in any one direction we will be too "weak" to perform adequately in other areas. The idea can now be found in the Freudian theory of the libido, but it was also part of the folk wisdom of the past and was applied most frequently to sexual activity, since it was regarded as the greatest drain on this source of vitality,[22] and therefore could account for the observed differences between men:

> if I were so lusty as some of my own tribe, it were no great labor to commit a burglary upon a maidenhead; but all my nourishment runs upward into brains . . .
>
> (*The Witty Fair One,* II.ii.p.24)

and even between the generations:

> An old man's generative spirit runs all into brain, and that runs after covetousness too, gets wealth not children.
>
> (*A Mad Couple Well Matched,* III.i.p.207)

This conception of psychological economy takes on a special significance in *Michaelmas Term* because of the social dimension of the play, for the opposition between the classes can also be understood

---

22 "Since each such act, they say,/ Diminisheth the length of life a day" (Donne's "Farewell to Love," ll. 24–25); cf. his "Progress of the Soul," ll. 208–10, Shakespeare's Sonnet 129 ("The expense of spirit"), *The Atheist's Tragedy,* IV.i.1–42, and *The Second Maiden's Tragedy,* I.i.49–53.

as a consequence of their commitment to mutually exclusive "expenses of spirit." The asexual acquisitive man is the merchant, too busy amassing wealth to have any energy left over for love, and the contrary traits attach to the gallant, who uses up so much energy on the pleasures of the town that none remains for his business affairs or country estate. The result is a "natural" sexual and financial competition between the two which yields another universal law, implied in the speech of Shortyard just quoted and in Quomodo's double entendre playing upon his name:

> But now to thee, my true and secret Shortyard,
> Whom I dare trust e'en with my wife;
> Thou ne'er didst mistress harm,, but master good;
> There are too few of thy name gentlemen,
> And that we feel, but citizens in abundance.
>
> (I.i.85–89) [23]

and stated very clearly by Quomodo a few lines later in a succinct summation of the role of the sex-money equation in the class conflict:

> There are means and ways enow to hook in gentry,
> Besides our deadly enmity, which thus stands:
> They're busy 'bout our wives, we 'bout their lands.
>
> (ll. 105–7)

According to this law it is also appropriate that Lethe, who is the furthest removed from any economic base and has the highest social pretensions (he claims to have a place at Court), should be the most lecherous of all the characters. We can see then why it was possible to explain the outcome of the triangles in terms of the men's social status as well as their activity in the two arenas, since, again, one implies the other.

This sociopsychological opposition does not figure in the subplot of *A Mad World*, where no attempt is made to stress the class distinction between Brothel and Harebrain, or the latter's sexual inadequacy (which presumably can be inferred from his wife's availability and his own obsessive jealousy, and perhaps by innuendo from the speech quoted earlier on restricting her "to her stint" [24]). But it is frequently exploited in Middleton's other city comedies and those of his contemporaries, although usually not through an equivalence-plot

---

23 Because of the bawdy meaning of "yard," his name provides another link between the two arenas, for its primary sense refers to the inaccurate measuring rods used by cloth-sellers to cheat customers (hence he did "master good").

24 And from the fact that an earlier version of his name, preserved in the quarto, was Shortrod—cf. Shortyard, and Sir Tristram Shorttool in *Lady Alimony*. We are also told Sir Bounteous is impotent (I.i.149–53, III.ii.85–88, V.i.102–4), but this seems to be a result of age (see II.iv.59–64, quoted above).

format. In the contest between citizen and gentleman the citizen's wife occupies a pivotal position; as a woman she is not affected by the law of inverse proportion, because she does not engage in trade herself and in the sexual act is viewed as the recipient rather than the expender of energy, yet she obviously is affected by the very different appeals of the two personality types contending for her: she has a direct interest both in improving the family fortunes by helping her husband fleece the gallant, and in satisfying her own emotional needs with the gallant at her husband's expense. Hence her decision will have more general social implications, since it determines the direction in which the money flows. If she acts on the second motive she is a conservative force funneling some of the newly acquired wealth of the bourgeoisie back to the gentry from whence it came—this is the role of Thomasine, who in effect pays Easy for his services with the lands stolen by Quomodo; and a similar exchange is the basis of the much more brutally frank relationship of the Jeweler's Wife and impoverished Knight in *The Phoenix* (she calls him her "Pleasure," he calls her his "Revenue"),[25] and of Prudence Gallipot, the apothecary's wife, and Laxton (who reneges on his part of the bargain) in *The Roaring Girl*. When governed by the first motive, however, she is an agent of social change who accelerates the rise of her own class and the decline of the class enemy. In a relatively innocent version of this process, alluded to in a number of plays,[26] the shopkeeper simply makes use of his wife's charms to lure in customers, but in its fullest development he becomes the wittol who trades her sexual favors for financial success. Such a situation is glanced at in *Michaelmas Term* in another double entendre joining the two spheres:

> Is not wholesale the chiefest merchandise? Do you think
> some merchants could keep their wives so brave, but for
> their wholesale?
>
> (IV.ii.13–15)[27]

And it is directly represented in several of Middleton's comedies: Peter Purge in *The Family of Love* is a wittol, we saw, as is Knavesby in *Anything for a Quiet Life*, and the most memorable of them all is Jack Allwit of *A Chaste Maid in Cheapside*, who for many years has

---

25 Cf. *Epicene*, II.v.122–23: "it shall give it knighthood's name for a stallion to all gamesome citizens' wives."

26 Mistress Mulligrub, the vintner's wife in *The Dutch Courtesan*, says that "a fine-fac'd wife in a wainscot carved seat is a worthy ornament to a tradesman's shop, and an attractive, I warrant; her husband shall find it in the custom of his ware"; but she operates in the other direction by loaning money to "squires, gentlemen, and knights" in exchange for "a piece of flesh" (III.iii.10–28). Cf. *A Mad Couple Well Matched*, II.i.p.186: "they but set us there for show to draw in custom."

27 In the quartos, "hole-sale."

prostituted his wife to the dissolute Sir Walter Whorehound, until their lucrative arrangement terminates, fittingly, with the knight in debtors' prison and the Allwits embarking on a new commercial enterprise with the capital they have accumulated from him. The following chapter will consider this remarkable portrayal, which is the crowning achievement of Middleton's exploration of the sex-money equation in the context of the class conflict.

That conflict was a very prominent feature of the period, but we should not be confused about the "realism" of this dramatic treatment of it, for the Elizabethans certainly did not believe the shopkeeper's wife was the key to the vast economic revolution they were witnessing. The triangle of citizen, wife, and gallant in these plays is typically surrounded with authentic detail, but it is not to be accepted as a literal transcription of reality; it is, rather, more in the nature of a myth used to express and comment on the changes taking place—a kind of sexualization of the cash nexus. But that does not mean the equation of the two areas necessarily implies a Marxist perspective in which economics becomes the fundamental "ground" and sex part of the secondary "superstructure," because this body of drama makes no doctrinaire commitment to the primacy of either (in fact we saw that the resolution of one area into the other proceeded in opposite directions in *A Mad World* and *Michaelmas Term*). It would be no less true to say that a basic psychological reality is being translated into a sociological myth. This might explain why both of these comedies reverse the standard practice with respect to the relative seriousness of the sexual underplot and financial main action. It might also explain why so many plays built on this triangle, including *Michaelmas Term,* reverse the actual historical process by allowing the representative of the older order to defeat the capitalist. We can blame that on the class bias of the playwrights, to be sure, but I think something else in involved since it is still the more satisfying outcome even for us in our thoroughly bourgeois culture. This suggests that what we are really responding to is an opposition not so much of historically delimited social classes as of universal character types crystallized around the two terms of the equation—an opposition between the "money-oriented" compulsive driven to hoard his emotional and physical "capital" and the "sex-oriented" profligate who squanders his energies and possessions for immediate gratification. And in such a confrontation the latter type seems to be inherently more congenial.

Perhaps an explanation can be found in an earlier example of this genre of comic intrigue. Many plays of Plautus and Terence depicted a contest between the same two personality types for the same two stakes, money and a woman, with the victory always going to the sex-oriented contender. However, these men were not differentiated by social status but by generation; they were father and son. Some Freudian critics have argued that the Roman formula was really a disguised fulfillment of the repressed wishes of the Oedipus complex, and we should consider whether that insight might not also apply here. The gallant in these comedies often seems almost childishly irresponsible in comparison to the citizen, who is generally much older (indeed the quotation from *A Mad Couple Well Matched* made his miserliness and sexlessness a function of age) and so can serve as a "displaced" paternal figure. (Sometimes he is actually a relative of the gallant— never his father, which would preclude any social distinction, but an uncle or other older kinsman—although then the stake is only financial because of the incest taboo.) And since the gallant gets not only his wealth but also his wife—or his daughter or niece, in another "displaced" version seen in *The Family of Love, A Fair Quarrel, A Trick to Catch the Old One,* and *A New Way to Pay Old Debts*[28]—this triangle is even closer to the Freudian paradigm than Roman comedy, where the girl is not a member of the family. Moreover, it has been asserted that the Oedipal pattern is itself related to the myths and rituals based on the cycle of the seasons, the son to the fertile spring and the father to sterile winter, so that from this perspective too our preference for the amorous gallant over the avaricious merchant seems to go beyond the particular terms of their conflict to a more universal opposition it reflects. It is impossible to prove (or disprove) this sort of theory, but we can point to at least one Renaissance dramatist who saw such a natural cycle in the effect of the sex-money equation upon the class struggle of his day:

> we that had
> Our breeding from a trade, cits, as you call us,
> Though we hate gentlemen ourselves, yet are
> Ambitious to make all our children gentlemen:
> In three generations they return again.
> We for our children purchase land; they brave it
> I' the country; beget children, and they sell,
> Grow poor, and send their sons up to be prentices.
> There is a whirl in fate: the courtiers make
> Us cuckolds; mark! we wriggle into their
> Estates; poverty makes their children citizens;
> Our sons cuckold them: A circular justice!
> The world turns round . . .
> (*The Gamester,* I.i.p.201)

---

28 In *A Trick* and *A New Way* the citizen and gallant are related but incest is avoided by giving one of them a "double" who is not in the family: Witgood takes the property of his uncle, Lucre, and the niece of Lucre's fellow usurer, Hoard; Overreach loses his property to his nephew, Wellborn, and his daughter to Wellborn's counterpart, Allworth. On this whole point see the discussion of the *Stichus* in Appendix A.

III

At this point the reader may have concluded that every equivalence plot equated some activity to sex, and he would not be so very far from right. For an explanation we have only to look at the nature of sexuality itself, which, because it is one of the most powerful and at the same time most repressed of our instincts, enters into so many different kinds of significant relationships, both analogical and causal, with so many other areas of life. But there are exceptions in the drama of the period. In Jonson's *The Staple of News,* for instance, although a sexual element is introduced (in the courting of the symbolic Lady Pecunia), it is not part of the inter-plot equation, and since that equation is also atypical in other respects an analysis of it should provide an appropriate conclusion to the survey of the equivalence structure. The older critics seem to have found this the most admirable of Jonson's later works, but that admiration was usually limited to a subordinate component of the play, the brilliant satire on the infant newspaper industry contained in the two episodes of the Staple. "It is in them alone," according to one well-known commentary, "that the claim of this drama to a place in the first rank of Jonson's comedies must rest." [29] The main plot, the story of the three Pennyboys who contend for Lady Pecunia, attracted much less of their attention, and most of them objected to what they regarded as the unfortunate combination of this generalized "allegory" on the use of wealth with the "realistic" and topical satire of the News Office, and to the resultant loss of unity in the work as a whole.

It is not surprising that more recent studies of the play, following the current trend, try to prove it really is unified; but they do this by a simple assimilation of these two parts to each other, arguing that the Staple material is also concerned with "man's greed" and so "the venting of news, like everything else in the play, falls within the orbit of that religion of money whose centre is Pecunia." [30] This view presents some serious difficulties. While it is true that the News Staple is a commercial enterprise and seeks the patronage of Pecunia, the two scenes showing its operation do not focus on avarice, like the episodes in Volpone's sickroom or Subtle's laboratory to which these critics

---

[29] C. H. Herford and Percy Simpson, *Ben Jonson,* 2 (Oxford, 1925), 178. Cf. A. W. Ward, *A History of English Dramatic Literature to the Death of Queen Anne,* 2 (London, 1899), 404; A. Thorndike, *English Comedy* (New York, 1929), p. 186; John Palmer, *Ben Jonson* (London, 1934), p. 268; F. S. Boas, *An Introduction to Stuart Drama* (London, 1946), p. 125 (he takes the Staple as the "main theme").

[30] Edward Partridge, *The Broken Compass* (London, 1958), p. 187; cf. Freda Townsend, *Apologie for "Bartholmew Fayre"* (New York, 1947), pp. 83, 85; Helena Baum, *The Satiric and the Didactic in Ben Jonson's Comedy* (Chapel Hill, 1947), p. 81; John Enck, *Jonson and the Comic Truth* (Madison, 1957), p. 217; C. G. Thayer, *Ben Jonson: Studies in the Plays* (Norman, 1963), pp. 177, 179, 182–83.

have compared them, since the dupes are not after money but news, and the men who sell it to them spend very little time contemplating their loot. Actually the emphasis throughout these scenes is not on the power of money, or any other motivation of the persons involved (most of the customers are mere blanks and even the managers are pale and undeveloped figures beside the magnificent swindlers of *Volpone* or *The Alchemist*), but on the fantastic nature of the business itself and the fantastic product it dispenses.

In terms of this emphasis and the connections of character and incident established by the action, the Staple seems to be more closely affiliated to two other components of the play than to Pecunia—two components which lend themselves even less readily to the attempt to reduce the entire comedy to a portrayal of money-worship. One is the society of "jeerers," the shabby set of pretenders to the various professions who are identified by their favorite game of insulting outsiders and each other; and the other is the Canters' College projected at the height of the festivities in Act IV. In combination with the News Office they form a triadic relationship which is seen, on the simplest level, in the overlap of characters: Cymbal, the governor of the Staple, is also "grand captain of the jeerers"; his cousin Fitton is a jeerer and one of the Staple's "emissaries" or reporters; and Canters' College is to include Fitton and Picklock, another Staple emissary, as well as the remaining jeerers—Doctor Almanac, Captain Shunfield, and Madrigal the poet. More important is the line of action that connects them in the central portion of the comedy. When Pennyboy Junior and Pecunia leave the Staple in III.ii for the Devil Tavern, Cymbal declines their invitation to join them but sends Fitton and Picklock along as his representatives; and as soon as they depart the other jeerers enter the Staple and learn where they are dining. Thus it is really the News Office that brings all these men together in Act IV in the ensemble scene at the tavern, and out of the jeering that follows from this gathering is evolved the scheme for the College. As a result of this chain of events, therefore, the three components seem to fall into place as parts of a single continuum. It is a most unusual construct since these components are not really episodes (though they are embodied in them) but conceptions, ideal entities as it were, yet together they function as a subplot which, like the Pistol scenes of *Henry V* or the Dampit scenes of *A Trick to Catch the Old One*, has an internal coherence of its own that serves to unify it and to relate it to the main action.

The Staple, the society, and the College are fundamentally similar in nature. They are all concerned exclusively with language—more specifically, with certain abuses of language—and each of them institutionalizes this concern in an organization whose sole purpose is to exploit and magnify one of these abuses. The Staple collects and sells gossip; the jeerers make a game of trading and savoring insults; the College will treat as an academic discipline the various obscurantist jargons comprehended under "canting." These organizations arrange themselves into a kind of hierarchy which corresponds to their order in the causal sequence connecting them in Acts III and IV (which is also the order of their introduction in the expository dialogue in Act I, and of their first appearances on stage [31]), and seems to be determined by several related criteria. Although all three satirize real abuses, successively more fanciful elaborations are imposed on this reality in the institutional *reductiones ad absurdum:* the idea underlying the Staple is not so far removed from the news offices of Jonson's day, or for that matter, our own; the jeering contest is based on a more extravagant conceit; [32] and most fantastic of all (though not without its bitter kernel of truth) is the university devoted to the "professing" of cant. Yet the abuses themselves are growing more universal, for journalism was at this time a new and relatively limited phenomenon, compared to the activity ridiculed in the jeerers, while we are informed in the authoritative summation of Pennyboy Canter that "All the whole world are Canters" (IV.i.56). And in their motives and consequences they become increasingly serious. The News Office simply caters to harmless childish curiosity. Jeering is less innocent and more destructive, since those who engage in it "dare to stand/ No breath of truth," as Pennyboy Canter explains, and

> Dare put on any visor, to deride
> The wretched, or with buffoon license jest
> At whatsoe'er is serious, if not sacred.
>
> (V.vi.3–4, 9–11)

But canting is worst of all because, again according to Pennyboy Canter, it deliberately divorces words from meaning ("it affects the sense it has not"—IV.iv.75), and so uses language against itself, undermining its very existence as a medium of communication.

Finally, this temporal and hierarchical arrangement of the three institutions determines their connection to the main plot. It places them in relation not only to language but also to wealth, the central issue of that plot; but here the attempt to reduce everything to the "religion of money" runs into further difficulty, for the sequence up

---

[31] In the opening episode we first hear of the Staple at I.ii.22, the jeerers at line 65, and canting at I.iii.15; the Staple itself is first seen in the second episode (I.iv–vi), the jeerers in the third (II.i–iv), and the College is proposed in IV.iv.
[32] Gifford says the game of jeering "was unquestionably played in society" at this time (*The Works of Ben Jonson* [London, 1816], 5: 263), and Knights calls it "a fashionable craze" (*Drama and Society in the Age of Jonson*, p. 219), but neither offers any evidence.

this scale is moving away from "man's greed": the Staple is in business to make money (although we saw this is not stressed), but jeering has nothing to do with money, and the College is created to give money away. The effect of these institutions upon the careers of the Pennyboys is also developed in terms of this sequence. To the young prodigal, Pennyboy Junior, the Staple is merely an incidental diversion; he visits it in I.v and again in III.i to show it to Pecunia, spends some of his money there very foolishly, and that is all. He must take Pecunia to the Staple, but the jeerers come to them at the tavern, where in the course of the drunken party they grow increasingly intimate. He shares her with them in a kind of partnership (he urges her to kiss them, they urge her to live with him); they combine forces to throw out his miserly uncle, Pennyboy Senior (at which point the merging of the two groups has progressed so far that the uncle calls Pecunia and her servants "Women jeerers" and complains of being "Jeer'd by confederacy"); and at the height of the revelry he includes them in Canters' College. And the College itself marks his greatest involvement in the "language" sequence, since he is completely identified with it as its inventor and cofounder.

A similar process can be traced in the relation of Pennyboy Senior to the first two institutions. He has only one contact with the Staple, in III.iv when Cymbal asks him for Pecunia's patronage. But the jeerers make him their target on three separate occasions arranged in an order of increasing intensity: in II.iv they visit his home to see Pecunia, and only begin their jeering game in reaction to his attack; when he appears at the tavern in IV.iii they take the offensive; and in V.v they deliberately seek him out to play their game against him. Canters' College is planned in IV.iv just after he is routed from the tavern, but even that constitutes a significant relationship, for it makes this grandiose scheme for wasting money dependent upon the violent rejection of the restraints imposed by the principle of parsimony he represents. This same sequence also holds for Pennyboy Canter, the disguised father of Pennyboy Junior. Although he accompanies his son on his two visits to the Staple, he has nothing to say to the newsmongers; but in the tavern episode he is drawn into a running quarrel with the jeerers which culminates in his demonstration that they are all canters and gives his son the idea for the College; and this in turn so exasperates him that he casts off his disguise and removes Pecunia, destroying the whole project. Then in Act V we learn that as a consequence of his intervention in the College he has also destroyed the Staple (V.i), and terrified the jeerers to the point where the news of his approach drives them from the home of Pennyboy Senior (V.v). Thus in this cumulative sequence he has by the end of the play defeated all three of the linguistic institutions.

On the causal level, then, the Staple, jeerers, and College are related to the main action through the opposition there between the prodigal Pennyboy Junior and the miserly Pennyboy Senior, for in that opposition all three institutions are lined up in their sequential order on the prodigal side. Indeed the stages of Pennyboy Junior's involvement with them, corresponding to this order, are the principal means of dramatizing his growing financial recklessness. Hence the News Office does not figure in the main plot as an example of avarice, but as the first and most innocent step in his spending spree. The jeerers, themselves former prodigals who have wasted their inheritances (which accounts for their hostility to his uncle), become his parasites and tempters on this spree, where their role is symbolized in their attempt to win over Pecunia for him by promising her complete "liberty" (IV.ii.168–75). And Canters' College is the supreme expression of his prodigality, and therefore the immediate cause of his downfall.

Although the three institutions serve this important causal function in the main action, the sequence they make up can still stand in its own right, independent of its effect on the Pennyboys. On the formal level it constitutes a separate subplot, related to the Pennyboy plot by an analogy that equates their subject matters—language and money. The emphasis of this equation is on the abuses in each area, because they are the primary concern of the individual plots and so of the parallel between them, and it is in these terms that the equation momentarily becomes an identity in the climactic fusion of the project for Canters' College, which is at the same time the greatest misuse of language and of wealth. But the equation also presents a positive norm for the two areas in the person of Pennyboy Canter, who not only speaks throughout as a chorus criticizing both kinds of abuses but also directly intervenes in both actions to rectify them—in the money-plot by converting his son and brother from their extreme aberrations to the golden mean he stands for, and in the language-plot, as was seen, by overthrowing the Staple, the jeerers, and the College.

This equivalence, like those of the other plays, is also expressed in the diction of the two plots, especially in the ironical praises heaped upon the three institutions and upon Pecunia to signify the distorted attitudes toward language and wealth. The College is called "A divine whimsy! And a worthy work,/ Fit for a chronicle . . . To all ages" (IV.iv.99–100); the jeerers "are the gallant spirits o' the age!/ The miracles o' the time!" (IV.ii.140–41); the Staple is

the house of fame, sir,
Where both the curious and the negligent,

The scrupulous and careless, wild and stay'd,
The idle and laborious, all do meet,
To taste the cornucopia of her rumors,
Which she, the mother of sport, pleaseth to scatter
Among the vulgar.

(III.ii.115–21)

And Pecunia is also divine, "The talk o' the time! th' adventure o' the age," "The Venus of the time and state," the "state and wonder/ Of these our times," who "dazzle[s] the vulgar eyes" and is courted by "All sorts of men, and all professions!"; her "bounties" or "favors" are "scattered" abroad; and winning her would be "A work of fame," a "work . . . worthy of a chronicle." [33] These similarities should not be surprising, for the institutions and Pecunia are conceived at analogous levels of symbolic abstraction. What is surprising is the number of critics who have asserted that the Staple was "realistic" and therefore of a completely different order from the "allegorical" Pecunia and her servants. But Jonson himself speaks of "the allegory" of his News Office (in his address "To the Readers" preceding Act III), and this analysis has tried to show that the Office, the jeering ritual, and the College all deal with phenomena of real life by translating them into fantastic "imagin'd structures" (IV.iv.125). Their kinship to the lady can even be seen in their common origins, although, again, the derivation of Pecunia from Aristophanes' *Plutus* has been pointed out many more times than the connection of the linguistic organizations to the thinking-factory of *The Clouds* or the female governments in *The Thesmophoriazusae* and *The Ecclesiazusae*.

Certainly there are important differences between an allegorical character engaged in literal activities and an allegorical activity carried on by literal characters. Jonson's decision to include both may have been dictated by the nature of the two subjects in the equation, money being a concrete thing and language a mode of behavior. But it more likely reflects his moral conception of them, since the right use of the former turns out to be an Aristotelian mean between two opposite extremes, and so can easily be dramatized in the contrasting mistaken ways that Pennyboy Junior and his uncle handle an "imagin'd" character personifying wealth, while the right use of the latter is not a mean [34] but a Platonic ideal of truth, which is more easily rendered through the satirical exposure of a series of "imagin'd" in-

<hr>

[33] I.vi.63, 66, 86, 93; II.i.32; II.v.34; Intermean II.18–19; III.ii.238–39; IV.ii.175; IV.iv.131–32.
[34] Larry Champion sees the golden mean as a "theme" that "radiates" through all elements of the play, including the "diseased appetite for news" (*Ben Jonson's "Dotages"* [Lexington, 1967], pp. 61, 70–71). Cf. Robert Knoll, *Ben Jonson's Plays* (Lincoln, 1964), p. 174.

stitutions symbolizing increasingly serious abuses of language. However, this is a difference between two allegorical approaches, not between allegory and realism.

Realism does enter the play, in the Intermeans of the lady critics and the two episodes in Pennyboy Junior's lodgings that begin Acts I and V. But these are meant to contrast with both the linguistic and the financial allegories of the equation—the Intermeans at the end of each act, and the Pennyboy Junior episodes in a sort of frame bounding the central portion of the play. The first scene in Pennyboy's room is pitched at a realistic level to establish a base for the fantasies to follow; and the second (which opens with his soliloquy recalling his situation in I.i) brings us abruptly down to earth after the collapse of the ultimate fantasy, Canters' College, at the end of Act IV, and then proceeds to the "fresh cheat," Picklock's scheme to defraud the Pennyboys, which does not involve Pecunia or the linguistic institutions but real money and real words (in Pennyboy Canter's deed and Picklock's confession, heard by a witness, that becomes a legal "fact" used to defeat him), and thus provides the kind of grounding for Pennyboy Junior's reform and reconciliation with his father that is needed before the action rises again to its symbolic close in the trial of Pennyboy Senior's dogs, his rescue from the jeerers, and the final disposition of Pecunia. These two framing episodes, then, tend to confirm the hypothesis developed here, for they "place" the Staple, jeerers, and College on the same plane of reality (or unreality) as Pecunia and her train, as parallel components of the comic allegory that enacts the inter-plot equation.

However, Jonson's handling of these institutions leaves something to be desired. One would think the hierarchy into which he ordered them might call for a rounding out of the descent from the College by the inclusion of a final Staple scene in Act V (presumably following the last appearance of the jeerers in V.v); at any rate, Jonson felt uncomfortable enough about this to have one of his ladies in the fourth Intermean complain of the sudden dropping of the Staple, as if to forestall criticism.[35] But his treatment of the jeerers is open to more serious objection. They never really come into focus because they must wear too many hats—as practitioners of their game, pretenders to the various professions, suitors of Pecunia, and tempters of Pennyboy Junior; and their jeering is a pretty dreary exercise com-

---

[35] In *The New Inn* he again drops his subplot before Act V and offers an excuse in the Epilogue. This play sets up the same kind of equation between two virtues embodied in parallel "imagin'd structures," with the same moral contrast: the "court" of the main plot deals with love, which emerges as a Platonic ideal, and the belowstairs "militia" with courage, defined as a "mean 'twixt fear and confidence" (IV.iv.40).

pared to the hilarious contest of "vapors" in *Bartholomew Fair* from which it derives. (This is partly a consequence of the prior failing, since much of the effectiveness of the vapors game depends on its relation to the character of Humphrey Wasp, as we will see, whereas the jeerers have no character to exploit in this way.) And while the idea of the College is rich in comic possibilities, they remain largely unrealized in the brief space allotted to it. It can scarcely be denied that lapses of this sort show a decline in artistic power from the period of the major comedies. But these failures in execution of the overall design should not blind us to the integrity of the design itself, or to the integral part played in it by this unusual adaptation of the equivalence-plot format.

6

The Limits of Multiplicity

The preceding chapters have attempted to show how the various modes of integration were employed to unify the multiple plots of Renaissance drama, but the assimilative power of these modes, either alone or in combination, is obviously not unlimited and must break down if taxed beyond a certain point. We might then go on to consider the more general question of how much "multiplicity" can be successfully integrated into a single dramatic whole. As with other problems of this sort, we should not expect some theoretical, a priori answer, since there is no way for a critic to know what can be done in an art form until an artist has actually done it. We will find the answer, I believe, in two plays reserved for this chapter and for this purpose, written by the two most inventive and effective authors (with the inevitable exception) of multiple-plot drama in the period, Thomas Middleton's *A Chaste Maid in Cheapside* and Ben Jonson's *Bartholomew Fair*. They do not represent a new category of integration, but rather utilize all of the categories in highly complex structures which bring together more separate lines of action than any of the works yet examined, and realize more completely the full potentialities inherent in the convention of the multiple plot.

These two plays are certainly very different in many important respects, including the manner in which their complex unity is attained, but there are a number of external and perhaps coincidental resemblances—they were produced at about the same time (probably between March 1613 and October 1614); they are both realistic comedies dealing with the same segments of society in contemporary London; and we will see in the next chapter that each is the dramatist's last play of this type, marking the end of a definite stage in his career. Their critical receptions have also been similar. Until recently they were relatively neglected by the commentators and rarely reprinted, the standard school anthologies almost without exception limiting their selection of each writer's efforts in this genre to his earlier work (usually *A Trick to Catch the Old One* for Middleton, and Jonson's *Volpone* or *The Alchemist*); but now more and more people are coming to realize that they must be ranked among the greatest comedies of the age, and some are prepared to claim that they represent the culminating achievements of their authors in this field.[1]

Although the critics responsible for this revaluation have approached the plays from many different points of view, they are virtually all agreed in locating their distinctive excellence in what we have called their "multiplicity"—in the marvelous richness and variety of incident, character, and tone that the dramatist has been able to shape into an artistic unity. But while this is continually affirmed, it is not easy to learn from these accounts in any meaningful detail exactly how the plays are unified, for most discussions of them have been directed mainly toward an examination of certain of their components—the rhetoric, diction, or imagery, the setting or atmosphere, specific episodes or themes, and the like—or else toward generalizations about the playwright's realism and irony and moral or esthetic creed. Yet if they are such impressive feats of integration, it should be possible to explain this at a level somewhere between these particular parts and intellectual abstractions, because however important they may be to the total dramatic experience, they cannot themselves determine the actual arrangement of the material in the concrete form in which it appears. That would be determined at the structural level, where the diverse elements will be organized into a pattern of rela-

---

[1] For this new estimate of *A Chaste Maid* see Una Ellis-Fermor, *The Jacobean Drama* (London, 1936), p. 135; Richard Barker, *Thomas Middleton* (New York, 1958), p. 78; Samuel Schoenbaum, "*A Chaste Maid in Cheapside* and Middleton's City Comedy," *Studies in the English Renaissance Drama in Memory of Karl Julius Holzknecht* (New York, 1959), p. 289; R. B. Parker, "Middleton's Experiments with Comedy and Judgement," *Jacobean Theatre* (London, 1960), p. 188; and the introductions to the editions of Alan Brissenden (London, 1968), p. xv, and of Charles Barber (Berkeley, 1969), p. 2. The new enthusiasm for *Bartholomew Fair* does not usually go quite so far, but see Freda Townsend, *Apologie for "Bartholmew Fayre"* (New York, 1947), p. 71; Wallace Bacon, "The Magnetic Field: The Structure of Jonson's Comedies," *HLQ*, 19 (1956), 145; H. R. Hays, "Satire and Identification: An Introduction to Ben Jonson," *KR*, 19 (1957), 276; John Enck, *Jonson and the Comic Truth* (Madison, 1957), p. 189; C. G. Thayer, *Ben Jonson: Studies in the Plays* (Norman, 1963), p. 128.

tionships that in turn will establish their emotional and intellectual significance. And since these are the two most complicated structures of this sort we have encountered, they should provide a fitting climax to our study of the Renaissance multiple plot, as well as a final test of the method of analysis worked out for that study.

I

The basic pattern of *A Chaste Maid in Cheapside* can be viewed as an expansion of the triple hierarchy, since it includes four distinct plots arranged in an order of descending importance.[2] As in the case of many of the three-level dramas, this is also the order of their inception. The action opens with the main plot, which centers on the efforts of Touchwood Junior to win Moll Yellowhammer (the "chaste maid" of the title) despite the violent opposition of her parents, who want her to marry Sir Walter Whorehound. The second plot, beginning in the second scene, deals with the Allwit household, where Sir Walter has for years been carrying on an affair with the wife and supporting the complaisant husband. The third scene initiates the third action, the story of the barren couple, Sir Oliver and Lady Kix, who finally acquire a child through the ministrations of Touchwood Senior. And in the fourth plot, which does not get under way until Act IV (and so is the briefest and least developed), Tim Yellowhammer courts and weds a supposed Welsh heiress only to discover she is Whorehound's former mistress.

The material connections of the plots rest on family ties and geographic proximity—the Touchwoods are brothers, Moll is Tim's sister, Kix is a kinsman of Whorehound, some members of the Kix, Allwit, and Yellowhammer households are neighborhood acquaintances —and these are used to bring almost all the characters together in the two ensemble scenes that frame the central action, the Allwit christening in III.ii and the mock funeral of Moll and Touchwood in V.iv. They are also used to generate the causal connections among the plots, primarily through Sir Walter, who is actively engaged in plots one, two, and four, and is vitally affected by plot three, because his inheritance depends on the Kixes' remaining childless and is lost forever when Lady Kix is impregnated by Touchwood Senior. But Touchwood undertakes this task to help his brother by impoverishing, and so disqualifying, his rival for Moll's hand (just as he aids him more directly in the planning and execution of each of the three

---

2 In counting the plots some critics ignore the Tim-Welshwoman sequence, and include the single episode of Touchwood Senior, his wife, and the Wench in II.i; but this does not become another line of action, its chief purpose being to contrast Touchwood's amazing fertility with the Kixes' childlessness, and so establish his credentials for solving their problem.

attempts to spirit Moll away). Whorehound's scheme to marry Moll, therefore, links the first plot to the third; and it links both to the second, for Allwit tries to stop the marriage in order to preserve his arrangement with Whorehound, and this domestic threesome finally breaks up because of Whorehound's duel with Touchwood Junior in plot one, which leads to his repentance and rejection of the Allwits, and Lady Kix's pregnancy in plot three, which removes any inducement on their part to hold him. Finally, Tim's relation to his sister connects his plot with the first, since his marriage to the Welshwoman is a consequence of Whorehound's courtship of Moll, and his parents' discovery that this woman (whom Sir Walter introduced as his wealthy niece) is really a penniless whore is one of the factors, along with the disinheriting of Sir Walter, that reconciles them to their daughter's marriage to Touchwood Junior. The connection is rather weak, but in the first three plots these interactions are so skillfully developed that each plot affects and is affected by the others, the whole complex system being made to turn on the competition of Whorehound and Touchwood in the main action for the "chaste maid." This elaborate causal integration of the disparate plots is itself a remarkable structural achievement, one of the most remarkable of its kind in the period.

The formal integration of this structure, which is still more elaborate, is articulated through the analogical interrelationship of these four lines of action. Each of them is based on a sexual triangle involving two men and a woman; and in their treatment of this triangle the first and fourth plots make up a comparable pair, as do the second and third. Both plots of the first pair are stories of young couples who eventually marry, conceived in such a way that one seems the exact opposite of the other. This is evident from the behavior of Yellowhammer and his wife, for they do everything they can to prevent the first marriage, but fail, and then come to approve of it, whereas they aggressively promote the second, are successful, and later regret it. Whorehound's roles in these actions are also opposed; in the first he tries to get the girl and fails, in the second he is trying to get rid of the girl and succeeds. As these differences suggest, the difficulties faced by the couples are reversed: the courtship of Moll and Touchwood is over and their only problem is getting married, hence the major scenes of this plot portray their attempts to elope and finally the wedding itself, but in the other plot the only problem, and subject of the only big scene (IV.i), is Tim's courtship, while the marriage itself is not even presented.

All of this, however, is a result of the more basic contrast in the nature of their emotional attachment—the contrast between a couple whose love triumphs over external pressures, and a couple who have nothing but these pressures to bring them together. And that in turn depends on the contrasting natures of the characters. Touchwood is, along with his brother, the chief wit or manipulator in the play, and Moll is the only maid and apparently, except for the wife of Touchwood Senior, the only chaste woman; their wedding thus represents the most desirable union possible in this world. Tim, on the other hand, though a Cambridge scholar, is the fool of the play, and the Welshwoman, although she passes for a virgin, is the most disreputable woman in it, so that their wedding marks the lowest point on the same scale of value, the key terms of which are expressed, appropriately enough, in Tim's school logic when he demonstrates that *"stultus est animal rationale,"* and offers to "prove a whore to be an honest woman" (IV.i.1–43). The other principal value in this world is also at issue, for Moll has a dowry of "two thousand pound in gold" while the Welshwoman's "two thousand runts" turn out to be as illusory as her maidenhead. Therefore in all significant respects— emotional, intellectual, moral, and financial—the fourth plot is the antithesis of the first.

A similar relationship emerges from the juxtaposition of plots two and three, since they too share a common situation which invites comparison between them, but develop it in contrasting ways. These plots are distinguished from the first pair because they are concerned, not with the romantic problems of youth that terminate in wedlock, but with the domestic affairs of older married people in established households. (A further difference can be seen in the role of Whorehound, who is largely a passive character here, acted on by the course of events, whereas his active intervention was what set plots one and four in motion.) Each of them centers upon a triangle consisting of a long-married couple and another man who cuckolds the husband and begets his children. However, the second plot opens with the expected birth of the Allwit child, who is really Whorehound's, while the birth of the Kixes' baby, really sired by Touchwood Senior, is awaited at the end of the third. This temporal opposition extends throughout the two sequences, which proceed in reverse order. At the beginning of plot two we are shown an apparently stable *ménage à trois* which has been flourishing for many years but is destroyed by the subsequent action; the action of plot three produces such a *ménage,* and when Kix in the final scene invites Touchwood to move in with them to father more children, he is creating a replica of the Allwit household that will presumably continue well into the future (with the difference that it includes the cuckolder's own wife [3]). An-

---

[3] Oliver tells Touchwood to "go to your business roundly;/ Get children, and I'll keep them" (V.iv.75–76), a comically ambiguous reference to Touchwood's legitimate offspring and to the additional "physic" he must administer if the Kixes are to realize their dream of being "Circled with children" (III.iii.91).

other element in the contrast is the happiness of the participants, since it apparently depends on this unusual domestic arrangement. The Allwits, we see at once, are completely satisfied with it, and their peace is only disturbed when they are threatened with the loss of Whorehound; but the Kixes are introduced in the midst of a quarrel which has been going on intermittently for years, and is only resolved when Touchwood moves in—indeed, Kix is just as elated by this prospect at the end of his plot as Allwit was by Whorehound's visit at the beginning of his. Similarly, Whorehound seems to have been quite contented as a member of the Allwit family, and the final blow in his catastrophe (which includes other factors) comes when they throw him out, whereas Touchwood Senior is first presented at the bottom of his fortunes and attains his greatest happiness when he joins the Kixes.

Underlying this inversion in the direction of the plots is a more fundamental contrast in personalities. Although both husbands are cuckolds, Allwit is aware of it, which makes him a scoundrel, but Kix is not, and so is only a fool. This determines their status in the triangles—Allwit is well paid by Whorehound to put up with him and is victimizing him, while Kix is paying Touchwood Senior and is to be regarded as his victim. The motives of the wives are also very different; Lady Kix accepts the situation because she desperately wants a child (though this too has its financial side), and Mistress Allwit, so far as we can tell, because it is lucrative. But the most crucial opposition is in the nature of these two marriages. The Kixes, for all their bickering, show a real devotion to each other, which is presented comically in the intervals between the fights but is made quite believable and is even commented on with a certain sympathy by Touchwood (III.iii.43–48). The Allwits, on the other hand, never fight, but neither do they feel any affection; their marriage is nothing more than an efficient business partnership, as becomes clear (if any doubt remained) in their revealing conversation at the close of V.i. This opposition between the couples is also reflected in their attitude toward the cuckolder—the Allwits, who have been maintained for years by Whorehound, reject his appeal for help without a qualm when they can get no more out of him; but the Kixes, even though they have paid Touchwood, are genuinely grateful and press further rewards on him beyond their original bargain. And it is extended to the cuckolder's motivation, for Whorehound, as his name implies, is satisfying his lust, while Touchwood takes on the task (though he certainly enjoys it, and the money) primarily to help his brother. Therefore, these plots have been contrasted in the same emotional, intellectual, moral, and financial terms that differentiated the other pair, so that a kind of proportion is established, the first being related to the fourth as the second is to the third.

These formal relationships, together with the causal interactions already discussed, can explain how the four plots are integrated into a single whole, but they cannot in themselves explain the "final" significance of this integration, since that depends not only on the means by which unity is achieved, but also on what is being unified. Each of the plots has its own distinctive tone or character which, weighted and brought into proper focus through this cohesive structure, contributes to the total effect. And the arrangement of the plots in terms of these individual tones coincides with this structure, as in the three-level hierarchies, for the order of their introduction, which we found was the order of descending importance determined by the causal system, is at the same time the order of decreasing seriousness.

The first action is the most serious. Its story of young lovers overcoming the opposition of coldblooded "practical" parents derives from one of the most venerable dramatic formulas going back, as was seen, to classical New Comedy, and beyond that, according to the anthropologists, to the primitive fertility rituals associated with the cycle of the seasons.[4] The plot is practically a textbook illustration of this theory, with its magical triadic sequence of elopements, each bringing the lovers closer to annihilation—the first in Act III leading to Moll's imprisonment, the second in Act IV to a kind of "death by water," the third in Act V to the counterfeit of death itself—and its magical resurrection when they rise from their coffins to marry, using death to outwit the "death forces" that separated them, and taking their funeral cerements, as Touchwood Senior suggests, to create new life:

> Here be your wedding sheets
> You brought along with you; you may both go to bed
> When you please to.

(V.iv.43–45)

And since the formula had become one of the standard conventions of Renaissance romantic comedy, this would immediately enlist the audience on the side of the lovers and, to some extent, guide their response. The convention itself, however, does not determine the tone; in fact most plots of this general type tend toward much greater comic elaboration, usually in the clever tricks the lovers play on the parents or on the obnoxious suitor favored by them. Except for that brief opening episode where Touchwood buys his wedding ring from Moll's unsuspecting father, there is none of this here; the first two stratagems are simple straightforward flights, and the mock funeral is not treated comically. The emphasis throughout is not on the cleverness of Moll and Touchwood at all, but on the venality and cruelty of Moll's par-

---

[4] On this aspect of the play see R. B. Parker's introduction to his edition (London, 1969), pp. xlvii–lvi, and Arthur Marotti, "Fertility and Comic Form in *A Chaste Maid in Cheapside*," *CompD*, 3 (1969), 65–74.

ents, which makes the lovers more sympathetic and their plot more serious.

The fourth action, which was shown to be the opposite of the first in its basic design, is also at the opposite emotional pole. It is a farcical or "clown" subplot that relies heavily on a kind of verbal slapstick. And it functions as a foil since it completely reverses the romantic formula by permitting the avaricious older generation (the Yellowhammers and Whorehound) to manipulate and bring together a desentimentalized young couple (a fool and a whore) in what is a travesty of a love-match. But this inversion had itself become a dramatic convention, with its own stock situations and scenes, such as the fool's inept courtship and the whore's passing herself off as an heiress. Clearly these two conventions reinforce each other when they are juxtaposed, for the marked contrasts between them serve to make the romantic plot seem even more serious and the other even less, and similarly, to increase our sympathy for the first pair of lovers and our alienation from their debased counterparts, particularly the clown, as his role is defined by the convention and the context of the other plot (where Tim consistently takes the side of his parents against his sister). It is true that our feelings are only weakly engaged in this farcical action, but they do require his comic punishment, which is provided appropriately by the marriage to a whore.

Therefore these plots, romance and antiromance, while they are the furthest apart, fit neatly together because of their conventional nature and the symbiotic relationship that obtains between the "straight" model and its foil. It would not be difficult to imagine a comedy limited to those two actions (both padded out with additional incidents), along the lines of some of the direct contrast structures of Chapter 2, though it would be difficult to imagine it eliciting much critical interest. For the special flavor of this play depends to a considerable extent on the other two plots, whose unique contribution lies in their striking unconventionality. This is why we cannot speak of either of them as a foil or parody, since there is no identifiable norm that would make such concepts meaningful. Yet it is possible to locate them on the overall emotional scale in the same terms applied to the first pair. The second plot is the more serious of the two in its treatment of the marital triangle and its conclusion in V.i, with the near-death of Sir Walter and his bitter denunciation of the Allwits (although I would argue that even this moment, which some view as the most profound in the play, is partially undercut by the comic efforts of the Allwits to placate him, and then by their brazen about-face when they return the denunciation). In contrast, the continual squabbles and reconciliations of the Kixes, and the hilarious prescription of Touchwood's "physic" in III.iii, the major scene of the third plot, approach closer to the level of plot four. These actions can also be differentiated, like the other pair, by our feelings for the characters, since the sordid relationship of Whorehound and the Allwits makes them antipathetic—much more so, certainly, than Tim and the Welshwoman—whereas we regard Touchwood Senior and the Kixes with amiable amusement.

The four plots, therefore, have been selected and arranged in a scheme that exhausts the possibilities of comic action defined by these variables (understanding that the term "serious" here marks only the upper limit of the comic spectrum, without passing over into a different genre): the first is serious-sympathetic comedy, the second serious-unsympathetic, the third farcical but sympathetic, and the last farcical-unsympathetic. And their outcomes confirm this analysis; both sympathetic actions end very happily for all the major characters concerned except Whorehound (even Moll's parents finally welcome her marriage), while in the other two everyone is forced to accept, more or less grudgingly, some kind of defeat. Whorehound is a special case since he is affected by all four resolutions and cannot react differently to each, as the Yellowhammers do in plots one and four; but his downfall is associated primarily with plot two because it is placed in the Allwits' home and their rejection of him is made to seem the last crushing blow.

In this structure the sex-money equation plays a very important role, although here, unlike *A Mad World, My Masters* and *Michaelmas Term,* it is not divided between separate plots but lies at the heart of all four, we saw, and so serves to unify them in terms of a common rather than an analogous subject matter. The two areas of the equation are combined in the comparison of the two dominant families, the Allwits and the Yellowhammers,[5] that develops through their parallel alliances with Whorehound in which they both trade him sex for money, the Yellowhammers selling their daughter to him (for social position as well), and Allwit his wife. Of course the first is a perfectly respectable transaction and the second outrageously indecent, but that I think is the point. For Allwit is simply carrying this commercialization of love to its logical conclusion, as we discover from his demonstration, in the famous soliloquy at the beginning of I.ii, that cuckoldom is "The happiest state that ever man was born to" (the counterpart of Tim's proof at the outset of his plot that a fool is a rational animal and a whore an honest woman). His argument is couched entirely in the economic terms of profit and loss, and is irrefutable if life is reduced to these terms, since then love it-

5 The function of the family units is discussed by Ruby Chatterji, "Theme, Imagery, and Unity in *A Chaste Maid in Cheapside,*" RD, 8 (1965), 106–16.

self becomes a commodity to sell, and its physical and emotional demands an expense to be avoided:

> He gets me all my children, and pays the nurse
> Monthly or weekly; puts me to nothing
>   . . . I am as clear
> From jealousy of a wife as from the charge:
> O, two miraculous blessings! 'Tis the knight
> Hath took that labor all out of my hands:
> I may sit still and play; he's jealous for me,
> Watches her steps, sets spies; I live at ease,
> He has both the cost and torment.
>
>   (I.ii.18–19, 48–54) [6]

Allwit's household is thus a *reductio ad absurdum* of the values of the Yellowhammers and their middle-class world—indeed, given those values, he is really less absurd than they precisely because he has gone all the way and so can exploit Whorehound, whereas Whorehound is exploiting them. There is no incongruity, therefore, in his displays of moral indignation during the christening party in III.ii, or the interview with Yellowhammer in IV.i, or the rejection of Whorehound in V.i, for this hypocritical combination of self-righteousness and self-interest (also found in the Glisters and Purges of *The Family of Love*) is the essence of the bourgeois respectability which he has every right to claim, and which takes a much crueler form in the Yellowhammers' persecution of Moll. The Yellowhammer family, beneath its proper façade, is just as much a business partnership as the Allwits, their fundamental similarity in this respect being confirmed by the parallel between the last two scenes that focus on them, in which they lose their sexual merchandise: in V.i the Allwits, after vainly trying to calm down the apparently dying Sir Walter, abandon him and agree on the next best course, to let out lodgings, whereupon Allwit exclaims, "In troth, a match, wench"; and in the next scene the Yellowhammers vainly try to cheer up their apparently dying daughter until her "death" ends their hopes of a marriage to Sir Walter, and then agree to settle for Tim's wedding with the words, "Mass, a match!"

Because it epitomizes this conception of the sex-money equation, the Allwit plot can be called the satirical center of the play; but that does not mean we should follow some of the critics in writing off the main-plot romance as a mere "neutral frame" on which to "hang the

---

6 Unlike the typical sexual contest between citizen and gentleman (seen in *Michaelmas Term*), there is no suggestion that Allwit cannot satisfy his wife; he merely regards it as an unprofitable expenditure of energy. In *The Life of Mother Shipton*, a Restoration imitation, Shiftwell, who takes Allwit's role, is made a lecherous man himself, which destroys the point.

more interesting comedy of fleshly passions and follies," [7] for the story of Moll and Touchwood, although not as intriguing as plots two or three, is at the structural center, modifying and being modified by these subordinate actions, not only in the causal connections between them (which were all seen to work through the main action), but also in the emotions they arouse. The very audacity of the Allwit plot and of its comic replica in the Kix plot is emphasized, and at the same time kept within appropriate bounds, because it is framed by the conventional main action and the equally conventional inversion of that action in plot four. And conversely these unconventional plots create the general environment that gives the love story its special significance, perhaps most impressively in the much admired "realistic" episodes of the promoters and the christening. They are included partly for their independent satiric import, but they also help to define with marvelous vividness the identity of "Cheapside," the home of the Yellowhammers and Allwits and the center of the middle-class world whose sordid carnality and commercialism, shown in these scenes corrupting the "religious wholesome laws" of Lent and the sacrament of baptism, constitute the real enemy of Moll and Touchwood, and the background against which the triumph of their love is made to stand out as something uniquely attractive—as the comic miracle expressed in the title of *A Chaste Maid in Cheapside*.

II

The integration of Jonson's *Bartholomew Fair* follows a very different and unusual pattern that many would not call a multiple plot at all. Indeed a number of critics claim it has no plot,[8] and this is true in the sense that we cannot find any central line of action which holds everything together. But if the play is unified, as virtually everyone acknowledges, it must have a structure, an organizing principle, to determine the roles of the characters and the sequence of their activities. In the search for such a structure it does not help very much to be told, as we sometimes are, that "the fair itself" is the real sub-

---

[7] Madeleine Doran, *Endeavors of Art* (Madison, 1954), pp. 150, 291; cf. Muriel Bradbrook, *The Growth and Structure of Elizabethan Comedy* (London, 1955), p. 162.

[8] E.g., T. S. Eliot, "Ben Jonson," *Selected Essays* (New York, 1932), p. 134; Henry Wells, *Elizabethan and Jacobean Playwrights* (New York, 1939), pp. 55–56; T. M. Parrott and Robert Ball, *A Short View of Elizabethan Drama* (New York, 1943), p. 143. In *Apologie for "Bartholmew Fayre"* Freda Townsend also asserts the play is without a plot (p. 73), but then produces a list of "five separate actions" in it, and an explanation of its unity that Wallace Bacon claims—quite rightly, I believe—is too vague and metaphorical. He finds it is unified by the fair, which "acts as a magnetic center" and so "determines the pattern—the structure—of elements, as a magnet will arrange iron filings in a clearly observable pattern" ("The Magnetic Field," pp. 123–24, 148, 151–53).

ject or protagonist of the drama. The fair is certainly a crucial element in the action, but it is not what the action is about and does not define its course. For all their bustling movement, the fair and the "Bartholomew-birds" who inhabit it are dramatically static, ending up just as they began without being altered in any way by the events of the play. It is the visitors to the fair who are affected by it, rather than the other way around, and everything significant that happens there happens to them. It cannot even be said that these events are arranged to provide a progressively deeper insight into the fair, for it turns out to be the fair (or more strictly, their response to it) that exposes the visitors, and not the reverse. The action, then, while precipitated by the fair, is concerned with these visitors, and its main stages are demarcated by their careers: it begins when they decide to attend the fair, its central portion follows them through their day at Smithfield, and it ends when they decide to leave the fair and return to their normal environment.

Therefore, the major division of characters will be between the people of the fair who make up the dramatic world in which the action takes place, and the outsiders whose visit to this world constitutes the action itself. But among the visitors further divisions must be noted, for they start out in distinct groups, and it is in terms of their respective roles in these groups that the structure is developed. There is the Cokes party, consisting of Bartholomew Cokes, esquire, of Middlesex; his betrothed, Grace Wellborn; her guardian's wife, Dame Alice Overdo, who is Cokes's sister; and Cokes's governor, Humphrey Wasp. Another is the Littlewit party, which includes John Littlewit, a proctor; his wife, Win-the-fight; her widowed mother, Dame Purecraft; and their spiritual adviser, Zeal-of-the-land Busy, who is Dame Purecraft's suitor. The two gallants, Tom Quarlous and his friend, Ned Winwife, who is also courting Purecraft, form a third group. And Adam Overdo, Alice's husband and judge of the court of pie-powders, operates all by himself in disguise as an outsider spying on the fair.

Jonson attached considerable importance to this division, since he is careful to establish it before the action really gets under way. In the expository first act in Littlewit's house each of the first three groups is introduced as an entity that existed prior to this occasion; during the course of the act these groups come to independent decisions to see the fair, for quite different reasons, and set out by themselves; and later at the fair they arrive at separate times, still intact, and go their respective ways. And Judge Overdo introduces himself at the beginning of Act II in a soliloquy that emphasizes his isolation from the other visitors who have just left for the fair, as well as from the denizens of the fair we are about to meet. Moreover, the first two of these parties, which make up the main body and dramatic center of the visitors, have been constructed as parallel collections. Both of them are temporary households (Cokes, Grace, and Wasp came up from the country two days ago to stay at the Overdo home, and Busy has been boarding with Littlewit for three days), and their family relationships are so symmetrically arranged that every person in one group has his counterpart in the other.

Cokes and Littlewit, who are linked in the first speech of the play where the proctor comments on the marriage license he has drawn up for the squire, have equivalent roles, since each is the ostensible leader of his party, the head of the household, as it were, and at the same time its most foolish member (both their names imply this, "cokes" meaning a stupid dolt). And each is responsible for bringing his group to the fair because he feels a proprietary interest in it and wants to show it to his fiancée or wife. Cokes insists,

> 'twas all the end of my journey, indeed, to show Mistress
> Grace my Fair; I call't my Fair because of Bartholomew;
> you know my name is Bartholomew, and Bartholomew
> Fair.
>
> (I.v.64–67)

Littlewit's response, harking back to his opening soliloquy ("That was mine afore, gentlemen; this morning, I had that i'faith, upon his license"), reinforces the connection between them, and as soon as Cokes leads the first party off, he says to his wife,

> we must to the Fair too, you and I, Win. I have an affair
> i'the Fair, Win, a puppet-play of mine own making—say
> nothing—that I writ for the motion-man, which you must
> see, Win.
>
> (ll. 145–48)

Therefore these are the two visitors who feel most at home in the fair and most thoroughly enjoy it, and partly as a result their careers there are similar.

Wasp and Busy are also associated in Act I at the beginning of scene iv when, immediately after Quarlous's long description of the Puritan prepares us for his entrance, Wasp walks in instead. They are the most implacable foes of the fair in their parties. This hostility is one manifestation of a general censoriousness that places them both in positions of power; for while they are the only members of these groups who are not related (or about to be) by ties of blood or marriage, and are even in a sense dependent on the head of the family (this is more true of Wasp, but we also learn that Busy is sponging off Littlewit), they have made themselves, by their moral bullying, the real leaders of their parties, whom the two ostensible leaders fear and in their characteristic ways have to appease: Cokes is always trying to placate Wasp, and Littlewit must continually resort to devious tricks to get around Busy. And again, because of their equivalent attitudes and roles, they suffer similar fates at the fair.

Finally, the four women are paired off at the outset in terms of family relationships. Win, Littlewit's wife, is the counterpart of Grace, the fiancée of Cokes (who links them in I.v.83–85 when he wishes he might marry Win); and Dame Purecraft, Win's mother, corresponds to Dame Overdo, the wife of Grace's guardian (as indicated at I.ii.27 by another of Littlewit's anticipatory connections). The two older women also have certain traits in common: they are both overawed by the moral bully of their group and are both critical of the fair, although their opposition is relatively mild and derivative, Dame Purecraft taking her opinions at second hand from Busy, and Dame Overdo from her absent husband (rather than from Wasp), whose authority she is forever citing. However, unlike the four men, this initial parallelism among the four women does not remain fixed, since in response to the pressures of the fair a new combination is brought about: the wives, Dame Overdo and Win, become associated and eventually meet the same fate, and so do the two unmarried women, Grace and Dame Purecraft. This rearrangement, in fact, will be found to mark a major turning point in the play.

Although the eight visitors have been paired off in this way, there are important differences within each pair which result from a more general contrast between the two groups themselves, since each group has its characteristic social and ethical tone that is set in the first act and confirmed by the events of the fair. The Littlewit party is composed of middle-class "city" Puritans who, whatever their individual peculiarities, all tend to be less innocent and straightforward than their counterparts in the Cokes party, which comes from a higher social stratum with a stronger "county" flavor. The distinction is clear in the case of the two fools: Cokes is a natural simpleton going through the fair with the spontaneous enthusiasms of a child on a lark, but the equally stupid Littlewit is, as his name suggests, an intellectual pretender who prides himself on his "pretty conceits" and on the "pretty passages" of his inane puppet-play. It also appears in the original pairing of the women, for Dame Overdo's insistence upon the authority of "Master Overdo's name" and her "Justice-hood," though vain and silly, is without any ulterior motive, while Dame Purecraft's strident profession of the creed of "our zealous brother Busy" is a calculated pose, as she reveals in her confession to Quarlous, adopted to make money; and the quiet, unaffected confidence in her own integrity and good breeding that governs the conduct of Grace (the only noncomic character in either group) is the opposite of Win's moral hypocrisy, which has been "bred i' the family" and enables her to evade the prohibitions of her mother and Busy, and even those imposed by her marriage vows, once the temptation presents itself. Later, when Dame Overdo is paired with Win as a "bird o' the game," some sense of this distinction is preserved; we see how easily Win is taken in by the pimps in IV.v, whereas Dame Overdo's fall occurs offstage, and at the puppet-play Win is shown being courted by Edgworth and obviously enjoying her new vocation, while the older woman remains in a drunken stupor.

This differentiation of the groups is most obvious and most significant in their moral leaders, Wasp and Busy; but here the contrast has been extended to include another critic of the fair, the solitary Judge Overdo, who is treated in parallel with the other two and juxtaposed to them in a comic hierarchy that corresponds to the order of their introduction at the beginning of the play, and of their deflation and conversion at the end. Wasp, who is the first of the three to appear (I.iv) and the first to abandon his role as censor (V.iv), is the simplest and funniest. He is an irascible "dry-nurse" whose inflated sense of his own importance depends on his absolute authority over his loved and badgered child, and his hostility to the fair is not ideological but wholly and frankly personal; he dislikes it because he sees it as a threat to Cokes and to his control of him. Busy, the second to enter (I.vi) and to meet his downfall (V.v), is more complex and more serious, for his objections to the fair are based on a general doctrine that he manipulates to impose his will upon others and to serve his own interests. He is the consummate hypocrite of the play, whose prodigious talents in this field are but palely reflected in the two women of his party. And Adam Overdo, the last to appear (II.i) and last to capitulate (V.vi), is the most complicated and serious portrait of the three. The essential difference between his attack on the fair and Busy's does not seem to be that one represents the church and the other the state, as some critics would have it, or that one is a Puritan and the other Anglican, but that the Puritan prophet cynically uses his brand of ideology (which to be sure is theological) to delude others, while the ideology of the Anglican judge (which is political and legal) is only used to delude himself.[9] His behavior springs from the conviction, expressed and nurtured in the elaborate rationalizations of his soliloquies, that his investigation of the fair's "enormities" and the successive martyrdoms this brings upon him will make him a savior of

---

[9] See Jonas Barish's excellent study of these characters in *Ben Jonson and the Language of Prose Comedy* (Cambridge, Mass., 1960), pp. 197–211. Jackson Cope shows that Overdo also thinks in scriptural imagery ("*Bartholomew Fair* as Blasphemy," *RD*, 8 [1965], pp. 128–30).

the commonwealth and admit him to the exalted company of Roman sages in whom he finds his sanction. Thus the hierarchy into which these enemies of the fair arrange themselves is formed on two variables: Wasp's opposition is practical and sincere, Busy's theoretical and hypocritical, and Overdo's theoretical and sincere. All three men have similar careers at the fair—they all come to grief there and eventually have to surrender their claims of moral superiority over their fellow visitors as well as the fair; but the amount of comic suffering they must undergo in the process is commensurate with their places on this scale of self-righteous pretension.

The two remaining visitors, Quarlous and Winwife, stand apart from and above the rest by reason of their social status and, more important, their insight. They become the "wits" of the play, not primarily by tricking the "gulls" (for there is much less intrigue of this sort here than in Jonson's preceding comedies), but by understanding and judging them. As with the other outsiders, it is their reaction to the fair that characterizes them: they do not eagerly enter into it on the level of the simple fools, Cokes and Littlewit, nor do they try like Wasp, Busy, and Overdo, the "careful" fools,[10] to attack or reform it, but tend to regard it with tolerant amusement. In fact their original motive for going to Smithfield was not to see the fair itself but the "sport" they expected Cokes and his party would afford them there (I.v.138–43), and during most of Acts II through IV their principal occupation is to observe and savor the follies of the other visitors. And since it was shown that this is precisely what the basic scheme of the play requires the audience to do, these men can be said to function as our representatives at the fair, guiding our response, in the manner of a chorus, to the comic behavior it brings out in the Cokes and Littlewit parties. Quarlous is more impulsive and belligerent than Winwife, and twice loses his choric detachment when he finds himself embroiled with the fair people, but their roles are equivalent and so are their fates at the end.

We are now in a position to see the broad outlines of the structure, which can be traced in terms of what happens to this system of associations and differentiations within the body of visitors once they descend on the fair It is quickly stated. At first these groups preserve their distinct identities, remaining intact and isolated from each other; but as they become caught up in the fair they gradually disintegrate until every person is on his own, and at the same time the

---

10 Quarlous makes the distinction: "I would fain see the careful fool deluded! Of all beasts, I love the serious ass, he that takes pains to be one, and plays the fool with the greatest diligence that can be." He is speaking of Wasp, but Grace adds that Overdo "is answerable to that description in every hair of him" (III.v.264–70, cf. ll. 27–33).

contacts between groups gradually increase, contributing to this breakdown and eventually producing a rearrangement of the two main parties in which each member is joined to his counterpart in the other party, and then is brought to the puppet-show that assembles all the visitors, in their new relationships, for the resolution. This movement should occasion no surprise since it is very similar to that employed in *The Alchemist* (and to a lesser extent in *Volpone*), where the originally separate victims, whom the cozeners are trying to keep apart, begin to collide with each other in a steadily increasing tempo to form more complex combinations leading to the final unraveling. The obvious difference is that *Bartholomew Fair* has no master schemers who attempt to manipulate all the visiting groups and prevent their meeting, which is another way of saying that this time Jonson has not organized his structure around a central intrigue plot. Here events are brought about, not by the clever plans of a Volpone and Mosca or a Face and Subtle, but by "Luck and Saint Bartholomew" (V.i.1); yet behind it all can be discerned the author's hand shaping the material to create an equivalent sense of pace and pattern.

This can be demonstrated by observing the stages in the interaction, disintegration, and realignment of the groups of visitors. With the interactions a momentum is developed not only in the number of encounters between groups, but also in the nature of the groups involved, since the first external contacts of the two main parties are with Overdo, Quarlous, and Winwife, who function as roving observers, and only then does the thrust of the action build up to meetings of the main parties themselves, initially by a series of near-misses between those members who are not counterparts, and finally by the pairing off of the parallel members, the only ones in these parties who even see each other before the puppet-show. Act II brings Overdo (i), then Quarlous and Winwife (v), and then the Cokes party (vi) to the fair; but the two gallants do not notice Overdo and leave before Cokes arrives, so there is no contact between groups until the last scene (vi), where Cokes's pocket is picked while he listens to Overdo's oration, and Overdo (still unrecognized in his disguise) is beaten by Wasp for the crime.

In Act III this process gradually accelerates. Quarlous and Winwife finally see some other visitors, although at first without speaking to them: they merely watch, unobserved, as the Littlewit party enters the pig-booth (ii), and as Overdo makes another brief appearance (iii). Then their first real meeting occurs in scene iv, when they join the Cokes party, engaging Grace in conversation, while Cokes's second purse is stolen and Overdo, who has returned in the wake of the pickpocket (making the first time three groups of visitors are on stage together), is again blamed for it and arrested. Cokes, Wasp, and

Mistress Overdo depart, but they leave Grace with Quarlous and Winwife, which begins the break up of their group; and the gallants take her away just as the Littlewits emerge from the booth, so that the first possible contact between members of the two main parties is narrowly averted (v). But now it is the turn of the Littlewit group to come apart: Busy overthrows the gingerbread stand, and when he is arrested Dame Purecraft follows him, while Littlewit brings Win back into the booth to find her a privy (vi).

Act IV carries this process much further and steps up its tempo. Overdo and Busy, still accompanied by Purecraft, are held in custody (i). Cokes, who has left Wasp and his sister to see Overdo taken to the stocks, just misses the two Puritans of the other main party, is robbed again, and wanders off alone (ii). Quarlous parts company with Grace and Winwife to see Wasp in the game of "vapors" (iii). The game ends in Wasp's arrest, separating him from Dame Overdo and thus completely dissolving their party (iv), and she enters the booth to relieve herself just in time to avoid meeting Littlewit, who comes out with Win and leaves her there while he visits the puppet-tent. Only at this point, in scene v, do members of the two main groups finally meet: Win and Dame Overdo, now both deserted and thrown together in the pig-booth, allow the pimps to enlist them as "birds o' the game." And in the last scene (vi) the second such combination is brought about when Wasp joins his counterpart Busy, along with Overdo, in the stocks, although they soon escape and go their separate ways. (Here again a meeting between nonparallel members of the main parties is prevented since Wasp escapes first before Purecraft arrives to comfort Busy.) The first three scenes of Act V complete this movement. Purecraft has left Busy, marking the final stage in the dissolution of the Littlewit party, and proposes to Quarlous (in his disguise as Trouble-all, the madman) just after they run into Winwife and Grace, who is now her counterpart in the Cokes party (ii). And in scene iii Cokes and Littlewit, the last of these parallel characters, meet at the tent where Littlewit's play is to be presented and have a fine time discussing the puppets and admiring each other's wit before the rest of the audience appears.

This puppet-show eventually draws in all of the visitors, who present themselves in the new alignment which the fair precipitated out of the original groups. Cokes and Littlewit were paired off when they met there; Win and Dame Overdo come in together, masked and gaudily dressed, with the pimps and bullies; Grace enters with Winwife, and Dame Purecraft with Quarlous; and the three enemies of the fair, now completely isolated, are introduced in parallel, each one coming forward to assert his prerogative as censor and to suffer his comic deflation, in the sequence defined by their relative complexity and seriousness. As soon as Wasp arrives in scene iv he begins to scold Cokes in his usual manner, but when Cokes reminds him of the stocks, he quickly surrenders:

> Does he know that? Nay, then the date of my authority is out; I must think no longer to reign, my government is at an end.
>
> (V.iv.97–99)

In the next scene Busy enters to attack the play as an "abomination," but is ignominiously defeated in debate with the puppet and forced to abandon his position:

> Let it go on. For I am changed, and will become a beholder with you!
>
> (V.v.116–17)

Then in the last scene Overdo, who has been lurking in the background all along, finally intervenes to condemn the many "enormities" he has uncovered, and to straighten out the confusion produced by the fair, separate the innocent from the guilty, and restore the earlier grouping of the visitors, by imposing a physical arrangement upon his audience that will freeze them in their proper relationships. He starts by commanding them all, "Sit still, I charge you," and proceeds to place them where they belong: Trouble-all (really Quarlous in disguise) is ordered to "come hither" under his protection, Edgworth the cutpurse to "stand there," Littlewit to "stand by" Dame Purecraft, Cokes and Wasp to "stand you both there in the middle place," Ursula and Nightingale to "stand you there, you, songster, there," and Quarlous (once he is unmasked) to "Stand you there." But since the workings of the fair have destroyed his neat, static categories, he is dealt a series of surprises culminating in the discovery that one of the "twelve-penny ladies" is his own wife. This brings him up short and allows Quarlous to launch his counterattack against Overdo's stupidity and moral rigidity, which he couches in the same language ("Nay, sir, stand not you fix'd there, like a stake in Finsbury to be shot at . . ."), and to recount how he has defeated each of the three enemies of the fair—by getting Cokes's marriage license from Wasp, Dame Purecraft from Busy, and the blank warrant from Overdo that terminates his guardianship of Grace. The result is Overdo's complete capitulation, the last of the three, which he explicitly equates with the first:

> Nay, Humphrey, if I be patient, you must be so too; this pleasant conceited gentleman hath wrought upon my judgment, and prevail'd.
>
> (V.vi.105–7)

The fair metes out parallel fates not only to these three censors but to each pair of visitors it has brought together. The two married women, Dame Overdo and Win, who fell in with the pimps because of the same call of nature, have changed least of all and simply return, slightly tarnished, to their husbands. The two fools, Cokes and Littlewit, are liberated through no fault of their own from their moral oppressors, but otherwise remain unaltered; they have both lost their women (one permanently, one temporarily) by abandoning them at the fair, but Cokes could not care less, and the doting Littlewit has already proved in Act I that he is incapable of jealousy. The lives of Grace and Dame Purecraft, however, are really transformed, since they have both exchanged very undesirable suitors (Cokes and Busy) for very desirable husbands, the best available in the world of the play. And the friends who wed them, Winwife and Quarlous, are receiving complementary rewards, the two richest prizes of this world, which they acquire in the same fortuitous way: Winwife wins his wife in a lottery, when the mad Trouble-all marks his word rather than Quarlous's in the tablet; and Purecraft proposes to Quarlous because he disguised himself as Trouble-all, for a completely different purpose, and she was advised to marry a madman by the fortune-tellers of Cow Lane. (To emphasize the similarity, we are told that Trouble-all acts as "a fortune-teller" in marking the tablet, and both matches are called the work of "fortune." [11]) As another unintended result of this disguise, Quarlous secures Overdo's blank warrant which is used to free Grace from his control. None of this was planned by the two gallants who came to Smithfield merely to enjoy the "sport," and while they are clever enough to take advantage of these windfalls blown their way by the fair, and so in a sense deserve them, they really owe their parallel triumphs to the same ruling deities responsible for pairing the fates of all the other visitors—"Luck and Saint Bartholomew."

The nature of the sequence and the resolution would seem to indicate what has happened as a result of eliminating the central intrigue found in *Volpone* and *The Alchemist* (or of substituting this particular form of providence for it): each visitor's career has become a kind of "plot" in itself, with its own beginning, middle, and end, much like the independent lines of action in more orthodox multiple-plot drama. The number and variety of these "plots," their simultaneous development, and their accelerating interaction, account in large part for the extraordinary "multiplicity" of the play, registered by the critics in such terms as "kaleidoscopic," "crowded can-

---

[11] See IV.iii.22, 51, 101; V.ii.31, 84. Fortune also decreed that these men reverse the positions they originally held in Act I, where Winwife came to court Purecraft and Quarlous warned him against "widow-hunting."

vas," "sprawling vitality," "riotous carnival," and "comic saturnalia."
And this conception of "plot" also allows us to explain the cohesion
of that multiplicity, since the relationships which cut across the separate groups of visitors can then be seen to take on the function
of the usual modes of inter-plot integration, connecting each of the
comparable pairs from the two main parties in an analogy, with both
positive and negative aspects, and the three censors in a hierarchic
scale. The network of these connections serves to combine the groups
themselves into one dramatic entity, a single, corporate body of
"action" which moves into and out of the "background" of the fair
while remaining distinct from it, and so constitutes the organizing
principle of the entire play. There are of course many more such
connections here than in the other works we have examined because
there are many more "plots" in this special sense, but that appears to
be a difference in degree rather than in kind, for I think the analysis
has shown that the underlying formal patterns are essentially the
same, and that they determine both the multiplicity and the unity
of the dramatic structure.

This account of the structure, concentrating as it has on the formal
or spatial relations among the visitors, has necessarily slighted certain
other temporal connections that run through the middle portion of
the action and help to order and give direction to their experience at
the fair. One such thread is provided by the tribulations of poor
Cokes, the "clown" of the play, who in two triadic sequences is progressively stripped by Edgworth of his possessions (his silver purse in
Act II, his gold purse in III, and some of his clothes in IV), and by
the disintegrative forces of the fair, as we saw, of his three companions (Grace in Act III, Wasp and Dame Overdo in IV)—all of
which in his muddled recapitulation he attributes to the two prov-
idential deities governing this world:

> Bartholomew Fair, quoth he; an' ever any Bartholomew
> had that luck in't that I have had, I'll be martyr'd for him,
> and in Smithfield too . . . I ha' lost myself, and my cloak
> and my hat, and my fine sword, and my sister, and Numps,
> and Mistress Grace (a gentlewoman that I should ha' mar-
> ried), and a cut-work handkercher she ga' me, and two
> purses today.
>
> (IV.ii.71–73, 81–85) [12]

A more important sequence of this sort is built around the three
enemies of the fair; each of these acts brings one of them his big scene,
where he is given the maximum opportunity to display his character-

---

[12] After stealing his first purse Edgworth says, "This fellow was sent to us by fortune for our first fairing" (II.vi.63–64).

istic censorious obsession and is promptly punished for it. In II.vi Overdo tries to reform Edgworth by his harangue on "the fruits of bottle-ale and tobacco," but is beaten by Wasp, who assumes he was really setting up Cokes to be robbed. III.vi contains Busy's attack on "the merchandise of Babylon" in the gingerbread and hobbyhorse stands that leads to his arrest. And in IV.iv Wasp enters the game of "vapors," whose rules seem designed to exhibit his irascibility in its purest form (just as the puppet-show exhibits Littlewit's capacities as a producer of "wit" and Cokes's as a consumer), and is also arrested. Apparently the sequence proceeds down the scale formed by these men (rather than the order followed in Act V) so that the number of discomfitures each undergoes will correspond to his place on it: Overdo is beaten in II.vi, brought to the stocks in IV.i, and finally put in them in IV.vi (which is legally part of the same penalty delayed in IV.i, but dramatically quite distinct); Busy suffers just the last two of these; and Wasp only the last. This order also produces a cumulative effect in the number of censors punished each time: in II.vi it is Overdo alone, in IV.i he is joined by Busy, and in IV.vi all three are in the stocks together, a climax that visually establishes their kinship and suggests a temporary resolution to their quarrel with the fair, preparing us for their permanent submission in the next act.

The analysis has also slighted the denizens and activities of the fair itself, that contribute so much to our pleasure and have been the source of so much recent speculation—especially Ursula and her booth, the mad Trouble-all, and the puppet-show (a double-plot play in its own right based on the equivalence of "love" and "friendship"). But if this approach is valid, it should be possible to fit them into the scheme outlined above in terms of their effect on the visitors. For the structural emphasis adopted here may help to counteract what seems to be an increasing tendency to magnify the importance of the "Bartholomew-birds" by sentimentalizing them (or diabolizing them, which is really another form of sentimentality). We are told, for example, that the fair is meant to embody a "spirit of warmth and animal appetite" which "the play itself is primarily recommending," that Ursula presides over it "like the life force" or "a kind of universal mother" or "earth itself, the great Mother, Demeter, and Eve" (when she is not *Ate, Discordia* herself" at her "diabolic furnace," sitting "like Cerberus at the gate of her particular hell" and recalling "the ancient Vice, that Vicar of Hell"), and that Jonson presents "her unequivocal triumph" and the fair's.[13] Yet it is difficult to find any warrant for

---

[13] Bacon, "The Magnetic Field," p. 146; Barish, *Ben Jonson and the Language of Prose Comedy*, pp. 222–24; Cope, "*Bartholomew Fair* as Blasphemy," pp. 142–44; Enck, *Jonson and the Comic Truth*, pp. 191, 198; Robert Knoll, *Ben Jonson's Plays* (Lincoln, 1964), p. 157; Thayer, *Ben Jonson*, p. 133.

such views in the concrete movement of the play. The fair remains the same squalid, though certainly lusty, background from the beginning to the end, and while it may be said to defeat its severest critics, Wasp, Busy, and Overdo (although in a more significant sense they defeat themselves), it never seriously threatens Quarlous and Winwife, who actually are given an "unequivocal triumph," and whose attitude toward the fair people is anything but sentimental.[14] Yet theirs is the position that is confirmed by the formal and final synthesis of the multiple-plot structure which, in its crucial realignment of characters and distribution of rewards and punishments, pronounces the authoritative judgment upon this brilliant comic universe.

---

[14] Barish believes that the simple fools among the visitors are also "vindicated" and "triumph" (pp. 212, 230, 236), and that Quarlous and Winwife (who never get sentimental about them, either) end up "at the comic tribunal of the puppet play . . . with almost as much to answer for as the rascals of the Fair itself" (p. 195). But Cokes and Littlewit seem even sillier in Act V than in Act I, and the gallants are not accused of anything at the tribunal—rather it is Quarlous who does the accusing in his definitive attack on Overdo. I think James Robinson, in "*Bartholomew Fair*: Comedy of Vapors," *SEL*, 1 (1961), 74, also sacrifices these gallants to his general theme, which is nearly the opposite of Barish's; and for other attempts to debase Quarlous see Cope, who compares him to Satan (pp. 150–51), and Ray Heffner, "Unifying Symbols in the Comedy of Ben Jonson," *English Institute Essays, 1954* (New York, 1955), pp. 94–95.

7

Beyond the Categories

The warning, in the introductory chapter, that this investigation of multiple-plot drama would not lead to easy generalizations has been borne out by the analyses of the individual plays exemplifying the principal categories of integration, to the extent that they succeeded in conveying the remarkable variety of forms and effects comprehended under each category. Any conclusion we might draw from those analyses about the nature of the multiple plot could do little more than recapitulate this diversity in a summary which added nothing to our understanding. But that is a consequence not only of the material itself but also of our mode of approach to it, which has focused so exclusively upon the specific structure of each dramatic work in its own unique terms. Rather than remain within these limitations, it might be more helpful in this final chapter to open up the investigation by exploring—even if very briefly—some other ways of treating the subject.

Probably the most obvious of these alternatives is the historical approach. Although we have arranged the plays, for our special purpose, according to their logical relationships in the categories, they are also related to each other chronologically in the sequential evolution of the multiple-plot convention during this period. And from the individual analyses we have accumulated enough data to describe the broad outlines of that sequence: there is an early, formative stage, marked by a relatively crude and simpleminded use of the convention and some uncertain experimentation, that extends from the inception of secular drama in the 1560s to about 1590; then the stage of major achievement, beginning in the early 1590s and ending around 1615, from which most of the exemplary plays were drawn; and a longer final stage, down to the closing of the theaters in 1642, where we find, if not "decadence," at least a significant decline in the inventiveness with which the convention is employed and in its effectiveness.[1] But such an outline is not very enlightening; in fact it could be applied almost unchanged to many other aspects of English Renaissance drama —to the development of the various genres, or the verse medium, or the plotting and characterization. Nor is this surprising since the multiple plot is just one element of the drama and would be expected to mature, in the hands of the same playwrights, at about the same pace as the others.

If, however, we wish to proceed beyond this kind of generalized description to the concrete details and causal explanations of the history, we run into real difficulties, particularly in the crucial initial stage when the secular drama was emerging out of the Morality. One problem is simply the inadequacy of our information; we do not know enough about the number of plays of this period that have been lost, or the representativeness of those that have survived, or even their dates, to be able to judge with any accuracy the effect of the Morality tradition—either in itself or in relation to other possible influences —upon the first multiple plots. But the possibility of other influences raises still more serious problems, for we saw in the preceding chapters that the conceptions underlying the categories of multiple-plot integration—analogical comparison and contrast, hierarchy, foil and parody, and equivalence—could be found in the universal processes of the mind, quite apart from their literary manifestations, and the earliest plays we examined would seem to confirm this. Medwall's *Fulgens and Lucrece,* often described as the first English secular drama, already has a fully developed subplot, and similar or even more elaborate structures appear in many of the transitional works of the 1560s—in *Cambyses,* for example, and *Appius and Virginia, Damon and Pythias,* and *Horestes.* In an important sense, therefore, the multiple plot required no prior literary "cause," since it was always there.

Even if we confined our causal explanations to the field of literature, there is no reason why they would have to be located within the drama. The multiple plots of such narratives as Ariosto's *Orlando Furioso,*[2] or Spenser's *Faery Queen,* or Sidney's *Arcadia,* may well have

---

[1] For an interesting explanation of this decline see Norman Rabkin, "The Double Plot: Notes on the History of a Convention," *RD,* 7 (1964), 55–69.
[2] Some of them would also be familiar with the writings of Cinthio and other continental critics in defense of Ariosto's plot structure.

influenced playwrights groping for some kind of coherent form. They may also have been influenced by the tradition of "tragical histories," going back to Boccaccio's *De Casibus Virorum Illustrium* and Lydgate's *Fall of Princes* and revived in the immensely popular *Mirror for Magistrates* and its progeny, where a number of independent stories were collected to exemplify a common lesson (the capriciousness of Fortune, or the retribution of an avenging Deity [3]), or by another type of collection, best known to us in Boccaccio's *Decameron* and Chaucer's *Canterbury Tales*, in which the stories were combined around a single narrative frame and often, in the subdivisions, a single subject ("Here beginneth the seventh day of the Decameron wherein . . . is discoursed of the tricks which or for love or for their own preservation women have heretofore played their husbands"). The unity of these works, such as it was, entailed the kind of serial multiplicity discussed at the beginning of Chapter 2, rather than a real multiple-plot structure with its simultaneous actions, but they could have suggested or reinforced the idea of such a structure in the drama.

The problems of this history do not disappear even if we ignore these other possible sources or influences and restrict our causal account to the drama itself, for while everyone would accept the general proposition that the playwrights learned from each other, we can seldom be certain that any one of them knew any particular work of his predecessors, or that he saw in it what we would have liked him to see. There can be no doubt, however, that each man knew his own earlier work and learned from it, so that we should be able to reconstruct an intelligible line of development in the handling of the multiple plot by a single dramatist, especially if we deal with a single recognizable stage in his career and a single genre. It is only possible to sketch in a few examples, using for this purpose the comedies of the three best writers of multiple-plot drama in the period. The evolution of Ben Jonson's dramaturgy is in this respect fairly obvious. Very early, in the *Every Man* plays and *Cynthia's Revels,* he tried to encompass a wide range of material through what has been called a "loose multiplicity" of separate actions held together by a governing idea.[4] Then in *Volpone* he adopted a much tighter and narrower mode of construction, combining one subplot (of Wouldbe and Peregrine) with one clearly defined main plot built around the master plan of Volpone and Mosca; but even here their relations to

---

3 The shift in emphasis from Fortune to retribution is discussed by Willard Farnham, *The Medieval Heritage of Elizabethan Tragedy* (Berkeley, 1936). In some of the later, more specialized collections the stories were also unified by a common subject matter—e.g., John Reynolds's *The Triumphs of God's Revenge against the Crying and Execrable Sin of Murther.*
4 C. H. Herford and Percy Simpson, *Ben Jonson,* 1 (Oxford, 1925), 70. Freda Townsend traces this evolution of Jonson's "multiplicity" in *Apologie for "Bartholmew Fayre"* (New York, 1947).

their victims—Voltore, Corbaccio (with his son Bonario), and Corvino (with his wife Celia)—although similar in nature, really constitute three coördinate strands that do not merge until the trial. This pattern is not followed in *Epicene,* but in *The Alchemist* it is carried much further; the subplot proper is eliminated and the chief cozeners, Face and Subtle, generate a series of schemes which have greatly increased in number, relative independence, and variety, each of their seven victims introducing a different problem that runs throughout the play, so while this is strictly speaking a single-plot drama, that plot consists of seven coördinate quasiplots which enter into the final explosion and resolution. *Bartholomew Fair,* then, can be seen as the logical next step, for now the central confidence game has disappeared completely (to be replaced by "Luck and Saint Bartholomew"), and we are left with a collection of separate characters—more, and more varied than in *The Alchemist*—pursuing their separate purposes in quasiplots that have become, as we found in our previous analysis, the real plots of the play, in terms of which its integration is achieved. But Jonson did not attempt to go beyond this point, and it is difficult to see how he could have without abandoning any hope of unity (which is why we took the play as a "limit of multiplicity"). In his next comedy, *The Devil is an Ass,* he reverted to a much more orthodox and much less interesting plot structure, and began his long and painful descent into "dotage."

The development of Thomas Middleton's technique in his early city comedies is more difficult to trace because their dating is so uncertain, yet it seems to be in some ways similar to Jonson's. He too sought to cover a broad spectrum in *The Phoenix* and *Your Five Gallants,* two of the least effective of these plays, by adding together a number of almost independent actions very loosely connected, in the apt image of R. B. Parker, "like a multi-ringed circus with a single ring-master." [5] In *A Mad World, My Masters, Michaelmas Term,* and *A Trick to Catch the Old One,* which are the best plays of this early group (and may well be the last of them), he made use of a tighter double-plot structure, but with a consequent narrowing of focus. Then several years later when he wrote *A Chaste Maid in Cheapside* he was able to secure the breadth resulting from a greater number of disparate actions, without any sacrifice of formal coherence, by returning to and expanding upon yet another structural pattern he had tried out, without much success, in his first experiments—the three-level hierarchy of *The Family of Love.* Gerardine and Maria, the main-plot lovers of *The Family,* reappear as Touchwood Junior and

---

[5] "Middleton's Experiments with Comedy and Judgement," *Jacobean Theatre* (London, 1960), p. 185.

Moll Yellowhammer, and the third-level clowns, Lipsalve and Gudgeon, as Tim and his Tutor; but the second level of the Glisters and
Purges is split into two plots, the Allwit action providing the more
serious social satire, and the Kixes an innocent comic counterpart. A
comparison of the two plays shows very vividly Middleton's growth
over the intervening years in his ability to integrate the separate
levels and to exploit the material within them—most obviously by
avoiding any direct representation of the lovers' emotion (which produced a jarring note in the earlier play) and concentrating instead on
their conflict with the girl's parents, and by shifting the emphasis of
the subplot triangle from the adulteress to the cuckold, which enables
him to build out of the unrealized potentialities of Purge's role the
splendidly audacious character of Allwit, one of the great comic cre-
ations of the Renaissance stage. In this play we can also see a much
more effective use of the sex-money equivalence found in *A Mad
World, My Masters* and *Michaelmas Term,* and of the Dampit role
of *A Trick to Catch the Old One,* which is taken over by Sir Walter
Whorehound in a similar downward "Progress" that provides a negative moral base for the comic actions, while at the same time, unlike
Dampit's sequence, becoming an essential part of those actions and
helping to unify them. And although the scheme through which this
unity is attained is very different from that of *Bartholomew Fair,*
it also represents the author's climactic "limit of multiplicity" and
marks the end of a definite stage in his career. Thereafter he was to
turn his attention to tragicomedy, and to structures (such as the three-
level hierarchy of *A Fair Quarrel*) that were generally less ambitious.

The evolution of multiplot technique in Shakespeare's comedies
is more complicated, as one would expect, and more difficult to sum-
marize so briefly, but it is possible to see it advancing slowly and un-
certainly toward the "reversed" hierarchy we discovered in *As You
Like It.* Although the chronological sequence of his earliest plays
is still disputed, it is clear that from the very beginning he was
deliberately experimenting with various ways of combining three
distinct levels of comic action, and that he gradually came to associate
these levels with three distinct kinds of love, which results in a comic
form quite different from Jonson's and Middleton's. In *The Comedy
of Errors* he borrows the story of the twin brothers from Plautus's
Menaechmi (a one-level play) but invests it with greater romantic
sentiment, and adds by way of contrast the more farcical confusion
of their twin servants, adapted from Plautus's *Amphitryon,*[6] and
the more serious frame story of their father, Aegeon. This arrangement is turned around in *The Taming of the Shrew,* where the low-

---

[6] It may also owe something to *Stichus* (see Appendix A).

comic Sly episode is used as a frame, and the two principal actions depict the sharply differentiated love stories of Bianca and her sister Kate—one rather prettified and conventional, the other much more robust and realistic. *The Two Gentlemen of Verona* does not fit this pattern, but in *Love's Labor's Lost* we have a triple hierarchy that seems to foreshadow *As You Like It;* the attitude toward love embodied in the courtship of Berowne and Rosaline sometimes approaches the complex perspective of the later Rosalind, and his behavior and that of his companions in the main-action romances is made to seem less artificial and ridiculous in comparison with Don Armado, whose infatuated wooing, like Silvius's, is so much more fantastically elevated above reality than their own (and addressed to a woman so much below theirs), while Costard on the third level represents the same sort of frank sexuality as Touchstone. (The episodes devoted to Holofernes and Sir Nathaniel make up a fourth component, integrated with the others through the equivalence of love and language which operates in all three levels of the romantic hierarchy.) The plot combination of *A Midsummer Night's Dream* also points in this direction, since the "madness" of the young lovers in the woods is played off against the realistic, mature love in the frame story of Theseus and Hippolyta, and the earthy practicality of Bottom, who functions as a desexualized Costard or Touchstone in his encounter with Titania. *The Merchant of Venice* poses a special problem because one of its main plots is not concerned with romance (although it is related to the romantic actions in the love-friendship equation that unifies the play). And we have already seen how *Much Ado about Nothing* utilizes the standard three-level formula, and how that formula is inverted in the more successful structure of *As You Like It,* which marks the climax of this sequence. The plots of *Twelfth Night* follow a quite different scheme (an inferior scheme, I believe, although many would disagree), and *The Merry Wives of Windsor* and the "bitter comedies" of Shakespeare's next period really belong to different subgenres.

The role of the comic genre itself in the foregoing accounts suggests another possible approach to this subject, for though our investigation has been based on universal formal categories applicable to all dramatic genres (as evidenced by the range of examples in each of the central chapters), it could with equal validity have been organized around these genres and subordinated the categories to them. This, again, might be done historically, by tracing the evolution of multiple-plot comedy, tragedy, history, and so on, but it might also proceed analytically by considering the logical relationship of the multiple plot to each kind of drama. There clearly is such a relationship, since it is not coincidental that the two plays which seemed to realize the fullest potentialities of "multiplicity" were both comedies, or that the development of the three greatest practitioners was most evident within this same genre. The multiple plot is apparently more effective in comedy than in tragedy, as some of the better playwrights recognized: Shakespeare used a subplot in only one of his major tragedies, and Jonson, Chapman, and Webster avoided it in theirs. Indeed, the number of multiple-plot tragedies of the first rank in this period is quite small, while it is almost impossible to think of a good single-plot comedy.

A historical explanation can be found for this in the classical models that exercised such a profound influence upon the Renaissance stage, since the subplot is never used in the tragedies of Seneca (or of the Greeks) but is an important element in most of Terence's comedies, as we will later see. However, I think there are more fundamental reasons underlying the Renaissance practice, and the Greek and Roman as well, which inhere in the nature of the two genres. One such reason is related to the different kind or degree of probability required of them. In a successful tragedy the lines of causation leading to the catastrophe should seem inevitable and should spring directly from the character of the protagonist and his immediate situation, whereas in comedy we do not expect this sense of inevitability and in fact welcome the crossing of separate lines of causation (which is often amusing in itself) and the surprising complications and reversals resulting from it. But that is just what must happen in the double plot if it is successfully integrated on the causal level, where each action should significantly affect the outcome of the other. Thus the demands of the double plot in this respect appear to be entirely appropriate to comedy and in direct conflict with the demands of tragedy. And this is borne out by the fact that in most of the multi-plot tragedies we examined, the causation only proceeds "downward" —that is, the main action alters the course of the subplot, but is not altered by it. The absence of reciprocal connections preserves the integrity of the tragic plot, but at the expense of weakening the integrity of the plot combination.

Another and probably more basic explanation of the relationship of the multiple plot to these two genres involves the final rather than the efficient level of integration. For reasons that we cannot go into here, the tragic effect is by its very nature more homogeneous and more concentrated than that of comedy. This may be seen, for instance, in the much greater dependence of tragedy upon a single dominant protagonist (even in plays like *Romeo and Juliet,* where the two lovers are treated as a single dramatic entity). And its bearing on the multiple plot is obvious enough, because the more separate comic actions that are added to a comedy, at least up to a point, the more "comic" the play becomes, while increasing the number of tragic actions in a play would certainly not make it more "tragic." Nor is this difficulty avoided by employing less serious subplots, since they may also dilute the concentration of the tragedy. We have found some important exceptions, in which the contribution of the subplot outweighs its disadvantages, but the tendency seems to hold as a general rule, and to be confirmed by the actual tragic production of the period.

There are of course many more problems to be considered in this type of approach. It would examine the relation of the multiple plot to the other genres prominent in the period, including tragicomedy and the history play (in which the clown subplot often has the special purpose, as Empson noted, of representing the "nation" whose fate depends upon and gives weight to the actions of the exalted personages of the main plot). It would also break down these genres into their constituent species or traditions, when they qualified the character of the plot combination (as we saw in comparing Jonson's and Middleton's comedies of intrigue with Shakespearean romantic comedy). And it would attempt to explain how the various combinations or modes of integration operated in each kind of drama. These questions cannot be taken up here, but they will at least indicate some of the possibilities of what appears to be a very promising line of inquiry.

Finally, we should ask if it is possible to surmount the categories and the history and the genres by approaching the multiple plot on a more abstract level, in terms of its general nature and general contribution to the theater. There may seem to be nothing to discuss at such a level, since throughout this study we have insisted that no multiplot structure could be understood apart from its specific function within its concrete dramatic context. But if we strip away all of these particulars we are still left with something—with the fact of "multiplicity" itself. And multiplicity is an important value in its own right, because it grows out of one of the most basic impulses of artistic expression, the impulse to encompass as much as possible. This is the goal of the "coverage" which Empson deals with, and which in earlier dramatic criticism was frequently called "variety," as it is in Sir George Etherege's *She Would If She Could:*

> COURTALL. That which troubles me most is we lost the hopes of variety, and a single intrigue in love is as dull as a single plot in a play, and will tire a lover worse than t'other does an audience.
>
> FREEMAN. We cannot be long without some underplots in this town; let this be our main design, and if we are

anything fortunate in our contrivance we shall make it a
pleasant comedy.

(III.i.86–91) [7]

The banter of these Restoration wits reduces this (and everything else)
to the trivial, but variety can mean much more than the titillation of
jaded audiences. It is closely related, I think, to the Aristotelian conception of "magnitude," although that too is presented in quite super-
ficial terms:

> The limit, however, set by the actual nature of the thing
> is this: the longer the story, consistently with its being com-
> prehensible as a whole, the finer it is by reason of its mag-
> nitude.[8]

Like the other definition from the *Poetics* that initiated our study,
this is much too restrictive, since magnitude is not just a matter of
physical length but also, more significantly, of the depth or breadth
of experience, both internal and external, conveyed by the action (although that will affect its length as well). It does, however, state a
valid criterion, and one directly relevant to this inquiry, for while the
multiple plot is not the only means of achieving magnitude—as *Hamlet* can testify—it was one of the most common and most effective
means employed in the drama of the period.

The magnitude of a play can be enlarged by the multiple plot, according to Empson, in two related senses—in the range of life it includes, and in the range of responses it elicits from the audience. And
both kinds of expansion, corresponding to our material and final
causes, were demonstrated by the analyses of the exemplary plays,
where we found in almost every case that each plot in the combination portrayed a different area of experience or society and produced
a different emotional tone. But it is not possible to "cover" all areas
or all emotions, and even if it were, this would conflict with the criterion of unity which, as Aristotle realized, determines the optimum
magnitude ("consistently with its being comprehensible as a whole")—
or in our earlier formulation, sets the "limits of multiplicity." For the
impulse toward unity is as basic as the impulse toward inclusiveness,
and the tension between the two, although varying in emphasis at dif-

---

7 Dennis Davison (ed.), *Restoration Comedies* (London, 1970). Note also the implicit
assumption of a special connection between the "under-plot" and comedy.
8 *Poetics* vii.1451^{a}10–12. Cf. Jonson's version in *Timber*: "And every bound, for
the nature of the subject, is esteem'd the best that is largest, till it can increase
no more; so it behooves the action in Tragedy or Comedy to be let grow, till the
necessity ask a conclusion" (ed. Herford and Simpson, 8 [1947], 646–47).

ferent times and in different genres, seems to be an essential condition of the drama, if not of all art.

Dramatic inclusiveness, however, involves a formal as well as a material and final dimension, and it is here that the multiple plot provides the opportunity for resolving this tension. While a play cannot cover everything, it can seem to do so with a limited number of separate actions, if they have been defined by the formal structure in such a way as to exhaust the possibilities of the subject.[9] But this structure can do more than that, for the scheme which so defines these actions will at the same time integrate them, through one or more of the categories, as the constituent parts required to make up the complete whole. The very exhaustiveness of the plot combination, in other words, becomes its principle of unity. We have seen many exhaustive schemes of this sort which differentiate and integrate the plots—in terms of social classes, in *The Shoemakers' Holiday* and *A Woman Killed with Kindness,* or moral positions, in *The Atheist's Tragedy* and the three censors of *Bartholomew Fair,* or two extremes and a mean, in *The Family of Love* and *As You Like It,* or the permutations of a "nuclear" parallel situation, in *A Fair Quarrel* and *Hyde Park.* In these and numerous other works the multiple plot supplied the playwrights with a means for satisfying both of the opposing demands, for generating and controlling the variegated panoramic richness which is one of the most characteristic and most glorious attributes of this great theater. It is therefore in large part responsible for that richness, and beyond its particular functions in the individual plays, this is what constitutes its principal general contribution to the drama of the English Renaissance.

---

[9] On this point see L. A. Beaurline, "Ben Jonson and the Illusion of Completeness," *PMLA,* 84 (1969), 51–59.

Appendix A

The Double Plot in Roman Comedy

All students of English Renaissance drama agree that it originated in the happy confluence of the native and classical (or more specifically, Roman) theatrical traditions. They have not always agreed, however, in determining the relative weight to be attached to these two sources, and on this question I think we can trace a major shift in opinion occurring at about the same time as the other critical revolutions already referred to. It is most evident in the field of tragedy, where the discussion has centered, although it also involves the less serious genres. The older view, typified by Cunliffe's *The Influence of Seneca on Elizabethan Tragedy* (1893) and introduction to *Early English Classical Tragedies* (1912), Manly's *The Influence of the Tragedies of Seneca upon Early English Drama* (1907), the introduction to Kastner and Charlton's edition of *The Poetical Works of Sir William Alexander* (1921), and Lucas's *Seneca and Elizabethan Tragedy* (1922), stressed the classical contribution; but since the publication of Willard Farnham's *The Medieval Heritage of Elizabethan Tragedy* and Howard Baker's *Induction to Tragedy* during the 1930s we find an increasing concentration on the influence of the native tradition, which still continues in such recent works as Bernard Spivack's *Shakespeare and the*

Allegory of Evil and David Bevington's *From "Mankind" to Marlowe.* There seem to be several reasons for this change of emphasis, including the general reassessment of the Renaissance as an organic outgrowth of the Middle Ages rather than a sharp break from them, the great expansion of our knowledge of early English drama (and contraction of our Latin), and the special interest of some of the newer schools of criticism in the primitive elements which stand out more prominently in this naïve drama than in the sophisticated products of the Roman stage—although it will be shown that they too preserve some archaic material.

In relation to our investigation this new emphasis has certainly been vindicated, since we saw that many of the characteristic multiple-plot patterns appear in embryonic form in the late Moralities and semi-Moralities marking the transition to the secular theater. One cannot assume, however, that their development was not also influenced by the other tradition, even though this possibility is usually overlooked. Some of the Roman comedies contain types of subplots which are quite similar to those we have just examined, and could easily have served as their models. For the works of Plautus and Terence had acquired a very considerable authority in England during this period; many of the playwrights would have studied them (and even acted in them) at school, and the more learned would also have been aware of the substantial body of reverential commentary already built around them by the continental critics, some of it dealing explicitly with the double plot.[1] There is to be sure seldom any certain way of deciding whether a particular aspect of English multiplot drama derived from them (either directly or via the Italian *commedia erudita*) or from the Morality tradition, or both, or evolved spontaneously out of the internal logic of the artistic structure. But even if these comedies are only early analogues rather than actual sources of this drama, they are still worth examining for the light they can shed on the general functions of the subplot.

I

Of the eighty-odd plays that have survived from classical antiquity, only those of Terence contain a fully developed double plot, which he regularly constructs by combining the stories of two pairs of young lovers. This is one of the most striking features of his dramaturgy; virtually all of the commentators from Donatus and Evanthius down to the present discuss it, and virtually all of them find that it contributes significantly to his artistic achievement. They also seem to

---

[1] See Marvin Herrick, *Comic Theory in the Sixteenth Century* (Urbana, 1950), pp. 112–16.

agree about this contribution, for while these discussions have been as various as the points of view brought to bear on the subject, the specific advantages claimed for the Terentian "duality-method" [2] usually come down to the same two basic points: the enrichment of the comic complication that results from the causal interaction of the two plots, and the illuminating contrasts this provides between the parallel characters—the two *adulescentes,* the two *senes,* and sometimes others —of these plots. There is, however, another important dimension of this duality which should be considered in any attempt to account for its effectiveness and for its possible influence upon later drama.

That dimension becomes evident as soon as the comparison is extended beyond the individual characters in these two romantic stories to the nature of the two romances themselves. In each of the four comedies built on the double-plot structure (this does not include *The Woman of Andros,* since Charinus's affection for Philumena never leads to any action that might constitute a separate plot [3]), the parallel love affairs are differentiated along the same lines: one pair of lovers (Clinia and Antiphila in *The Self-Tormentor,* Chaerea and Pamphila in *The Eunuch,* Antipho and Phanium in *Phormio,* Aeschinus and Pamphila in *The Brothers*) eventually unite in a legal and socially accepted marriage, while the other pair (Clitipho and Bacchis, Phaedria and Thais, Phaedria and Pamphila, Ctesipho and Bacchis respectively) only form an irregular sexual liaison. From this follows another major difference in the nature of the action appropriate to the two kinds of romance: in the "marriage-plot" the central problem is always the social status of the young woman, which seems to disqualify her as a wife, and so the resolution typically turns on a *cognitio* revealing her true parentage; in the "liaison-plot," on the other hand, the problem is not the woman's status (which never changes) but the ability of the young man to obtain or keep her, and it is resolved through some stratagem, usually financial, initiated by him or his allies to that end. This does not mean all four plots of each type are identical, for the pattern admits of considerable variation in detail from play to play, and a few do not exactly fit in all respects; thus the marriage in *The Brothers* requires no *cognitio,* and the money to maintain the liaison in *The Eunuch* is not acquired by the usual trickery. But as a general formula it indicates a fundamental contrast between the combined plots which is developed so consistently in these plays that it must

---

[2] As Gilbert Norwood terms it in *The Art of Terence* (Oxford, 1923).
[3] Charinus's plea to undertake such an action is explicitly rejected by Davus, the chief manipulator (709–13). It has been suggested that the inclusion of Charinus (who according to Donatus was not in the Menandrian original) represents Terence's first tentative approach to the dual structure he was to develop in the four later plays.

have been the result of Terence's conscious intention, either in his initial choice of Greek models or in his alterations of them.

A few modern critics have noted this contrast,[4] but too often it has been ignored, especially by those who wish to reduce all the products of New Comedy to a single archetype. Moses Hadas, for example, asserts that in this genre the following story is "repeated with only minor changes from play to play":

> a young man is in love with a girl owned by a white slaver who is about to dispose of her elsewhere; his cunning servant defrauds the young man's father of the necessary sum; the girl is discovered to be of good birth (having been kidnapped or exposed in infancy) and hence an eligible bride.[5]

Gilbert Norwood constructs a similar "composite photograph" of the plots of Plautus and Terence:

> A young Athenian is in love with a charming but friendless girl who is the purchased slave of a *leno* . . . He wishes to purchase her and keep her as his mistress . . . Here intervenes his slave, loyal to his young master but otherwise conscienceless, who saves the situation by an elaborate ruse either to defraud the hero's father of the needed sum or to induce the slave-owner to part with the girl. When discovery of this deception arrives, all is put right by a sudden revelation that the heroine is really of Athenian birth (but kidnapped or lost in babyhood) and can therefore marry the hero.[6]

And another such "conventional" plot, couched in Freudian terms, is presented by Northrop Frye.[7] All of these formulations conflate the two distinct kinds of romantic attachment and of dramatic action which Terence separates by his dual structure, so it is not surprising that they have prevented many commentators from appreciating this aspect of the structure and have even led to some unjust criticisms of it, such as the complaint that "the dualism" of *The Eunuch* "would have been perfect had Thais been legally possible as a wife for Phaedria." But that would have meant a second marriage-plot with a second *cognitio*, which is just what Terence always avoids.

---

4 See Philip Harsh, *A Handbook of Classical Drama* (Stanford, 1944), p. 316, and George Duckworth, *The Nature of Roman Comedy* (Princeton, 1952), pp. 157–58.
5 *Roman Drama* (Indianapolis, 1965), p. ix. No extant Greek or Roman comedy fits this description.
6 *Plautus and Terence* (New York, 1932), p. 12.
7 "The Argument of Comedy," *English Institute Essays, 1948* (New York, 1949), pp. 58–59.

One reason for avoiding this duplication seems obvious enough: the use of two coincidental discoveries of long-lost daughters would make them both much less probable. It would also make them much less interesting, because of the predictable and boring repetition. The sense of fascinated excitement Terence is able to engender depends in large measure on the range of situation and incident provided by his formula, since it brings together two very different comic worlds— one presided over by a benevolent Fate, where the principal errors and ironies result from an essential ignorance, shared by all the characters, which is innocent of human contrivance and is finally dispelled in a happy and equally uncontrived revelation of the truth; and the other controlled by a shrewd schemer who deliberately arranges most of the confusion and invites us to enjoy the cleverness of his deceptions and the ridiculous discomfitures of his victims. In terms then of both credibility and variety, it is easy to see the advantages of this plot combination.

This may account for the combination on the formal level of the contrasts between the two kinds of actions, but we have still to consider the final effect of the contrast between the two kinds of romance portrayed in them. It is not a simple matter, since it involves the emotional and moral coloring of those romances, and that is determined not by the real-life attitudes toward marital and extramarital love in Terence's society in second-century Rome, or in the fourth-century Athens of his models, but by a theatrical convention which has created an artificial exotic world of its own kept at some distance from the audience, the world of the *palliata*.[8] Some of the nuances of feeling implied in this contrast, therefore, may well be irrecoverable. Because they are defined by the convention, Terence can assume these affective values in his representation, which is concerned not so much with the romantic affairs themselves as with the conflicts precipitated by them between the two young men and their fathers (or between the two fathers in *The Brothers* and to a lesser extent in *The Self-Tormentor*). There are very few scenes bringing the young lovers together (indeed the girl is rarely seen); their emotional relationship has usually been established before the play opens and undergoes no real development, being treated in terms of the convention as a *donnée*. And the attempts to describe the passion of the *adulescens*, either in his own words or indirectly through others, are seldom very helpful in distinguishing these two sorts of love. In the liaison-plot as in the marriage-plot this passion is called *amor*, and in both he typically re-

---

8 Walter Chalmers discusses this point in "Plautus and His Audience," *Roman Drama* (London, 1965).

acts to the threatened loss of his beloved with the same despairing thoughts of death or exile,[9] and to their prospective union or reunion with the same rhapsodic delight.

Terence does, however, include some explicit statements of this distinction. In *The Self-Tormentor* Clitipho compares the haughtiness and avarice of the *meretrix* he loves to the virtuous modesty of the *virgo* loved by Clinia (223–27), and in a later scene Bacchis enlarges on this comparison from the woman's point of view (381–95); each young man in *Phormio* contrasts his plight with his cousin's, Phaedria arguing that Antipho is more fortunate in having married a respectable lady (162–72), and Antipho that Phaedria is better off since his problem was solved as soon as he paid the slave-dealer (820–27); and in *The Brothers* a number of people point out the difference between Aeschinus's attachment to Pamphila, whom he had promised to marry, and his supposed infatuation with the slave-girl he bought for Clitipho (326–34; 469–77, 724–25).[10] But it is through the action itself that the distinction emerges most clearly. In the marriage-plots of *The Self-Tormentor, Phormio,* and *The Brothers* the young man has been living with a decent girl, though apparently of humble or foreign birth, whom he already regards as his wife,[11] so when the discovery occurs it does not alter his attitude toward her but simply allows their relationship to be regularized. The liaison-plots can have two kinds of women—in *The Self-Tormentor* and *The Eunuch* a professional courtesan whose favors the youth has enjoyed for some time, and in *Phormio* and *The Brothers* a music-girl owned by a slave-dealer and at first unattainable—yet the liaisons themselves are akin in that they always require money (to maintain the courtesan or buy the girl) and are always transitory, the thought of marriage never crossing anyone's mind. There also seems to be a calculated effort to debase these affairs even further. In the first two plays the young man complains of his mistress' infidelity or cupidity, the usual stigmata of the *meretrix,* and his romantic posturings are severely qualified during the final episode by the ease with which he consents to share her with a rival in *The Eunuch* or, in *The Self-Tormentor,* to abandon her completely. The other two denouements leave the youth in undisputed possession of

[9] Cf. *Self-Tormentor,* 190, 398–400; *Eunuch,* 888; *Phormio,* 200–1, 484, 551–52; *Brothers,* 275, 332. The reference texts are the Loeb Classical Library editions of Terence (ed. John Sargeaunt) and of Plautus (ed. Paul Nixon).
[10] These comparisons are not found in *The Eunuch,* the least typical play of this group, since Chaerea thinks Pamphila is a slave; but see 624–26, 864–71, and 923–40, which imply the contrast with Thais.
[11] See *Self-Tormentor,* 99, 105; *Brothers,* 332–34, 473; in *Phormio* they are legally married. The initial situation in *The Eunuch* again is different because of Pamphila's status, but Chaerea is eager to wed her as soon as she becomes eligible. And since we are told at the outset she is probably a citizen (110), this action arouses the same expectations as the other marriage-plots.

the slave-girl, but the carnal basis of his affection is emphasized by his eagerness to rush her off to a drunken bedroom "party" [12] (in marked contrast to the climax of the marriage-plots, which is never accompanied by this sense of sexual urgency because the union has already been consummated); and the closing lines here, too, serve to belittle their relationship, in the condescending permission he is given to take her home, as if she were a new toy or pet puppy he would soon outgrow.

This suggests that the distinction between the two kinds of romance has been designed as a contrast in emotional tone—that the marriage-plot is meant to be elevated above the plot with which it is combined. The difference already noted between the two types of action contributes to this same effect; the liaison-plot seems more farcical because it is resolved through the trickery of a contest of wits and butts, and the marriage-plot more serious because of the resolving role of a benign Fortune operating above (and often defeating) the plans of the human intriguers. The tonal contrast is also enforced by the nature of the issue that determines each resolution. In the liaison-plot this issue—the goal of the scheming and the means of uniting the lovers—is typically *money*, as Antipho points out when he compares his own problem in marrying Phanium with Phaedria's in obtaining Pamphila:

> I rejoice, considering how things are with me, that my cousin has attained his object. How sensible it is to cherish such desires that when things go wrong you can easily set them right. With him the moment he found the money he got clear of his anxiety . . .
>
> (*Phormio*, 820–23)

And this colors the entire plot; it reduces the action to a confidence game and the romance to a commercial transaction, and it reduces our concern for both because they are made to turn upon an external object, the loss or gain of which does not really change the characters or their place in the world.

In the marriage-plot, on the other hand, the crucial issue is someone's *identity*. It is not a very profound conception of identity, to be sure, since it is defined only in familial and social terms, but it is still much more internal than money and much more serious, in that it does produce a radical and permanent alteration in people's lives, as signified by the public acceptance of the marriage at the close of these plots. This relative scale of value is clearly indicated in *Phormio* by the fact that Chremes is prepared to spend a large sum to dissolve

---

12 *Phormio*, 829–37; *Brothers*, 284–87, 521–31, 589 (cf. *Self-Tormentor*, 902–6).

Antipho's marriage so that he can wed Chremes' daughter. For here money plays a very different role than in the liaison-plot. It is never used to obtain access to the girl (even in *The Eunuch*, where she is supposedly a courtesan's slave [13]), nor is it acquired by trickery from the *senex*; rather, it is willingly given to the youth along with the girl because it is subordinated to the marriage. Thus the combination seems to recapitulate the historical opposition between two marital customs, the liaison-plot based on the system of bride-price, in which the man buys his wife from her family, and the other on the dowry system in which the bride's family pays the groom.

The kinds of love and action and issue in both plots, then, work together to create the two contrasting tones; and since the marriage-plot is the more important in each play (though in some the difference in magnitude is not very great), the liaison-plot can be said to serve as a "foil" to enhance its superior values. This effect is not as fully realized as it might have been, because Terence so seldom focuses on the romances as such, yet it provides an artistic rationale for the pattern he adopted in all his double plots. (He may also have been striving for this effect in his two single-plot comedies, both essentially of the "marriage" type, by including a contrast between his chaste heroine and a courtesan—Chrysis, the supposed sister of Glycerium in *The Woman of Andros,* and Bacchis, the supposed rival of Philumena in *The Mother-in-Law.*)

It is in this foil relationship underlying the pattern, rather than the specific details of the two actions, that these plays may have exercised their most significant influence upon the double plot of English Renaissance drama, although even the details are preserved in some of the earlier and more slavishly imitative "classical" comedies. In *Mother Bombie,* for instance, John Lyly followed the exact prescription of Terence's dual resolution, which he apparently understood better than most modern commentators: the more serious main-plot lovers, Maestius and Serena, are finally brought together by the discovery of their true parentage, and the more comic subplot pair, Candius and Livia, by a trick of the pages (the equivalent of the clever Roman slave or parasite) that fools their parents—but this ends in another marriage rather than concubinage, as required by post-Roman morality. In the later drama, however, the anachronistic *cognitio* is abandoned and the main plot is usually resolved instead by some alteration of the characters' feelings for each other, which permits an even sharper emotional contrast with the subordinate lovers, as does the greatly expanded roles of the women. Yet despite these modifications resulting from the new theatrical and social conventions,

---

[13] See 926–29, and cf. *Brothers,* 348–49.

the basic Terentian pattern can still be discerned in the use of what Jonson called "the sub-couple" [14] to set off the sentimental romance of the main action, and the traits they are given for this purpose—earthiness, cynicism, cunning, and the like—often could have been derived from the intriguers of Terence's liaison-plots. Shakespeare was apparently very fond of this arrangement, since most of his comedies include deromanticized subcouples of this general type, and we found many other examples in the works of his contemporaries, as well as in the formula of our own musical comedy. One cannot prove a direct line of transmission from Rome to Elizabethan London, still less to Broadway, but the continued popularity of this combination of love stories testifies to the effectiveness of Terence's original conception.

II

The surviving comedies of Plautus exhibit a much greater structural variety than those of his successor, but none of them approaches the complexity of the Terentian "duality-method." Although some contain a second pair of young lovers (Pistoclerus and Bacchis of Athens in *The Two Bacchides,* Callidamates and Delphium in *The Haunted House,* Antamoenides and Anterastilis in *The Carthaginian,* Lesbonicus and Callicles' daughter in *The Three Penny Day*), they are more like the dramatically inert Charinus and Philumena in Terence's *The Woman of Andros,* for their relationship does not generate a separate line of action of its own. There are two distinct intrigues, or combinations of intrigue and discovery, in *The Two Bacchides* and *The Carthaginian,* as well as *Curculio, Epidicus,* and *The Braggart Warrior,* but in each case these are developed successively instead of through alternating scenes, and involve only one romantic couple. Thus they are all essentially single-plot plays.

In a number of them, however, we do find another type of "duality" quite unlike Terence's, a subordinate level which is worked out in semidetached episodes rather than a complete subplot, and centers not on a second young gentleman who is the protagonist's peer but on a character socially and emotionally far beneath him—a low-comic slave. The commentators have noted that Plautus uses much more of this independent "servile" buffoonery than Terence; it has even been explained as a consequence of his single plots, which tend to be so thin that they call for this sort of padding. In some plays it is merely padding, introduced for its own sake without any significant relation (beyond a generalized "comic relief") to the main action, but in others it sets up a formal analogy to that action along lines very similar to

---

14 *A Tale of a Tub,* V.x.91.

the clown material discussed in Chapter 4. As in the later drama, the analogous episode often represents an imitation, conscious or unconscious, by the clown of his "betters," here usually his owner or his owner's son. There is an obvious example in Act IV, scene iii, of *The Three Penny Day*, where Lesbonicus's slave, Stasimus, laments the loss of his ring during a session in the grogshop, paralleling on a small scale Lesbonicus's own profligacy which precipitated the major intrigue. *The Haunted House* opens with an argument between Theopropides' slaves, Grumio and Tranio, that prepares for the opposition of Theopropides and his son Philolaches on which the action turns: Grumio, in charge of the family farm, is loyal to the father and just as stodgy, while Tranio, who runs the city house, assists and resembles the prodigal son. And in *The Two Bacchides* Chrysalus and Lydus present another belowstairs version of the same contrast between the values of the two generations in the main plot, although they never confront each other, and are comically transposed: Chrysalus, the clever ally of Mnesilochus, is the slave of his father Nicobulus, a typical severe *senex*, but Lydus, the old-fashioned disciplinarian, belongs to the more easygoing Philoxenus, father of Mnesilochus's friend.

The romance of the young lovers, which provides—along with the conflict of generations—the central motivation in most of these plays, is also sometimes set off by a low-comic flirtation between a male and female slave. Sceparnio's clumsy pawing of Ampelisca in *The Rope*, II.iv, invites such a comparison with Plesidippus's efforts to rescue his beloved Palaestra, Ampelisca's fellow fugitive; and the saucy interchange between Paegnium and Sophoclidisca in *The Girl from Persia*, II.ii, bears a similar relationship to the love of their masters, Toxilus and Lemniselenis. These slave courtships, with their farcical bawdry,[15] are pitched at a level much further below the principal romance than were Terence's subcouples, and so should produce a more striking "foil" contrast, but they turn out to be much less significant in the total economy of the play because, like the servile analogues to the opposition between *adulescens* and *senex* already noted, they are limited to single scenes which remain relatively isolated from the main plot and establish only a very rudimentary and vague parallel to it.

The most fully developed and integrated of the Plautine clown-slave actions do not function primarily as foils but as parody. In *Truculentus* we again find the juxtaposed romances of two slaves, Truculentus and Astaphium, and their masters, the country youth Strabax and Phronesium, the avaricious courtesan; but this slave courtship

---

[15] In the scene from *The Rope* Sceparnio wears a phallus (see 429), apparently the only instance of this in all of the New Comedy, according to Harsh.

takes up two scenes that form a little sequence of their own depicting the downward "Progress" of the titular character: in the first (II.ii) he truculently rebuffs Astaphium when she comes to bring his master to her mistress, and threatens to warn the boy's father about the affair; in the second (III.ii) he seeks her out and eagerly offers to pay for her favors. And since in III.i we saw Strabax slip over to Phronesium with a bag of his father's money for the same purpose, the placing of Truculentus's visit to Astaphium immediately after this scene confirms our impression that the slave is imitating his master. Thus the effect is similar to that of the third-level plots in such plays as *The Atheist's Tragedy* and *The Lady of Pleasure,* where the clowns were also corrupted by the example of their betters. Truculentus's comically inept propositioning of the maid debases Strabax's behavior with the mistress, and at the same time renders it more culpable because it has brought about his slave's downfall as well as his own. But the parodic thrust extends beyond this to the entire main action, which is organized around Phronesium's easy success in fleecing a series of lovers (Diniarchus and Stratophanes and Strabax). Truculentus, with his strict "country" morality, was the only one in the play to hold out against this "city" debauchery, so that the sudden collapse of his principles emphasizes the universal power of female sexuality and the helplessness and ludicrousness of the men who succumb to it.

There is a more elaborate parodic analogy in *Casina,* where the rivalry of Lysidamus and his son Euthynicus for the slave-girl Casina is mirrored in the efforts of their respective slaves, Olympio and Chalinus, to marry her. In this case the analogy entails a direct causal connection as well, since each of the masters delegates his own slave as a proxy to obtain the girl for himself. The opening movement, up to the slaves' drawing of lots in II.vi, is structured by this symmetrical two-level competition, with Lysidamus's wife, Cleustrata, taking the side of her son (who like Casina never appears). The first scene shows Olympio threatening to punish Chalinus for disputing his claim to Casina. The next (II.i) shows Cleustrata, in a soliloquy, threatening to punish Lysidamus for pursuing the girl. She and her husband argue in II.iii over which slave shall marry Casina, paralleling the initial confrontation of the slaves themselves. Then in II.iv Lysidamus fails to persuade Chalinus to abandon his suit, and in II.v Cleustrata similarly fails to persuade Olympio. After Olympio wins the lottery, however, the balance shifts; now he and his master are competing for Casina's maidenhead, while Chalinus and his mistress plan a trick (disguising Chalinus as the girl) which results in the comic discomfiture of both Olympio and Lysidamus during the final act. The formal analogy therefore relates the two slaves not only to the sexual rivalry of their masters but also to the generational conflict between them, with Olympio turning out to be as foolish as the father, who is the chief butt of the intrigue, and Chalinus as clever as the mother, who is her son's surrogate and chief wit (again the father's servile ally is from the country and the son's from the city). As a consequence the deflationary parody is directed primarily at Lysidamus, since he is the "dirty old man" guilty of the two unforgivable sins—trying to cross young love and letting himself be gulled. But even though our sympathies are wholly with the son, who will eventually marry Casina,[16] the slaves' buffoonery must to some extent color his romance as well (which may be one reason why he is kept off stage and replaced by the mother). This can be demonstrated by comparing the play to *The Merchant*, which also portrays a competition-by-substitute between father and son for a girl, where their proxies are not two clownish slaves but a respectable neighbor and his son. The result is a more sentimental love interest and a much duller comedy.

The "duality" in *Amphitryon* is worked out on the same two levels, although the sexual conflict of the main plot does not pit father against son but mortal against god, and the servile conflict, while built on an analogous wit-butt relationship, does not involve a woman. On one level Jupiter impersonates Amphitryon in order to take his place and get at his wife Alcmena; on the other Mercury impersonates Amphitryon's slave, Sosia, in order to take his place and assist Jupiter. It it true that Mercury is not the slave of Jupiter but his son (and of course a god), yet he is given all the traits of the *dolosus servos,* including the bawdry, buffoonery, and physical slapstick, and even the insolence that evokes the standard promises of punishment from his "master." He also shares the slave's special familiarity with the audience, which he exploits in one of his entrances to identify his role:

> Get away, get out, get off the street, every one! Let no man be so bold as to block my path. For damme, just tell me why a god like me hasn't as much right to hector people that hinder him as your paltry slave in the comedies? He brings word the ship is safe, or the choleric old man approaching: as for me, I hearken to the word of Jove and at his bidding do I now hie me hither.
>
> (984–89) [17]

---

[16] The Epilogue says she will be revealed as the daughter of a neighboring couple, Alcesimus and Myrrhina, making her an eligible bride. As in *The Merchant,* these neighbors are allies of the principal contenders, the husband aiding Lysidamus and the wife Cleustrata, but their role is much less important than that of the two slaves.
[17] Compare the typical entrance of the Morality Vice, ordering the audience to "Make way!"

And this servile role produces a causal as well as an analogical connection between the two levels, along the same lines as *Casina:* like Chalinus, Mercury makes a fool of his slave-adversary in the subordinate action because he is helping his master make a fool of his adversary's master in the main action.

As a result of the double impersonation, the structure forms a more intricate pattern of symmetrical alternation than in *Casina.* It too begins with a low-comic confrontation of the slaves, during which Mercury in his disguise utterly confuses and routes the real Sosia, thus preparing for and contributing to the later confusion and defeat of Amphitryon. The next scene consists of Mercury's soliloquy foretelling that defeat and the final reconciliation. In I.iii Jupiter, disguised as Amphitryon, takes leave of Alcmena after their long night together, and threatens Mercury with a beating to silence his sly interjections. Act II presents the real Amphitryon's parallel meetings with slave and wife: in the first scene he threatens to beat Sosia for his story about a "twin," and in the second he greets Alcmena after their long separation, but her strange welcome leads to a bitter argument between them, contrasting to the tender parting of I.iii (it is also punctuated by Sosia's running commentary, just as that was by Mercury's, only now Alcmena wants Amphitryon to punish Sosia for his remarks, whereas then she protected Mercury from Jupiter's wrath). Act III opens with Jupiter's prophetic soliloquy, like Mercury's in I.ii. He returns to Alcmena in III.ii and is berated by her because of the treatment she received from her husband in II.ii, causing another reversal which he himself points out:

> this love affair of mine lately occasioned [Amphitryon's] guiltless self some consternation, it is turn about now, and my guiltless self has to suffer for the scorn and contumely he heaped on her.
>
> (894–96)

But he talks himself back into her good graces and bed, and orders off *both* slaves, sending Sosia on an errand (III.iii) and placing Mercury on guard to keep Amphitryon from entering the house (III.iv). Amphitryon arrives in Act IV and confronts Mercury, who holds him off by dousing him with slops. There is a large lacuna in the manuscripts here, but from surviving scraps of dialogue we can reconstruct the three remaining encounters required by this pattern: Alcmena shuts out her husband (having admitted his double in III.ii); he attacks the real Sosia for the dousing administered by the false Sosia (the converse of Alcmena's earlier attack on the false Amphitryon for the abuse she had suffered from the real one); and finally the two prin-

cipals, Amphitryon and Jupiter, meet face to face in a violent quarrel
that brings us back full circle to the quarrel of their slaves in I.i, and
like it ends with the impostor's victory. This is the climax and com-
pletion of the parallelism; neither Mercury nor Sosia figures in the
happy resolution.

Prior to this resolution the servile subaction has much the same
parodic effect as in *Casina,* for although Mercury and Sosia, unlike
Chalinus and Olympio, have no woman to fight over,[18] their conflict
is equated to that of their masters in the romantic triangle of the
main plot, not only by the formal analogies and causal interactions
between the two levels in the sequence just traced, but also by the
kind of "emulation" we found in many Renaissance clown episodes.
This is explained by Sosia:

> to my way of thinking, an honest servant ought to stick to
> this principle: be like what his betters are, model his expres-
> sion on theirs, be in the dumps if they are in the dumps,
> and jolly if they are happy

> (959–61)

and a little later by Mercury:

> My father calls me; I come, obedient to his hest and will.
> I am a good son to my father, as a son should be. I back
> him up in his gallantries, encourage him, stand by him, ad-
> vise him, rejoice with him. If anything gratifies my father,
> it gratifies me infinitely more.

> (991–94)

The two masters are then doubly responsible for the buffoonery of the
slaves, who are following their orders and their example; consequently
that buffoonery will reflect on them both—primarily, as in *Casina,* on
the butt of the intrigue, Amphitryon, but also to a lesser degree on
Jupiter, since his behavior (before the thunderclap which ends Act IV
and introduces a new note of solemnity) consistently belies his divine
status and so becomes subject to this further deflation. That is the chief
function of the subaction, for the main plot itself is a "high" comic
parody of the serious legend, and therefore the slaves' "low" comic
parody of this plot makes a special contribution to the overall effect,

---

[18] Sosia once refers to "my lady friend" (659), who could be Alcmena's maid
Bromia, and Mercury could have used his disguise to take the same advantage of
her that his father took of her mistress. Perhaps he did in the Greek original,
or in the missing portion of Plautus's play. Molière provided such a belowstairs
Alcmena for these men in his adaptation, and so did Shakespeare when he im-
ported them, as the two Dromios, into *The Comedy of Errors.*

which Mercury in the Prologue defines as a combination of these two
levels:

> I'll convert this same play from tragedy to comedy . . . I
> shall mix things up: let it be tragi-comedy. Of course it
> would never do for me to make it comedy out and out,
> with kings and gods on the boards. How about it, then?
> Well, in view of the fact that there is a slave part in it, I
> shall do just as I said and make it tragi-comedy.
>
> (54–63)

The slave-clowns in *Stichus* have a different role because there is
no real main plot for them to parallel. In fact the absence of such a
plot has led many critics to deal quite harshly with the play. But while
it cannot be defended on esthetic grounds, it should be of considerable
interest to dramatic historians and theoreticians, particularly those
with an anthropological or psychological orientation, since this very
deficiency would seem to indicate that the play preserves a simpler
and purer version of the primitive ritual pattern which also underlies
the more sophisticated productions of Plautus and Terence. Its artistic "formlessness" stands much closer than these other dramas to that
original preartistic "form," and so renders it more accessible to us.
In this sense *Stichus* is, I think, the most archaic of all the surviving
examples of New Comedy.

The play consists of three distinct episodes, which grow progressively less serious. In Act I Antipho, a widower, tries to persuade his
two daughters, Panegyris and Pamphila, to divorce their husbands, the
brothers Epignomus and Pamphilippus, who have been away three
years on a trading voyage to recoup their lost fortunes. Although the
women placate him with cajolery and caresses, they reject his advice.
In Acts II–IV the two husbands return triumphantly, laden with
merchandise and slaves, to be reunited with their wives and reconciled to their father-in-law; but they laugh off his request for one
of the slave-girls, and the request of their former parasite, Gelasimus,
for an invitation to the family feast they are planning to celebrate
their homecoming. And the final act portrays the drunken revelry of
the brothers' two slaves, Stichus and Sangarinus, who are having their
own homecoming feast with their common mistress, Stephanium, the
maid of Pamphila.

The situation itself is very familiar, embodying the same formula
found in most of the New Comedy—the victory of young love over
the opposition (on the usual financial considerations) of the older
generation. The striking difference is that here no line of action is
required to defeat the opposition and bring about the victory—no

intrigue, no recognition, no "plotting" at all. In Aristotle's terminology, there is only the "beginning" and "end" of a plot without any "middle" to provide a causal link between them.[19] But if the play is an archaic survival, this would mean that the "middle," where the principal dramatic interest of the other comedies lies, is a later addition to the formula, which was once limited to these two terminal stages. And this hypothesis is confirmed by the relation of those stages to the presumed source of classical comedy—a ritual ceremony based on the natural cycle of the seasons. Translating the play into that cycle, we can see that the first stage is winter, the domain of the "dying year god," represented by the old sterile father, and that his daughters represent the earth, lying fallow under his rule and longing for the spring. In urging them to divorce their husbands and come back to his house he is trying to perpetuate his rule, to make them abandon hope that spring will return. But it does return in the second stage, with the arrival of the young men who bear the riches of the earth and will fertilize their wives to produce new human life as well. And the festive meal or *komos* at the end is the celebration of this triumph of youth over age, spring over winter, and life over death, a sacred Communion which in an earlier period would be shared by the actors with their audience (and which retains something of its original religious significance in the statements by both husbands of their intention to sacrifice to the gods before feasting).

This also accounts for the unusual prominence given to the meal—it takes up about one-sixth of the text, and an even greater proportion of the acting time because of the elaborate stage business. In most New Comedies, which concentrate upon the complications of the "middle," it has completely disappeared, although vestiges of it survive in a few of them (and in many Renaissance comedies) where the characters are invited to a dinner at the very end.[20] But here all the preceding action is for the sake of the *komos* and leads directly to it: first in the hopes of the wives awaiting their husbands' return, and then in the preparations initiated by the husbands as soon as they land. The entire play *is* a celebration, and because there is no plot development to obscure it, its ritual basis is much clearer than in the more dramatic comedies.

Even the two subsidiary "actions" that occur during the homecoming episode point in this direction, since they are not required by the causal sequence, such as it is, but function primarily to establish the

---

[19] *Poetics* vii.1450^{b}27–35.
[20] See the conclusions of Menander's *The Grouch*, Plautus's *The Two Bacchides*, *Curculio*, *Pseudolus*, and *The Rope*, and Terence's *Phormio*. *The Comedy of Asses* and *The Girl from Persia* present this final feast, but it is much tamer than Stichus's. It appears at the end of about half of Aristophanes' comedies.

significance of the *komos*. In its original form (as in the final act of this play) the *komos* apparently involved a communal sharing of both food and sex, and in each of the minor actions one of these ingredients is withheld from someone by the brothers organizing the festivities: Gelasimus's scheme to cadge a free meal is frustrated by Epignomus in III.ii and Pamphilippus in IV.ii, and in IV.i Antipho's scheme to get a free flute-girl meets the same fate. Antipho can dine with them because he is part of the family and has surrendered gracefully to the new generation, but as the impotent winter king he is incapable of participating in the more literal ceremonies of the fertility rite:

> Even now, the rapscallion takes himself for a young blade.
> I'll give him a girl—to serenade the old codger at night in
> bed. For good Lord, I can't imagine what other use he has
> for one.
>
> (571–73)

Gelasimus, however, cannot even be fed, since he is the outsider who is trying to intrude upon the festival and must be mocked and expelled by the true "initiates." His final rejection, which comes immediately before the feast itself, is treated as a joke by the brothers (as is their rejection of Antipho's plea in the preceding scene), yet his decision to hang himself in despair suggests that it once had a serious import. The primitive *komos* served to reaffirm the spiritual and physical community of the audience, bound together through the tribal ties of blood and marriage, and that community was defined by those it excluded as well as by those who were included in it and were therefore alone permitted to join the ritual.[21]

More to our purpose is the role of the slaves in this *komos,* since we still need to understand why their celebration is presented not merely as a parallel to that of the main plot but as a *substitute* for it. I think this can also be explained in terms of the original ritual, if we recall some of the traits of the clown discussed in Chapter 4. For one thing, he is closer to the audience than any other character, and so is better able to break down the separation between them and the performance at the point when they must make the transition from observers to participants. The slaves in Act V address the audience and stage-musician directly, and even ply the musician with wine from their feast, which originally would have circulated through the entire tribe as the "play" drew to a close and merged into the communal orgy. And the sheer animality of the clown, his freedom from civilized restraints, makes him especially suitable for such an orgy. Because their status reduces them to this appetitive level, the behavior of Stichus, Sangarinus, and Stephanium can be much grosser and

---

21 Compare the fates of Shakespeare's Shylock, Don John, Jaques, and Malvolio.

wilder than their masters', and therefore much more like the primeval *komos.*

The combination of their servile status and orgiastic indulgence also emphasizes the saturnalian function of the ritual. There are incidental traces of such a function in several of Plautus's other comedies, where the nature of the intrigue makes the master temporarily dependent upon his slave and the slave takes advantage of this situation to force his master to beg for help; [22] but *Stichus* ends with an actual slave saturnalia. It is explicitly defined from the outset as a special holiday during which the slaves are given the privileges of free men. Stichus's first speech, when he and Epignomus enter the play in III.i, is a request that he "have this one day off," and Epignomus replies in kind: "The day is yours, I shan't bother you. Be off where you like . . . I put this day at your disposal" (421–24, 435). Pamphilippus also puts his home at the slaves' disposal, so for this one day they can act as masters of the household and their feast can be on an equal footing with Epignomus's, which is taking place next door at the same time and under the same circumstances, as Stichus points out to Sangarinus upon his arrival:

> the dinner's all cooked, and you and I've been given the run of your house here—what with the party at our place, and your master and his wife dining there, along with Antipho and my master too.
>
> (662–65)

During the meal itself the two slaves consciously imitate the etiquette of a formal banquet, giving orders to imaginary servants, discussing the reclining arrangement, and bestowing upon each other the titles of mock-officials ("I appoint you Director of the Cask"; "I elect you Commandant of this banquet") whose duties would be equivalent to the *Saturnalicius princeps* or the later Lord of Misrule. And this festival license is sharply separated from normal life not only by the restriction to a single day but also by Stichus's reassurance to the onlookers, when he is granted the holiday, which distances it from their own world and cancels out any threat it might pose:

> Yes, and you people needn't be surprised that we slavelings have our liquor and love affairs and dinner engagements: all that's permitted us in Athens.
>
> (446–48)

---

[22] Olympio briefly lords it over Lysidamus in *Casina,* III.vi; Libanus and Leonida over Argyrippus in *The Comedy of Asses,* III.iii; and Epidicus and Pseudolus over their masters (Periphanes and Simo) at the close of the two plays named for them. This aspect of Plautine comedy is discussed in Erich Segal's *Roman Laughter* (Cambridge, Mass., 1968), chap. 4.

As "slavelings," furthermore, it is appropriate for them to have a common mistress, which makes their celebration seem more saturnalian than that of their masters, who are monogamously paired off with Antipho's daughters. But I think this deviation from the parallel between the two levels suggests a more basic affinity, for the sexual relations of the main characters are not quite as proper as they may appear. Northrop Frye argued that the conflict of the generations in New Comedy is a "displaced" version of the Oedipal triangle, and this interpretation is borne out in several of Plautus's plays where the father desires the same girl as his son—in *Casina* and *The Merchant*, as we saw, and in *The Comedy of Asses* and *The Two Bacchides*.[23] Even when he does not, he usually opposes his son's efforts to get the girl, so that it is possible to regard her as a "displaced" mother figure, and therefore to corroborate the anthropological explanation of the conflict in psychological terms: the union of the young lovers, which represents the victory of spring over winter that preserves the life of the community, also becomes the fulfillment of the individual's Oedipal fantasies. The same situation obtains in *Stichus,* although there the old man is the father of the girl rather than of his young rival. But that is another common form of Oedipal displacement, found in the many folktales and legends where a jealous, possessive father places obstacles in the path of his daughter's suitors or locks her up from them.[24] Antipho, in urging Panegyris and Pamphila to divorce their husbands, is really trying to keep them for himself. A number of details in their initial interview point to this concealed motivation—his flustered response to the kisses and caresses they shower upon him, in what seems a deliberate attempt to exploit his incestuous desires; his announcement of his intention to remarry, which he later admits was a ruse designed to "test" them; and his final revelation:

> But here's the true cause of my coming to you and wishing
> a conference with you both: my friends are advising me to
> take you away to my own home.
>
> (127–28)

And it comes still closer to the surface after the arrival of his sons-in-law, because as soon as he realizes he has permanently lost his daughters to them, he asks for a flute-girl as a replacement:

---

23 Note also the rivalry of uncle and nephew in *The Pot of Gold.*
24 *The Merchant of Venice* combines two versions of this formula—one in the Jessica–Lorenzo plot, another (with a benign father) in the plot of Portia and her caskets.

> I gave you my daughter to pass your nights with pleasantly:
> and now I consider it a fair return for you to give me a girl
> to pass my nights with.
>
> (547–48)

But while the suggestions of incest in the main plot center around Antipho's attachment to his daughters, I think they also carry over to the younger generation. These two sisters are themselves married to two brothers, so that the four of them almost form a single family; they live in adjoining houses, the husbands went together on their voyage, the wives waited together for their return, and now they will all share one great banquet to celebrate their joyous reunion.

There is no indication that this sharing will include sex as well as food, but it certainly does in the parallel slave banquet—in fact that seems the most important aspect of their festivities, emphasized repeatedly in the conversation of the two men, in Stephanium's insistent impartiality ("I love you both . . . I'm longing to be with you both"), and in the unabashed eroticism of the action. And its larger meaning is also emphasized, for although Stichus and Sangarinus are introduced as "rivals" for Stephanium (434) and appear to be competing for her approval in their drunken dancing contest (somewhat like the servants in *Fulgens and Lucrece*), the saturnalian spirit not only suppresses their jealousy but actually transforms it into a bond of unity:

> Jolly fine it is to have your rival for your pal,
> Sharing both one loving cup, and both one loving gal.
> I am you and you are I; we're soul-mates rare, we two;
> When our sweetheart is with me, why, she is still with you.
> And still with you, she's still with me;
> We therefore feel no jealousy.
>
> (727–31)

The mystical sense of identity expressed in this song takes us back to the primitive *komos*, where the communal intercourse presumably had the same ritual purpose as the communal eating and drinking. This is confirmed in a few other Roman comedies which conclude with two rivals resolving their quarrel by agreeing to share their sweetheart between them, but she is always a professional courtesan.[25] Panegyris and Pamphila are respectable matrons, and so are prohibited by the

---

25 *Truculentus* and *The Eunuch*; at the end of *The Two Bacchides* both fathers are invited to share their sons' mistresses as well as their dinner. The arrangement in *Stichus* resembles that in *The Comedy of Errors*, where two brothers are matched to two sisters in the main plot, and their two servants to the same kitchen wench in the subplot; but since both actions turn on innocent "errors," they can toy more openly with the incest taboo: Antipholus of Syracuse almost sleeps with his sister-in-law, and the two servants involved with Nell are actually brothers.

dramatic and social conventions from contributing in this way to the union of their menfolk—here husbands and father—who like Stichus and Sangarinus are joined at the end in a common bond ("there is peace and fellowness between us three"). That I believe is the principal reason why the slave feast is substituted for theirs, since it can enact the "real" orgy which is but palely reflected in the more sedate ceremony next door. The main thrust of the parallel then is to equate the higher level to the lower, but the effect is not parodic in our usual sense because it does not so much deflate the masters' feast as extend or deepen its significance. It shows what is really happening beneath the civilized façade of that feast, or rather what would have happened in an earlier time before the ritual evolved into art, and its function therefore precedes our artistic distinction between foil and parody.

Appendix B

List of Plays

This list includes every English play written before 1642 that is mentioned in the text, with the probable date (or date limits) of its first production, the author, and the modern edition used (if one has been quoted or cited), followed by the page numbers of all references to it. Titles of works discussed in some detail are in **boldface italic**. For all of Shakespeare's plays the edition of G. B. Harrison (New York, 1948) has been used, for all of Jonson's the edition of Charles Herford and Percy and Evelyn Simpson (11 vols., Oxford, 1925–52), and for all of Dekker's that of Fredson Bowers (4 vols., Cambridge, 1953–61). "Dodsley" stands for Robert Dodsley's *A Select Collection of Old English Plays*, revised by W. C. Hazlitt (4th ed., 15 vols., London, 1874–76). Dates of production are taken for the most part from Samuel Schoenbaum's revision of Alfred Harbage's *Annals of English Drama, 975–1700* (London, 1964).

The Alchemist, 1610, Ben Jonson, 132, 184–85, 193, 208, 211, 218
Alphonsus, Emperor of Germany, 1587–99, anon. (Chapman on title page), 78

The Antiquary, 1634–36, Shackerly Marmion, ed. Dodsley, Vol. XIII, 59
Antonio's Revenge, 1599–1601, John Marston, 78

M. L. Wine, Regents Series (Lincoln, 1965), 181

Eastward Ho, 1605, Ben Jonson, John Chapman, and John Marston, 88–90

The English Traveler, 1621–33, Thomas Heywood, 6

Enough is as Good as a Feast, 1559–70, W. Wager, 24

Epicene; or, The Silent Woman, 1609, Ben Jonson, 112–13, 181, 218

Every Man in His Humor, 1598, Ben Jonson, 217

Every Man out of His Humor, 1599, Ben Jonson, 217

A Fair Quarrel, 1615–17, Thomas Middleton and William Rowley, ed. Martin Sampson, T. M. (New York, 1915), 3, 7–9, 58, 66–75, 85, 94, 110, 124, 153–54, 158–60, 164, 167, 183, 219, 224

The False One, 1619–23, John Fletcher and Philip Massinger, 131

The Family of Love, 1602–4, Thomas Middleton, ed. A. H. Bullen, *Works of T. M.* (Boston, 1885), Vol. III, 56, 58–66, 70, 74, 75, 103, 107, 110, 125, 181, 183, 201, 218–19, 224

The Famous Victories of Henry V, 1583–88, anon., 117

Friar Bacon and Friar Bungay, 1589–92, Robert Greene, 3, 11–12, 138, 141, 145, 151

Fulgens and Lucrece, 1490–1501, Henry Medwall, 7, 10, 141, 148–50, 216, 244

The Gamester, 1633, James Shirley, ed. William Gifford and Alexander Dyce, *Dramatic Works and Poems of J. S.* (London, 1833), Vol. III, 96–97, 110, 138, 183

The Great Duke of Florence, 1627, Philip Massinger, ed. Arthur Symons, Mermaid Series (London, 1887), 175

Hamlet, 1599–1601, William Shakespeare, 111, 113, 144, 223

Hengist, King of Kent; or, The Mayor of Queenborough, 1615–20, Thomas Middleton, ed. R. C. Bald (New York, 1938), 113

Henry IV, Part 1, 1596–98, William Shakespeare, 11–12, 63, 104–8, 113, 125–26, 138, 140, 142–43, 146

Henry IV, Part 2, 1597–98, William Shakespeare, 117, 138, 140, 142–43

Henry V, 1599, William Shakespeare, 14, 18, 51, 110, 116–20, 122–24, 126, 128, 132, 134, 138, 143, 185

Hoffman; or, Revenge for a Father, 1602, Henry Chettle, 126, 138

Holland's Leaguer, 1631, Shackerly Marmion, 7

The Honest Whore, Part 2, 1604–5, Thomas Dekker, 3

Horestes (The Interlude of Vice), 1567–68, John Pickering, 7, 111, 216

Hyde Park, 1632, James Shirley, ed. Edmund Gosse, Mermaid Series (London, 1888), 7, 14, 96–101, 149, 224

If It Be Not Good, the Devil Is in It (If This Be Not a Good Play, the Devil Is in It), 1611–12, Thomas Dekker, 138, 141

The Insatiate Countess, 1610–13, John Marston and William Barkstead, 125, 138, 147

The Jew of Malta, 1588–90, Christopher Marlowe, 78, 131, 136

List of Plays

1604–7, Thomas Middleton, ed. Martin Sampson, *T. M.* (New York, 1915), 16, 99, 127–37, 168, 175, 178, 183, 185, 193, 218–19

Troilus and Cressida, 1601–2, William Shakespeare, 11, 146, 151, 160–68

Twelfth Night; or, What You Will, 1600–1, William Shakespeare, 220, 241

The Two Gentlemen of Verona, 1590–94, William Shakespeare, 220

Two Lamentable Tragedies (Two Tragedies in One), 1594–98, Robert Yarington, 17

The Virgin Martyr, 1620, Thomas Dekker and Philip Massinger, 29

Volpone; or, The Fox, 1606, Ben Jonson, 2–3, 9, 155, 177, 184–85, 193, 208, 211, 217–18

The Weeding of the Covent Garden; or, The Middlesex Justice of Peace, 1632, Richard Brome, 7

The Welsh Ambassador; or, A Comedy in Disguises, 1623 (?), Thomas Dekker (and John Ford?), 113

What You Will, 1601, John Marston, ed. H. Harvey Wood, *Plays of J. M.,* Vol. II (Edinburgh, 1938), 175

A Wife for a Month, 1624, John Fletcher, 69

The Winter's Tale, 1610–11, William Shakespeare, 113

Wit at Several Weapons, 1609–20, John Fletcher (and Thomas Middleton and William Rowley?), 110

The Witch of Edmonton, 1621, Thomas Dekker, John Ford, and William Rowley, 141

The Witty Fair One, 1628, James Shirley, ed. Edmund Gosse, Mermaid Series (London, 1888), 179

The Woman Hater; or, The Hungry Courtier, 1606, Francis Beaumont and John Fletcher, ed. George Williams, *Dramatic Works in the B. and F. Canon,* gen. ed. Fredson Bowers, Vol. I (Cambridge, 1966), 11–12, 151–54, 168, 172

A Woman Killed with Kindness, 1603, Thomas Heywood, ed. R. W. Van Fossen, Revels Series (London, 1961), 2–3, 6, 19, 93–97, 99, 145, 224

Women Beware Women, 1620–27, Thomas Middleton, 110

Your Five Gallants, 1604–7, Thomas Middleton, 218

Select Bibliography

This bibliography does not include unpublished material, except in section I, or material not in English. Section V is limited to the major writers of multiple-plot drama in the period and to critical studies that deal directly with the interplot relationships in this drama. Articles later incorporated into books by their authors are not listed separately, and introductions to editions of the plays are excluded, except for a few of special significance. In the case of Shakespeare, it was only possible to give a small sampling of the very considerable body of literature that might be cited, with special emphasis on the seven plays discussed in this book.

Under each dramatist in section V studies covering two or more works are listed before those devoted to single works; under Shakespeare and Middleton there is a further subdivision by genre. Playwrights are arranged alphabetically, and plays chronologically. No attempt was made to provide cross-references to the general studies in sections I and II.

Perhaps it is necessary to add that no evaluation is implied in this selection, which is based solely upon the relevance of the items to multiple-plot analysis.

I. General Studies of the Multiple Plot

Armbrister, Victor. "The Origins and Functions of Subplots in Elizabethan Drama." Ph.D. dissertation, Vanderbilt University, 1938 [summary published by the Joint University Libraries, Nashville, 1938].

Bradbrook, Muriel. *The Growth and Structure of Elizabethan Comedy*. London: Chatto & Windus, 1955.

———. *Themes and Conventions of Elizabethan Tragedy*. Cambridge: University Press, 1935.

Doran, Madeleine. *Endeavors of Art: A Study of Form in Elizabethan Drama*. Madison: University of Wisconsin Press, 1954.

Empson, William. *Some Versions of Pastoral*. London: Chatto & Windus, 1935.

Fergusson, Francis. *The Idea of a Theater*. Princeton: Princeton University Press, 1949.

Fletcher, Angus. *Allegory: The Theory of a Symbolic Mode*. Ithaca: Cornell University Press, 1964.

Rabkin, Norman. "The Double Plot in Elizabethan Drama." Ph.D. dissertation, Harvard University, 1959.

———. "The Double Plot: Notes on the History of a Convention." *Renaissance Drama* 7 (1964): 55–69.

Smith, L. G. "The Sub-Plot in Jacobean Drama, with Special Reference to Shakespeare, Heywood, Middleton and Fletcher." Master's thesis, King's College, London, 1957.

II. General Studies of the Fool and the Clown

Baskervill, Charles Read. *The Elizabethan Jig and Related Song Drama*. Chicago: University of Chicago Press, 1929.

Busby, Olive. *Studies in the Development of the Fool in the Elizabethan Drama*. London: Oxford University Press, 1923.

Chambers, E. K. *The English Folk-Play*. Oxford: Clarendon Press, 1933.

———. *The Mediaeval Stage*. 2 vols. London: Oxford University Press, 1903.

Cole, Douglas. "The Comic Accomplice in Elizabethan Revenge Tragedy." *Renaissance Drama* 9 (1966): 125–39.

Disher, M. Willson. *Clowns and Pantomimes*. London: Constable, 1925.

Empson, William. *The Structure of Complex Words*. Norfolk: New Directions, 1951.

Kaiser, Walter. *Praisers of Folly: Erasmus, Rabelais, Shakespeare*. Cambridge, Mass.: Harvard University Press, 1963.

Moore, John Brooks. *The Comic and the Realistic in English Drama.* Chicago: University of Chicago Press, 1925.

Nicoll, Allardyce. *Masks, Mimes and Miracles: Studies in the Popular Theatre.* New York: Harcourt, Brace, 1931.

Swain, Barbara. *Fools and Folly during the Middle Ages and the Renaissance.* New York: Columbia University Press, 1932.

Welsford, Enid. *The Fool: His Social and Literary History.* London: Faber & Faber, 1935.

Willeford, William. *The Fool and His Scepter.* Evanston: Northwestern University Press, 1969.

Winslow, Ola. *Low Comedy as a Structural Element in English Drama from the Beginnings to 1642.* Chicago: University of Chicago Libraries, 1926.

Wright, Louis. "Variety-show Clownery on the Pre-Restoration Stage." *Anglia* 52 (1928): 51–68.

III. General Studies of Comic and Realistic Elements in the Mystery Cycles

Auerbach, Erich. *Mimesis: The Representation of Reality in Western Literature.* Translated by Willard Trask. Princeton: Princeton University Press, 1953.

Janicka, Irena. *The Comic Elements in the English Mystery Plays against the Cultural Background (Particularly Art).* Poznan, 1962.

Kinghorn, A. M. *Mediaeval Drama.* London: Evans Brothers, 1968.

Kolve, V. A. *The Play Called "Corpus Christi."* Stanford: Stanford University Press, 1966.

McAlindon, T. "Comedy and Terror in Middle English Literature: The Diabolical Game." *Modern Language Review* 60 (1965): 323–32.

McCollom, William. "From Dissonance to Harmony: The Evolution of Early English Comedy." *Theater Annual* 21 (1964): 69–96.

Robinson, J. W. "The Art of the York Realist." *Modern Philology* 60 (1963): 241–51.

Rossiter, A. P. *English Drama from Early Times to the Elizabethans.* London: Hutchinson, 1950.

Salter, F. M. *Mediaeval Drama in Chester.* Toronto: University of Toronto Press, 1955.

Speirs, John. *Medieval English Poetry: The Non-Chaucerian Tradition.* London: Faber & Faber, 1957.

Williams, Arnold. *The Drama of Medieval England*. East Lansing: Michigan State University Press, 1961.

Wood, Frederick. "The Comic Elements in the English Mystery Plays." *Neophilologus* 25 (1940): 39–48, 194–206.

1. The Towneley (Wakefield) *Secunda Pastorum*

Cantelupe, Eugene and Griffith, Richard. "The Gifts of the Shepherds in the Wakefield *Secunda Pastorum:* An Iconographical Interpretation." *Mediaeval Studies* 28 (1966): 328–35.

Chidamian, Claude. "Mak and the Tossing in the Blanket." *Speculum* 22 (1947): 186–90.

Gardner, John. "Structure and Tone in the *Second Shepherds' Play*." *Educational Theatre Journal* 19 (1967): 1–8.

Johnson, Wallace. "The Origin of the *Second Shepherds' Play:* A New Theory." *Quarterly Journal of Speech* 52 (1966): 47–57.

Manly, William. "Shepherds and Prophets: Religious Unity in the Towneley *Secunda Pastorum*." *PMLA* 78 (1963): 151–55.

Morgan, Margery. " 'High Fraud': Paradox and Double-Plot in the English Shepherds' Plays." *Speculum* 39 (1964): 676–89.

Peel, Donald. "The Allegory in *Secunda Pastorum*." *Northwest Missouri State College Studies* 24 (1960): 3–11.

Ross, Lawrence. "Symbol and Structure in the *Secunda Pastorum*." *Comparative Drama* 1 (1967): 122–49.

Thompson, Francis. "Unity in *The Second Shepherds' Tale*." *MLN* 64 (1949): 302–6.

Watt, Homer. "The Dramatic Unity of the *Secunda Pastorum*." *Essays and Studies in Honor of Carleton Brown*. New York: New York University Press, 1940.

Zumwalt, Eugene. "Irony in the Towneley *Shepherds' Plays*." *Research Studies of the State College of Washington* 26 (1958): 37–53.

IV. General Studies of Comic Elements and Double Plot in the Morality Plays

Bevington, David. *From "Mankind" to Marlowe: Growth of Structure in the Popular Drama of Tudor England*. Cambridge, Mass.: Harvard University Press, 1962.

Craik, T. W. *The Tudor Interlude: Stage, Costume, and Acting*. Leicester: Leicester University Press, 1958.

Dessen, Alan. "The 'Estates' Morality Play." *Studies in Philology* 62 (1965): 121–36.

Farnham, Willard. *The Medieval Heritage of Elizabethan Tragedy.* Berkeley: University of California Press, 1936.

Happé, P. "The Vice and the Folk-Drama." *Folklore* 75 (1964): 161–93.

Mares, Francis. "The Origin of the Figure Called 'the Vice' in Tudor Drama." *Huntington Library Quarterly* 22 (1958): 11–29.

Spivack, Bernard. *Shakespeare and the Allegory of Evil.* New York: Columbia University Press, 1958.

Wickham, Glynne. *Shakespeare's Dramatic Heritage.* New York: Barnes & Noble, 1969.

Williams, Arnold. "The English Moral Play before 1500." *Annuale Mediaevale* 4 (1963): 5–22.

Wilson, F. P. *The English Drama, 1485–1585.* Oxford History of English Literature, vol. 4, part 1. Oxford: Clarendon Press, 1969.

V. Studies of Individual Playwrights and Plays

A. FRANCIS BEAUMONT and JOHN FLETCHER

Appleton, William. *Beaumont and Fletcher: A Critical Study.* London: Allen & Unwin, 1956.

Leech, Clifford. *The John Fletcher Plays.* London: Chatto & Windus, 1962.

Waith, Eugene. *The Pattern of Tragicomedy in Beaumont and Fletcher.* New Haven: Yale University Press, 1952.

Wallis, Lawrence. *Fletcher, Beaumont & Company: Entertainers to the Jacobean Gentry.* New York: King's Crown Press, 1947.

1. *The Knight of the Burning Pestle* (Beaumont)

Doebler, John. "Beaumont's *Knight of the Burning Pestle* and the Prodigal Son Plays." *Studies in English Literature* 5 (1965): 333–44.

2. *A King and No King* (Beaumont and Fletcher)

Mizener, Arthur. "The High Design of *A King and No King.*" *Modern Philology* 38 (1940): 133–54.

Turner, Robert. "The Morality of *A King and No King.*" *Renaissance Papers* 1960: 93–103.

3. *The Maid in the Mill* (Fletcher and Rowley)

Steiger, Klaus. " 'May a Man be Caught with Faces?': The Convention of 'Heart' and 'Face' in Fletcher and Rowley's *The Maid in the Mill.*" *Essays and Studies* 20 (1967): 47–63.

B. GEORGE CHAPMAN

MacLure, Millar. *George Chapman: A Critical Study*. Toronto: University of Toronto Press, 1966.

Spivack, Charlotte. *George Chapman*. Twayne's English Authors, vol. 60. New York: Twayne, 1967.

1. *The Gentleman Usher*

Weidner, Henry. "The Dramatic Uses of Homeric Idealism: The Significance of Theme and Design in George Chapman's *The Gentleman Usher*." *ELH* 28 (1961): 121–36.

2. *The Widow's Tears*

Herring, Thelma. "Chapman and an Aspect of Modern Criticism." *Renaissance Drama* 8 (1965): 153–79.

Schoenbaum, Samuel. "*The Widow's Tears* and the Other Chapman." *Huntington Library Quarterly* 23 (1960): 321–38.

Weidner, Henry. "Homer and the Fallen World: Focus of Satire in George Chapman's *The Widow's Tears*." *Journal of English and Germanic Philology* 62 (1963): 518–32.

Williamson, Marilyn. "Matter of More Mirth." *Renaissance Papers* 1956: 34–41.

C. THOMAS DEKKER

Conover, James. *Thomas Dekker: An Analysis of Dramatic Structure*. The Hague: Mouton, 1969.

Price, George. *Thomas Dekker*. Twayne's English Authors, vol. 71. New York: Twayne, 1969.

1. *The Shoemakers' Holiday*

Burelbach, Frederick. "War and Peace in *The Shoemakers' Holiday*." *Tennessee Studies in Literature* 13 (1968): 99–107.

Toliver, Harold. "*The Shoemaker's Holiday*: Theme and Image." *Boston University Studies in English* 5 (1961): 208–18.

2. *The Honest Whore, Part 1* (with Middleton) and *Part 2*

Manheim, Michael. "The Thematic Structure of Dekker's *2 Honest Whore*." *Studies in English Literature* 5 (1965): 363–81.

Ure, Peter. "Patient Madman and Honest Whore: The Middleton-Dekker Oxymoron." *Essays and Studies* 19 (1966): 18–40.

3. *The Witch of Edmonton* (with Ford and Rowley)

Sackville-West, Edward. "The Significance of *The Witch of Edmonton*." *Criterion* 17 (1937): 23–32.

D. John Ford

Anderson, Donald. "The Heart and the Banquet: Imagery in Ford's *'Tis Pity* and *The Broken Heart*." *Studies in English Literature* 2 (1962): 209–17.

Leech, Clifford. *John Ford and the Drama of His Time*. London: Chatto & Windus, 1957.

Oliver, H. J. *The Problem of John Ford*. Carlton: Melbourne University Press, 1955.

Ornstein, Robert. *The Moral Vision of Jacobean Tragedy*. Madison: University of Wisconsin Press, 1960.

Ribner, Irving. *Jacobean Tragedy: The Quest for Moral Order*. New York: Barnes & Noble, 1962.

Sensabaugh, George. *The Tragic Muse of John Ford*. Stanford: Stanford University Press, 1944.

———. "John Ford Revisited." *Studies in English Literature* 4 (1964): 195–216.

1. *The Broken Heart*

Blayney, Glenn. "Convention, Plot, and Structure in *The Broken Heart*." *Modern Philology* 56 (1958): 1–9.

McDonald, Charles. *The Rhetoric of Tragedy: Form in Stuart Drama*. Amherst: University of Massachusetts Press, 1966.

2. *'Tis Pity She's a Whore*

Kaufmann, R. J. "Ford's Tragic Perspective." *University of Texas Studies in Literature and Language* 1 (1960): 522–37.

3. *The Fancies Chaste and Noble*

Sutton, Juliet. "Platonic Love in Ford's *The Fancies, Chaste and Noble*." *Studies in English Literature* 7 (1967): 299–309.

E. Robert Greene

Sanders, Norman. "The Comedy of Greene and Shakespeare." *Early Shakespeare*, edited by John Russell Brown and Bernard Harris. Stratford-upon-Avon Studies, vol. 3. London: Edward Arnold, 1961.

F. Thomas Heywood

Brown, Arthur. "Thomas Heywood's Dramatic Art." *Essays on Shakespeare and Elizabethan Drama in Honor of Hardin Craig*, edited by Richard Hosley. Columbia: University of Missouri Press, 1962.

Townsend, Freda. "The Artistry of Thomas Heywood's Double Plots." *Philological Quarterly* 25 (1946): 97–119.

1. *A Woman Killed with Kindness*

Canuteson, John. "The Theme of Forgiveness in the Plot and Subplot of *A Woman Killed with Kindness*." *Renaissance Drama* n.s. 2 (1969): 123–41.

Cook, David. "*A Woman Killed with Kindness:* An Unshakespearian Tragedy." *English Studies* 45 (1964): 353–72.

Coursen, Herbert. "The Subplot of *A Woman Killed with Kindness*." *English Language Notes* 2 (1965): 180–85.

Spacks, Patricia. "Honor and Perception in *A Woman Killed with Kindness*." *Modern Language Quarterly* 20 (1959): 321–32.

Ure, Peter. "Marriage and the Domestic Drama in Heywood and Ford." *English Studies* 32 (1951): 200–16.

Van Fossen, R. W., ed. *A Woman Killed with Kindness*. Revels Plays. Cambridge, Mass.: Harvard University Press, 1961. Introduction.

2. *The English Traveler*

Grivelet, Michel. "The Simplicity of Thomas Heywood." *Shakespeare Survey* 14 (1961): 56–65.

Rabkin, Norman. "Dramatic Deception in Heywood's *The English Traveller*." *Studies in English Literature* 1(1961): 1–16.

See also Ribner (V.D).

G. BEN JONSON

Bacon, Wallace. "The Magnetic Field: The Structure of Jonson's Comedies." *Huntington Library Quarterly* 19 (1956): 121–53.

Barish, Jonas. *Ben Jonson and the Language of Prose Comedy*. Cambridge, Mass.: Harvard University Press, 1960.

Beaurline, L. A. "Ben Jonson and the Illusion of Completeness." *PMLA* 84 (1969): 51–59.

Campbell, Oscar. *Comicall Satyre and Shakespeare's "Troilus and Cressida."* San Marino: Huntington Library, 1938.

Champion, Larry. *Ben Jonson's "Dotages": A Reconsideration of the Late Plays*. Lexington: University of Kentucky Press, 1967.

Enck, John. *Jonson and the Comic Truth*. Madison: University of Wisconsin Press, 1957.

Gibbons, Brian. *Jacobean City Comedy: A Study of Satiric Plays by Jonson, Marston and Middleton*. London: Rupert Hart-Davis, 1968.

Heffner, Ray. "Unifying Symbols in the Comedy of Ben Jonson." *English Institute Essays, 1954*. New York: Columbia University Press, 1955.

Kernan, Alvin. *The Cankered Muse: Satire of the English Renaissance.* New Haven: Yale University Press, 1959.

Knoll, Robert. *Ben Jonson's Plays: An Introduction.* Lincoln: University of Nebraska Press, 1964.

Partridge, Edward. "Ben Jonson: The Makings of the Dramatist (1596–1602)." *Elizabethan Theatre,* edited by John Russell Brown and Bernard Harris. Stratford-upon-Avon Studies, vol. 9. London: Edward Arnold, 1966.

———. *The Broken Compass: A Study of the Major Comedies of Ben Jonson.* New York: Columbia University Press, 1958.

Thayer, Calvin. *Ben Jonson: Studies in the Plays.* Norman: University of Oklahoma Press, 1963.

Townsend, Freda. *Apologie for "Bartholmew Fayre": The Art of Jonson's Comedies.* New York: Modern Language Association, 1947.

1. *A Tale of a Tub*

Bryant, J. A. *"A Tale of a Tub:* Jonson's Comedy of the Human Condition." *Renaissance Papers* 1963: 95–105.

2. *Cynthia's Revels*

Gilbert, Allan. "The Function of the Masques in *Cynthia's Revels.*" *Philological Quarterly* 22 (1943): 211–30.

Talbert, Ernest. "The Classical Mythology and the Structure of *Cynthia's Revels.*" *Philological Quarterly* 22 (1943): 193–210.

3. *Poetaster*

Nash, Ralph. "The Parting Scene in Jonson's *Poetaster* (IV, ix)." *Philological Quarterly* 31 (1952): 54–62.

Talbert, Ernest. "The Purpose and Technique of Jonson's *Poetaster.*" *Studies in Philology* 42 (1945): 225–52.

Waith, Eugene. "The Poet's Morals in Jonson's *Poetaster.*" *Modern Language Quarterly* 12 (1951): 13–19.

4. *Volpone*

Arnold, Judd. "The Double Plot in *Volpone:* A Note on Jonsonian Dramatic Structure." *Seventeenth Century Newsletter* 23 (1965): 47–48, 50–52.

Barish, Jonas. "The Double Plot in *Volpone.*" *Modern Philology* 51 (1953): 83–92.

Davison, P. H. *"Volpone* and the Old Comedy." *Modern Language Quarterly* 24 (1963): 151–57.

Dessen, Alan. *"Volpone* and the Late Morality Tradition." *Modern Language Quarterly* 25 (1964): 383–99.

Donaldson, Ian. "Jonson's Tortoise." *Review of English Studies* 19 (1968): 162–66.

Hawkins, Harriett. "Folly, Incurable Disease, and *Volpone*." *Studies in English Literature* 8 (1968): 335–48.

Levin, Harry. "Jonson's Metempsychosis." *Philological Quarterly* 22 (1943): 231–39.

Litt, Dorothy. "Unity of Theme in *Volpone*." *Bulletin of the New York Public Library* 73 (1969): 218–26.

Mills, Lloyd. "Barish's 'The Double Plot' Supplemented: The Tortoise Symbolism." *Serif* 4 (1967): 25–28.

Nash, Ralph. "The Comic Intent of *Volpone*." *Studies in Philology* 44 (1947): 26–40.

Weld, John. "Christian Comedy: *Volpone*." *Studies in Philology* 51 (1954): 172–93.

5. *Epicene*

Donaldson, Ian. " 'A Martyrs Resolution': Jonson's *Epicoene*." *Review of English Studies* 18 (1967): 1–15.

Salingar, L. G. "Farce and Fashion in *The Silent Woman*." *Essays and Studies* 20 (1967): 29–46.

6. *The Alchemist*

Blissett, William. "The Venter Tripartite in *The Alchemist*." *Studies in English Literature* 8 (1968): 323–34.

Dessen, Alan. "*The Alchemist:* Jonson's 'Estates' Play." *Renaissance Drama* 7 (1964): 35–54.

Ellis-Fermor, Una. *The Jacobean Drama*. London: Methuen, 1936.

Goodman, Paul. *The Structure of Literature*. Chicago: University of Chicago Press, 1954.

7. *Bartholomew Fair*

Cope, Jackson. "*Bartholomew Fair* as Blasphemy." *Renaissance Drama* 8 (1965): 127–52.

Hays, H. R. "Satire and Identification: An Introduction to Ben Jonson." *Kenyon Review* 19 (1957): 267–83.

Potter, John. "Old Comedy in *Bartholomew Fair*." *Criticism* 10 (1968): 290–99.

Robinson, James. "*Bartholomew Fair:* Comedy of Vapors." *Studies in English Literature* 1 (1961): 65–80.

H. THOMAS KYD, *The Spanish Tragedy*

Freeman, Arthur. *Thomas Kyd: Facts and Problems*. Oxford: Clarendon Press, 1967.

Hunter, G. K. "Ironies of Justice in *The Spanish Tragedy*." *Renaissance Drama* 8 (1965): 89–104.

Murray, Peter. *Thomas Kyd.* Twayne's English Authors, vol. 88. New York: Twayne, 1969.

Wiatt, William. "The Dramatic Function of the Alexandro-Villuppo Episode in *The Spanish Tragedy*." *Notes & Queries* n.s. 5 (1958): 327–29.

I. JOHN LYLY

Best, Michael. "Lyly's Static Drama." *Renaissance Drama* n.s. 1 (1968): 75–86.

Hunter, G. K. *John Lyly: The Humanist as Courtier.* Cambridge, Mass.: Harvard University Press, 1962.

Huppé, Bernard. "Allegory of Love in Lyly's Court Comedies." *ELH* 14 (1947): 93–113.

Knight, G. Wilson. "Lyly." *Review of English Studies* 15 (1939): 146–63.

Powell, Jocelyn. "John Lyly and the Language of Play." *Elizabethan Theatre,* edited by John Russell Brown and Bernard Harris. Stratford-upon-Avon Studies, vol. 9. London: Edward Arnold, 1966.

Stevenson, David. *The Love Game Comedy.* New York: Columbia University Press, 1946.

1. *Love's Metamorphosis*

Parnell, Paul. "Moral Allegory in Lyly's *Loves Metamorphosis*." *Studies in Philology* 52 (1955): 1–16.

J. CHRISTOPHER MARLOWE, *Doctor Faustus*

Bluestone, Max. "*Libido Speculandi:* Doctrine and Dramaturgy in Contemporary Interpretations of Marlowe's *Doctor Faustus*." *Reinterpretations of Elizabethan Drama,* edited by Norman Rabkin. New York: Columbia University Press, 1969 [includes survey of views on the subplot, and full bibliography].

Bradbrook, Muriel. "Marlowe's *Doctor Faustus* and the Eldritch Tradition." *Essays on Shakespeare and Elizabethan Drama in Honor of Hardin Craig,* edited by Richard Hosley. Columbia: University of Missouri Press, 1962.

Crabtree, John. "The Comedy in Marlowe's *Dr. Faustus*." *Furman Studies* 9 (1961): 1–9.

Hunter, G. K. "Five-Act Structure in *Doctor Faustus*." *Tulane Drama Review* 8 (1964): 77–91.

Ornstein, Robert. "The Comic Synthesis in *Doctor Faustus*." ELH 22 (1955): 165–72.

See also Bevington (IV).

K. JOHN MARSTON

Caputi, Anthony. *John Marston, Satirist*. Ithaca: Cornell University Press, 1961.

Finkelpearl, Philip. *John Marston of the Middle Temple: An Elizabethan Dramatist in His Social Setting*. Cambridge, Mass.: Harvard University Press, 1969.

1. *Histriomastix*

Kernan, Alvin. "John Marston's Play *Histriomastix*." *Modern Language Quarterly* 19 (1958): 134–40.

See also Gibbons (V.G), Kernan (V.G), McDonald (V.D).

L. PHILIP MASSINGER

Dunn, T. A. *Philip Massinger: The Man and the Playwright*. Edinburgh: Thomas Nelson & Sons (for University College of Ghana), 1957.

1. *The Roman Actor*

Davison, Peter. "The Theme and Structure of *The Roman Actor*." *Journal of the Australasian Universities Language and Literature Association* 19 (1963): 39–56.

See also the general studies of Beaumont and Fletcher (V.A).

M. THOMAS MIDDLETON

COMEDIES AND TRAGICOMEDIES

Dunkel, Wilbur. *The Dramatic Technique of Thomas Middleton in His Comedies of London Life*. Chicago: University of Chicago Libraries, 1925.

Parker, R. B. "Middleton's Experiments with Comedy and Judgement." *Jacobean Theatre*, edited by John Russell Brown and Bernard Harris. Stratford-upon-Avon Studies, vol. 1. London: Edward Arnold, 1960 [includes *Women Beware Women*].

Schoenbaum, Samuel. "*A Chaste Maid in Cheapside* and Middleton's City Comedy." *Studies in the English Renaissance Drama in Memory of Karl Julius Holzknecht*, edited by Josephine Bennett *et al.* New York: New York University Press, 1959.

———. "Middleton's Tragicomedies." *Modern Philology* 54 (1956): 7–19.

1. *The Phoenix*

Davidson, Clifford. "*The Phoenix:* Middleton's Didactic Comedy." *Papers on Language and Literature* 4 (1968): 121–30.

Dessen, Alan. "Middleton's *The Phoenix* and the Allegorical Tradition." *Studies in English Literature* 6 (1966): 291–308.

2. *Michaelmas Term*

Chatterji, Ruby. "Unity and Disparity: *Michaelmas Term.*" *Studies in English Literature* 8 (1968): 349–63.

3. *A Mad World, My Masters*

Slights, William. "The Trickster-Hero and Middleton's *A Mad World, My Masters.*" *Comparative Drama* 3 (1969): 87–98.

4. *A Chaste Maid in Cheapside*

Chatterji, Ruby. "Theme, Imagery, and Unity in *A Chaste Maid in Cheapside.*" *Renaissance Drama* 8 (1965): 105–26.

Marotti, Arthur. "Fertility and Comic Form in *A Chaste Maid in Cheapside.*" *Comparative Drama* 3 (1969): 65–74.

Parker, R. B., ed. *A Chaste Maid in Cheapside.* Revels Plays. Cambridge, Mass.: Harvard University Press, 1969. Introduction.

5. *The Spanish Gypsy*

Burelbach, Frederick. "Theme and Structure in *The Spanish Gipsy.*" *Humanities Association Bulletin* 19 (1968): 37–41.

TRAGEDIES

Hibbard, G. R. "The Tragedies of Thomas Middleton and the Decadence of the Drama." *Renaissance and Modern Studies* 1 (1957): 35–64.

Jump, J. D. "Middleton's Tragedies." *The Age of Shakespeare,* edited by Boris Ford. Pelican Guide to English Literature, vol. 2. Baltimore: Penguin Books, 1955.

Schoenbaum, Samuel. *Middleton's Tragedies: A Critical Study.* New York: Columbia University Press, 1955.

Tomlinson, T. B. *A Study of Elizabethan and Jacobean Tragedy.* Cambridge: University Press, 1964 [includes *Chaste Maid in Cheapside*].

6. *Women Beware Women*

Ricks, Christopher. "Word-Play in *Women Beware Women.*" *Review of English Studies* 12 (1961): 238–50.

7. *The Changeling* (with Rowley)

Bawcutt, N. W., ed. *The Changeling.* Revels Plays. Cambridge, Mass.: Harvard University Press, 1959. Introduction.

Farr, Dorothy. *"The Changeling." Modern Language Review* 62 (1967): 586–97.

Hébert, Catherine. "A Note on the Significance of the Title of Middleton's *The Changeling." College Language Association Journal* 12 (1968): 66–69.

Holzknecht, Karl. "The Dramatic Structure of *The Changeling." Renaissance Papers* 1954: 77–87.

Williams, George, ed. *The Changeling.* Regents Renaissance Drama. Lincoln: University of Nebraska Press, 1966. Introduction.

See also Gibbons (V.G), Ornstein (V.D), Ribner (V.D).

N. GEORGE PEELE

Sampley, Arthur. "Plot Structure in Peele's Plays as a Test of Authorship." *PMLA* 51 (1936): 689–701.

1. *The Arraignment of Paris*

Lesnick, Henry. "The Structural Significance of Myth and Flattery in Peele's *Arraignment of Paris." Studies in Philology* 65 (1968): 163–70.

Von Hendy, Andrew. "The Triumph of Chastity: Form and Meaning in *The Arraignment of Paris." Renaissance Drama* n.s. 1 (1968): 87–101.

2. *David and Bethsabe*

Blair, Carolyn. "On the Question of Unity in Peele's *David and Bethsabe." Studies in Honor of John C. Hodges and Alwin Thaler,* edited by Richard Davis and John Lievsay. Knoxville: University of Tennessee Press, 1961.

Ewbank (née Ekeblad), Inga-Stina. "The House of David in Renaissance Drama: A Comparative Study." *Renaissance Drama* 8 (1965): 3–40.

3. *The Old Wives' Tale*

Bradbrook, Muriel. "Peele's *Old Wives' Tale:* A Play of Enchantment." *English Studies* 43 (1962): 323–30.

Goldstone, Herbert. "Interplay in Peele's *The Old Wives' Tale." Boston University Studies in English* 4 (1960): 202–13.

O. WILLIAM SHAKESPEARE (a sampling)

Frye, Dean. "The Question of Shakespearean 'Parody'." *Essays in Criticism* 15 (1965): 22–26.

Goldsmith, Robert. *Wise Fools in Shakespeare.* East Lansing: Michigan State University Press, 1955.

Hotson, Leslie. *Shakespeare's Motley*. New York: Oxford University Press, 1952.

Levin, Harry. "The Shakespearean Overplot." *Renaissance Drama* 8 (1965): 63–71.

Moulton, Richard. *Shakespeare as a Dramatic Artist: A Popular Illustration of the Principles of Scientific Criticism*. 3d rev. ed. Oxford: Clarendon Press, 1893.

Palmer, John. *Comic Characters of Shakespeare*. London: Macmillan, 1946.

Righter (Barton), Anne. *Shakespeare and the Idea of the Play*. London: Chatto & Windus, 1962.

Traversi, Derek. *An Approach to Shakespeare*. 3d rev. ed. Garden City: Doubleday, 1969.

Van Doren, Mark. *Shakespeare*. New York: Henry Holt, 1939.

COMEDIES

Barber, C. L. *Shakespeare's Festive Comedy: A Study of Dramatic Form and its Relation to Social Custom*. Princeton: Princeton University Press, 1959 [includes *Henry IV*].

Bonazza, Blaze. *Shakespeare's Early Comedies: A Structural Analysis*. The Hague: Mouton, 1966.

Brown, John Russell. *Shakespeare and his Comedies*. 2d rev. ed. London: Methuen, 1962.

Evans, Bertrand. *Shakespeare's Comedies*. Oxford: Clarendon Press, 1960.

Leech, Clifford. *"Twelfth Night" and Shakespearian Comedy*. Toronto: University of Toronto Press, 1965.

Wilson, John Dover. *Shakespeare's Happy Comedies*. London: Faber & Faber, 1962.

1. *The Comedy of Errors*

Baldwin, T. W. *On the Compositional Genetics of "The Comedy of Errors."* Urbana: University of Illinois Press, 1965.

Williams, Gwyn. *"The Comedy of Errors Rescued from Tragedy."* *Review of English Literature* 5 (1964): 63–71.

2. *The Two Gentlemen of Verona*

Brooks, Harold. "Two Clowns in a Comedy (to say nothing of the Dog): Speed, Launce (and Crab) in *The Two Gentlemen of Verona*." *Essays and Studies* 16 (1963): 91–100.

3. *The Taming of the Shrew*

Greenfield, Thelma. "The Transformation of Christopher Sly." *Philological Quarterly* 33 (1954): 34–42.

Seronsy, Cecil. " 'Supposes' as the Unifying Theme in *The Taming of the Shrew.*" *Shakespeare Quarterly* 14 (1963): 15–30.

4. *Love's Labor's Lost*

Hoy, Cyrus. *The Hyacinth Room: An Investigation into the Nature of Comedy, Tragedy, and Tragicomedy.* New York: Knopf, 1964.

Westlund, Joseph. "Fancy and Achievement in *Love's Labour's Lost.*" *Shakespeare Quarterly* 18 (1967): 37–46.

5. *A Midsummer Night's Dream*

Dent, Robert. "Imagination in *A Midsummer Night's Dream.*" *Shakespeare Quarterly* 15 (1964): 115–29.

Young, David. *Something of Great Constancy: The Art of "A Midsummer Night's Dream."* New Haven: Yale University Press, 1966.

6. *The Merchant of Venice*

Auden, W. H. *The Dyer's Hand, and Other Essays.* New York: Random House, 1962.

Donow, Herbert. "Shakespeare's Caskets: Unity in *The Merchant of Venice.*" *Shakespeare Studies* 4 (1968): 86–93.

7. *Much Ado about Nothing*

Fergusson, Francis. *The Human Image in Dramatic Literature.* Garden City: Doubleday, 1957.

McCollom, William. "The Role of Wit in *Much Ado About Nothing.*" *Shakespeare Quarterly* 19 (1968): 165–74.

Rossiter, A. P. *Angel with Horns, and Other Shakespeare Lectures.* New York: Theatre Arts, 1961.

Smith, Denzell. "The Command 'Kill Claudio' in *Much Ado.*" *English Language Notes* 4 (1967): 181–83.

Storey, Graham. "The Success of *Much Ado About Nothing.*" *More Talking of Shakespeare*, edited by John Garrett. London: Longmans, Green, 1959.

8. *As You Like It*

Draper, R. P. "Shakespeare's Pastoral Comedy." *Études Anglaises* 11 (1958): 1–17.

Gardner, Helen. "*As You Like It.*" *More Talking of Shakespeare*, edited by John Garrett. London: Longmans, Green, 1959.

Jenkins, Harold. "*As You Like It.*" *Shakespeare Survey* 8 (1955): 40–51.

Mincoff, Marco. "What Shakespeare Did to *Rosalynde.*" *Shakespeare Jahrbuch* 96 (1960): 78–89.

9. *Twelfth Night*

Draper, John. *The "Twelfth Night" of Shakespeare's Audience.* Stanford: Stanford University Press, 1950.

Salingar, L. G. "The Design of *Twelfth Night.*" *Shakespeare Quarterly* 9 (1958): 117–39.

10. *The Merry Wives of Windsor*

Green, William. *Shakespeare's "Merry Wives of Windsor."* Princeton: Princeton University Press, 1962.

11. *All's Well That Ends Well*

Hapgood, Robert. "The Life of Shame: Parolles and *All's Well.*" *Essays in Criticism* 15 (1965): 269–78.

Price, Joseph. *The Unfortunate Comedy: A Study of "All's Well that Ends Well" and Its Critics.* Toronto: University of Toronto Press, 1968.

12. *Measure for Measure*

Lawrence, William. "*Measure for Measure* and Lucio." *Shakespeare Quarterly* 9 (1958): 443–53.

Stevenson, David. *The Achievement of Shakespeare's "Measure for Measure."* Ithaca: Cornell University Press, 1966.

13. *The Winter's Tale*

Brown, John Russell. "Laughter in the Last Plays." *Later Shakespeare,* edited by John Russell Brown and Bernard Harris. Stratford-upon-Avon Studies, vol. 8. London: Edward Arnold, 1966.

Pyle, Fitzroy. *"The Winter's Tale": A Commentary on the Structure.* London: Routledge & Kegan Paul, 1969.

14. *The Tempest*

James, David. *The Dream of Prospero.* Oxford: Clarendon Press, 1967.

Zimbardo, Rose. "Form and Disorder in *The Tempest.*" *Shakespeare Quarterly* 14 (1963): 49–56.

15. *The Two Noble Kinsmen* (with Fletcher?)

Bertram, Paul. *Shakespeare and "The Two Noble Kinsmen."* New Brunswick: Rutgers University Press, 1965.

Edwards, Philip. "On the Design of *The Two Noble Kinsmen.*" *Review of English Literature* 5 (1964): 89–105.

See also Leech (V.A).

HISTORIES

Bethell, S. L. "The Comic Element in Shakespeare's Histories." *Anglia* 71 (1952): 82–101.

16. *Henry IV, Part 1* and *Part 2*

Barish, Jonas. "The Turning Away of Prince Hal." *Shakespeare Studies* 1 (1965): 9–17.

Brooks, Cleanth and Heilman, Robert. *Understanding Drama.* New York: Henry Holt, 1945.

Dickinson, Hugh. "The Reformation of Prince Hal." *Shakespeare Quarterly* 12 (1961): 33–46.

Jenkins, Harold. *The Structural Problem in Shakespeare's "Henry the Fourth."* London: Methuen, 1956.

Knowles, Richard. "Unquiet and the Double Plot of 2 *Henry IV.*" *Shakespeare Studies* 2 (1966): 133–39.

Kris, Ernst. "Prince Hal's Conflict." *Psychoanalytic Quarterly* 17 (1948): 487–506.

Leech, Clifford. "The Unity of 2 *Henry IV.*" *Shakespeare Survey* 6 (1953): 16–24.

Ross, Lawrence. "Wingless Victory: Michelangelo, Shakespeare, and the 'Old Man'." *Literary Monographs* 2, edited by Eric Rothstein and Richard Ringler. Madison: University of Wisconsin Press, 1969.

Toliver, Harold. "Falstaff, the Prince, and the History Play." *Shakespeare Quarterly* 16 (1965): 63–80.

Wilson, J. Dover. *The Fortunes of Falstaff.* Cambridge: University Press, 1943.

17. *Henry V*

Battenhouse, Roy. "*Henry V* as Heroic Comedy." *Essays on Shakespeare and Elizabethan Drama in Honor of Hardin Craig,* edited by Richard Hosley. Columbia: University of Missouri Press, 1962.

Gilbert, Allan. "Patriotism and Satire in *Henry V.*" *Studies in Shakespeare,* edited by Arthur Matthews and Clark Emery. Coral Gables: University of Miami Press, 1953.

Goddard, Harold C. *The Meaning of Shakespeare.* Chicago: University of Chicago Press, 1951.

Hotson, Leslie. *Shakespeare's Sonnets Dated, and Other Essays.* New York: Oxford University Press, 1949.

TRAGEDIES

18. *Troilus and Cressida*

Ellis-Fermor, Una. *The Frontiers of Drama.* London: Methuen, 1945.

Gérard, Albert. "Meaning and Structure in *Troilus and Cressida*." *English Studies* 40 (1959): 144–57.

Kimbrough, Robert. *Shakespeare's "Troilus and Cressida" and Its Setting*. Cambridge, Mass.: Harvard University Press, 1964.

Knights, L. C. *Some Shakespearean Themes*. London: Chatto & Windus, 1959.

Morris, Brian. "The Tragic Structure of *Troilus and Cressida*." *Shakespeare Quarterly* 10 (1959): 481–91.

Rabkin, Norman. *Shakespeare and the Common Understanding*. New York: Free Press, 1967.

19. *King Lear*

Elton, William. *"King Lear" and the Gods*. San Marino: Huntington Library, 1966.

Heilman, Robert. *This Great Stage: Image and Structure in "King Lear."* Baton Rouge: Louisiana State University Press, 1948.

Kernan, Alvin. "Formalism and Realism in Elizabethan Drama: The Miracles in *King Lear*." *Renaissance Drama* 9 (1966): 59–66.

Kernodle, George. "The Symphonic Form of *King Lear*." *Elizabethan Studies and Other Essays in Honor of George F. Reynolds*. Boulder: University of Colorado Press, 1945.

Price, Thomas. *"King Lear:* A Study of Shakspere's Dramatic Method." *PMLA* 9 (1894): 165–81.

Ribner, Irving. *Patterns of Shakespearean Tragedy*. London: Methuen, 1960.

P. Cyril Tourneur

Murray, Peter. *A Study of Cyril Tourneur*. Philadelphia: University of Pennsylvania Press, 1964.

Peter, John. *Complaint and Satire in Early English Literature*. Oxford: Clarendon Press, 1956.

1. *The Revenger's Tragedy* (Middleton?)

Adams, Henry. "Cyril Tourneur on Revenge." *Journal of English and Germanic Philology* 48 (1949): 72–87.

Foakes, R. A., ed. *The Revenger's Tragedy*. Revels Plays. Cambridge, Mass.: Harvard University Press, 1966. Introduction.

Lisca, Peter. *"The Revenger's Tragedy:* A Study in Irony." *Philological Quarterly* 38 (1959): 242–51.

Salingar, L. G. *"The Revenger's Tragedy* and the Morality Tradition." *Scrutiny* 6 (1938): 402–24.

2. *The Atheist's Tragedy*

Kaufmann, R. J. "Theodicy, Tragedy and the Psalmist: Tourneur's *Atheist's Tragedy.*" *Comparative Drama* 3 (1969): 241–62.

See also Kernan (V.G), McDonald (V.D), Ornstein (V.D), Ribner (V.D), Schoenbaum, *Middleton's Tragedies* (V.M), Tomlinson (V.M).

Index

The plays indexed in Appendix B are not included here. For the basic concepts used throughout the book, only the most important discussions and examples are indicated.